An Introduction
to the Study of
Public Policy

Third Edition

An Introduction to the Study of Public Policy

Third Edition

Charles O. Jones

University of Virginia

Brooks/Cole Publishing Company

Monterey, California

To Joe B. and Dan
with love, from their father

Consulting Editor: *Bernard Hennessy*

Brooks/Cole Publishing Company
A Division of Wadsworth, Inc.

Printed in the United States of America
10 9 8 7

Library of Congress Cataloging in Publication Data

Jones, Charles O.
   An introduction to the study of public policy.

   Bibliography: p.
   Includes index.
   1. United States—Politics and government.
2. Public administration—Decision making.   3. Policy
sciences.   I. Title.
JK271.J62   1984   353.07′2   83-18834
ISBN 0-534-03093-9

Subject Editor: *Marquita Flemming*
Production Editor: *Penelope Sky*
Manuscript Editor: *Charles Hibbard*
Permissions Editor: *Mary Kay Hancharick*
Interior and Cover Design: *Katherine Minerva*
Cover Illustration: *David Aguero*
Art Coordinator: *Judith L. Macdonald*
Interior Illustration: *John Foster*
Typesetting: *TriStar Graphics, Minneapolis, Minnesota*
Printing and Binding: *Malloy Lithographing, Inc., Ann Arbor, Michigan*

To the Students

I have made many changes in *An Introduction to the Study of Public Policy* for this third edition. Anyone who presumes in the first place to write a text on the policy process had better be prepared to make major revisions along the way. Perhaps no area of study in social science has changed more in the past two decades. The whole field of public policy has developed manifold approaches and points of departure. Consequently, the function of this book has changed even though its approach has not. Originally, the book was to serve as a general introduction to public policy. Now I see it as quite specialized in its focus. It is really more about the *politics of the policy process* than about the ways of doing policy analysis. There are now many "how to do it" books; mine is really a "what to look for" book. And my purpose is more to promote understanding of how the process might work under varying conditions than it is to teach students how to make policy decisions.

The most important addition to this edition is the new opening chapter. In my own courses on the policy process I have found it necessary to discuss how changes in political institutions have affected policy development, implementation, and evaluation. That was not necessary when these institutions were more stable. But a decade and more of reform has made a difference.

In other chapters, I have tried to incorporate the best thinking on the respective topics (including some of my own!). The greatest changes are in the chapters dealing with agenda-setting, budget making, and evaluation. The reason is quite simple: scholars are now doing more work on each of these topics. I confess that I am least satisfied with the chapter on evaluation, and yet I worked harder on it than on any of the others. The subject is just very difficult, and has many ramifications for policy decisions and the policy process. I hope I have revealed these complex dimensions with sufficient clarity to promote classroom discussion.

Finally, I have included a number of new cases. In teaching, I find it helpful to withdraw from the more conceptual and theoretical matters and talk about what actually happened, and when, and where. I have retained some cases from the previous editions simply because they are such fine illustrations of particular aspects of the process. Besides, I think it is useful for students to be introduced to policy conflicts in different eras.

In preparing this edition I have again profited a great deal from my students, at Wellesley College, the University of Arizona, the University of Pittsburgh, and now at the University of Virginia. I introduced courses on the policy process at each of these institutions, beginning at Wellesley in 1960. The students put up with me while I struggled to develop my ideas, and added to my education by sharing their insights and their experiences with public problems. I write in a more or less conversational style, because I want to continue talking with students: examining various analytical concepts and practical case studies, and raising questions. I invite you to join in the discussion and, from your own experience and learning, to challenge my understanding of concepts. It would please me to be told by your professors that this book was torn apart and reassembled in more intelligent form by their classes. I ask only that you let me know what you know. Nothing would be more unfair than for a student who has something to teach to keep that knowledge from a teacher who has something to learn.

Acknowledgments

I have many people to thank for their assistance in producing this book. Robert Gormley, then with Wadsworth Publishing Company, found my ideas appealing and encouraged me to write. With every edition I have wanted the reactions of Randall B. Ripley, whose own work on public policy is referred to frequently in these pages. Appreciation is due to reviewers James S. Fleming, Rochester Institute of Technology; Randall Ripley, Ohio State University; and A. B. Villanueva, Western Illinois University: each offered sensible criticisms. Richard I. Hofferbert, State University of New York at Binghamton, made excellent suggestions for chapters 4 and 9, many of which I tried to incorporate.

Several others helped this edition into print. Nancy Lawson, White Burkett Miller Center for Public Affairs; Randa Murphy, American Enterprise Institute; and my wife Vera each typed portions of the manuscript. No author has ever been better served! At Brooks/Cole Publishing, I worked with Henry Staat, Marquita Flemming, and Penelope Sky. Each was encouraging, helpful, and cooperative.

I also want to acknowledge several graduate students who assisted me in policy courses, helping me to organize my thinking and teaching: Christopher J. Bosso, Dieter Matthes, and Margaret E. Scranton at the University of Pittsburgh, and Randall Strahan at the University of Virginia. Others contributed to my understanding of how things work, through their own research and thinking on public policy issues: Lynn Brown, David Epperson, Robert Healy, David Kozak, Layne Hoppe, Sharon Lukish, George McClomb, Kevin Neary, Joseph McCormick, Charles Stubbart, Robert Thomas, Elaine Todres, and Jack White. Mark Rozell produced the index and assisted in updating the bibliography.

Previous editions of this book were dedicated to the late John M. Gaus. This third edition is dedicated to two young men whom Professor Gaus knew as growing boys. Knowing his regard for them, and of his love and respect for all young people, I am confident he would endorse the change. The Jones boys have made their parents very proud and I simply felt like acknowledging that fact.

Charles O. Jones

Contents

Chapter Four:
Getting Problems to Government
51

Chapter Five:
Formulating Proposals
76

Chapter Ten:
Conclusion as Prelude
233

Chapter One

"The Causes of Policy Failures Are, at Root, Political"

On July 1, 1965, George W. Ball, then under secretary of state, wrote to President Lyndon B. Johnson about a compromise solution for South Vietnam. At this crucial juncture in decision making (before committing large numbers of troops to a war in Southeast Asia), Ball warned:

> ■ The decision you face now . . . is crucial. Once large numbers of US troops are committed to direct combat they will begin to take heavy casualties in a war they are ill-equipped to fight in a non-cooperative if not downright hostile countryside.
>
> Once we suffer large casualties we will have started a well-nigh irreversible process. Our involvement will be so great that we cannot—without national humiliation—stop short of achieving our complete objectives. *Of the two possibilities I think humiliation would be more likely than the achievement of our objectives—even after we had paid terrible costs.*[1]

President Johnson gave Ball an opportunity to express his concerns before other national security advisers. At the meeting Ball stated, "We cannot win, Mr. President. The war will be long and protracted. The most we can hope for is a messy conclusion. There remains a great danger of intrusion by the Chinese. But the biggest problem is the problem of the long war."[2] This advice was received by a president who apparently had already made up his mind on another course of action. In forwarding major options (including Ball's compromise), to President Johnson, National Security Adviser McGeorge Bundy remarked, "My hunch is that you will want to listen hard to George Ball and then reject his proposal."[3] In his study of "the Americanization of the war in Vietnam," Larry Berman concludes that the president had already decided on the more aggressive option. Berman refers to Ball's "hour of cogent but fruitless analysis. He never had a chance. Johnson simply used the occasion to let everyone believe that all sides had been considered."[4] Not even Johnson's close friend Clark Clifford could alter the course. At a small meeting at Camp David, Clifford repeated earlier warnings about the dangers of committing ground troops. "I can't see anything but catastrophe for my country," Clifford said. But as Berman notes, "Clifford's warning was heard but ignored. There

1

was now too much momentum, too many advocates of escalation to stop the buildup."[5]

The purpose of this recounting is not to second-guess the president in regard to this significant decision, tempting as that exercise might be. Somebody is always right at some point in the complex thinking process necessary to choosing among policy options. More importantly, we are not normally in a position to back up and try again. Thus, it is never quite clear how things might have turned out had we selected a different option. History is easier to make than to reconstruct.

The point is rather to illustrate the importance of *how* decisions are made. Whose advice was sought? How was that advice delivered? What questions were asked? How was the giving of advice managed? Who had the final say? These are but a few of the many questions associated with the processes of decision making. The case of Vietnam piques our interest in the process because the results have been judged to be so disastrous. This conclusion is supported by the titles of many books on the subject:

Larry Berman, *Planning a Tragedy* (1982)
Joseph Buttinger, *Vietnam: The Unforgettable Tragedy* (1977)
Chester L. Cooper, *The Lost Crusade* (1970)
Robert L. Galluci, *Neither Peace nor Honor* (1975)
Ernest Gruening and Howard Beaser, *Vietnam Folly* (1968)
Paul Kattenburg, *The Vietnam Trauma in American Foreign Policy* (1980)
John Mecklin, *Mission in Torment* (1965)
Arthur M. Schlesinger, Jr., *The Bitter Heritage* (1967)
Sir Robert G. K. Thompson, *No Exit from Vietnam* (1969)
Ralph K. White, *Nobody Wanted War* (1968)

Few events in American history have had a more profound effect than this "tragedy," "lost crusade," "folly," "trauma." Yet failure typically stimulates inquiry: How could that have happened? What went wrong? Such questions naturally lead one to the processes by which problems are defined, options identified, and decisions made.

I have begun with the Vietnam example because it is dramatic and therefore quickly makes the point that a disaster encourages study of how it happened. But many less dramatic cases on the domestic front contribute to the present preoccupation with the policy process. Concerns about program success and an escalating budget have directed attention to the health of the present system. Book-length studies offer the following conclusions about program failure.

Economic Development

■   A major criticism that can be made of the EDA public works program in Oakland [California] is that it closed off the possibilities of learning. Far from being a model from which the organization could learn success, it was not even an experiment from which the organization could learn from failure. (Jeffrey Pressman and Aaron Wildavsky, *Implementation*, 2d ed., 1979, p. 125)

National Institute of Education

■   NIE's initial belief structure had been generated from the expectations surrounding its creation. There was optimism and confidence that good people, unsullied by special interest group demands, could rationally deduce a plan that would lead to success for education R&D [research and development]. Over time a series of failures led to a reassessment of the *means* to success. The belief structure was altered. But the assumption that success was achievable through intentional action went unchallenged. (Lee Sproull et al., *Organizing an Anarchy,* 1978, p. 216)

Public Housing

■   If public agencies are judged by the policies they generate and policies in turn are evaluated by reference to their human consequences, then the people of the United States have a monstrosity on their hands—blundering, incompetent, insensitive, expensive, and unable or unwilling to learn and improve. The thirty-five year history of public housing in St. Louis suggests institutional arrangements for creating and administering public policy that are grossly inadequate to contemporary needs and a value system distorted to the point of being perverse. (Eugene Meehan, *The Quality of Federal Policymaking,* 1979, p. 194)

General Social Welfare

■   Little is known about how to produce more effective health, education, and other social services. Unfortunately, moreover, neither social service systems nor federal programs are organized to find out. (Alice M. Rivlin, *Systematic Thinking for Social Action,* 1971, p. 7)

Nursing Home Care

■   It is the combination of the tendency of policy-makers to make mistakes and their inability to undo them that creates policy failure. The problem is not so much that planners in 1935 or 1955 or 1965 were wrong, but that we are still living with their decisions. *The causes of policy failure are, at root, political.* They spring less from the nature of business enterprise or large formal organizations or the propensity of human beings to make mistakes than from the ways Americans have organized to govern themselves, and the attitudes they hold about government. (Bruce C. Vladeck, *Unloving Care,* 1980, p. 264. Emphasis added)

These quotations represent a small sample of the material that one could compile concerning such varied federal programs as environmental protection (Bernard J. Frieden, *The Environmental Protection Hustle*), health care delivery (Robert R. Alford, *Health Care Politics*), the space program (Ian Mitroff, *The Subjective Side of Science*), poverty relief (James T. Patterson, *America's Struggle Against Poverty, 1900–1980*), swine flu immunization (Arthur M. Silverstein, *Pure Politics and Impure Science*), and mass transit (Michael N.

Danielson, *Federal–Metropolitan Politics and the Commuter Crisis*). In these and many other studies of the development and implementation of public policy (see bibliography), one is treated to analyses of failure or a catalog of unexpected consequences. Either way, one is drawn to consider the reasons for these unsatisfactory results.

But there is more. The rapid, virtually uncontrolled increases in the federal budget also have contributed to the unusual amount of interest in how policy is made and administered. Three developments in particular appear to be responsible for the greater interest in the budget. First is its growth in terms of unadjusted dollars (that is, not accounting for inflation). It was not until 1962 that federal budget outlays exceeded $100 billion. Since then the increases have been spectacular: $211.4 billion in 1971, $657.2 billion in 1981, more than $800 billion for 1983, and nearly $850 billion projected for 1984. When adjusted for inflation these figures are much less startling, but most people react to the totals as they see them, not to some recalculation.

The second development is the increase in the annual deficit and the contribution that increase makes to the federal debt. Before the 1970s it was extraordinary for the annual deficit to exceed $10 billion in other than war years (this occurred only twice—in 1959 and 1968). Now we are asked to accept deficits in excess of $100 billion. Further, the total debt has now exceeded the $1 trillion mark. Again, these numbers should be corrected in some fashion if comparisons are to be made. Thus, for example, the total debt as a percentage of gross national product (GNP) has actually declined since the 1960s. Our present interest, however, is in explaining the rising concern about the institutions and how they work. In that connection, any budget figure that exceeds $1 trillion is likely to command attention.

A third possible explanation for growing public interest in the budget is the growth in the so-called "uncontrollables."

■   A large share of the nondefense budget for the years immediately ahead is determined by decisions made in previous years. Such outlays have been considered relatively "uncontrollable" because they can be altered only if the basic legislation authorizing such spending is changed. Uncontrollable outlays have increased from slightly less than 60 percent of total outlays in fiscal 1967 to 76.6 percent in fiscal 1982.[6]

"Uncontrollable" programs include government pensions, disability benefits, health care, unemployment compensation, and food stamps—in fact, any program that defines eligibility or entitlement and is thus required to pay out benefits to those who meet the criteria.

When one places concerns about how well programs are working alongside worries about escalating, even uncontrolled, budgets, the recent interest in the effectiveness of the policy system seems appropriate. Perhaps this interest reflects a natural development in a maturing government. Now that the federal government has so greatly expanded its domestic agenda, it may well be time to explore how everything is working.

The Nature of the System

Clearly it is no simple task to provide a brief overview of the political system. A government as complex as ours does not lend itself to summation. Still, the policy process works within a constitutional and historical context that must be acknowledged. Almost by definition democratic systems are the most difficult to characterize. In part the problem is definitional. Nobody knows for sure what a democracy is because democracies tend to be in a state of development. E. E. Schattschneider explains:

■ Out of the experiences and ideas of many people in many places in the course of centuries there has come a good deal of agreement about what democracy is, but nobody has a monopoly of it and the last word has not been spoken. It is still being invented and it is still hospitable to a multitude of interpretations, none final. *The result of this condition is that people who like democracy have had to learn to live with a certain amount of confusion about what they believe.*[7]

So our system is characterized by ambiguity and continuous development with regard to both ends and means. Still, there is a firm shell within which all this uncertain activity takes place. This shell is the Constitution as it is expressed in the everyday workings of the political institutions. Schattschneider likens government to "an oyster, hard on the outside and soft on the inside, and the outside and inside are utterly dependent on each other."[8] What follows is an attempt to describe the American oyster, in general and in its particulars.

The System in General

The Founding Fathers were not a trusting lot. They believed in original sin and were determined to prevent the apple from being totally consumed. These beliefs are evident throughout the deliberations that led to the Constitution but are most clearly stated in *The Federalist*.

■ The accumulation of all powers, legislative, executive, and judiciary, in the same hands, whether of one, a few, or many, and whether hereditary, self-appointed, or elective, may justly be pronounced the very definition of tyranny. Were the federal Constitution, therefore, really chargeable with the accumulation of power, or with a mixture of powers, having a dangerous tendency to such an accumulation, no further arguments would be necessary to inspire a universal reprobation of the system. (No. 47)

James Madison invoked the "celebrated" Montesquieu on this point: "When the legislative and executive powers are united in the same person or body, there can be no liberty." The solution was found in the problem itself. In what is justifiably one of the most often quoted passages in *The Federalist*, the authors explained:

■   The great security against a gradual concentration of the several powers in
the same department, consists in giving to those who administer each department the necessary constitutional means and personal motives to resist encroachments of the others. . . . Ambition must be made to counteract ambition.
The interest of the man must be connected with the constitutional rights of the
place. It may be a reflection on human nature, that such devices should be
necessary to control the abuses of government. But what is government itself,
but the greatest of all reflections on human nature? If men were angels, no
government would be necessary. If angels were to govern men, neither external nor internal controls on government would be necessary. In framing a
government which is to be administered by men over men, the great difficulty
lies in this: you must first enable the government to control the governed; and
in the next place oblige it to control itself. A dependence on the people is, no
doubt, the primary control on the government; but experience has taught man-
kind the necessity of auxiliary precautions. (No. 51)

It seems that the Framers were more concerned about *preventing tyranny*
than they were about *facilitating policy development.* This statement is important to our purposes. Apparently the Framers were willing to live with the
consequences of protracted action, even if it meant stalemate, in order to
avoid despotism. As a result it is difficult for a national majority either to shape
itself or to act. As Robert A. Dahl and Charles E. Lindblom point out, "the
strategic consequence of this arrangement . . . has been that *no unified, cohe-
sive, acknowledged, and legitimate representative-leaders of the 'national majority' exist in the United States.*"[9]

More relevant to our purposes here is that the several types of separation,
checks, and balances, have encouraged *formalism.* Each branch and level of
government naturally becomes protective of its authority, thus preserving the
form of the system and making abrupt change difficult. Encroachments by one
branch into the accepted jurisdiction of another are quickly registered, and
protests, or counteractions, follow, just as the Framers hoped. Consequently,
there remains an attentiveness to form.

At the same time, however, accommodations are required if the system is to
act at all. A government dedicated entirely to preventing tyranny may fail to
cope with public problems. This is not the place to list all of the means by
which our political institutions connect with each other and with the general
public. Much of this book is about those connections. Rather, I will simply
introduce the broad features of the processes of accommodation. This can be
done most expeditiously by answering a number of basic questions.

1. *How does one gain access to the formal structure?* The quick answer is, by
commanding the resources necessary to get involved (see the discussion of
preferential pluralism in question 2). Beyond that point, it should be noted that
the structure is relatively porous. There are many access points for those in
the know, which also suggests that a loss in one decision-making arena may be
appealed to another.

2. *Who gets access?* For much of our history those with resources have tended to have the most access. Where resources are equally divided there is no problem. In the absence of this equality, access tends to be characterized by a kind of *preferential pluralism,* in which the more affluent and knowledgeable individuals and groups have an advantage. In recent decades access has been extended to certain low-income groups through the government agencies that administer welfare programs, though resources have by no means been equalized.

3. *How do decisions get made?* Bargaining becomes a way of life in a system of separated institutions and layered governments. Policy making can be likened to a flea market, with no one accepting the first price mentioned, yet with each requiring the goods of another. Any bargains struck must, however, be displayed at some point. One cannot escape the formalism. Agreements reached in a subcommittee, or the cabinet room, or a private office normally must be trotted out and shown to others if they are to have the force of law. Prolonged and successful efforts to conceal agreements typically result in demands for reform in the direction of more openness.

4. *What do decisions look like?* If everyone is protecting turf and bargaining is the principal decision-making style, then one does not expect large changes in social policy to occur very often. As Paul R. Schulman observes: "Large-scale policy objectives . . . are not easily reconciled to the dominant political environment of pluralistic bargaining and scarce resources." [10] Building on the base, or *incrementalism,* tends to characterize many government programs. The increments may vary considerably, but change tends to occur by modifying the base, not by scrapping it altogether and starting over.

To make our divided and separated institutions work, then, we have devised a relatively porous system of access and relied on bargaining to develop compromises, which in turn tend to produce policy increments. These features describe an *accommodative formalism*—that is, a sensitivity to structure combined with an acknowledgment of the need for change.

The result of this continuous interplay between structural maintenance and facilitation of change is a brand of contextual change and reform that constantly attends to what *has been* in directing the state toward what *should be.* Listen to Burke lecture the French on this point (in his *Reflections on the Revolution in France*):

■   You had all these advantages in your ancient state; but you chose to act as if you had never been molded into civil society, and had everything to begin anew. You began ill because you began by despising everything that belonged to you. [11]

And in commenting on his own country's "discontents," he advised:

■   Our constitution stands on a nice equipoise, with steep precipices and deep waters upon all sides of it. In removing it from a dangerous leaning towards one side, there may be a risk of oversetting it on the other. Every project of a material change in a government so complicated as ours, combined at the same time with external circumstances still more complicated, is a matter full of difficulties: in which a considerate man will not be too ready to decide; a prudent man too ready to undertake; or an honest man too ready to promise. They do not respect the public nor themselves who engage for more than they are sure that they ought to attempt, or that they are able to perform.[12]

However persuasive this line of argument may be (and it does not convince most social activists), one must acknowledge the frustrations it engenders as an operating base for a political system. It is maddening for those who want short-run social change. The basic Burkean approach is, when in doubt, either don't do it at all, study it, or do it just a little bit. This adherence to the status quo dampens the enthusiasm of the participants and explains the incremental-ism so characteristic of the policy product.

On the other hand, constitutionalism of this sort encourages interest group or pressure politics. Where process is emphasized—providing the means for defining problems and making policy rather than dictating what shall be—each interest must get involved. Otherwise there may be no increments, or those that are developed may have an adverse effect. A third result possible in our system is occasional crisis politics. Major decisions are often postponed, plan-ning is frequently avoided, and coordination among public and private actions is seldom attempted or achieved. Then we are suddenly faced with violent urban unrest, campus disorder, long lines at gas stations, signs declaring "Pol-luted Water: No Swimming," cities choked with traffic, bankrupt railroads with obsolete equipment, unsafe toxic waste dumps, and so on. Crash pro-grams are then instituted that seldom can be expected to have more than marginal impact.

A fourth, but by no means final, result is the marshalling of symbols, both to preserve the existing order and to integrate change. Flag, Constitution, institu-tions, basic democratic principles—all are trumpeted frequently, either to pre-vent action or to promote it. There is, then, a sort of functional mythology characteristic of our system—less prominent than in authoritarian regimes but more important than many of us like to acknowledge.

I make these observations to illustrate a commonplace: there are definite consequences and costs associated with the American brand of governing. These results contribute to our understanding of the context within which policy processes develop and work.

The System in Particular: The Institutions

The description in the previous section suggests that the particulars of insti-tutional arrangements may vary considerably from one era to the next. It is altogether fitting, therefore, that a few pages be devoted to developments in the past twenty-five years that have influenced present arrangements. In this section I discuss institutional developments; in the next section I review issue developments.

The Presidency

In a book for the 1950s, Clinton Rossiter likened the president to "a kind of magnificent lion who can roam widely and do great deeds so long as he does not try to break loose from his broad reservation."[13] Rossiter acknowledged that there were restraints on his use of power but "the President is not a Gulliver, immobilized by ten thousand tiny cords."[14]

▪ He will feel few checks upon his power if he uses that power as he should. This may well be the final definition of the strong and successful President: the one who knows just how far he can go in the direction he wants to go. If he cannot judge the limits of his power, he cannot call upon its strength. If he cannot sense the possible, he will exhaust himself attempting the impossible. The power of the Presidency moves as a mighty host only *with* the grain of liberty and morality.[15]

No scholar has since glorified the office to quite this extent, but James Mac-Gregor Burns, writing in the preface to the 1973 edition of his book *Presidential Government,* reported that even the Republican Nixon "supported a big, institutionalized Presidency." "Thus," according to Burns, "the basic tendencies toward presidential government . . . have continued under a Republican Administration."[16]

Changes in the office were, however, well underway by the time President Nixon was inaugurated. The conduct of the Vietnam War by President Johnson resulted in sharp criticism of presidential power. But having a Republican president test "the limits of his power," perhaps even, in Rossiter's words, "exhaust himself attempting the impossible," contributed to serious reappraisals of the presidency. Arthur M. Schlesinger, Jr., referred to the "imperial Presidency" that "was making a bold bid for power at home."

▪ The belief of the Nixon Administration in its own mandate and in its own virtue, compounded by its conviction that the republic was in mortal danger from internal enemies, had produced an unprecedented concentration of power in the White House and an unprecedented attempt to transform the Presidency of the Constitution into a plebiscitary Presidency.[17]

Whether Nixon's use of the office was "unprecedented" in either of the ways suggested by Schlesinger is a matter of opinion. What is a matter of record, however, is that the Vietnam War, civil disobedience, presidential–congressional conflicts on many issues, and, above all, Watergate as a significant trigger event, concentrated growing public concern about presidential power. Though the Nixon presidency set the issues in clear focus, we now can identify earlier events as also contributing to the mood for change: the Kennedy assassination, Johnson's landslide election in 1964, enactment of the Great Society programs, and the tumultuous 1968 Democratic convention. In retrospect, the 1960s and 1970s display the peaks and valleys of presidential power to a greater extent than any comparable period. By the end of the 1970s analysts recorded the end of the "imperial presidency." Fred I. Greenstein observes:

■   The older presidency-celebrating imagery of "lonely grandeur" and "awe-some power," and of the need for more power, cannot be resurrected. A common prescription during the Johnson and Nixon years—that the presidency be "demystified"—may slowly be coming to pass, particularly if the nation continues to undergo a series of one-term presidencies. . . . Today's presidency is an institution in search of new role definitions.[18]

Still, as Greenstein also notes, expectations of the president are high. And the size of the office, that is, the population associated with the White House, remains large. Thus we appear to be witnessing high expectations of a president served by more people sharing less power for a shorter period of time. Taken together these developments should have a profound effect on the policy process.

The Congress

If the presidency has changed, can Congress be far behind? In his review of Congress in the 1970s, Samuel C. Patterson records changes in membership, work load, committees and subcommittees, decision making, staffing, and leadership.[19] The compilation in *Vital Statistics on Congress, 1982* shows even more changes in congressional elections, campaign finance, continuity of membership, use of staff, and the like.[20] It is a fact that Congress tried to change itself more during the 1970s than during any previous decade in its history. There appear to have been several stimuli for reform: reaction to two quite different but equally aggressive, even threatening, presidents (Johnson and Nixon); an infusion of a young and restless new generation of legislators impatient with a seniority system; emergence of a number of difficult domestic and international issues (and a greater connection between the two types of problems); and continued public and media criticism of congressional effectiveness.

The outpouring of reform acts during the decade was extraordinary as Congress moved to reestablish itself as a premier policy-making branch of the government. First it sought to improve itself by:

1. Streamlining procedures
2. Modifying the seniority system
3. Creating policy analysis units (Office of Technology Assessment, Congressional Budget Office, Congressional Research Service)
4. Introducing computer technology
5. Enlarging personal and committee staffs
6. Altering committee and subcommittee jurisdiction and power
7. Increasing the role of party organization and leadership
8. Developing a coordinated budgetary process

All of these reforms have had important implications for the working of the national policy process, in terms of how, when, and where it works, as well as who works it. But the last change, in particular, has had a major impact by focusing attention more clearly on the broader policy issues. Thus, when a president like Ronald Reagan wished to concentrate on the scope and growth of the budget, the new congressional procedures facilitated this purpose.

Second, since increasing power of one institution normally comes at the expense of that of another, Congress made an effort to curb presidential prerogatives. The War Powers Act of 1973 was designed to reinject Congress into decisions associated with modern war making. The new budgetary procedures were important for Congress but were also directed at the president. Indeed, certain sections of the act curbed the presidential practice of impounding funds. The campaign finance laws were also changed to prevent the sort of excesses practiced by the Nixon campaign organization in 1972.

Third, Congress responded to public and media criticism by opening up virtually all committee and subcommittee meetings and enacting ethics codes.

In summary, Congress has changed itself quite considerably in structure, personnel, and participation in national decision making. The net result for the policy process appears to be an institution with many more claims but not necessarily the means for consolidating these claims into coherent policy proposals. Put differently, Congress has expanded its horizons but not its vision. It has high expectations of itself as a policy-making unit. And it has experienced a quantum increase in population (through staff increases). Thus on Capitol Hill we witness more people seeking to participate more actively in more policy activities—all with fewer means for cooperation and consolidation than in the past.

The Court

Joel B. Grossman and Richard S. Wells point out that

■ Convincing ourselves that the Supreme Court is a political institution is easy. Defining with some precision the precise role that it plays in the American political system is, of course, more difficult.[21]

The reason, in part, is that the Supreme Court is set apart from many of the ordinary forces of politics, yet still feels their effects. It has been said that the Court follows the election returns, but it does so in quite a different manner from the other branches, and for different stakes. The justices naturally pay attention to changes in social and political moods; it would be hard as prominent citizens not to do so. Beyond this attentiveness, however, is the fact that these changes determine the Court's agenda. The Court exists to resolve conflicts; it is not surprising, then, that major public policy issues often find their way onto the judicial docket. Nor is it astounding to learn that the Court's role in public policy is less publicized than that of the White House or Congress. Thus we can accept Anthony King's assessment that "of the great national trinity of political institutions in the United States, the presidency, Congress, and the Supreme Court, the presidency would seem to have changed most, the Supreme Court least."[22]

We may also accept the proposition that changes in the Court are related to the dynamics of the other institutions, are dependent on what they do, or do not do. Thus our perception of the Court's impact on public policy is likely to lag behind that of the president and Congress. We expect the latter to play major roles, but, as Robert A. Dahl observes, "Americans are not quite willing to accept the fact that the Court *is* a political institution and not quite capable of denying it."[23]

As a political institution the Court's policy role interacts with the roles played by Congress and the president, though it is somewhat less publicly acknowledged. Thus, for example, if all major interests are being satisfied by the representative and bureaucratic processes of the legislature and executive, there is no need for these interests to appeal to the courts. The 1960s and 1970s, however, were not characterized by a high level of policy satisfaction. The Court's agenda was full, mostly with matters that were ignored or refused by the popularly elected policy-making institutions. Martin Shapiro describes the results.

■ In the past twenty-five years the Supreme Court has been a major domestic policy maker in the United States. It has initiated at least five major policies. The first is school desegregation. The second is reapportionment. . . . The third is a major reform of the criminal justice system. . . . The fourth is an emascula-tion of federal and state obscenity laws. . . . The fifth is the opening up of birth control and abortion services to millions of working-class women and girls.[24]

Shapiro also notes that "the Court could readily anticipate more political opposition than support" on these issues. None was politically sexy.

■ Few American politicians even today would care to run on a platform of desegregation, pornography, abortion, and the "coddling" of criminals. If, as we are often told, the Supreme Court follows the election returns, it neverthe-less does not act in a directly election-oriented way.[25]

These decisions did not always please Congress and the president. President Nixon, in fact, "promised in the 1968 campaign to remake the Court in his own conservative image."[26] He had the unusual opportunity of appointing four justices, including the chief justice, in his five and one-half years in office (Carter had no appointments in four years), and he was true to his word. He appointed only political conservatives to the bench. Not even these appoint-ments could save the president during Watergate, however. The final blow to the president came when the Court required the release of the Watergate tapes (*United States* v. *Nixon*, 1974).

In summary, it is true, as King asserts, that the Court has not experienced such dramatic change as have Congress and the presidency in the past two and one-half decades. Still, its role in the policy process has been steady— perhaps enhanced, yet always difficult to specify—throughout the period. Fail-ure of Congress and the president to deal with difficult policy issues, the quantum growth of national programs, presidential appointments reflecting apparent shifts in political mood, and the institutional crises in the other branches (notably Watergate and Abscam) have all contributed to defining the Court's role. My colleague Henry J. Abraham refers to the Court as "the most dazzling jewel in the judicial crown of the United States," and quotes Alpheus T. Mason's reference to the Court as "the American counterpart of the British Crown."[27] As long as we believe in the truth of these descriptions, the Court will maintain its mysterious power.

The Bureaucracy

Compared to the Court, it is easy to document changes in bureaucracy over the past two and one-half decades. Doing so results in some interesting surprises. In a government growing as fast as ours it is to be expected that bureaucracy will expand. In 1960 all governments (federal, state, and local) spent just over $150 billion; in 1982 they spent well over $1 trillion.

Congresses and presidents plan for and approve expenditures, but it takes bureaucracies to see that the money gets spent. More programs costing more money typically require more bureaucracy. But this growth in the number of bureaucrats occurs in many places, not just in the federal agencies, as is so often believed. In fact, during the 1970s, when the federal budget experienced record increases, federal civilian employment stayed virtually the same (between 2.7 and 2.8 million). But there were changes in the distribution of these employees and substantial growth in other sectors as well.

At the beginning of the 1970s the Department of Defense, the Postal Service, and the Veterans Administration accounted for more than 70 percent of federal civilian employees. By the end of the decade these agencies accounted for less than 60 percent of employees. Meanwhile the Departments of Health, Education, and Welfare (HEW) (later divided into two departments), Justice, Labor, and the Treasury grew from a combined total of less than 10 percent to nearly 14 percent of employees. Health, Education, and Welfare grew more than 50 percent during the 1970s. Defense declined by nearly 20 percent during the same period. Thus within the agencies there were important shifts that reflected the new domestic priorities.

These changes do not tell as much of the story as do the figures associated with other bureaucratic sectors. First we must rid ourselves of the common notion that all bureaucrats work for the federal government. If we define bureaucracy as being associated with hierarchical organizations, specialization, formal rules, and the like, then it shows up in many public and private places. It is in these other places that we have witnessed such impressive growth. Government programs beget bureaucracy, and bureaucracy begets more bureaucracy in at least three ways.

First, federal domestic programs typically seek to expand or supplement state and local activities. Often a condition for receiving grants is that a state or local agency expand its bureaucracy in terms of functions and personnel. Federal agencies themselves expand less than those at lower levels, where most actual program administration takes place. Data on government employment show precisely this outcome. Whereas federal civilian employment has remained relatively steady in the last two decades, state and local employment has *more than doubled*. A vast intergovernmental bureaucracy has emerged to cope with national domestic problems. This complex network of administrators is not well understood by most students of public policy.

Second, those seeking to control or influence the bureaucracy find that they must expand their operations. Presidents, Congresses, private interests, even government agencies (federal, state, local, and foreign) want to affect the decisions made by bureaucrats, especially as administrative discretion increases. As Anthony Downs points out, however, tracing the work of bureaucracy can itself result in large organizations. He speaks of the "Law of Control Duplication: *Any attempt to control one large organization tends to generate another.*"[28] Thus we have witnessed the growth of White House and congressional staffs, lobbying organizations, and units within agencies that are designed to monitor what is going on inside and outside their own organizations.

Third, the complexity itself encourages the idea that government agencies cannot handle all the work assigned to them. One may expect the growth of consulting firms that also duplicate the jurisdictions of the agencies they work for. Any analysis of bureaucratic growth must include the proliferation of the so-called "beltway bandits"—those firms (many of which are located near the Capital Beltway in Washington) that do the work of government agencies under contract. They constitute a form of satellite government.

Enough has been said to illustrate the truly intricate and profound changes that have occurred within the bureaucracy. Hugh Heclo summarizes the developments as follows:

■ New policies associated with our modern age of improvement have tended to promote the idea of government by remote control. Political administration in Washington is heavily conditioned by an accumulation of methods for paying the bills and regulating the conduct of intermediary organizations. This pattern is consistent with a long tradition of fragmented and decentralized administration. . . . Rather than building and staffing its own administrative facilities for these programs, the federal government has preferred to act through intermediary organizations—state governments, city halls, third party payers, consultants, contractors, and many others.[29]

A final note. One should not conclude that this elaborate network is monolithic or intentionally dictatorial. Far from it. According to Guy Benveniste, the crisis is of a quite different order: "The environment in which every large organization operates has become so complex and therefore so uncertain that organizations do not function well."[30] If bureaucracy overruns us it will be a result more of ignorance than intent.[31]

Political Parties

William J. Keefe observes that

■ Any attempt to unravel the mysteries of American political parties might well begin with recognition of this fact: The parties are less what they make of themselves than what their environment makes of them.[32]

The environment has never been supportive of strong, centrally organized, and policy-active national parties. The decentralized nature of our election system, among other features, has prevented the emergence of the kind of political parties characteristic of European parliamentary systems, for example. Yet the nomination and election of presidents traditionally served as a unifying force— an event that every four years brought together the disparate elements of the parties. It is generally conceded that reforms in the nominating process and campaign finance have had the effect of weakening the national parties. Austin Ranney asserts that "the parties' traditional roles in choosing presidential candidates and in financing and directing presidential campaigns have diminished so greatly that presidential politics has become, in substance if not in form, something closely approaching a no-party system."[33] As Nelson W. Polsby points out, however, "in many respects, the Republican party remains unreformed."[34] The changes in the nominating process were initiated in the Democratic party and were far more extensive in that party than in the Republican party. Of course, the Democrats were successful in changing federal and state laws regarding campaign finance and presidential primaries, and these changes affected both parties.[35]

As regards political parties and the electorate, the following trends are relevant:[36]

1. Greater popular participation in the selection of delegates to national nominating conventions (as a consequence of the increase in number of presidential primaries)
2. Fewer people voting in general elections, both presidential and midterm elections (though the 1982 midterm elections showed slight increases)
3. More people eligible to vote than ever before
4. Fewer individuals identifying with a party—more professing to be independents
5. More split-ticket voting (even among strong partisans), thus giving Republicans more wins than would be predicted from their numbers
6. Profound impact of the media, particularly television, on the costs, style, and substance of campaigns

Not surprisingly, these trends affect a party's claim to legitimacy in governing. But parties face other problems in governing that have been accentuated of late. For example, commanding the allegiance of members of Congress has never been a simple task for party leaders. If anything, it has been made more difficult by the growth of campaign contributions from political action committees (PACs), the election of a new generation of postreform independent-thinking members, and the decentralizing effect of many reforms (see the section on the Congress). Further, frequent split-ticket voting has given us Republican presidents and Democratic Congresses in four of the last eight presidential-year elections, and a Republican president, Democratic House, and Republican Senate in another (1980). It is exceedingly difficult to have party government when the major policy-making institutions are controlled by different parties. Finally, in recent years a number of major domestic issues have arisen that cut across partisan attachments—for example, civil rights, energy shortages, environmental concerns, and a whole series of economic and budgetary matters.

Some mention should be made of the organizational strength of the national Republican party during the post-Watergate era. As James W. Ceaser observes, the Republican party "appears more healthy and vigorous than at any other time in recent memory."[37] The national party headquarters has demonstrated an impressive capacity to raise money and to engage in the "high tech" politics of the computer and television age. This effort has permitted the party to take advantage of divisions in the Democratic party and to win despite the fact that only about one-fourth of the voters identify with the Republican party.

In summary, political parties have been affected by the social and political environment. They are not strong enough either to resist change or to redirect the political system once change has occurred. Therefore one cannot look to the parties to remedy the faults that are observed in present trends. Instead, they tend to facilitate whatever is happening.

Interest Groups

The First Amendment is unequivocal in stating that "Congress shall make no law . . . abridging . . . the right of the people . . . to petition the Government for a redress of grievances." The people have been petitioning for redress throughout American history. It seems, however, that more government programs spawn more grievances. Another striking change, then, is the increase in interest group activity. As Speaker of the House of Representatives Thomas P. O'Neill (D–Massachusetts) observed, "Everybody in America has a lobby."[38] Those who were successful in the past want to protect their gains; those who were unsuccessful want to try again; and still others want to prevent success by the first two groups.

Interest group activity has escalated for several reasons. First and foremost is the expansion of the federal domestic agenda (see chapter 4 for a discussion of agenda). In particular, the Great Society programs of the Johnson Administration greatly enlarged the so-called welfare entitlements—benefits for those meeting various criteria (e.g., medicare, medicaid, aid to dependent children, food stamps, unemployment benefits, housing assistance, retirement support). Those receiving benefits naturally want to keep them.

Second is the response from those who see welfare programs and other entitlement programs competing for the support they themselves enjoyed in the past. Thus experienced groups have had to intensify their efforts in the policy process, especially during recent periods of budgetary conservatism.

Another development of importance in expanding interest group activity has been the growth in the number of so-called public interest groups. Not a new phenomenon by any means, these groups proliferated as a legitimate means of expression during the turbulent 1960s. Jeffrey M. Berry defines these groups as being those that seek "a collective good, the achievement of which will not selectively or materially benefit the membership or activists of the organization."[39] Members do benefit—there may even be material rewards. The causes are more general, however, and success presumably is shared with everyone. The several types of public interest groups include those like Common Cause and Ralph Nader's task groups that get involved in many issues as well as those with more specific mandates, such as environmental, consumer, and civil rights organizations. Another variant is the so-called single-issue group, of which the antiabortion and antinuclear power advocates would be prime examples. The public interest groups are important in the policy process not only for the demands they make but also for their insistence on citizen participation. Thus they have been a major force in opening the process to new actors.

Interest groups have not only expanded in number; many have extended their involvement to all stages of the policy process. The more sophisticated groups have always known that it is important to follow through to insure that a program is implemented as intended. Victory in lawmaking is meaningless if the law is ignored or subject to feeble administration. Many groups now monitor what happens beyond program approval; in addition, they frequently support provisions that call for public participation in later stages. This change may be the most significant in assessing interest groups. It may be said to incorporate another development—the greater involvement in political campaigns. Thus groups, often acting through political action committees, participate directly in elections.

What is happening with interest groups in the policy process must be placed alongside what is happening with political parties and elections. This comparison reveals what Richard A. Brody refers to as "the puzzle of political participation in America."[40] Parties are said to be declining and voting turnout is down. Yet "politics one-on-one," as Brody calls it, is increasing. It seems that many Americans are simply not satisfied to allow elected representatives full discretion in making policy decisions. They want to be involved themselves, and at many more points in the decision-making process.

Intergovernmental Relations

"No changes in the political system have been greater than those that have come to federalism."[41] The developments are dramatic. Mention has already been made of the growth of bureaucracy at the state and local levels, as stimulated by the requirements and demands of federal programs. The details of this growth will be discussed later (see chapter 8), but you should be alerted to the possible effects of changing relationships among the layers of government.

Perhaps we should begin with the statement that no one fully comprehends the intricacies of the present patterns of intergovernmental relations.[42] The variation in specific connections between federal, state, and local officials— and further, between them and various quasi-public and private groups and individuals—is simply awesome. I am not speaking here solely of the broad trends in federalism, as discussed later in this section, but rather of the day-to-day contacts required to develop and implement policy programs. Over time these contacts presumably result in networks of decision making that are crucial to the workings of government. Yet it takes dedicated study of specific programs—medicare, pollution control, housing, job training, economic development, etc.—to identify who works with whom and how. Sheer numbers—of states, of localities, of officials, of clienteles, of programs—complicate even the most dedicated effort to learn more. It is worth noting in this connection that I spent five years working on just one policy area, that of air pollution control. I had neither the time nor the resources to do a study of all federal–state–local contacts in this one area. I concentrated on just one county and one state and produced a book of several hundred pages.

We can, however, spot general trends in intergovernmental relations. These trends may not provide the kind of information and understanding identified above, but they do suggest a shift in the balance or locus of power in the federal government. The growth of federal programs in the 1960s saw a quantum increase in the role of the national government vis-a-vis state and local governments. Not unexpectedly, charges were soon leveled against the "feds" that they were arrogant, insensitive, and inflexible. Major changes were made in the 1970s as the national government experimented with various means to introduce more flexibility without completely losing control (e.g., through revenue sharing and block grants—see chapter 8). In his State of the Union Message in 1982, President Reagan proposed a "new federalism" for restructuring federal–state–local authority in various public policy areas.[43] Here was an effort to swing the pendulum back to the state and local governments. These trends coincide with the expansive, consolidative, and contractive eras identified in the following section and illustrate the dynamic nature of these crucially important intergovernmental associations.

This much we know for certain: study of domestic policy making and implementation cannot be limited to what happens in Washington, D. C. This has always been true, but the quantum increase in federal programs in the 1930s and 1960s encouraged some observers to concentrate on the national level to the exclusion of the lower levels. That error should not be repeated by this generation of policy scholars.

Summary

A weakened presidency, a more pretentious Congress, a steady Court, an expanding bureaucracy, enfeebled political parties, disinterested voters, burgeoning group activity, and a changing intergovernmental policy structure—these developments both reflect and contribute to the social change that has characterized recent decades. Anthony King concludes that "American politics have become, to a high degree, atomized."[44] Majorities still must be gathered, but it is much more difficult to build lasting coalitions. James L. Sundquist sees a "crisis of competence in government" and concludes that "severe institution-tional and structural problems must be addressed."[45] However characterized, it is apparent that institutional changes require more analysis than in the recent past. Many of the changes are traceable to greater participation in all phases of the policy process and therefore will be treated at several points in this book.

The System in Particular: The Issues

In his profound essay in search of a new public philosophy, Samuel H. Beer declared that "in the early sixties the New Deal came to an end." He doubts that we have discovered a new public philosophy to direct the policy process but observes that "there is such a thing as equilibrium without purpose."[46] After Beer wrote those words a new president, Ronald Reagan, was elected. And as A. James Reichley points out, "Ronald Reagan has brought to the presidency an unusually coherent social philosophy."[47] It is much too early to judge whether President Reagan represents a new dominant approach; at present there is evidence on both sides of that issue. On the other hand, changes in the policy agenda are apparent that can be acknowledged for what they are.

Beer marks the early 1960s as ending the New Deal. Lyndon B. Johnson's Great Society programs completed much of the work left undone by the Roosevelt and Truman administrations. But Beer notes a shift in style from the power of ideas and pressure politics to the technocracy of professional policy analysts. As he points out, "the antipoverty program was not shaped by the demands of pressure groups of the poor—there were none—but by the deliberations of government task forces acting largely on the research-based theories of two sociologists."[48] This "technocratic takeover" was followed by a romantic revolt of the "counterculture" that stressed equalitarianism. Both movements led to expanded government—the first in a quantum increase in social programs, the second in a spate of new regulations (many of them in the civil rights and environmental areas). The election of Richard M. Nixon to the presidency in 1968 signalled a shift in emphasis. In his 1970 State of the Union Message Nixon identified a new issue: "the effectiveness of government." Thus we entered a period in which *consolidation* and *reorganization* were paramount issues. Even with the major distractions of Watergate and an energy crisis during the 1970s, one can recognize consistent attention to the more consolidative proposals throughout the Nixon, Ford, and Carter presidencies. Despite this attentiveness, however, the budget soared, seemingly impervious to efforts designed to control it. Therefore, conditions were as ripe as they have been in decades for the Reagan approach.

If the New Deal and the Great Society were *expansive* in nature, and the Nixon–Ford–Carter efforts more *consolidative*, then it is appropriate to label the Reagan era as *contractive*. The Reagan philosophy applies to more than federal government programs, however. As Reichley describes it, the Reagan approach is based on four tenets: supply-side economics, a federalism that returns many programs to state and local levels, a "conservative nationalism" in foreign and defense policy, and a "traditional morality" that stresses family and religion.[49] These issues clearly represent contraction with a purpose. Much more is involved than merely reducing the budget.

Conclusion

In a sense this chapter is about the roots of and response to the recent discontent with our government. Early in the chapter I provided illustrations of this discontent with government programs and their costs. I then sought to identify general characteristics of the political system, arguing that they constitute a type of accommodative formalism by which we try to maintain our past while adjusting to our present. The last two sections concentrated on institutional and issue changes during the past two decades. These changes represent our accommodations during a period of extraordinary discord. They should help us to understand the context of the policy process as well as its internal dynamics.

The rest of the book will introduce a framework for analyzing the policy cycle, from identifying and defining problems to judging whether a particular program works. In what follows, an effort will be made to deemphasize institutions as such (the presidency, Congress, bureaucracy, etc.) and to encourage the tracing of public problems, proposals, programs, and decisions. In chapter 2, I define terms, identify various approaches, specify my own preferences, and introduce the framework in broad outline. The remaining chapters expand on this outline. Each includes illustrations of policy action on contemporary problems.

"The causes of policy failure are, at root, political." I have used this quote from Bruce C. Vladeck as the chapter title because I am anxious that you associate politics with the policy process. That is really what this book is about. A working assumption for this effort is that public policy, like politics, concerns "who gets what, when, how."[50]

Notes

1. Reprinted in Neil Sheehan et al., *The Pentagon Papers* (New York: Bantam Books, 1971), p. 450. Emphasis in original.
2. Larry Berman, *Planning a Tragedy* (New York: Norton, 1982), p. 109.
3. Berman, p. 191.
4. Berman, pp. 108–109.
5. Berman, p. 121. Emphasis added.
6. Joseph A. Pechman, ed., *Setting National Priorities: The 1982 Budget* (Washington, D. C.: The Brookings Institution, 1981), p. 46.
7. E. E. Schattschneider, *Two Hundred Million Americans in Search of a Government* (New York: Holt, Rinehart & Winston, 1969), p. 42.
8. Schattschneider, p. 24.
9. Robert A. Dahl and Charles E. Lindblom, *Politics, Economics and Welfare* (New York: Harper & Row, 1953), p. 336. Emphasis in original.

10. Paul R. Schulman, *Large-Scale Policy Making* (New York: Elsevier, 1980), p. 20.
11. Ross J. S. Hoffman and Paul Levack, eds., *Burke's Politics* (New York: Knopf, 1949), p. 296.
12. Hoffman and Levack, p. 37.
13. Clinton Rossiter, *The American Presidency* (New York: New American Library, 1956), p. 53.
14. Rossiter, p. 52.
15. Rossiter, p. 53.
16. James MacGregor Burns, *Presidential Government* (Boston: Houghton Mifflin, 1973), pp. x, xi.
17. Arthur M. Schlesinger, Jr., *The Imperial Presidency* (Boston: Houghton Mifflin, 1973), p. 377.
18. Fred I. Greenstein, "Change and Continuity in the Modern Presidency," in *The New American Political System*, ed. Anthony King (Washington, D. C.: American Enterprise Institute, 1978), p. 83.
19. Samuel C. Patterson, "The Semi-Sovereign Congress," in King, Ch. 4.
20. Norman J. Ornstein et al., *Vital Statistics on Congress, 1982* (Washington, D. C.: American Enterprise Institute, 1982).
21. Joel B. Grossman and Richard S. Wells, *Constitutional Law and Judicial Policy Making*, 2d ed. (New York: Wiley, 1980), p. 7.
22. Anthony King, "The American Polity in the Late 1970s: Building Coalitions in the Sand," in King, p. 373.
23. Robert A. Dahl, "Decision-Making in a Democracy: The Supreme Court as National Policy-Maker," *Journal of Public Law*, vol. 6 (1957), p. 279.
24. Martin Shapiro, "The Supreme Court: From Warren to Burger," in King, p. 179.
25. Shapiro, p. 181.
26. Grossman and Wells, p. 1338.
27. Henry J. Abraham, *The Judicial Process*, 4th ed. (New York: Oxford University Press, 1980), p. 179.
28. Anthony Downs, *Inside Bureaucracy* (Boston: Little, Brown, 1967), p. 148.
29. Hugh Heclo, "Issue Networks and the Executive Establishment," in King, p. 92. See also David Nachmais and David Rosenbloom, *Bureaucratic Government USA* (New York: St. Martin's Press, 1980) for details on growth in these other sectors.
30. Guy Benveniste, *Bureaucracy* (San Francisco: Boyd & Fraser, 1977), p. 4. See also the analysis of Hugh Heclo in *A Government of Strangers* (Washington, D. C.: The Brookings Institution, 1977).
31. In comments on this book in manuscript, James S. Fleming made the following interesting observation at this point: "But we are still overrun." He also noted that "as technocratic ways become more and more the norm of modern thinking, there is a great danger that the technocratic majority will tyrannize itself, leading to all the repressiveness and stifling of dissent that de Toqueville saw as inherent in traditional, pretechnocratic majorities." Quoted by permission.
32. William J. Keefe, *Parties, Politics, and Public Policy in America*, 3d ed. (New York: Holt, Rinehart & Winston, 1980), p. 1.
33. Austin Ranney, "The Political Parties: Reform and Decline," in King, p. 213. See also the historical analysis of James W. Ceaser, *Reforming the Reforms: A Critical Analysis of the Presidential Selection Process* (Cambridge, Mass.: Ballinger, 1982).
34. Nelson W. Polsby, *Consequences of Party Reform* (New York: Oxford University Press, 1983), p. 53.
35. Polsby also points out that the media are now the "leading intermediaries in the . . . presidential nominating process." P. 142.
36. See Keefe, Chs. 3, 4; Ranney; and Raymond E. Wolfinger and Steven J. Rosenstone, *Who Votes?* (New Haven: Yale University Press, 1980).
37. Ceaser, p. 155.
38. Quoted in *Time*, August 7, 1978, p. 15.
39. Jeffrey M. Berry, *Lobbying for the People* (Princeton, N. J.: Princeton University Press, 1977), p. 7.
40. Richard A. Brody, "The Puzzle of Political Participation in America," in King, Ch. 8.
41. William J. Keefe et al., *American Democracy* (Homewood, Ill.: Dorsey Press, 1983), p. 66.
42. This is not to disparage the many fine scholars in this field, for example, Deil Wright, David Walker, Martha Derthick, Michael Reagan, and Mavis Reeves. They would be among the first to agree with the statement. There is no more challenging field of study than intergovernmental relations.
43. See Timothy J. Conlan and David B. Walker, "Reagan's New Federalism: Design, Debate and Discord," *Intergovernmental Perspective*, vol. 8 (Winter 1983), pp. 6–22.
44. King, p. 39.

45. James L. Sundquist, "Congress, the President, and the Crisis of Competence in Government," in *Congress Reconsidered*, ed. Lawrence C. Dodd and Bruce I. Oppenheimer (Washington, D. C.: Congressional Quarterly Press, 1981), p. 370.
46. Samuel H. Beer, "In Search of a New Public Philosophy," in King, p. 44.
47. A. James Reichley, "A Change in Direction," in Pechman, p. 229.
48. Beer, p. 16.
49. Reichley, pp. 236–259.
50. Harold D. Lasswell, *Politics: Who Gets What, When, How* (New York: Meridian Books, 1958).

Chapter Two

Studying the Policy Process

In the line of Democratic presidents, Lyndon B. Johnson was followed by Jimmy Carter. These two presidents offer a striking contrast in substance and style. To be sure, others in the same line during this century—Woodrow Wilson to Franklin D. Roosevelt to Harry S Truman to John F. Kennedy to Lyndon B. Johnson—also varied in personal style. But the differences between Johnson and Carter appear to be greater by several orders of magnitude. They go beyond problems in dealing with a Democratic Congress. If anything, Johnson's favorable experience in that regard (prior to the escalation of the Vietnam War) was extraordinary. The differences are rooted in the public problems the two presidents perceived and the proposals they offered for treating these problems. A reading of the State of the Union Messages of each shows that Johnson was primarily an initiator, proposing new, substantive programs that expanded the role of the federal government. Carter was primarily a fixer, stressing reform and reorganization. New programs, when he offered them, tended to be procedural, organizational, regulatory in nature. These differences suit the shift from expansive to consolidative issues noted in chapter 1.

This change in style is sufficiently dramatic to invite study of the issues themselves. We are naturally attracted to the study of presidents because they are such prominent political figures. But the differences between a Johnson and a Carter should encourage us to review the social and economic context in which each served. This is not an argument for ignoring presidents as personalities; any such suggestion should be justifiably rejected. Rather it is a brief in favor of paying attention to issues: how they are perceived and acted on and how they change over time. It is entirely possible (perhaps even predictable) that we will uncover a different set of political dynamics with such an approach, one that may contribute to an understanding of the difficulties in coalition building pointed out by Anthony King:

■ American politicians continue to try to create *majorities;* they have no option. But they are no longer, or at least not very often, in the business of building *coalitions.* The materials out of which coalitions might be built simply do not exist. Building coalitions in the United States today is like trying to build coalitions out of sand. It cannot be done.[1]

Jimmy Carter, like Lyndon Johnson, had to create majorities for his proposals. He found it very difficult, however, to rely on the old coalitions. He certainly was not able to rely on the congressional Democratic party as a coalition of supporting interests, whereas Johnson often was. It is also worth noting that the complex issues associated with the Vietnam War drastically altered Johnson's support in the later years of his administration. Clearly issues (and their social and political contexts) are important topics for analysis in the study of politics.

In this chapter I briefly compare different process approaches to the study of politics, define core terms associated with the study of the policy process, introduce the basic elements of a framework of analysis (with caveats), identify various uses of the framework (as associated with differing goals), and summarize my own views on the characteristics of the policy process.

Studying Process and Defining Policy

Some people are primarily interested in the *substance* of issues; that is, in the nature of the problems and how they can be solved. For example, they want to understand the essential elements of inflation, unemployment, or trade imbalances in order to identify alternative courses of action for solving these problems. Their expertise is related to these substantive issues, for example, as labor, economic, education, or trade specialists.

Many political scientists (including myself) are more interested in *process* than substance. For them *substance* (e.g., inflation and actions to curb it) is merely a way to study *process.* Their expertise develops out of knowledge about the organization, routines, and decisions of government and other public agencies. This focus on process encourages specialization; for example, on Congress, the presidency, or budget making. Clearly this book is directed primarily to those interested in process.

A common dictionary definition of *process* is "a series of actions or operations definitely conducing to an end." Obviously *process* is associated with all forms of social behavior. Political scientists traditionally have been interested in *institutional processes,* that is, those "series of actions or operations" associated with legislatures, executives, bureaucracies, courts, political parties, and other political institutions. Many, if not most, political science courses focus on these processes: what they are, how they work, what they produce, and how they connect. Generalizations are developed about such processes as budget making, administrative rule making, congressional voting, priority setting, making appointments, reorganization, and committee decision making. More often than not, these generalizations cut across substantive issues.

Focusing on *group processes* is also popular. In this approach it is assumed that groups are absolutely crucial in political decision making. One studies the role of interest groups but also looks for groups within political institutions.[2] The latter groups may not always coincide with the organizational framework of the institution. They are defined in terms of who participates and interacts with whom in a particular matter. It may well be, for example, that not all members of a congressional standing committee participate in exploring solutions to a problem, whereas lobbyists, bureaucrats, and private consultants do. The student of group processes attempts to identify this cross-institutional participation and generalize about its nature. Various *elite* theories propose that decisions are actually made by small groups that may or may not communicate with their publics. In this view the group process is really an *elite* process.[3]

Attention in this book is directed to *policy processes*. The focus here is on public problems and how they are acted on in government. It is assumed that problems themselves help to shape the structure and organization of government, and that often cross-institutional and intergovernmental connections will emerge to treat these problems. Generalizations are developed about issues or issue areas (see chapter 3 for the distinction) as well as the activities associated with resolving them.

Here then are three process approaches (four, if one counts elitism separately) that differ in terms of the focus of analysis and the nature of the generalizations. They are not incompatible—far from it. Nor is one more legitimate than the others; rather, each contributes to a fuller understanding of the others. Each is an effort to describe and analyze reality: for example, committees as institutional groups are real; interactions among outside formal groups are real; public problems are very real. Finally, each emphasis may reveal an aspect of the political or decision-making system that is obscured by the others. We will concentrate on the policy process in this book, using the other approaches where appropriate to clarify aspects of that process.

Defining the term *policy* is a first order of business. The task is not an easy one, however. We hear the word practically every day, but it is used to refer to highly diverse sets of activities or decisions. In a single day one can hear a United States senator proclaim that "this country no longer has a Latin American foreign *policy*," a mayor announce a change in traffic control *policy* for the central business district, the gas man state that company *policy* now requires that the meter be near the road, and a student advisor explain that departmental *policy* requires course distribution among fields. Listen to S. David Freeman as he discusses energy policy in this country:

■ America's energy policy amounted to a blind act of faith that the oil companies and the utilities would indefinitely continue to deliver the goods. . . . Even after the fuel shortages became a reality in the winter of 1972–73, the federal government played down the seriousness of the problem. . . . Government policy was to rely on the oil companies, and their policy was to put profits ahead of the public interest.[4]

Freeman uses the term rhetorically to characterize failure to act and accusingly to condemn the oil companies.

In fact, the word *policy* often is used interchangeably with *goals, programs, decisions, laws, standards, proposals,* and *grand designs.* Such substitution need not create problems in everyday conversation among decision makers and their associates. Normally in such technical or administrative intercourse the word has a specific referent that is understood by all parties. For example, a group of air pollution control officials may all understand that "hazardous air pollutants *policy*" refers to Section 1857c-7 of the Clean Air Amendments of 1970. They are all experts and know the law. Shorthand communication of this type is familiar to us all.

Those studying the policy process do not have the advantage of a common reference. A definition is required, one that helps the student determine what to look for in "policy." The definition I favor is offered by Heinz Eulau and Kenneth Prewitt:

■ Policy is defined as a "standing decision" characterized by behavioral consistency and repetitiveness on the part of both those who make it and those who abide by it.[5]

This definition leaves us with the problems of judging how long a decision must stand, what constitutes behavioral consistency and repetitiveness, and who actually constitutes the population of policy makers and policy abiders, but it does identify some of the components of public policy.

Here then are two broad uses of the term *policy:* one as a word substitute or shorthand where common understanding is assumed; another as a set of characteristics to be specified and then identified through research. Clearly the second is more applicable to the present enterprise. For the purpose here is to encourage study of public policy and how it is made. We do not plan to conduct research on policy questions as such. The plan is rather to provide a basis for understanding the "behavioral consistency and repetitiveness" associated with efforts in and through government to resolve public problems. Used in this way, *policy* is a highly dynamic term. As Eulau and Prewitt point out, "What the observer sees when he identifies policy at any one point in time is at most a stage or phase in a sequence of events that constitute policy development."[6] To put it another way, we freeze the action for purposes of analysis. Whatever we learn must be specified in terms of the questions we seek to answer, the time frame within which our research is conducted, and the institutional units being studied. Therefore any reference to "defense policy," "farm policy," or "social security policy" should lead us to ask, What do you mean by that? Are you speaking of national goals? Current statutes? Recent decisions? Or are you characterizing certain behavioral consistencies by decision makers? The point of asking these questions is not to enforce one particular definition of the term *policy,* but rather to clarify meanings and thereby improve understanding.

One final note on this matter. Eulau and Prewitt also observe that "policy is distinguished from policy goals, policy intentions, and policy choices."[7] What this suggests is that it is helpful to distinguish the several components of public policy. For example:

Intentions: The true purposes of an action

Goals: The stated ends to be achieved

Plans or proposals: Specified means for achieving the goals

Programs: Authorized means for achieving goals

Decisions or choices: Specific actions taken to set goals, develop plans, implement and evaluate programs

Effects: The measurable impacts of programs (intended and unintended; primary and secondary)

One can reasonably use the term *policy* as an *adjective* with each of these components, but it does become somewhat confusing if the term is used interchangeably with all of them.

We should also note the more legal terms associated with public policy making: *legislation, laws, statutes, executive orders, regulations, legal opinions.* These too are often called policy. For our purposes, however, they are simply *the formal ingredients or legal expressions of programs and decisions.*

A Policy Process Framework

In his 1971 State of the Union Message, President Nixon proposed a plan to share federal revenues with the state and local governments.

■   I propose that the Congress make a $16 billion investment in renewing State and local government—with $5 billion of this in new and unrestricted funds, to be used as the States and localities see fit, and with the other $11 billion provided by allocating $1 billion of new funds and converting one-third of the money going to the present narrow-purpose aid programs into Federal revenue sharing funds for six broad purposes—urban development, rural development, education, transportation, job training, and law enforcement—but with the States and localities making their own local decisions on how it should be spent.[8]

Revenue sharing, as this program came to be called, has now been in existence for more than a decade. Suppose one wanted to analyze it in order to learn something about the nature of the policy process that would produce such a plan. A number of questions come to mind that derive from a logical set of activities associated with the working of government.

Activities	*Questions*
1. Perception/definition	What is the problem to which this proposal is directed?
2. Aggregation	How many people think it is an important problem?
3. Organization	How well organized are these people?
4. Representation	How is access to decision makers maintained?

5. Agenda setting	How is agenda status achieved?
6. Formulation	What is the proposed solution? Who developed it and how?
7. Legitimation	Who supports it and how is majority support maintained?
8. Budgeting	How much money is provided? Is it perceived as sufficient?
9. Implementation	Who administers it and how do they maintain support?
10. Evaluation	Who judges its achievements and by what methods?
11. Adjustment/termination	What adjustments have been made and how did they come about?

Note that these are all "who," "what," and "how" questions, and it is assumed that "when" will be asked throughout since timing is normally very important. The point is that we are primarily interested in *the politics of the policy process* and are, therefore, naturally inclined to ask those questions that Harold D. Lasswell (1963) identified as central to that inquiry. Lasswell proposed seven "how" questions deriving from the following functional activities: intelligence, recommendation, prescription, invocation, application, appraisal, and termination. My list was developed from Lasswell's and is offered in the same spirit: "Classifications are serviceable when they are tentative and undogmatic, and when they guide scholarly activity in directions that are presently accepted as valuable." [9] This statement makes an important point for this book. My principal purpose here is to provide means by which students can learn more about the dynamics of policy development and execution. This book offers a map or guide, to give direction and to identify features that might be missed otherwise.

The policy activities listed can be grouped in sequence of government action. The first five are associated with getting the problem to government and the next three with direct action by the government to develop and fund a program. Implementation is really the government returning to the problem, and the last two activities (evaluation and adjustment/termination) can be thought of as returning the program to government (for review and possible change).

Each activity may also be thought of as yielding a product that often contributes to the next activity (but see the caveats noted below). For example, perception and definition can result in a clearly specified *problem;* formulation in a definite *proposal or plan.* Table 2.1 summarizes the activities, as categorized in government, with the potential products at each point.

A few caveats are in order before proceeding. They are necessary to remind the reader once again that the framework offered here is primarily heuristic, not prescriptive. One must therefore understand the following points.

**TABLE 2.1   The policy process:
A framework for analysis**

Functional activities	Categorized in government	With a potential product
Perception/ definition		Problem
Aggregation	Problems to government	Demand
Organization		
Representation		Access
Agenda setting		Priorities
Formulation	Action in government	Proposal
Legitimation		Program
Budgeting		Budget (resources)
Implementation	Government to problems	Varies (service, payments, facilities, controls)
Evaluation	Program to government	Varies (justification, recommendation, change, solution)
Adjustment/ termination		

1. While the sequence itself appears logical, it is not necessarily followed in order. As will be noted later, in some cases legitimation may actually precede formulation; that is, support is available for doing something, anything, about a problem before an actual plan has been developed.

2. Likewise the activities are not akin to a relay race in which the definers pass the baton to the aggregators, who pass it in turn to the agenda setters, and so on. There may be overlapping of activities, and some may not even occur at all.

3. I have not proposed any criteria for judging whether an activity has been completed. This is not to say that such criteria do not exist or are never applied, but rather to suggest that formulating them would be premature and, if attempted, would be subject to change as one moved from one issue or activity to the next. Thus, for example, the question of what constitutes completed or acceptable problem definition or program development must be left open, perhaps to be itself the subject of research.

4. Neither should one be misled into imagining that all problems on the agenda of government emerge from the private sphere of social interaction. Government itself is a major source of its own agenda items, either as a consequence of the effects of existing programs or as a result of specific issue searches (see chapter 4).

5. The activities are not necessarily identified solely with particular institutions. Implementation need not be engaged in only by bureaucrats, nor legitimation only by legislators. The framework should encourage one to identify those who participate in an activity, regardless of their institutional base; that is, identification should be based on the nature of the activity.

With this introduction to the framework and the proper warnings as to its use, we turn next to various purposes and goals of policy actors.

Working the Policy Process: Four Perspectives

Participants vary in how they view the policy process and in what they seek to gain from it. At a minimum we can identify *rationalists, technicians, incrementalists,* and *reformists*. All four types of actors will typically be involved in any complex issue. However, at any one time or for any one issue, one or more of the groups may dominate. The four types of participants vary in the roles they play in the policy process, the values they seek to promote, the source of goals for each, and their operating styles.

Rationalists

"The main characteristic of . . . different forms of rationality is that they involve reasoned choices about the desirability of adopting different courses of action to resolve public problems."[10] This process of reasoned choice (1) identifies the problem, (2) defines and ranks goals, (3) identifies all policy alternatives, (4) forecasts consequences of each alternative, (5) compares consequences in relationship with goals, and (6) chooses the best alternative.[11] This approach is associated with the role of the *planner* and *professional policy analyst*, whose training stresses rational methods in treating public problems. Often the methods themselves are valued by the rationalist and therefore are promoted. It is assumed that goals are discoverable in advance and that "perfect information" is available.[12] The operating style tends to be that of the comprehensive planner; that is, one who seeks to analyze all aspects of the issue and test all possible alternatives by their effects and contribution to the stated goals. Most readers probably find this approach appealing. It strikes one as commonsensical to be as comprehensive as possible. Unfortunately, both institutional and political characteristics frequently interfere with the realization of so-called rational goals.

Technicians

A technician is really a type of rationalist, one engaged in the specialized work associated with the several stages of decision making. Technicians may well have discretion, but only within a limited sphere. They normally work on projects that require their expertise but are defined by others. The role they play is that of the *specialist* or *expert* called in for a particular assignment. The values they promote are those associated with their professional training, for example, as engineers, physicists, immunologists, or statisticians. Goals are typically set by others, perhaps any of the other three types identified here (or a mix of them). The operating style of the technician tends to be abstracted from that of the rationalist (who tends to be comprehensive). The technician displays confidence within the limits of training and experience but considerable discomfort if called upon to make more extensive judgments.

Incrementalists

I associate incrementalism with politicians in our policy system. Politicians tend to be critical of or impatient with planners and technicians, though dependent on what they produce. Incrementalists doubt that comprehensiveness and rationality are possible in this most imperfect world. They see policy development and implementation as a "*serial* process of constant *adjustment* to the outcomes (proximate and long-range) of action."[13] For incrementalists, information and knowledge are never sufficient to produce a complete policy program. They tend to be satisfied with increments, with building on the base, with working at the margins. The values associated with this approach are those of the past or of the status quo. Policy for incrementalists tends to be a gradual unfolding. Goals emerge as a consequence of demands, either for doing something new or, more typically, for making adjustments in what is already on the books. Finally, the operating style of incrementalists is that of the bargainer—constantly hearing demands, testing intensities, and proposing compromises.[14]

Reformists

Reformists are like incrementalists in accepting the limits of available information and knowledge in the policy process, but are quite different in the conclusions they draw. Incrementalists judge that these limits dictate great caution in making policy moves. As David Braybrooke and Charles Lindblom note, "Only those policies are considered whose known or expected consequences differ incrementally from the status quo."[15] This approach is much too conservative for reformists who, by nature, want to see social change. They would agree with David Easton that "we need to accept the validity of addressing ourselves directly to the problems of the day to obtain quick, short-run answers with the tools and generalizations currently available, however inadequate they may be."[16] The emphasis is on acting now because of the urgency of problems. This is the approach taken by self-styled citizen lobbyists. The values are those related to social change, sometimes for its own sake but more often associated with the special interests of particular groups. Goals are set within the group by various processes, including the personal belief that the present outcomes of government action are just plain wrong. The operating style of reformists has become very activist, often involving demonstrations and confrontation.

Given the striking differences among these four types of participants (see table 2.2), it is not surprising that each group is highly critical of the others. It is alleged, for example, that rationalists simply do not understand human nature. Braybrooke and Lindblom state that the rationalist's "ideal is not adapted to man's limited problem-solving capacities."[17] Technicians are criticized

TABLE 2.2   **Working the policy process: Four perspectives**

Perspective	Characteristics				Criticism
	Roles	Values	Goals	Style	
1. Rationalist	Policy analyst/ planner	Method	Discoverable	Comprehensive	Failure to acknowledge limits
2. Technician	Expert/ specialist	Training/ expertise	Set by others	Explicit	Narrowness
3. Incrementalist	Politician	Status quo	Set by new demands	Bargaining	Conservative
4. Reformist	Citizen lobbyist	Change	Set by substantive concerns	Activist	Unrealistic, uncompromising

for their narrowness. Incrementalists rely too much on the status quo and fail to evaluate their own decisions.[18] Reformists are indicted for their unrealistic demands and uncompromising nature.

Different eras do appear to evoke different perspectives: the incrementalism of the 1950s, the reformism of the 1960s and 1970s, the rationalism of the late 1970s and the early 1980s (particularly in energy, environmental, and economic planning). But in every era our politics is characterized by a mix of participants within and among the institutions. Thus each group is forced at some point to deal with or encounter the others. The product may favor one perspective at a given stage of the policy process (see table 2.1), but the multiplicity of institutions, governments, and decision making insures a melding over time.

It is interesting to speculate how various domestic and foreign issues might have been resolved had one perspective dominated to the exclusion of all the others. In a most interesting account, Graham T. Allison plays this game with the Cuban missile crisis of 1962. He identifies three models (or perspectives) of decision making: rational actor, organizational process, and governmental (bureaucratic) politics. He concludes that:

■ . . . while at one level three models produce different explanations of the same happening, at a second level the models produce different explanations of quite different occurrences. . . . Spectacles magnify one set of factors rather than another and thus not only lead analysts to produce different explanations of problems that appear . . . to be the same, but also influence the character of the analyst's puzzle, the evidence he assumes to be relevant, the concepts he uses in examining the evidence, and what he takes to be an explanation. . . . Different conceptual lenses lead analysts to different judgments about what is relevant and important.[19]

Allison argues that "the best analysts of foreign policy manage to weave strands of each of the three conceptual models into their explanations."[20] Perhaps, then, our system works best when there is a blending of perspectives.

Initial Realities and Personal Perspectives

Students of the policy process, too, have perspectives that unquestionably influence how they approach their work. I, for example, tend toward the incrementalist perspective because of my interest in process over substance (see the distinction made earlier in this chapter). As pointed out, I stress the importance of understanding the "how" of public policy (see the questions listed on pages 27–28). The study of process can lead one to agree with Martin Rein that:

■ Policy analysis is essentially involved with intractable problems. End values, societal goals, etc., are inherently controversial. Policy analysis involves the use of social science tools that produce inherently uncertain and incomplete findings, and these doubtful findings are then brought forward in an attempt to understand goals which are ambiguous and conflicting and where the elusive question of priorities is always dominant.[21]

If Rein is correct, one does not expect the rational–comprehensive approach to succeed often. Rather, Braybrooke and Lindblom's description of "disjointed incrementalism" seems apt, even as the ultimate consequence of large-scale reform:

■ It is decision making through small or incremental moves on particular problems rather than through a comprehensive reform program. It is also endless; it takes the form of an indefinite sequence of policy moves. Moreover, it is exploratory in that the goals of policy making continue to change as new experience with policy throws new light on what is possible and desirable. In this sense, it is also better described as moving away from known social ills rather than as moving toward a known and relatively stable goal.[22]

The advantage of incrementalism is that one never has to test the validity of a new idea or proposal. New decisions build on a given base, with a bit more of this or that added to existing programs. What can go wrong with this process? Obviously many things can go wrong if the basic program is judged to be misguided or the increments are never examined carefully for what they add. Our experiences in Vietnam and with nuclear power can be cited as cases in point. Thus there are also distinct disadvantages that lead many policy scholars and activists to reject incrementalism in favor of more rational and reformist approaches to decision making. For others the problem is to maintain an appropriate level of democracy in making policy. A high degree of public access allows people to move in and upset the most orderly and rational plans. Conversely, left alone, "the best and brightest," as David Halberstam called our Vietnam War architects, can provide and implement options that turn out to be no more than increments toward disaster.

This discussion of decision-making preferences leads to the consideration of what I call "initial realities." The statements listed below provide a set of orienting propositions for much of what follows. Not everyone would agree with these, nor is there any reason why you should accept them uncritically. I am simply setting forth the basic tenets of my approach. Here then are the "initial realities."

About problems

1. Events in society are interpreted in different ways by different people at different times.
2. Many problems may result from the same event.
3. Not all public problems are acted on in government.
4. Many private problems are acted on in government.
5. Many private problems are acted on in government as though they were public problems.
6. Most problems are not solved by government, though many are acted on there.
7. "Policy makers are not faced with a *given* problem." [23]
8. Most people do not maintain interest in other people's problems.
9. Public problems may lack a supporting public among those directly affected.

About decision making

1. Many policy actors proceed as if goals were unambiguous.
2. Most decision making is based on little information and poor communication.
3. Problems and demands are constantly being defined and redefined in the policy process.
4. Policy makers sometimes define problems for people who have not defined problems for themselves.
5. Most people do not prefer large change.
6. Most people cannot identify a public policy.
7. All policy systems have a bias.
8. No ideal policy system exists apart from the preferences of the architect of that system.
9. Most decision making is incremental in nature.
10. People have varying degrees of access to the policy process in government.

About programs

1. Programs requiring intergovernmental and public participation invite variable interpretations of purpose.
2. Inconsistent interpretations of program purposes are often not resolved.
3. Programs may be implemented without provisions for learning about failure.
4. Programs often reflect an attainable consensus rather than a substantive conviction.
5. Many programs are developed and implemented without the problems ever having been clearly defined.

Taken together, these propositions suggest a highly relative and pluralistic decision-making system characterized by compromise, incrementalism, and continual adjustment, yet subject to biases in one direction or the other. Over time this system may be self-correcting with regard to the many social and economic interests that make up the polity; in the short run it tends to favor those groups with enough resources to make a lot of noise (preferential pluralism; see chapter 1).

Summary

As a final exercise for this chapter I summarize the previous material in a manner that focuses attention on what is to follow. As I understand it, the American way of making public policy goes something like this:

1. A problem is identified and a judgment made that government action is required. The process by which this happens is variable, both across issues and over time. It also is subject to mixed signals.
2. A proposal is developed to treat the problem. This process too may vary considerably in terms of who participates and how. It may involve elaborate institutional processes for getting agreement.
3. Proposals are typically filtered through decision-making processes characterized by
   a. an incremental style (build on the base, rely on marginal decisions)
   b. a search for analogies and precedents (New problem? How did we handle a similar case? Any precedent for the proposal?)
   c. a highly segmented organization (highly balkanized bureaucratic structure in the executive; committee, subcommittee system in the legislature, and done in triplicate in the federal system)
   d. differential group access to Congress and the executive
   e. policy-centered networks (communication and contact over time among those interested and involved in a subject)
   f. bargaining expectations leading to compromise (thus encouraging incrementalism)
   g. short-run orientation (dictated in part by the two-year election cycle of Congress)
4. The policy result tends to be obtuse, indirect, circuitous, unintegrated.
5. Program implementation tends to be characterized by unsystematic experimentation (administrators gain experience in implementing a program, then propose a further increment; both good and bad programs often survive).
6. Policy evaluation tends to be program justification. Even bad programs develop a supporting clientele. Figure 2.1 further illuminates this process.

Now imagine that someone proposes a comprehensive, well-integrated program to deal with a large public issue, for example, a national energy or a national health care plan. If my description of the decision-making process is

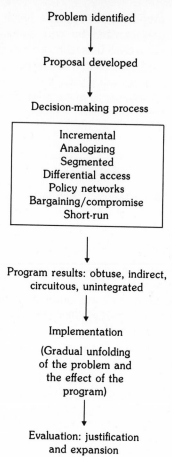

Problem identified

Proposal developed

Decision-making process

Incremental
Analogizing
Segmented
Differential access
Policy networks
Bargaining/compromise
Short-run

Program results: obtuse, indirect,
circuitous, unintegrated

Implementation

(Gradual unfolding
of the problem and
the effect of the
program)

Evaluation: justification
and expansion

FIGURE 2.1   The American way of making policy

accurate, the first thing one would expect is the disaggregation of the proposal. A comprehensive proposal, by definition, is an attempt to integrate and
coordinate existing programs. The beneficiaries of the existing programs quite
naturally resist, or at least are determined to measure how they will be affected. As a result of this disaggregation, one expects that any such comprehensive proposal will be moderated, compromised, de-escalated in order to suit
the special interests of various groups already comfortable with their piece of
the action.

Clearly there are important exceptions to this description. Much depends on
the social, economic, and political conditions that exist at a given time. If figure
2.1 provokes discussion and a search for exceptions it will have served an
important purpose. For present purposes table 2.1 and figure 2.1 serve as
useful guides to the rest of the book. We are now prepared to start at the
beginning—with the nature of public problems.

Notes

1. Anthony King, "The American Polity in the Late 1970s: Building Coalitions in the Sand," in *The New American Political System*, ed. Anthony King (Washington, D. C.: American Enterprise Institute, 1978), p. 391. Emphasis in original.
2. The classic work outlining this perspective is by David B. Truman, *The Governmental Process* (New York: Knopf, 1951).
3. For example, see C. Wright Mills, *The Power Elite* (New York: Oxford University Press, 1956).
4. S. David Freeman, *Energy: The New Era* (New York: Vintage Books, 1974), p. 4.
5. Heinz Eulau and Kenneth Prewitt, *Labyrinths of Democracy* (Indianapolis: Bobbs-Merrill, 1973), p. 465.
6. Eulau and Prewitt, p. 481.
7. Eulau and Prewitt, p. 465.
8. *Congressional Quarterly Weekly Report*, January 29, 1971, 264.
9. Harold D. Lasswell, "The Decision Process: Seven Categories of Functional Analysis," reprinted in *Politics and Social Life*, ed. Nelson W. Polsby et al. (Boston: Houghton Mifflin, 1963), p. 93.
10. William N. Dunn, *Public Policy Analysis: An Introduction* (Englewood Cliffs, N. J.: Prentice-Hall, 1981), p. 226.
11. Summarized from Dunn, who is citing Charles E. Lindblom.
12. See Fred M. Frohock, *Public Policy: Scope and Logic* (Englewood Cliffs, N. J.: Prentice-Hall, 1979), p. 45.
13. Frohock, p. 50. Emphasis in original. Incrementalism is associated with the many works of Charles E. Lindblom; see the Bibliography.
14. Amitai Etzioni is critical of incrementalism and proposes "mixed scanning" as an alternative. This approach encourages more attention to the contexts and horizons of decisions. It is offered as a compromise between rationalism and incrementalism. For details see *The Active Society* (New York: Free Press, 1968), Ch. 12.
15. David Braybrooke and Charles E. Lindblom, *A Strategy of Decision* (New York: Free Press, 1963), p. 85.
16. David Easton, "The Revolution in Political Science," *American Political Science Review*, 63 (December 1969): 1055.
17. Braybrooke and Lindblom, p. 48.
18. See Frohock, p. 60, for a summary of criticism of rationalists and incrementalists.
19. Graham T. Allison, *Essence of Decision: Explaining the Cuban Missile Crisis* (Boston: Little, Brown, 1971), p. 251.
20. Allison, pp. 258–259.
21. Martin Rein, *Social Science and Public Policy* (New York: Penguin, 1976), p. 74.
22. Braybrooke and Lindblom, p. 71.
23. Charles E. Lindblom, *The Policy-Making Process* (Englewood Cliffs, N. J.: Prentice-Hall, 1968), p. 13. Emphasis in original.

Chapter Three

The Nature of Public Problems

■ One disconcerting characteristic of policy problems is that they do not exist as units. The student of policy tends to think of "the problem" such as urban mass transportation as a unitary problem. In fact, there is no unity with respect to the problems people actually have, the way in which they perceive the problem or, as has been pointed out, of their interests and their values. Furthermore, since the policy process has a time dimension, each of these elements changes over time.[1]

It is true, as Raymond A. Bauer suggests in this passage, that we use the term *problem* very loosely in political discourse. Reference is made, for example, to "the" education, defense, environmental, employment, economic, or housing problem as though a chief problem designator existed somewhere making pronouncements to be universally accepted. The fact is that one person's problem may be another person's profit. Problems result from events that affect people differently. Not all problems become public; not all public problems become issues; and not all issues are acted on in government.

Clarification of terms must precede a survey of the several types of events and issues so important in setting the context of politics in this country. I offer the following:

Events: Human and natural acts perceived to have social consequences
Problems: Human needs, however identified, for which relief is sought
Public problems: Human needs, however identified, that cannot be met privately
Issues: Controversial public problems
Issue areas: Bundles of controversial public problems

A few comments and illustrations will help clarify this list. Events naturally vary immensely in effect. Wars and natural disasters touch millions of lives. Inventions like the internal combustion engine have altered our life-style dramatically. A new family in the neighborhood, however, normally has only limited consequences.

Events may cause problems to emerge and set the conditions for resolving them. Whether this happens depends on how observers perceive events. Those directly affected by a zoning variance that permits construction of a new shopping center and apartment complex, for example, may identify specific needs created by this event; others affected may not identify any particular resulting needs. Still others, perhaps a group of environmentalists not directly affected, may identify a need for those living in the area and oppose the variance. Congruity in identifying and acting on needs is by no means guaranteed, and therefore many problems may result from the same event. Conflict among problem definitions creates an issue.

Public and Private Problems

If a problem can be resolved without making demands on people not immediately affected, then it is private in nature. John Dewey explains it thus:

■ We take then our point of departure from the objective fact that human acts have consequences upon others, that some of these consequences are perceived, and that their perception leads to subsequent effort to control action so as to secure some consequences and avoid others. Following this clew, we are led to remark that the consequences are of two kinds, those which affect the persons directly engaged in a transaction, and those which affect others beyond those immediately concerned. In this distinction, we find the germ of the distinction between the private and the public.[2]

Note the coincidence with our definition of *problem*. Human acts have consequences on others, and some of these are perceived to create needs to the extent that relief is sought. If the transaction to control consequences (regulating needs) is relatively restricted in effect, it is private. If the transaction has a broad effect, it is public. According to Dewey, "the public consists of all those who are affected by the indirect consequences of transactions to such an extent that it is deemed necessary to have those consequences systematically cared for."[3] People take actions or propose actions to control their environments: to meet their needs, to solve their problems. Sometimes these actions have consequences for others. When these consequences are *perceived* by others and considered to be significant enough to be controlled, a public is born. As David G. Smith explains:

■ That which intervenes between the perceived problem and the governmental outcome is a *public*, a group of affected parties—aroused, engaged in conjoint activity, growing conscious of itself, organizing and seeking to influence officials.[4]

This concept of a public is important for these deliberations. Just as we have made a distinction between public and private problems, so too we can distinguish between public problems that have a supporting public and those that do not. The first type of problem is characterized by a group of concerned and organized citizens who intend to get action; the second is acknowledged as a problem that cannot be solved privately, but it lacks organized and active support. This distinction is critical for understanding the complex processes by which some problems reach government and others do not. As will be pointed out in chapter 4, the objective verification that a public problem exists (e.g., the many problems of the poor in this nation) is no guarantee that a public will emerge to press for relief. As noted in the lists of initial realities ("problems," no. 9, on page 34), "Public problems may lack a supporting public among those directly affected." Yet the government may act due to the demands of others. As another of the realities ("decision making," no. 4) states, "Policy makers sometimes define problems for people who have not defined problems for themselves."

A few examples should help clarify these concepts. A dispute between neighbors over planting a hedge might well be settled peaceably without involving others. Or a group of farmers might solve the problems created by a drought by establishing a relief fund during good years, collecting a percentage for each bushel of grain produced. They have needs but do not make demands on others. In both cases the matter at hand remains essentially private.

Should the injured neighbor organize some friends and demand that they help rip out the bushes, and should the hedge grower call in the police and some hedge-loving friends, we would have the makings of a public problem, even an issue. Should farmers demand government payments to see them through the drought period, then their personal needs would become a public problem. They are making demands on you and me, as taxpayers, for relief. We are drawn into resolving their problems.

Perhaps we taxpayers are of one mind about assisting drought-stricken farmers. They explain their problem, we agree to help, they get the money to keep going until the next crop period. No controversy arises over these actions, and therefore the public problem does not develop into an issue. Demands are seldom so easily met, however. Disagreements typically arise over priorities for allocating tax monies. There may even be conflict over the effects of drought on farmers (see below). The controversies characterizing issues vary greatly in intensity, scope, and complexity.

In still another variation, the affected farmers themselves might not act to solve the problems associated with drought. Some might simply give up, and others accept dry years as part of doing business and tighten their belts. Others might perceive serious consequences for consumers, however, and demand financial aid to prevent farmers from quitting or government support for research and irrigation facilities to reduce the effects of drought on food production. In this situation, problem definition and program development and implementation become more complicated. The public problem has shifted from those immediately affected to those experiencing the secondary consequences of drought. Conflict may well result when a program developed on the basis of one definition of the problem is administered to those who either do not perceive that problem or, if they do, are not moved to act.

Issue Areas

This discussion shows that a whole bundle of issues may be associated with any one event—for example, the Arab oil embargo; the hostage crisis in Iran; the rapid growth, then decline, of the school population; the deregulation of the airlines. For this reason I introduce the term *issue area*. What are often referred to as public problems—education, energy, mass transportation, housing—are in reality various conflicting demands for relieving several sets of needs. Complicating matters even more is the fact that needs and demands, and therefore conflicts and priorities, are constantly changing; issues therefore require almost continual definition and redefinition.

Political Systems and Problem Identification

One can distinguish among political systems by examining the characteristics of problem identification processes. In a democratic system problem identification is *intended* to be more subjective; in an authoritarian system it is *intended* to be more objective. In objectively defining problems an effort is made to employ scientific measures of the effects of events on people (this says nothing about the success of these measures, of course). There is little or no reliance on how the people interpret effects of events. Subjective processes, on the other hand, place a great deal of reliance on how those affected by an event interpret their needs. Elections and other representative processes presumably tap the public's subjective views.

Both objective and subjective measures are, in fact, relied on by all political systems. Again an illustration is useful. Start with the flight to the suburbs from a neighborhood in any core city. Owner-occupied housing units become rental units and deteriorate—the classic slum. There are objective measures of what has happened. The Bureau of the Census, or the local housing unit, can describe the "problems" of this neighborhood. Statistics are available showing the declining property values, condition of the housing, number of people occupying the units, increased crime rate, the number of units, and so on. Based on available data, political decision makers may logically designate this area for urban renewal. It is a story told many times.

Forget the objective data for a moment now and consider events from the perspective of the people living in the area. The "slum" designation (based on measures relied on by housing agencies) may not summarize their interpretation of the problems at all. They see a failure to enforce housing codes on landlords; a reduction of law enforcement (perhaps an increase of police harassment); reduction of other services in the area; government loan guarantees and tax breaks for buying, not renting (thus encouraging the "white flight" and perpetuating ghettos); low-quality schools; and so forth. These are, or may be, subjective analyses of the flight to the suburbs that lead to a set of programs quite different from those of urban renewal. In a democracy we presumably intend to err in the direction of the subjective. As is obvious with the urban renewal example and others to be noted later, we are not always true to our intentions.

A Philosophical Note

One final point should be emphasized before closing this definitional essay. The distinction between public and private problems is in part philosophical. It rests on one's interpretation of what can and cannot be treated privately. I might judge that people should be more self-reliant, and should manage their own affairs without calling upon others. Others may even quote the Scriptures in support of a more community-oriented approach. I have sought to provide an objective basis for determining the difference by emphasizing John Dewey's distinction between consequences affecting "the persons directly engaged in a transaction" (private) and those affecting "others beyond those immediately concerned" (public). Presumably we could develop measures of each that would allow us to distinguish empirically between public and private problems.

Quite definitely philosophical, however, is the judgment of whether problems, public or private, should be treated by government. I do not intend to resolve that puzzle here. Rather I will alert you to the varying forms of problems that do receive governmental attention: public problems with strong organizational support from attentive publics, public problems without publics (at least among those directly affected by an event), and private problems of various types.

A Catalog of Major Issue Areas

One of the many advantages of an open society is that evaluations of social progress come from a variety of sources. We do not have to await the announcement of a five-year plan to determine what should be done. We get frequent private and public assessments. The president's State of the Union Message and economic and budget messages, counterprograms and messages from congressional Democrats and Republicans, counterpart messages and assessments by state and local officials—all constitute official evaluations of where we are and what we must do. In addition we have any number of critical and analytical reviews from private agencies and interest groups. The Brookings Institution, an independent organization devoted to nonpartisan research, has for the past several years offered an analysis of the president's budget that has become a justly respected document. Groups like Common Cause, a citizen lobby, and the Ralph Nader Center for Study of Responsive Law are devoted to a kind of government watchdog function, and their reports naturally become sources of information on public problems. While admittedly not altruistic in their endeavors, many national interest groups also perform similar functions as they search for policies, problems, and events that may affect their clienteles. Finally, the Gallup and Harris polls in particular provide continuing data on what problems the general public judges to be important at any one time.

Taken together these various sources suggest a number of issue-area categories, that is, broad classifications of "bundles of controversial public problems." As a minimum these would include:

Foreign
  Relations with nations (individually and in alliances)
  Economic assistance to other nations
Defense
  U. S. forces
  Security assistance to other nations
  Arms control
Domestic
  Human resources (includes health, education, welfare, job training)
  Physical and natural resources (includes environment, energy, transportation, housing, agriculture, science, technology)
  Civil rights
  Social control (includes law enforcement, drug control, community support)
  Economic control
  Government organization
  Taxation
  Financial assistance to state and local governments
  Government spending

Clearly the significance of these categories will vary over time or from one State of the Union Message to the next. During the late 1960s and early 1970s, foreign and defense issues (the Vietnam War in particular), campus unrest, pollution, crime, and economic problems were of central concern. In 1975 the president's message dealt primarily with the economy and energy. International problems were mentioned last, at which time world economic distress was emphasized. Vietnam, that word that symbolized conflict and frustration in American politics for nearly a decade, was mentioned just once in passing in the 1975 message. In 1982 President Reagan stressed economic recovery and a very old concern: the federal–state–local division of responsibility. He vowed "to make our system of federalism work again."

Another sign of the times is the extent of involvement of the national government in each of the categories. Actually, lists of issue areas for 1970, 1950, 1930, and 1910 would show a decrease in the number of categories and government programs associated with each. The 1980s began with a serious national debate on the role of government, which the Reagan administration promised to reduce. Yet the budget and debt continued to increase at impressive rates.

The Budget as an Inventory of Major Issue Areas

The annual budget is the best statement we have of current and projected priorities, though it may not always be the most reliable inventory of major issue areas. No amount of rhetoric can match the actual allocation of resources to public problems for indicating government commitments. The federal budget is organized into several categories. The most useful one for present purposes is labeled "Meeting National Needs: The Federal Program by Function." Functions or needs are classified in the sixteen areas listed in table 3.1 (these sixteen are further subdivided into seventy-one subcategories of needs). These areas are not coterminous with the major departments and agencies; rather, they are cross-cutting in nature.

Several relevant observations can be made about the data in table 3.1. First, note that allocations to certain needs (natural resources and environment, agriculture, commerce and housing credit, community and regional development, and general purpose fiscal assistance—mostly revenue sharing with states and localities) peaked before 1981. Thus a shift away from these needs had already begun before the Reagan administration took office. Second, the columns indicating proposed changes show a rather bold reallocation of resources toward defense and a continuation of active growth rates for health and income security. Severe cuts are planned for energy; natural resources and environment; agriculture; commerce and housing credit (where offsetting receipts are expected to produce a surplus by 1985); community and regional development; education, training, employment, and social services; and revenue sharing. Third, a higher percentage of a larger budget is assigned to three needs—defense, health, and income security—leaving less and less for the other thirteen categories. In 1981 these three accounted for 68 percent of the outlays; by 1985 (as projected) they will account for 78 percent (due primarily to increases in defense allocations). These figures reveal the difficulties experienced by the president and Congress in responding to *new* needs. Defense, health, and income security are simply squeezing out other programs.

The trends in projected budgetary responses to needs are in line with one of the principal tenets of the Reagan philosophy: that the private sector should be free to solve more problems on its own. This view was reinforced with the decline in the economy in the late 1970s and early 1980s.

■ For most of the half-century during which the federal role was growing, the economy was expanding, first after the low point of the Great Depression, then during the boom of World War II, and finally during the great postwar expansion that, punctuated by brief recessions, lasted until the early 1970s. Beginning in the late 1960s, however, inflation became progressively more serious, and since 1974 the rate of growth of productivity has been negligible, about 1 percent a year. The administration maintains that reducing the size, cost and influence of government is a necessary precondition for bringing down inflation and restoring economic growth. Others believe that the economic role of the

TABLE 3.1   The budget and national priorities

Issue area	Peak year for outlays before 1982[a]	Proposed changes compared to peak year (in percent)	
		1983	1985
National defense	1981	+38	+83
	(159.8)	(221.1)	(292.1)
International	1981	+8	+17
affairs	(11.1)	(12.0)	(13.0)
General science,	1981	+19	+16
space, technology	(6.4)	(7.6)	(7.4)
Energy	1981	−59	−63
	(10.3)	(4.2)	(3.8)
Natural resources	1980	−28	−44
and environment	(13.8)	(9.9)	(7.7)
Agriculture	1978	−42	−40
	(7.7)	(4.5)	(4.6)
Commerce and	1980	−79	−100
housing credit	(7.8)	(1.6)	(expect offsetting receipts)
Transportation	1981	−16	−17
	(23.4)	(19.6)	(19.4)
Community and	1978	−34	−38
regional development	(11.1)	(7.3)	(6.9)
Education, training,	1981	−31	−43
employment, social services	(31.4)	(21.6)	(17.8)
Health	1981	+18	+42
	(66.0)	(78.1)	(93.5)
Income security	1981	+14	+29
	(225.1)	(261.7)	(290.1)
Veterans benefits	1981	+6	+17
and services	(23.0)	(24.4)	(26.9)
Administration of	1981	−2	−4
justice	(4.7)	(4.6)	(4.5)
General government	1981	+9	+7
(management)	(4.6)	(5.0)	(4.9)
General purpose	1978	−30	−26
fiscal assistance (to states/localities)	(9.6)	(6.7)	(7.1)

[a]Measured in billions of current dollars during the period 1973–1981.

Source: Originated from data in Office of Management and Budget, *The United States Budget in Brief: Fiscal Year 1983* (Washington, D.C.: Government Printing Office, 1982), pp. 80–84.

federal government was an important factor in assuring three decades of growth and price stability unprecedented in modern U.S. history.[5]

In summary, the Reagan administration would add a seventeenth need as a nonbudget item: reducing the role of government. Despite the administration's efforts to shift priorities, however, total budget outlays (and the deficits) continue to grow impressively. On the other hand, it is projected that by 1985, budget outlays will represent a smaller percentage of the gross national product (somewhat larger for defense; considerably smaller for nondefense items).[6]

The budget reflects one catalog of needs and how those needs are interpreted as priorities. However, the accelerated growth of certain budget items, combined with a stagnating economy, has reduced the capacity of the federal government to respond to new problems. Some people, including many in the Reagan administration, conclude that the biggest problem of all is the rejuvenation of the economy, and that that can occur only with a reduction in government spending and influence. Others doubt that this solution will work and call for increased government control of the economy. It is apparent that the two groups are in agreement on one point at least: that certain major problems are not being solved by the federal government. For both sides the budget is not the best inventory of major issue areas, a conclusion that has placed the budget front and center in the national policy-making system.

Issues and Events

What events have created the needs leading to major national issues? Again the discussion must be conducted at a general level and must be designed primarily to explain contemporary trends. I identify five broad categories of events influential in shaping issues: events of *discovery, development, communication, conflict,* and *control.* Broadly speaking, these events constitute what John Dewey calls the "human acts" that "have consequences upon others." They are the starting points for tracing the policy process for any one issue.

Discovery

Once basic physical and social needs are met, human beings demonstrate an impressive capacity for inventiveness. Scientific breakthroughs require resources, however, and not all social systems are equally accommodating to discovery (though they may benefit or suffer from what others find). Where resources are so limited that people go hungry and homeless, little can be allocated to science. Nations with vast resources, on the other hand, such as the United States and the Soviet Union, have encouraged scientific discovery, particularly in the post–World War II period. In this country most national government research is supported through the National Institutes of Health, the National Science Foundation, the National Aeronautics and Space Administration, and the Departments of Defense, Energy, and Agriculture. In all, several billion dollars are spent annually. By far the most is allocated to defense, but impressive amounts also go to nondefense areas. There is always something new to discover. "Scientific knowledge is systematic, enormous in its extent, powerful; but it is slight compared to what is not known."[7] As was stated in a recent five-year outlook:

■ The new capabilities and understanding from science and technology continue to mesh with the goals and needs of our society. The prevalence of chronic illnesses such as cancer and cardiovascular disease calls for better understanding of their nature and causes. Pressures on energy supplies are driving investigations of the chemistry of different coals, of the relative hazards of different fuels, and of the possible shapes of a more electricity-dependent society. Government programs—from allocation of funds for wastewater treatment plants to estimating the future number of annuitants of the Social Security System—demand continual refinement of demographic techniques and analyses.[8]

In a sense what this statement suggests is that discovery begets demands for more discovery. For example, if cures (or preventives) for cancer and heart disease were found, scientific attention might then turn to the effects on behavior of such breakthroughs, as well as associated problems of longevity.

Development and Application

Discovery itself has less impact than the application of findings. It is in the development and application of an idea, experiment, or finding that issues are raised. On August 6, 1945, a U.S. airplane dropped an atomic bomb on Hiroshima, Japan. Nearly five square miles of the city were obliterated, more than ninety-two thousand people were killed or declared missing. Two of the scientists involved in preparing the bomb recalled their reactions as follows:

■ *Frank Oppenheimer* (brother of J. Robert Oppenheimer): The announcement of Hiroshima . . . that the bomb had been dropped, and it had devastated. The first reaction was, "Thank God it wasn't a dud." But before that whole sentence of the broadcast was finished, one suddenly got this horror of all the people that had been killed. And I don't know why—up to then, I don't think we'd really—I'd really thought of all those flattened people.

■ *Hans Bethe:* The first reaction which we had was of fulfillment, now it has been done. Now the work that we have been engaged in for so many years has contributed to the war. The second reaction was, of course, one of shock and horror. What have we done? What have we done? And the third reaction: it shouldn't be done again.[9]

Yet it was done again. Just three days later another bomb was dropped on Nagasaki with equally devastating results. The nuclear era had begun with a vengeance. New problems and issues, both foreign and domestic, appeared on the government agenda.

The development of the internal combustion engine has been less dramatic than the dropping of atomic bombs, but it too has had a profound effect on people and government. In fact, the automobile has become such a part of our daily lives that it is hard to believe it has so recently arrived to shape our behavior. The statistics are really quite staggering: 8,000 automobiles registered for a nation of 76 million in 1900; nearly 120 million registered for a nation of 225 million by the 1980s. At its peak, annual automobile production reached two and one-half times the annual number of births in the United States. The sharp rise in petroleum prices and interest rates (themselves consequences of other events) arrested this growth in the early 1980s, with significant effects on the policy agenda.

The full impact of this discovery and development is measured by the incredible amount of resources devoted to its use and to cleaning up its effects. We must build roads (more than 3 million miles exclusive of city and town streets), repair automobiles (more than 400,000 business establishments employing 2 million people), take care of the residue (7 million cars junked each year), feed the creatures (more than 120 *billion* gallons of gasoline sold each year), treat the polluted air, control the traffic, bury the dead (50,000 each year), pave the central business districts for parking, spread 7 million tons of rock salt on highways in the winter, watch public transportation systems go bankrupt, and so on. This enormous public investment of time, energy, and resources explains why the energy shortage of the mid-1970s had a dramatic effect on the whole social system. Cars are more than just transportation; without them our cities are physically nonfunctional.

Communication

A revolution has been wrought in communication in my lifetime. Radio was in its infancy when I was born. Now practically every home has two or three. Most children own a radio; they can hold in the palm of their hand a device that will give them instant reports on what is going on in the rest of the world. Ninety-eight percent of American households have television sets (30 percent have two or more). Ninety-seven percent of American households have telephones. There are, on the average, nearly 800 million telephone conversations *daily* in this country. The typical home is, in fact, a small communications center, potentially providing more information, entertainment, and contact with the outside than was available to whole communities in the last century.

The total impact of these communication "events" is inestimable. Rather than attempting to assess it, one is advised to weigh the effect on the development of specific issues. Consider, for example, the role of television in the urban and campus disorders of the 1960s. "The whole world is watching" was an appropriate chant by street demonstrators during the 1968 Democratic convention in Chicago. Americans get daily news accounts of injustices, conflicts, discoveries, and decisions that were formerly directed to a privileged few. If information is power, then we have had a tremendous dispersal of power in the past three decades. National policy in Vietnam in the late 1960s was apparently very much influenced by media coverage of the war. On-the-spot coverage of battles, interviews with villagers, demonstrated inconsistencies (if not falsehoods) in discussing policies, soldier complaints about the conduct of the war—all combined with apparent effect on organization, policy, publicity, and, ultimately, strategy. By the late 1970s and early 1980s television coverage appeared to have become a part of the action on both sides in a whole series of miniwars or revolutions in Afghanistan, El Salvador, the Falkland Islands, Iran, Lebanon, and Poland.

Conflict

The fantastic events of discovery, development, and communication in my lifetime have certainly not rid us of conflict. Indeed, many breakthroughs in these other categories, particularly in meeting the needs of war, can be traced to conflict. The total impact of war on a society is obvious; the effects of specific commitments, strategies, and expenditures are less clear. Thus, for example, what is not done domestically because resources have gone to war can lead to serious conflicts at home. The sharp contrast between resource commitments to the declared "war on poverty" and to the undeclared war in Vietnam was sufficient to activate normally quiescent citizens.

The 1960s and 1970s witnessed at least as much domestic conflict as any decade in our history, with the exception of the 1860s. Violent riots in black ghettos, demonstrations, sit-ins, teach-ins, active participation in all phases of decision making, and citizen group organization all became commonplace in conflicts over women's rights, the environment, nuclear power, and abortion. Social and political organizations often found themselves unable to mediate the disputes or reduce the conflict.

The troubled economy of the 1980s may produce even more severe conflicts. Disputes over allocation of resources are avoided when decision makers are able to meet new demands by commanding more resources. That option is less available now, and decision makers are thus forced to meet new demands, or even maintain old programs, by reallocating resources (see the budget discussion beginning on page 44). Intense conflict over priorities such as defense, health, social security, energy, and the environment is inevitable under these circumstances.

Control

By *control events* I mean those private and public (with emphasis on the latter) sets of controls on social behavior. Since much of this book seeks to describe and analyze the U. S. national government—a major control mechanism—lengthy discussion is unnecessary at this point. It is sufficient to offer illustrations of major control events (or sets of events): the military draft, the income tax amendment, expansion of the meaning of the commerce clause in the Constitution, acceptance of Keynesian economics, passage of welfare programs (1930s, 1960s), enactment of regulations (1970s). Since most of these are properly considered in common parlance to be policies, we will discuss them specifically in later chapters.

Summary

I thought it useful to discuss the nature and trends of public problems and the events that cause them before reviewing the phases of the policy process. All one can do, however, is offer a sample of major issues to illustrate the scope of the government agenda. In all probability this chapter will soon be out of date, as new issues flood into the decision-making system. Yet the chapter also offers a set of categories and trends that are more lasting. The catalogs of issue areas and events are comprehensive enough to incorporate most public problems. Future agendas will be drawn from these catalogs, though quite possibly with revised priority.

Notes

1. Raymond A. Bauer and Kenneth J. Gergen, *The Study of Policy Formation* (New York: Free Press, 1968), p. 15.
2. John Dewey, *The Public and Its Problems* (New York: Holt, Rinehart & Winston, 1927), p. 12.
3. Dewey, pp. 15–16.
4. David G. Smith, "Pragmatism and the Group Theory of Politics," *American Political Science Review* 58 (September 1964): 602. Emphasis in original.
5. Joseph A. Pechman, ed., *Setting National Priorities: The 1983 Budget* (Washington, D. C.: The Brookings Institution, 1982), pp. 103–104.
6. Pechman, pp. 37, 102.
7. National Academy of Sciences, *Science and Technology: A Five-Year Outlook* (San Francisco: W. H. Freeman, 1979), p. 4.
8. National Academy of Sciences, pp. 1–2.
9. From the transcript for *The Day After Trinity: J. Robert Oppenheimer and the Atomic Bomb*, Public Broadcasting Service, April 29, 1981, pp. 22–23 (Kent, Ohio: PTV Publications).

Chapter Four

Getting Problems to Government

Functional activities	Categorized in government	With a potential product
Perception/ definition Aggregation Organization Representation Agenda setting	Problems to government	Problem Demand Access Priorities

Those who limit their study of public policy to actions taken within political institutions miss much that is important. The battle over policy may well be decided in the preliminary stages of issue emergence and agenda setting. William Solesbury summarizes what happens:

■   An issue originates with the idea in someone's mind that some real-world situation is unsatisfactory. But the vast majority of such ideas fail to become recognized as issues. The reason for this high failure rate is that public resources for responding to issues are relatively scarce, and this applies not only to the obvious resources of money and manpower but also to those of legislative time, political will, media coverage, and public concern. Nascent issues must compete for all these resources, and although some succeed in capturing a share of them, many more fail and never reach the stage of recognition which is the precursor to action. Political systems can cope with only a limited number of recognized issues at one time, and these are always subject to displacement by new emerging issues of greater appeal and force.[1]

This chapter focuses on the complex and often arbitrary processes that determine which issues are acted on in government. Attention is directed first to certain ordinary activities that are normally associated with the preliminary stages of the policy process. Agenda setting is then examined in greater detail, including analysis of various perspectives on the government's role in this important activity. Finally an effort is made to bring the discussion to life with case material.

Initial Functional Activities: Problem to Government

Perception and Definition

Imagine that you are riding in a subway car and witness a group of youngsters slashing seats and defacing the walls. The damage is obvious, the intent clear. You may register the event in your mind but judge it so common that it makes no further impression. Three months later the transit authority announces a fare increase to pay the costs of repairing damage caused by vandals. The earlier event now has more direct, personal relevance. What was initially *perceived* is now *defined* as a problem.

Witnesses to an event are likely to give differing accounts of what happened. Sometimes the accounts differ so much that it is inconceivable that all the witnesses perceived the same event. Furthermore, the individual who, by some objective measure, has misperceived an event may well consider that it has created "a human need for which relief is sought" (the definition of a problem). Of high relevance in relieving the need is that someone understand how those affected perceive the problem-causing event. What is it that they see as troublesome? This is no simple matter, but neither is it very important in most cases, because we routinely tolerate discomfort and compromise and half measures to solve our problems. The crucial point is reached when those affected decide that enough is enough—that, for example, the destruction of public property can no longer be tolerated. Policy actors who want continuing support must be sensitive to such stress points.

Perception is important in the policy process, therefore, because it conditions the definitions of problems. As used here, *perception* simply means the reception and registering of an event through sight, hearing, touch, and smell. Involved in that comprehension is an interpretation. The event is viewed in a particular way. Thus *perception refers to an event. Definition refers to a problem.* Something happens; someone perceives it in a particular way and defines it as a problem.

People "define" problems for themselves and for others. That is, they bring into sharp relief the social effects of events, frequently with the result that a problem is defined. Our interest picks up, of course, when the effects of events are defined as problems and efforts are made to resolve them.

Of course, many of the problems that eventually get to government are created by the implementation of policy. That is, government itself causes the event that is perceived and defined as a problem for an individual or group. Government is thus a major actor in contributing to its own agenda.

Consider the case of urban renewal. The steady deterioration of the central business district of a large city is perceived by a variety of individuals and groups. Some of them may consider the decay to be nothing extraordinary— just a part of life. For others, however, the deterioration creates a whole series of problems, and they therefore seek relief. Government is involved, and courses of action are developed, approved, and implemented.

Let us assume that the government authorizes the clearing of an area—removal of substandard dwellings and buildings—for subsequent redevelopment by private developers. The program is initiated in a large city. You are a private citizen living in the area to be cleared and operating a small drugstore there. The event of immediate relevance to you is the impending destruction of your home and business. The problems that have been defined by others cannot be solved without affecting you. What is your response? You may simply accept the circumstances and move away. You may have made an effort earlier to prevent the implementation of the policy decision. Someone else may become concerned about your plight and decide to represent you in the political process. In any case, your efforts or others' efforts in your behalf may constitute an event that still others perceive and define as a problem for themselves. Government activity has thus created new problems that may prompt further government involvement.

Government programs may also create dependencies among their clienteles, and those affected by reductions or changes will naturally organize to respond. Such resistance makes it much more difficult to modify government programs than one might think. The immediate reaction by affected publics to social security reform is a case in point. It took a special commission in 1982 even to get bipartisan agreement that a real problem existed with the social security system. Another excellent recent example is the flat tax proposal, which eliminates deductions for interest payments on home loans. We typically think first of welfare for the poor when discussing dependency on government. Yet the taxing system also provides welfare-like subsidies for the more affluent, whose sensory apparatus is often more finely tuned than that of the poor.

Aggregation and Organization

Implicit in the discussion of public problems is the notion of aggregation. Dewey talks about "those who are affected . . . to such an extent that it is deemed necessary to have . . . consequences systematically cared for." Aggregates are collections of persons who are affected by what goes on in society. But this collection of affected individuals may not be organized. Events occur every day—a teachers' strike, a crop failure, an increase in utility rates—that affect many people who do not organize in order "to have . . . consequences systematically cared for." In fact, organization is a major development in responding to events in society. The recent environmental and antinuclear movements are particularly noteworthy because they represent organized response by aggregates of normally quiescent citizens.

The number of people affected, the extent to which they aggregate, and the degree and type of organization all may influence the policy process and its outcomes. Let me reemphasize that these functional activities do not necessarily accompany all public problems, nor do they always occur in the same manner. In fact, one principal concern in policy study is the extent to which aggregation and organization do take place and the particular pattern that is involved.[2]

In his treatment of interest groups, David B. Truman makes a strong case that study of a group's formal organization will reveal features that are important for policy making. One can determine the degree of cohesion, expectations of permanence, internal division of labor, and formalized values, all of which can "intimately affect the survival and influence of the group."[3] The particular form of the structure depends on the nature and scope of the problems that unite members in the first place, the group's resources, its leadership, and its belief in democratic values. Not infrequently, of course, an "active minority" emerges to interpret the needs and wants of members.[4] This minority includes those who have the commitment, resources, and time to pursue the issue at hand. Again, the possibility of incongruity between the perceptions of those affected and the perceptions of their representatives develops.

Representation

With the fascinating concept of representation, we begin to work our way from the events in society to the actions designed to relieve the perceived tensions. Many books have been written on the subject of representation. About the best we can do here is acknowledge the almost limitless dimensions of the term. For example, representation is used to describe participation in the Miss America contest, an American Legionnaire's antics at his annual convention, the lawyer–client relationship, a national nominating convention, and the variety of relationships between legislators and constituents. It can be interpreted in terms of a "mirror reflection" or a trusteeship or a mandate to act as the represented would act if they could be there.[5] However developed, representation is never a neutral process—quite the opposite, in fact.

Fortunately we don't have to solve all the dilemmas raised by a full inquiry into the dimensions of representation. Our interest in it is primarily as a means of access to government for publics with problems. Representation can be the link between people, their problems, and government. We don't expect it to work in a particular way for everyone who has a need; some people get represented, others don't. What does interest us in this inquiry is the particular manner in which representation occurs for a specific public problem (and, for purposes of generalization, the similarities and differences among representational patterns). Involved are such considerations as the event and how it is perceived by the represented and the representative; the effects of the event and whether (and how) these are defined as problems by the represented and the representative; the extent to which those affected are represented at all; and the impact of the process.

Though this discussion is not confined to representation in any one institution, legislative representation illustrates the complexity of the process. One may be represented at many points and in various ways by legislator-representatives because they get involved in many of the functional activities of the policy process. Thus as you examine specific issue areas and public problems, consider that representation by and access to legislators may vary from issue to issue (the issue dimension), among the activities involved in the formulation of a course of action (formulation dimension), among the stages in the legislative process (legislative process dimension), among the actions in administering policy to the problem (administration dimension), or among the many service activities of legislative offices (constituency service dimension).[6]

The relationship among the several functional activities is important. For example, if representation forms a link between problem and action, it is critical to consider which perceptions, definitions, and aggregations get represented. If events can result in various problems (depending as they do upon definition), and some publics have more access than others to decision making, then obviously policy output is affected accordingly. Consider the person mentioned earlier, whose home and drugstore are being demolished for urban renewal. Though well aware of the deterioration of the area, she defines a different set of problems than does the department store owner in the nearby central business district or the commuter who speeds past the area on the freeway. She may see zoning violations, lack of police protection, inadequate lighting, lack of recreation facilities. Yet the area has been designated for urban renewal; other definitions of the area's problems are being represented. As the bulldozer flattens her home and store, we can imagine our friend saying, "Very interesting, but that is not exactly what I had in mind as a solution." For various reasons, her perceptions and definitions—even if aggregated with others in the same position (or perhaps because they are not aggregated)—are not reflected in the policy-making process.[7]

This case brings us to some intriguing elements of representation. How is it possible for a group of affluent representatives (whether they be legislators or bureaucrats) to know enough about poverty publics to represent their perceptions of events and definitions of problems? How can they identify with them? Isn't it highly probable that they will tend to represent those who are more like themselves? Is it possible for affluent representatives to empathize with poverty publics? A nice word, empathy, and it appears to be a significant element of representation as an activity. Henry Clay Smith defines empathy as "the tendency of a perceiver to assume that another person's feelings, thoughts, and behavior are similar to his own."[8] It seems that if representatives are to act for other people, or for a constituency, on the specific consequences of events in society, they must try to act in a way that leads them to make the underlying assumptions of "empathy." By the nature of the representative process, they try to create conditions whereby they can assume that others' "feelings, thoughts, and behavior are similar" to their own, given the case at hand. Can this be done with the problems of the poor? No doubt some representatives attain a high measure of empathic accuracy in such circumstances, but there are many obstacles to success.

Housing for the poor well illustrates these points. For the most part, federal public housing policy is based on very little information about either the problem as defined by ghetto residents or about the priorities of problems in the ghetto.[9] Nathan Glazer notes that we have only limited information about the effects of poor housing (thus raising the question as to what the real problems of the ghetto are).

■ What is the effect of substandard and crowded housing on the families that live in it? Here we reach into the murkiest of sociological depths. I have indicated how culture-bound are our definitions of "the standard" and "the crowded." We can find examples of entire societies living in housing that by our measures are substandard and crowded, and yet these conditions seem not to create a serious problem for family living.[10]

Federal housing policy has generally concentrated on the problems that were familiar to the policy makers. We work with what we know. Glazer speaks of "the consistent bias in this country in favor of the owner-occupied, single-family, free-standing house, with a bit of land around it." Slums get the attention of "reformers, writers, analysts," but

■ . . . it is the single-family, owner-occupied home—getting it built, getting it financed, saving it from banks, reducing its cost, increasing its amenities—that has received the chief attention of elected officials, administrators, and the majority of the American people, perhaps even the poor among them.[11]

The principal effort to aid the poor—public housing—has been a pitiful effort indeed. The number of units authorized by the Housing Act of 1949 (810,000 units over a six-year period) still had not been built in the 1970s. Too few units have been provided, they have been located in the most undesirable areas, the architecture is frequently unpleasant and sets off public housing as different, it has been limited to the poorest, and it breaks up communities. As Glazer notes, the poor themselves do not much like it: "While poor families on urban renewal sites have priority in entering public housing projects, only a minority do so."[12]

This dismal record was not established purposely. Most representatives have wanted to do the right thing. "Public housing is a graveyard of good intentions," concludes Glazer.[13] The failure is due in part to the difficulty of knowing what the problems are as defined by those experiencing them.

Interestingly, a related point can be made about many problems for affluent publics, though for quite different reasons. As described in chapter 3, the increasing use of the gasoline engine has had considerable impact. One effect that can readily be perceived by commuters is that of air pollution. This effect is defined by many as a problem, one of smell, sight, perhaps of physical well-being. Typically, the commuter identifies the source of the problem as the bus, truck, or car emitting oil smoke.[14] Less likely is the recognition that his or her own new car is also polluting the air, as approximately one gallon of gasoline in ten goes into the atmosphere through the crankcase and tailpipe. Here are consequences that may affect the physical well-being of affluent publics. Yet the precise effects of the consequences must be defined by technicians, since the ordinary citizen does not have the knowledge necessary to identify these effects. How can representatives know what to do? They are presumably able to achieve a higher degree of empathic accuracy with affluent publics, but what difference does it make if both they and their public lack the technical knowledge to determine effects? The result is that policy is based on technical information, modified to the extent that affluent publics make demands that are perceived by representatives.

Thus in the first case, that of public housing, one can legitimately raise the question of whether representatives can achieve empathic accuracy because of the marked differences between those who experience substandard housing and those who represent them. In the second case, that of air pollution, empathic accuracy is more likely but may be irrelevant to the hazards involved. The point of all of this is simply to alert you to complications inherent in the early stages of policy development and to illustrate the fascinating dimensions of one of the most fundamental of democratic concepts: representation.

Agenda Setting

It is useful at this point to remember that these early-stage policy activities are directed toward getting a problem to government. Gaining agenda status is therefore of special interest. In fact, the study of perception, definition, aggregation, organization, and representation typically stems from an interest in agenda setting. In other words, one begins with the current list of major issues being treated in government and studies how they got there.

In his study of agenda-setting strategies for pollution policies, Layne D. Hoppe makes a fundamental point of interest to students of public policy.

■ "Agenda" [comes] to have meaning in terms of specific patterns of action in government—particularly those in the early stages of policy development. An analysis of agenda-setting processes [becomes] an analysis of how problems developed, how they were defined, the courses of action formulated to act on these problems, the legitimation of one course of action over another, the emergence of policy systems designed to act on such problems on a continuing basis. The result [is] that it [is] most difficult to isolate an agenda-setting process as an identifiable, one-time, discrete process.[15]

This advisory serves to warn the student not to conceptualize the policy process as being segmented, with each activity clearly isolable from the others. It also suggests the pitfalls in any effort to identify various types of agendas, as though each were a definite "thing" existing in some governmental office as a kind of schedule of events.

Still, the term *agenda* is commonly used and does convey definite meaning as a list of items for action. In its most basic form the word simply means "things to be done." This definition is not very helpful, however, since there are things to be done at all levels and in most units of government. A reference point is needed. For example, one might refer to items to be taken up at a township meeting next Wednesday evening, proposals made in the president's State of the Union Message, or bills scheduled for committee attention. Roger

W. Cobb and Charles D. Elder have sought to clarify usage by distinguishing between the *systemic agenda* and the *institutional agenda*. The first is defined as "all issues that are commonly perceived by members of the political community as meriting public attention and as involving matters within the legitimate jurisdiction of existing governmental authority."[16] While each of us can doubtless nominate issues that meet these criteria (at least in our individual judgment), the concept itself is difficult to put into operation. Essentially it reduces to personal assessments of what *ought* to be acted on in government because of the scope of the problem, public concern, and the jurisdiction of government. We all have our lists of what ought to be done by government. Presumably the systemic agenda would be the composite of these lists. Unfortunately, such lists are not easy to compile, and we are therefore often left with individual and group assessments of what ought to be treated.

Cobb and Elder define the *institutional agenda* as "that set of items explicitly up for the active and serious consideration of authoritative decision makers."[17] The institutional agenda is of particular interest in this book because it refers to those matters that constitute much of the work of the policy process. It makes sense that the various national policy-making institutions—for example, the White House, departments or agencies, Congress and its committees—would have agendas. The State of the Union Messages, budget messages and resolutions, schedules of committee and subcommittee hearings, and legislative and court calendars are all formal expressions of institutional agendas. They show what is currently thought to deserve attention and resources.

A review of these agendas reveals a distinction between problems that are *new* and those that are *continuing*. Getting a problem on an agenda in the first place may require great persistence (see the child abuse case on page 69). Once agenda status is achieved, the next challenge is to maintain it: to convince decision makers that continuous government action is required to solve the problem. The politics of initiating action differs from that of maintaining action.

As institutional agendas grow, gaining status for a new problem becomes more difficult. In part this is a consequence of the scope of government activity: most problems are associated with the many programs already on the books. But, of course, in an expanding government the commitment of resources becomes such that little is left for new initiatives (a development that appears to characterize the early 1980s). Under these circumstances, institutional agendas become self-perpetuating: what was on the list last year turns up again this year.

Crisis may scramble institutional agendas. By its nature, a crisis breaks the ordinary pattern of doing business. It may even take a major disaster to get a new problem on the agenda. Oil spills, threat of a meltdown at Three Mile Island, the Arab oil embargo, riots in the streets, mine disasters, and air pollution episodes are all events that have had dramatic impact. If decision makers are prepared to act quickly, major changes may be effected in a short time. Public attention may not be sustained, however. Anthony Downs notes an "issue-attention cycle." "American public attention rarely remains sharply focused upon any one domestic issue for very long—even if it involves a continuing problem of crucial importance to society."[18] The trick, for those who want to see changes in the agenda, is to be prepared to act when the crisis occurs.

Among the possible effects of a crisis on institutional agendas are *displacement, expansion,* and *rippling.*[19] The first simply refers to one major issue losing its high ranking due to new events; for example, as energy issues displaced environmental issues following the Arab oil embargo in 1973. Issue expansion in this context refers to the discovery of related problems. Again the Arab oil embargo provides a good example. Analyzing the initial problem soon led to concerns about long-run dependence on foreign oil, instability in the Middle East, and even the way we have permitted cities to grow (creating difficult transportation problems). Rippling refers to the effect of priorities set at a higher level of government on the activities of lower levels or on the private sphere. Thus, for example, it has been difficult for state and local governments to resist when the national government identified a new issue and offered incentives for them to reorder their priorities. Rippling may also influence organization at the lower levels (for example, the many state and local environmental and energy units that were created after national priorities were set).

To summarize, *agenda* is a term commonly used to portray those issues judged to require public action. The *systemic agenda* is the broader set of issues in society, not all of which are treated in government. The *institutional agenda* consists of those issues regularly treated by decision makers in specific policy-making institutions (presidency, bureaucracy, Congress, the courts), each of which may have its own list. Because of the expansion of government during the 1930s and 1960s, the institutional agenda is now made up mostly of continuing problems. New problems must be fought for if they are to find a place on the agenda. Often crisis is required to rearrange priorities through displacement, expansion, and rippling.

Theories of Agenda Setting

Democracy is a system of government based on public participation. Since the satisfactory resolution of public problems is one major function of any government, we may expect democracies to be characterized by a high degree of public involvement in agenda setting, that is, in that important process by which problems deserving action are identified. At the same time, most theorists acknowledge that classical or pure democracy is unachievable in modern society. In fact, massive public participation in the detailed affairs of government can create chaos.

The "American Hybrid"

In the context of a democracy based on limited or specialized participation, the works of David B. Truman and Robert A. Dahl have made an important contribution to our understanding of agenda setting. Truman views the governmental process as a mosaic of interacting groups, both in and out of government itself. Problem identification occurs within the context of group life. With the effort of groups to solve their problems, Truman identifies an "inevitable gravitation toward government."

■ Herein lies the clue to the universal tendency of interest groups to resort to government action in the present day. Such groups will supplement their own resources by operating upon or through that institutionalized group whose powers are most inclusive in that time and place. . . . That institution today is government. . . .

  The effects of such reliance upon government are cumulative. Just as the direct and indirect effects of an interest group may disturb the equilibriums of related groups, so its operations through and upon government are likely to force the related groups also to assert their claims upon governmental institutions in order to achieve some measure of adjustment.[20]

Dahl posits "a preface to democratic theory" that incorporates much of the group approach but addresses the matter of how public policy is made. Selected quotes from this important work reveal his concept of what he terms "the American hybrid" of democratic decision making.

■ . . . on matters of specific policy the majority rarely rules. . . . elections are a crucial device for controlling leaders. . . . specific policies tend to be products of "minorities rule."[21]

Dahl argues in summary that:

■ A central guiding thread to American constitutional development has been the evolution of a political system in which all the active and legitimate groups in the population can make themselves heard at some crucial stage in the process of decision.[22]

Here then is an image of a working democracy as an interlacement of "active and legitimate groups" identifying problems and bargaining for solutions. Roger W. Cobb and Charles D. Elder list the following tenets of this revised democratic theory:

1. social pluralism
2. diverse and competing elites that are circulating and accessible
3. a basic consensus at least among the elites on the rules of democratic competition
4. elections that provide regular opportunities for citizens to participate in the selection of public officials

Cobb and Elder correctly refer to this as a system of limited participation and add that "there can be no doubt it is empirically more viable as a descriptive statement of functioning democracies than is classical theory."[23]

Bias in Agenda Setting

Although it may be descriptively accurate, some political scientists regard the revised theory as prescriptively undesirable. For the fact is that limiting participation to the "active and legitimate groups" in society by definition results in a biased agenda of public problems. *Active* implies organization, structure, leadership, support, and available resources. Not everyone in the society who has problems also has these advantages. *Legitimate* implies the meeting of some standards of social acceptability. Whatever those standards are, some groups are certain to be excluded. Perhaps we should be more blunt. It is, or should be, no news that the American system has been biased toward the affluent. Those with the resources to organize and communicate have an advantage in a system designed to respond to "active and legitimate groups." Indeed, even the problems of the poor are frequently represented by the affluent in our society. In recent decades that representation has resulted in many programs designed to relieve the problems of those identified as less advantaged. The test of true commitment to support for the poor may be upon us during the present era of concern over budget growth. That is, we may discover which problems have priority in times of perceived scarcity of resources: those of the affluent or those of the poor.

While many scholars have challenged the acceptability of "the American hybrid," E. E. Schattschneider, Peter Bachrach, and Morton S. Baratz have proposed particularly interesting and relevant analyses. In his book *The Semisovereign People,* Schattschneider clearly illustrates "the scope and bias of the pressure system." He challenges the notion that politically active group life is common in the United States. "The range of organized, identifiable, known groups is amazingly narrow; there is nothing remotely universal about it."[24] That which does exist, according to Schattschneider, "has an upper-class bias." This observation has important implications both for the question of what groups get from government and for the control of the agendas of government. For Schattschneider, competition is the essence of democracy, and he is distressed to find that it exists only to the extent of producing a "semisovereign people."[25]

Bachrach and Baratz posit "two faces of power": one in which decisions are made to favor one group or set of groups and a second in which conditions are created for excluding certain issues from consideration in government. They explain it thus:

■ Of course power is exercised when A participates in the making of decisions that affect B. Power is also exercised when A devotes his energies to creating or reinforcing social and political values and institutional practices that limit the scope of the political process to public consideration of only those issues which

are comparatively innocuous to A. To the extent that A succeeds in doing this,
B is prevented . . . from bringing to the fore any issues that might in their
resolution be seriously detrimental to A's set of preferences.[26]

Following Schattschneider, Bachrach and Baratz specify a "mobilization of
bias" in the political system, that is, "a set of predominant values, beliefs,
rituals, and institutional procedures . . . that operate systematically and consistently to the benefit of certain persons and groups at the expense of others."[27]
The means for sustaining this mobilization of bias is something called "nondecision making."

■ A nondecision, as we define it, is a decision that results in suppression or
thwarting of a latent or manifest challenge to the values or interests of the
decision maker. To be more nearly explicit, nondecision making is a means by
which demands for change in the existing allocation of benefits and privileges in
the community can be suffocated before they are even voiced; or kept covert;
or killed before they gain access to the relevant decision-making arena; or,
failing all these things, maimed or destroyed in the decision-implementing stage
of the policy process.[28]

It is unnecessary for our purposes to employ the rather awkward and inapt
term of "nondecision." We can simply record that governmental agenda-setting processes typically favor some groups and their problem definitions over
others, or even actively prevent access for certain interests. Actually there is
not very much new about the idea. It is a rather common theme throughout
much of American history—"the rich get richer" and all that. What is common knowledge often is not incorporated into intellectual discourse and theo-
rizing, however. Thus, whole books get written about the American political
system without so much as a mention of what and how problems get to
government, or the importance of finding out.

Agenda Setting: The Options

Having acknowledged the bias of a system that provides open access for
"active and legitimate groups," the social architect is faced with the difficult
problem of what should be done. Schattschneider was satisfied to provide for
competition. "Democracy is a competitive political system in which competing
leaders and organizations define the alternatives of public policy in such a way
that the public can participate in the decision-making process."[29] Presumably
for Schattschneider there are ways to define alternatives (including how problems are to be defined and priorities set) so that the public can participate.
Once that is done, it is up to the public to get cracking and involve themselves.
What if they don't? Schattschneider doesn't say, but his definition suggests
that the job is finished if competing leaders do what he proposes.

What becomes very evident in this review of theories is that agenda setting
is a complex and tricky business in a democracy. Simply maintaining an open
process favors the strong; doing anything else creates other biases. It is appro-

priate here to reiterate one of the initial realities: "All policy systems have a bias." At a minimum there appear to be the following agenda-setting options, each considered here with the problems it creates.

1. Let it happen.   In this first, highly pluralistic option, government takes a relatively passive role in agenda setting. It maintains channels of access and communication so that those affected can be heard, but it does not reach out either to assist individuals and groups to define problems and organize or to assume the task of problem definition and priority setting. This option is pluralistic in the sense that its success depends on many of the tenets of the group theory of politics: that people will define their own interests, organize, seek access, involve others in support of their cause, influence decision making, monitor implementation, and so on. There are countless examples associated with the normal course of farm, labor, business, and other sector policy making, wherein initiative is taken outside government to get it to act.

While "letting it happen" is attractive in concept, as Schattschneider and others point out, it also may be highly preferential. It simply ignores the uneven distribution of resources in the society. Nor do all groups have equal stature in the community. The fact is that a free system of this type favors those who have over those who don't; and that edge may well extend to how the process works as well as to what it produces.

2. Encourage it to happen.   In this second option, the government reaches out to assist people in defining and articulating their problems. The bias of a totally free system toward the strong over the weak is acknowledged and an effort is made to equalize resources so that the process of agenda setting does not favor one group or set of interests over another. Note that the emphasis here is in equipping people to participate, not in assuming the tasks of identifying and defining problems for them. Thus, for example, the poor, or those otherwise disadvantaged, are by some means provided with resources to get involved in politics and policy making—to make themselves heard, in Dahl's terms. The Economic Opportunity Act of 1964 (the War on Poverty) did provide means to this end by supporting community action agencies in poverty areas.

This option, too, presents problems. Government is put in the position of determining who needs assistance. Bias may just as easily result, as the rural poor might well have argued of the poverty program. Equally troublesome is the question of whether democratic government should be in the business of building up its own agenda by providing support for certain groups. There is also the question of government's ability to solve or even relieve the problems identified. Again, the poverty program of the 1960s demonstrated some of the risks involved in raising the hopes, but not necessarily the income level, of the poor.

3. Make it happen.   In this third option, government plays an active role in defining problems and setting goals. Policy makers do not wait for the system to work; they direct its operations by establishing problem-defining and

priority-setting mechanisms within government. Government must define problems, set priorities, and establish goals in all three options, but in the first two
these activities follow the signals and demands of the public. That is, political
decision makers are faced with the task of giving weight to this or that pressure that either has been freely expressed or has been encouraged by government. In the third case, however, decision makers do not await the emergence
of demands. They systematically review societal events for their effects and set
an agenda of government action.

The problems with this approach are, or should be, obvious. It places an
enormous burden on government. Surveying events, judging the consequences, and setting priorities in a complex society are difficult and demanding
responsibilities. Few governments have been able to accomplish these tasks
successfully. There is also the question of whether *democratic* government can
achieve these ends and remain true to its principles.

The tendency in this option is to develop technical means for agenda setting.
Comprehensive planning is stressed. However, a semblance of objectivity may
only mask the biases associated with choosing which issues will receive attention. Thus it may, in fact, be more difficult to identify the preferences of the
decision makers because of the methods employed; yet biases are bound to
exist.

Here then are three modes of government agenda setting in a democracy,
ranging from the more traditional role, in which decision makers await pressures to act, to the more activist roles of encouraging pressures from certain
groups (essentially providing support for the process) and actually monitoring
events to determine effects and judge where action is needed. The first, more
traditional, method seems to predominate even now in this country. We still
tend to "let it happen," even when preferential treatment and deliberateness
(if not downright sluggishness) invite legitimate criticism and/or social, economic, or political disaster.

The other options are based on the assumption that public problems deserving government action are either not being represented in the system or are
actively excluded by the "mobilization of bias." This conclusion has been
gaining support in recent decades, particularly in reference to various socially
and economically disadvantaged groups. I have already mentioned the development of community action agencies under the poverty program. Civil rights
and consumer-oriented agencies are other examples, as are various shifts to
affirmative action within established agencies. We have no examples as yet, at
least to my knowledge, of a *comprehensive* effort to "make it happen." The
five-year plans so popular at one time in Communist countries have not been
developed in the United States. Still, given the predominance of middle- and
upper-class representation in government, plans to relieve the problems of the
poor are typically designed by people who have limited subjective experience
of poverty. Put another way, the record of middle-class decision makers in
"making it happen" for lower-class publics illustrates both the methods and
some of the serious pitfalls of the third option. It should also be mentioned that

the recent stress on uncontrollable budget growth encourages more comprehensive analysis of national issues. Whether this shift will result in five-year plans is problematic, but in any case more people do seem to be paying attention to the scope of the government's agenda.

Dynamics of Agenda Setting

The routes that problems take to government are varied. Candidates learn about problems on the campaign trail, an enterprising journalist writes a series of articles on a local issue, Ralph Nader's group issues another report, a constituent complains to a member of Congress, a group of pensioners travel to Capitol Hill. No one yet has sought to catalog all the methods used for getting the government's attention, for the good reason that the task is overwhelming.

What can be done here is to provide a framework for studying the dynamics of agenda setting. We may not be able to spot all the variations, but at least we can guide the analysis, based on what is known about policy conditions and strategies. One place to start is with specific institutional agendas, to see whether there are certain common features. Jack L. Walker does this for agenda setting in the United States Senate. He identifies three features that enhance the probability that an issue will receive attention.

■   First, an item's attractiveness increases if it has an impact on large numbers of people. . . . Second, convincing evidence must exist that the proposed legislation is addressed to a serious and real problem. . . . Third, the case for inclusion on the agenda will be greatly strengthened if an easily understood solution exists for the problem being addressed. . . . These conditions are not sufficient in themselves to ensure success, but they certainly increase an issue's attractiveness and lower any barriers in its path.[30]

The first characteristic concerns the scope of the issue and possibly the support that can be mustered for it. Clearly such issues as inflation, energy shortages, and medical care will command the immediate attention of most decision makers. The second characteristic is related to the first: the problem or issue must be judged significant. One measure of its importance is the number of people who are affected. The third characteristic is the existence of a feasible solution, a feature that surely can be overridden by the first two. That is, if the issue affects large numbers of people, it may have agenda status whether or not a feasible solution is available.

Walker's list of features can be expanded considerably by thinking systematically about the following major elements of agenda setting:

1. The events themselves that trigger efforts to get problems to government (including whether and how problems are defined)
2. The organization and resources of those "who are affected"

3. The access or representation available to those groups
4. The structure of the policy process and the commitments of decision makers

Note that the first three of these elements more or less coincide with the functional activities discussed earlier: perception and definition, aggregation and organization, and representation. They are all parts of the process of getting problems on the agenda. The fourth element directs attention to the characteristics of the policy process at any one time. Those characteristics, too, have an effect on agenda setting since they involve the ways in which institutions work and decision makers think. The biggest problem in the world (by some objective definition) won't achieve agenda status if those who run the system don't perceive it as requiring attention.

These four elements can be further elaborated to (1) identify their major components and (2) provide a set of relevant questions for studying the dynamics of agenda setting for any one issue. What follows should be used by the reader as a guide to research and study of this important policy activity. Different issues should then be compared, to yield generalizations about agenda setting.

The events themselves
    Scope: How many people are affected?
    Perception: Who perceives what? How many people perceive consequences? What are the results of perception?
    Definition: Are the perceived consequences defined as a problem? If so, by whom? Are different problems defined by different people?
    Intensity: How intense are those who are affected? Does intensity vary among those affected?

Organization of groups
    Extent: How many members are there in the groups affected? What is their commitment to the group?
    Structure: What is the relationship between members and leaders—hierarchical? democratic? Is professional staff available?
    Leadership: How are leaders selected? How much authority do they have? How aggressive are they?

Access
    Representation: Are those affected by consequences represented by those in policy-making positions?
    Empathy: Are those in policy-making positions likely to empathize with those affected?
    Support: Can support be marshaled by those affected?

Policy process
    Structure: What are the relationships between policy actors and those affected—hierarchical? democratic? bargaining? What are the formal requirements of policy making?

Responsiveness: How responsive are policy actors to those affected? What have been the traditions regarding responsiveness?
Leadership: How are leaders selected? How much authority do they have? How aggressive are they?

It may be useful to illustrate the utility of the categories by examining strategies that involve various combinations of the second and third elements (organization and access or representation). Consider the following variations:

1. *A well-organized group with established access* (for example, the American Medical Association, the American Petroleum Institute)
2. *A well-organized group without established access* (for example, any group that, though well organized for other purposes, prefers not to go to government. Examples might be many professional groups earlier in the century)
3. *A poorly organized group with established access* (for example, the coal industry, farmers, or others with definite advantages in access but limited capacity for defining their interests)
4. *The poorly organized group without established access* (for example, many of the socially and economically disadvantaged groups in the society)

Presumably the first group will simply employ its advantages to get problems attended to in government. Its strategic planning is greatly simplified by its unity of purpose and political contacts. In fact, much of its effort may be directed toward containing the issue, so as not to incite others whose reactions might complicate matters.

The second group will probably capitalize on its organizational advantages to gain access to decision makers when necessary. Under the assumption that strong organization means effective leadership, unity of purpose, and available resources, any group in this second category has obvious potential political punch. Elected decision makers, in particular, can be expected to understand this and to pay close attention to the group's demands. A strong organization can normally depend on having access when it deems it necessary to go to government.

A group of the third type has the advantage of access but is incapable of exercising it effectively. In this case strategic planning must be directed toward developing the capacity of the group itself to identify problems and set priorities. Unless it is able to accomplish this, the group may find that problems are consistently defined for it by public decision makers, and that policies therefore are often inadequate.

Cobb and Elder contribute much to our understanding of the fourth group—essentially the outsiders in the political system, those with few resources to organize or gain access. They argue that agenda setting is facilitated through issue expansion: by involving other individual groups. They list four general types of groupings: identification groups (those that identify with another group's interests), attention groups (those aware of the issue at hand), the

attentive public ("a generally informed and interested stratum of the population"), and the general public ("less active, less interested, and less informed").
Their underlying proposition is that "the greater the size of the audience to
which an issue can be enlarged, the greater the likelihood that it will attain
systemic agenda standing and thus access to a formal agenda." [31]

I have already noted that issues of great scope are likely to be on governmental agendas. But I was speaking of those issues that result from large-scale,
dramatic events with immediate impact (natural disasters, war, the oil embargo). Cobb and Elder are speaking of expanding the scope of an issue as a
conscious agenda-setting strategy. Though they do not intend to limit this
approach to the poorly organized group without established access, I would
argue that they have well described the only strategy available to such groups.
The fact is that most policy making is limited to a relatively small number of
active participants precisely because it is conducted by and for groups in the
first three categories. In other words, issue expansion as an agenda-setting
strategy is the exception, not the rule, in American politics. And it is most
characteristic of groups without the advantages of organization and access.
During the 1960s in particular, we witnessed extreme forms of this strategy,
including violent protest. It was an era that Amitai Etzioni appropriately
dubbed "demonstration democracy." [32]

E. E. Schattschneider's analysis of this whole matter is particularly insight-
ful. On the one hand he notes that "democratic government is the greatest
single instrument for the socialization of conflict [read: expansion of the issue]
in the American community." [33] On the other hand, he introduces considerable
evidence to show the "scope and bias" of the decision-making apparatus.
While observing that "nationalization of politics inevitably breaks up old local
power monopolies . . . ," [34] he also notes that "a tremendous amount of conflict is controlled by keeping it so private that it is almost completely invisi-
ble." [35] And further: "It is the *loser* who calls in outside help." [36] Thus, we
must acknowledge that whereas expanding the issue may be a beneficial
agenda-setting strategy under certain circumstances, it often represents a last
resort for those with established access and/or strong organization.

Finally, I must mention those many citizen groups for whom expanded participation is a matter of principle. As discussed in chapter 1, certain public
interest groups have concentrated on increasing openness in all decision making. Where they are successful one finds a contagion of participation; by which
I mean simply that involvement of such groups often facilitates the participation of others (including the media), and their success in expanding a decision-
making population naturally results in more activity by those traditionally affected by the issue. Thus, for example, setting quotas on sugar imports is a
relatively limited government program. It has potentially broad public impact,
however, since sugar prices are affected. One can imagine the effect of citizen
group attention to these import quotas: greater awareness of their impacts,
demands for change, and more media and public concentration on the issue, all
stimulating increased activity by those supporting, and benefiting from, the

quotas. Once public perception has been penetrated, active participation may spread rather quickly.

We have only scratched the surface of the dynamics of agenda setting. I hope that enough has been said, however, to tempt students to pursue this line of inquiry. By now everyone acknowledges the importance of these early stages of decision making, but relatively little research has been conducted.[37] The task is difficult but is too important to be left undone.

Cases of Agenda Setting

I now offer real-life instances of agenda setting. The first, on child abuse, shows what combination of conditions is needed to succeed with a very old problem. The second illustrates what persistence can accomplish, even in the face of affected publics who show little interest in organizing on a life-and-death issue (auto safety). And the third identifies an emerging issue with widespread effect on the more affluent public.

A Federal Role in Curbing Child Abuse

The physical abuse of children is the sort of problem that evokes general public attention and sympathy. Yet for centuries it was dealt with almost exclusively in the private sector. According to Barbara J. Nelson, the issuance of a report by the Children's Bureau in 1957 constituted the "first major public sector" attention to this problem.[38] This report recommended state-level investigations of child "neglect, abuse, and abandonment." How did the issue develop and achieve agenda status?

Nelson's recounting of the story unfolds a complicated and lengthy *intergovernmental process* involving both public and private sectors. She establishes that the issue moved almost like a wave from a private research organization to the Children's Bureau in the Department of Health, Education, and Welfare and thence to the state legislatures and finally to Congress. The process spanned two decades. Initial interest in the Children's Bureau was a result of work done by the American Humane Association, a nongovernmental organization sponsoring research on child and animal protection. Once the issue was acknowledged, the bureau played an important role initially in maintaining and expanding public and media awareness. Possibly crucial to this expansion was a new and disturbing label, the "Battered Child Syndrome," which was the title of an article by a physician whose research was sponsored by the bureau. As Nelson observes, "From an agenda-setting perspective the effect of the label cannot be overestimated."[39] She records a significant increase in media attention following the publication of the article in the *Journal of the American Medical Association*.

Action in state legislatures was facilitated by media attention; by the development and promotion of model statutes or legislative guidelines by the Children's Bureau, the American Humane Association, the Council of State Governments, the American Academy of Pediatrics, and the American Medical Association; and by the fact that "support for child abuse legislation was a sure-win situation" for state legislators. Pressure was maintained to insure that laws were more than symbolic and that uniformity of law among the states was realized.

Recognition of the issue in Congress was somewhat slower, as may befit a federal system. Efforts were made to identify and act on the problem in the late 1960s, but with few results. According to Nelson, agenda setting in Congress proceeded as follows:

1. Attention to the the the dimensions of the issue by the Senate Subcommittee on Children and Youth (Committee on Labor and Public Welfare), chaired by Senator Walter Mondale (D.–Minnesota)
2. A decision by Mondale to focus on child abuse in a period otherwise inhospitable to social legislation. Mondale later joked that "not even Richard Nixon could be for child abuse." [40]
3. Committee hearings that resulted in considerable media attention to the issue
4. Passage in 1973 of a federal program providing aid for the prevention of child abuse and the treatment of abused and neglected children

With the enactment of the new program a National Center on Child Abuse and Neglect was created, thus insuring future attention to the issue. In 1978 the law was broadened somewhat and "a modest attack" was begun on a related problem: sexual abuse of children. Interestingly, the reauthorization of the 1973 act was used as a vehicle to draw attention to the related issue of child pornography. Here was another matter seeking agenda status, one that received quick action once recognition was achieved. [41] New problems are often acknowledged as a consequence of experience with established programs.

Government and Auto Safety

The previous case illustrates a problem with little active organizational support among those directly affected (a public problem without a public), yet with the potential for widespread attention and sympathy. The issue of automobile safety is quite different. The potential for public awareness was high, given the number of motor vehicles. But a public infatuated with the ownership of personalized transportation did not want to hear that cars were unsafe. Nor did manufacturers wish to have that point publicized, fearing both loss of sales and costly modifications in production.

The sheer number of motor vehicles insured that the issue of safety would eventually reach the agenda of government. It was destined to happen in the 1960s. "It took until 1948, fifty-five years, to produce the first 100,000,000 [motor vehicles]; the second took just fifteen years." [42] Accompanying this increase was a quite striking surge in deaths attributable to traffic accidents, which averaged more than 38,000 in the late 1950s and more than 54,000 in the late 1960s.[43] A person whose name has since become familiar to us all, Ralph Nader, wrote a book calling attention to this situation. *Unsafe at Any Speed* dramatically accused the automobile industry of failing to treat the problem. Nader even identified an "automobile accident industry" of "doctors, lawyers, engineers, and other specialists" who profited from but did not seek to prevent "the highway carnage."[44]

How did this issue reach national government agendas? How were public lethargy and the active opposition of a major industry overcome? The process began with the election of Abraham Ribicoff (D.–Connecticut) to the United States Senate in 1962.[45] Auto safety was for Ribicoff an issue whose time had come, as child abuse had been for Walter Mondale. Ribicoff had developed safety programs in Connecticut while governor and was determined to do the same nationally. He hired a young lawyer from Hartford, Ralph Nader, to serve as a consultant to the Subcommittee on Executive Reorganization, which Ribicoff chaired in 1965. The importance of Nader and his book (published in 1965) cannot be overemphasized. Like the "Battered Child Syndrome" label, Nader's book title focused public attention on a serious problem. It should also be pointed out that hearings on traffic safety had been conducted a decade earlier in the House (by Kenneth A. Roberts, D.–Alabama), but the time was not right for comprehensive safety legislation (though some laws affecting auto safety were passed, beginning in 1959).

The formidable automobile industry was in a difficult position once the issue had achieved a solid place on the congressional agenda. It is difficult for any corporation to oppose safe travel. The industry's position was further compromised, however, by an unseemly investigation and harassment of Ralph Nader, sponsored by the General Motors Corporation. With the barriers to agenda status lowered, action proceeded rather quickly. Among other supporting conditions were the growth of technical literature on traffic safety (more detailed definition of the problem) and increased attention in the mass media in response to activity in Congress. Jack L. Walker found that:

■ The amount of news generated on this topic declined fairly steadily from the mid-1960s until 1964 when it began to turn upward. There was a small increase in coverage during 1965—the year of the Ribicoff hearings—and then a massive upsurge in 1966, the peak year of traffic deaths and the year in which the highway safety act passed the Congress and was signed into law.[46]

The National Traffic and Motor Vehicle Safety Act, which also passed in 1966, included provisions for motor vehicle standards (including used vehicles), tire safety, and further research. The Highway Safety Act concentrated on supporting state highway safety programs. Passage of both laws had been achieved approximately eighteen months after the Ribicoff hearings—remarkably quickly for a major issue.

Even more impressive than the speed with which legislation was enacted the immediate attention given to other safety issues. Congressional action in one area appeared to have firmly established consumer safety as a topic of concern and lawmaking. Walker notes that:

■   Within the Congress, activist Senators were moving quickly to capitalize on the rising interest in safety by proposing new legislation. Senator Magnuson's Commerce Committee staff organized itself as a small factory for producing legislative proposals on safety.[47]

Soon investigations were conducted into meat, fish, and poultry inspections and the safety of diet pills. Laws were passed for toy safety, fire prevention, consumer product safety, coal mine safety, and occupational safety and health. Political entrepreneurs apparently act quickly once an issue area has been opened and resistance is low.

Tax Expenditures: An Emerging Issue

It is useful in this section to discuss one issue that has recently (at this writing) achieved agenda status. Tax expenditures refer to special deductions, exclusions, or credits that individuals or corporations may legitimately claim in calculating what they owe the federal government at tax time. For example, I am able to deduct the interest I pay on my home mortgage. I can also deduct charitable contributions, medical expenses, and professional expenses of various kinds (for example, the costs I incur in writing and publishing this book). Whereas many people get payments or subsidies from the federal government, tax expenditures permit one to keep more money than those not eligible to deduct or claim a credit. The term *expenditure* is a bit misleading, because the cost to the government is on the receipt side of the ledger: money is not forthcoming (or is paid back if the taxpayer has had too much withheld).

Tax inequity has long been a policy issue at the national level, but never before has there been such heavy concentration on total revenue loss through tax breaks. Agenda status for this issue was achieved in part because the Congressional Budget and Impoundment Act of 1974 required a listing of tax expenditures, which made the dimensions of the problem more apparent. The fiscal year 1983 budget was the first to estimate tax expenditures as outlays rather than revenue losses. "This is done by measuring the tax expenditure as the amount of outlays that would be required to provide an equal after-tax income to the taxpayer."[48]

It is estimated that tax expenditures in fiscal 1983 amounted to $317.1 billion, more than 40 percent of the total budget requested by the Reagan administration. If this amount were added to the budget, outlays for 1983 would exceed $1 trillion. The deficit would not change, however, since one is merely accounting for revenue not received.[49]

Here is a case of agenda setting resulting from demands for a more comprehensive analysis of the budget. The issue arises as one examines the budget in its many parts and seeks to understand how these parts are related. Congress did not have the capacity to conduct such an analysis before reforming its procedures (see chapter 7).

At this writing, proposals are before Congress to reduce tax expenditures, perhaps with a flat tax that does not permit deductions or other tax breaks (or permits only a limited number). Many flat tax proposals were introduced in 1982, all motivated by the desire for a simplified tax collecting system and fewer inequities. One such plan (introduced by Representative Richard A. Gephardt, D.–Missouri, and Senator Bill Bradley, D.–New Jersey) would use a 14 percent rate on income up to $25,000 ($40,000 for couples), with a sliding scale of 6 to 14 percent on additional income. It is safe to predict that any such proposal will be studied very carefully for its effects on the economy and the society. The tax structure has been used for many purposes besides raising revenue. Consider just the effects on charitable institutions of disallowing deductions for contributions. As Joseph Pechman, economist with the Brookings Institution, observed, "It might appear to be a good idea, but when they actually stare at it in the face, they'll see the problems, the practical political problems."[50]

Summary

Even this small sample of policy issues illustrates the varied channels to government. Note that in each case the problems associated with the agenda item were familiar to many in and out of government. A particular combination of factors was required, however, for the matter to become a priority. Labeling, widespread interest, limited (or neutralized) resistance, a persistent advocate in high places, media attention, and professional or technical analyses are a few of the conditions for agenda setting (several of which were mentioned earlier: see "Dynamics of Agenda Setting"). One cannot help observing that *coincidence* also plays a role in the process by which problems are acted on in government. It may be, however, that we simply have not studied these critical early stages of policy action well enough to identify the patterns. This possibility should help students of public policy set their own agendas for future study.

Notes

1. William Solesbury, "Issues and Innovations in Environmental Policy in Britain, West Germany, and California," *Policy Analysis* 2 (Winter 1976): 13.
2. Gabriel A. Almond and others use the term *aggregation* quite differently. They use it to refer to the conversion of demands into policy alternatives—our formulation and legitimation functions. See Gabriel A. Almond and G. Bingham Powell, Jr., *Comparative Politics: A Developmental Approach* (Boston: Little, Brown, 1966), chap. 5.
3. David B. Truman, *The Governmental Process* (New York: Knopf, 1951), p. 113.
4. Truman, pp. 139–155.
5. For a superb summary of the dimensions of representation, see Hanna F. Pitkin, *The Concept of Representation* (Berkeley: University of California Press, 1967).

6. I once discussed these dimensions in a seminar attended by a state legislator. He acknowledged the various dimensions of representation but provided an illustration that did not fit the categories. He had prepared an amendment and lined up the support necessary for passage. When the time came to introduce the amendment on the floor, he couldn't find it on his desk. The bill passed without the amendment while he continued to rummage through his papers. I resisted his suggestion for a sixth category—the "Stupidity Dimension."

7. For such examples see Herbert J. Gans, *The Urban Villagers* (New York: Free Press, 1962).

8. Henry Clay Smith, "Empathy," in *Empathy and Ideology*, ed. Charles Press and Alan Arian (Chicago: Rand McNally, 1966), p. 111.

9. The literature on public housing is abundant. For a sampling read Lawrence M. Friedman, *Government and Slum Housing* (Chicago: Rand McNally, 1968); Scott Greer, *Urban Renewal and American Cities* (Indianapolis: Bobbs-Merrill, 1965); Robert Taggart III, *Low-Income Housing: A Critique of Federal Aid* (Baltimore: Johns Hopkins University Press, 1970); Eugene J. Meehan, *The Quality of Federal Policymaking* (Columbia, Missouri: University of Missouri Press, 1979); and the many books by Charles Abrams, Daniel Wilner, Jane Jacobs, and Catherine Bauer.

10. Nathan Glazer, "Housing Problems and Housing Policies," *The Public Interest* (Spring 1967): 22.

11. Glazer, p. 29.

12. Glazer, p. 35.

13. Glazer, p. 38.

14. See, for example, the survey results in St. Louis on the awareness of pollution: U.S. Department of Health, Education, and Welfare, Public Health Service, *Public Awareness and Concern with Air Pollution in the St. Louis Metropolitan Area* (Washington, D.C., May 1965). In answer to the question of what air pollution meant to them, respondents most frequently mentioned odor (56 percent). Only 15.6 percent mentioned motor vehicle exhausts.

15. Layne D. Hoppe, "Agenda-Setting Strategies: Pollution Policy," unpublished Ph.D. dissertation, University of Arizona, 1969, p. 2.

16. Roger W. Cobb and Charles D. Elder, *Participation in American Politics: The Dynamics of Agenda-Building* (Boston: Allyn & Bacon, 1972), p. 85.

17. Cobb and Elder, *Participation in American Politics*, p. 86.

18. Anthony Downs, "Up and down with ecology—the 'issue-attention cycle,'" *The Public Interest* (Summer 1972): 39–41.

19. For a more complete discussion of these effects see Charles O. Jones and Dieter Matthes, "Policy Formation," in *Encyclopedia of Policy Studies*, ed. Stuart Nagel (New York: Marcel Dekker, 1982), chap. 6.

20. Truman, pp. 105–106.

21. Robert A. Dahl, *A Preface to Democratic Theory* (Chicago: University of Chicago Press, 1956), pp. 124, 131, 133.

22. Dahl, p. 137.

23. Roger W. Cobb and Charles D. Elder, "The Politics of Agenda-Building: An Alternative Perspective for Modern Democratic Theory," *Journal of Politics* 33 (November 1971): 895.

24. E. E. Schattschneider, *The Semisovereign People* (New York: Holt, Rinehart & Winston, 1960), p. 30.

25. See Schattschneider, pp. 140–141.

26. Peter Bachrach and Morton S. Baratz, *Power and Poverty: Theory and Practice* (New York: Oxford University Press, 1970), p. 7.

27. Bachrach and Baratz, p. 43.

28. Bachrach and Baratz, p. 44.

29. Schattschneider, p. 141.

30. Jack L. Walker, "Setting the Agenda in the United States Senate," in *Congress and Public Policy*, ed. David C. Kozak and John D. Macartney (Homewood, Ill.: Dorsey Press, 1982), p. 445.

31. Cobb and Elder, *Participation in American Politics*, p. 110.

32. Amitai Etzioni, *Demonstration Democracy* (New York: Gordon and Breach, 1970).

33. Schattschneider, p. 13.

34. Schattschneider, p. 11.

35. Schattschneider, p. 7.

36. Schattschneider, p. 16.

37. An exception is John W. Kingdon, *An Idea Whose Time Has Come: Agendas, Alternatives, and Public Policies* (Boston: Little, Brown, forthcoming).

38. Barbara J. Nelson, "Setting the Public Agenda: The Case of Child Abuse," in *The Policy Cycle,* ed. Judith V. May and Aaron Wildavsky (Beverly Hills: Sage Publications, 1978), p. 18.
39. Nelson, p. 26.
40. Quoted in Nelson, p. 33.
41. For details on the subsequent legislation see *Congress and the Nation,* vol. V (Washington, D. C.: Congressional Quarterly, Inc., 1981), pp. 691–693.
42. John Rae, *The American Automobile* (Chicago: University of Chicago Press, 1965), p. 237.
43. U. S. Department of Commerce, *Historical Statistics of the United States,* part 2 (Washington, D.C.: Government Printing Office, 1975), p. 719.
44. Ralph Nader, *Unsafe at Any Speed* (New York: Grossman, 1965), p. ix.
45. This story is recounted in Walker, pp. 435–439, and *Congress and the Nation,* vol. II, pp. 782–792.
46. Walker, p. 436.
47. Walker, p. 438.
48. Julie A. Carr, "Tax Expenditures," in *Setting National Priorities: The 1983 Budget,* ed. Joseph Pechman (Washington, D. C.: The Brookings Institution, 1982), p. 264.
49. Carr, p. 264.
50. Quoted in *Congressional Quarterly Weekly Report,* June 5, 1982, 1334.

Chapter Five

Formulating Proposals

Functional activities	Categorized in government	With a potential product
Formulation: research review projection selection	Action in government	Proposal or plan

One of the initial realities identified earlier quoted Charles E. Lindblom in stating that "Policy makers are not faced with a *given* problem." This statement summarizes much of what has been said so far in this book. Problems result from any major event; some are perceived and acted on by policy makers, many others are not. Again quoting Lindblom:

■ [Policy makers] have to identify and formulate their problem. Rioting breaks out in dozens of American cities. What is the problem? Maintaining law and order? Racial discrimination? Impatience of the Negroes with the pace of reform now that reform has gone far enough to give them hope? Incipient revolution? Black power? Low income? Lawlessness at the fringe of an otherwise relatively peaceful reform movement? Urban disorganization? Alienation?[1]

With this observation Lindblom illustrates another of the initial realities: "Many problems may result from the same event." But, as he suggests, decision makers "have to identify and formulate their problem." They have to make choices before they can decide on appropriate action. Thus we observe a sort of second-level process of problem definition engaged in by officials whose job is to direct the allocation of government resources. Typically they must look back to the event and the problems it causes and ahead to the options for solving those problems. As with all of the functional activities discussed here, formulation has both forward and reverse gears. This is not to say that both gears are always used. Sometimes a plan is produced with little attention given to what the problem is. It is normally characteristic of a policy cycle, however, that all activities are interdependent. It just so happens that not all policy action can be characterized by a cycle, a point we will have occasion to emphasize in chapter 9.

In this chapter, then, we turn our attention to policy action in government. What has happened has happened, and various people are moved to seek corrective action by government. What takes place now? If those in government get the message, they will typically do research, interpret the results, review and discuss alternatives, determine what is possible (often by projecting support and testing feasibility), refine proposals, make a final selection, and test that choice further. The subactivities associated with formulation are thus summarized as *research, review, projection,* and *selection.* They may occur very systematically—almost scientifically—or in quite haphazard fashion (see the distinction below between *formulation* and *planning*). Sometimes the process is reconstructed as having been rational and scientific, when in fact the decision itself was made quite haphazardly. And the time frame for formulation may be measured in minutes or years.

The result of all this activity may be nothing concrete. The problem may be solved outside government during the formulation process. Possibly the conflicts between the various definitions and interpretations of the problem are too great to resolve—and the conflicts may pass in time. On the other hand, the result may be a definite course of action. Typically, the government then attempts to legitimate this course of action so that it can be applied to the problem. Another round of activities ensues, involving more discussion, research, meetings, planning, testing, coordination. Strategies are developed, compromise points identified, concessions made, costs analyzed. Again, for the reasons already noted, no concrete program may be authorized. Much of what happens in government has no immediate programmatic result, though it may well lay the groundwork for subsequent policy development. Patience is a virtue in the American policy process.

What Is Formulation?

Formulation is a derivative of *formula* and means simply to develop a plan, a method, a prescription, in this case for alleviating some need, for acting on a problem. It is the first of the policy *development* phases or activities, and there is no set method by which it must proceed. That is, its distinguishing characteristic is simply that means are proposed to resolve somebody's perception of the needs that exist in society. How well this is done, who participates, and who gains an advantage varies from one issue or problem to the next.

Understanding of formulation as an activity is sharpened somewhat by distinguishing it from planning. Formulation is the more encompassing term; it includes both planning and far less systematic efforts to judge what should be done about public problems. Herbert J. Gans defines "social planning" as:

■   A method of decision making that proposes or identifies goals or ends, determines the means or programs which achieve or are thought to achieve these ends, and does so by the application of analytical techniques to discover the fit between ends and means and the consequences of implementing alternative ends and means.[2]

This definition emphasizes systematic methods of research, review, projection, and selection. It fits the more rationalist or technical approach identified in chapter 2, but typically excludes the less rigorous and more subjective methods of the politician as incrementalist or reformist (see table 2.1). Yet such persons may also be actively engaged in reacting to issues and automatically conjuring up proposals to resolve these issues. "Often these proposals are filtered through a screen of personal political experience."[3] In summary, formulation as used here incorporates both *rational planning* and what we might refer to as *subjective reacting*.

The preceding discussion encourages me to introduce other guidelines to broaden the scope of formulation as a policy activity.

1. Formulation need not be limited to one set of actors. Thus there may well be two or more formulation groups producing competing (or complementary) proposals.
2. Formulation may proceed without clear definition of the problem, or without formulators ever having much contact with the affected groups (see the list of initial realities).
3. There is no necessary coincidence between formulation and particular institutions, though it is a frequent activity of bureaucratic agencies.
4. Formulation and reformulation may occur over a long period of time without ever building sufficient support for any one proposal.
5. There are often several appeal points for those who lose in the formulation process at any one level.
6. The process itself never has neutral effects. Somebody wins and somebody loses even in the workings of science.

In a sense these guidelines constitute a set of initial realities for formulation. Suppose, for example, you are seriously affected by proposed tuition increases in your college or university. Your initial task is to organize others with similar views and make certain that university administrators understand your problem. Once those in authority begin to formulate proposals, you want to ensure that they are doing so in full knowledge of *your* interpretation of the problem rather than or in addition to that of state legislators, trustees, or budget officials. Thus, for example, you may want them to focus on equal opportunity for higher education as the issue, rather than on balancing next year's budget. You may even wish to formulate your own proposal and build support for it among various university clienteles. Such a proposal may include cost reductions, elimination of programs, fund raising, or more state or federal aid. If you lose within your institution, you may carry the battle to another decision-making point in the state or nation. These activities suggest one central point above all: *formulation is very much a political, though not necessarily a partisan, activity.* Not even use of the more neutral term *planning* can change that.

None of this is staggeringly profound; naturally you want to influence policy makers to be sympathetic to your view. Wanting sympathy and actually developing strategies to affect the perceptions of policy actors are quite different, however. The first may require only publicity; the second requires a knowledge and understanding of the intricate realities of decision making in government, and perhaps even a little empathy in order to judge how public officials look at problems.

Who Is Involved?

Who is involved in formulation? It is difficult to make a general statement. The most we can say is that participants vary. Who is involved in formulating a course of action to cope with the outbreak of herpes infections, or the escalating costs of hospital care, or huge grain surpluses that threaten the market, or the effects of acid rain? These are empirical questions for which data can be collected *once the activity of formulation itself is defined.*

Sources Inside Government

Though it is impossible to generalize across all issue areas about who will be involved in formulation, it is possible to identify places to look for participants. At the national level of decision making the search would normally begin in the executive branch, among both the bureaucrats and the political appointees. Typically we think of the executive as the source of planning. The president and close associates in the White House and cabinet frequently establish goals and set priorities that define boundaries for formulation of proposals. The actual development of plans and proposals normally occurs within the bureaucracy, with formal clearance of actions given by the upper echelons of political decision making. In some cases the president may judge that the departments and agencies are either incapable of developing suitable recommendations or are unlikely to do so. This conclusion may be a result of an assessment of their institutional bias or because no single agency has responsibility for the problem or problems identified. The president may thus rely on agencies outside government or appoint a special commission to develop proposals. It should also be noted that agencies, too, often rely on outside assistance, including state and local governments, universities, professional and other interest groups, congressional committee staff, private research organizations, and consulting groups.

Members of Congress are also frequently involved in formulation. In fact, it is quite conceivable that a particular formulation network is drawn entirely from legislative actors, to include staff persons, other legislative support units (e.g., the Congressional Research Service, Office of Technology Assessment, and General Accounting Office—all congressional agencies), and those groups outside government whose primary access is within the Congress. A sample of important issue areas in which members of Congress have played major roles in formulating proposals in recent years would include medical care for the aged, comprehensive health care, mass transit, air and water pollution control, environmental planning, and energy conservation. It should be pointed out that the voluminous congressional committee hearings and staff reports are perhaps the most readily available documentary sources for determining who is engaged in formulation within an issue area. These documents may reveal specific persons who have developed plans, what those plans include, how the members of Congress react, and what they propose either as modifications or substitutions. In fact, students of public policy are well advised to begin their analysis of problems on the national agenda by reading the relevant congressional hearings, reports, and debates. No other legislature—indeed, no other political institution—in the world provides such extensive public documentation of its policy actions.

Sources Outside Government

I have already suggested that our political system permits enormous input from sources outside government. Private interests and public institutions and agencies from other governmental levels may develop proposals for consideration within national policy-making units, and, as indicated above, Washington-based government formulators may seek advice, information, and recommendations from these other sources. Participation in public decision making by the bureaucratic, political (to include legislative), and private spheres has been characterized by many labels: subgovernment, cozy little triangle, iron triangle, whirlpool, subsystem, network. These connections are commonly painted in a sinister light. But as Roger H. Davidson observes:

■   Nothing is more natural than for interested individuals or groups to cluster about those government agencies whose decisions affect them directly. With the rise of the welfare state and its attendant philosophy of positive government, these relationships were formalized and invested with theoretical underpinnings of "interest group liberalism."[4]

Randall B. Ripley and Grace A. Franklin agree, noting that:

■   Subgovernments are important throughout a broad range of American public policy. They afford an important channel by which nongovernmental actors help determine policy and program content.[5]

In fact, it would be extraordinary in a democracy for a separation to be enforced among all those interested and affected by an issue. Much of the thrust of this book leads us to expect associations among such persons, both inside and outside government. We do, however, expect variation in participation between and within issues. That is to say, we do not expect to find the same people involved in aiding dependent children and protecting the wheat market. In addition, however, it may well be that the makeup of groups active in aiding dependent children varies over time and among the functional activities (defining the problem, formulating proposals, building support, etc.). I prefer the term *policy network* for these collections or communities of actors. I judge that their configuration and behavior are much more variable and complex than is conveyed by the popular term *cozy little triangle*. And as noted in chapter 1, the more neutral term alerts us to the changes that can occur, as with the growth in citizen participation during the 1960s and 1970s, a development that had significant effects on the policy process.

To illustrate the *possible* sources of participants in a policy formulation network, one need only turn to the *Washington Information Directory*, published by the Congressional Quarterly. This document is a handbook of the subgovernments, organized by substantive policy area. Table 5.1 displays the groups, agencies, and congressional committees and subcommittees from which one might expect networks to form just in the area of banking issues. There may be an occasional issue that involves persons from all these private and public organizations. Normally, however, only a few participants are active, depending on the issue itself, whom it affects, and what is being proposed. Now consider that the *Directory* provides information on public and private organizational units for well over *500 subject categories*. The banking entries noted in table 5.1 take up just two pages of the 930-page document. The complexities of national decision making are truly mind boggling.

Other nongovernmental sources of formulators include the many organizations and institutions in this country that provide public services. For example, the private foundations sponsor research and support public institutions (including governments) in various ways. The work of such national foundations as Ford, Rockefeller, Carnegie, Sloan, Russell Sage, and Mellon is familiar. These organizations produce ideas, recommendations, data, analyses, and even personnel to assist those formulating proposals. Two of the cases described at the end of this chapter—those concerning the poverty program and energy conservation—show the direct contribution of the Ford Foundation in policy formulation.

Equally significant in producing material of use in policy formulation are the nation's private or nonprofit research organizations (e.g., the Brookings Institution, American Enterprise Institute, the Urban Institute, the RAND Corporation). Often there are close ties between these organizations and the foundations that support them. Further, as with the RAND Corporation and others, some such operations are little more than extensions of government itself. Don K. Price explains:

■ We have seen the creation, under government auspices, of new private corporations to do government business. Most of them have been not-for-profit corporations, chartered under the law of some state—for example, the RAND Corporation, which makes technical and strategic studies for the Air Force; the Aerospace Corporation, which is the Air Force's systems engineer for the development of ballistic missiles; and the Institute for Defense Analyses, which evaluates weapons systems in relation to strategy for the Joint Chiefs of Staff and the Secretary of Defense.[6]

TABLE 5.1   Potential actors in policy networks: The case of
banking issues

Groups	Agencies	Committees
American Bankers Assn.	Federal Deposit Insurance Corp.	House: Committee on Banking, Finance, and Urban Affairs;
American Savings and Loan League	Federal Home Loan Bank Board	Subcommittee on Financial Institutions Supervision, Regulation, and Insurance
Assn. of Bank Holding Companies	Federal Reserve System	
Conference of State Bank Supervisors	National Credit Union Administration	House: Committee on Government Operations; Subcommittee on Commerce, Consumer, and Monetary Affairs
Consumer Bankers Assn.	Securities and Exchange Commission	
Credit Union National Assn.	Department of the Treasury	
Electronic Funds Transfer Assn.		Senate: Committee on Banking, Housing, and Urban Affairs; Subcommittee on Financial Institutions
Federal Home Loan Mortgage Corp.		
Independent Bankers Assn. of America		
Mortgage Bankers Assn. of America		
National Assn. of Federal Credit Unions		
National Assn. of Mutual Savings Banks		
National Assn. of State Credit Union Supervisors		
National Assn. of State Savings and Loan Supervisors		
National Savings and Loan League		
United States League of Savings Assns.		

Source: Compiled from Washington Information Directory, 1981–1982 (Washington, D.C.: Congressional Quarterly, Inc., 1981), pp. 59–61.

University research, too, has been heavily supported both by the foundations and the national government. In some cases this support is for specific projects, perhaps under contract arrangements with government agencies; in other circumstances support is provided for basic research with no specific product requested. The result has been a close working relationship between the academic community and government in policy formulation, particularly in the post–World War II period. As Charles V. Kidd concludes in his careful study of American Universities and Federal Research: "Universities need support for science from government and government needs knowledge obtainable only by university research. As a result, the two have been placed in a state of unprecedented mutual dependence."[7]

Finally, brief mention must be made of the increasing number of citizen organizations that have become active in national policy making. Perhaps most active on a wide range of issues is Common Cause, the citizen's lobby group organized by John Gardner (former secretary of Health, Education, and Welfare). But a large number of environmental and consumer protection groups have joined Ralph Nader's effort to investigate the public effects of government programs and develop counterproposals to those produced by government and special interests.

Here then are a few of the sources of policy formulation, of the information and recommendations that feed into decision making. The student of policy formulation must trace these developments for the issue or problem being examined and identify who is involved, how they interact, and what they produce.

Institutional Limits on Formulation

Though a major purpose of this text is to encourage students to discover cross-institutional and interlevel policy-related networks, still it is essential that institutional limits be acknowledged and assessed for their effect on policy formulation. For however individual decision makers may communicate and otherwise interact with those outside their agency or committee, they are circumscribed by certain features of the constitutional order and existing policy authority. We need do no more than mention the constitutional features of separation of powers, federalism, bicameralism, and checks and balances (see chapter 1). They are described and analyzed in countless texts on American government. Suffice it to say here that these principles do establish a decision-making context that cannot be ignored in the study of public policy. At a minimum, as structural features these characteristics segment the policy process, thus creating a requirement for cross-institutional contact if the work of government is to be done.

Less well described is the growth of peculiar policy relationships within agencies and committees that come to influence whether and how problems are defined and proposals developed. The incrementalism described by Lindblom comes about in part because institutional characteristics limit what can or will be done. More bluntly, don't expect any agency accustomed to doing things in a particular way to innovate very often. Rather, look for an effort to integrate new demands into an existing pattern of doing business.

Why is this so? Why should existing units either resist new demands or integrate them into familiar approaches? At the simplest level of analysis, people are most satisfied when tomorrow brings the same expectations and responsibilities as today. This is not only because they are comfortable with the familiar, however. Equally important are the networks of contacts and interactions that emerge over time as an institutional unit fulfills its conception of its responsibilities. For example:

1. Clientele or constituency relationships are established and protected.
2. All agencies (and committees) require support and have typically found means for gaining this support.

3. Definite patterns of communication exist within, between, and outside existing units.
4. Means are developed for defining problems and formulating proposals. These means strongly accommodate the interests presently served.

These interlacements are not easily broken, nor should they be if governmental stability is valued.

This is not to say that institutions are totally impervious to change or are incapable of doing things differently. Chapter 1 identifies many changes that have occurred in the past two decades. Normally, however, change occurs within the context of what is familiar and therefore comfortable. Recall another of the initial realities: "Most people do not prefer large change." Upsetting existing patterns often requires a dramatic event: economic collapse, war, riots. The most spectacular domestic event in this century was the Great Depression of the 1930s. Recent shocks with significant impact on institutional arrangements have been Watergate, energy shortages, record budget imbalances, and economic recessions. Among other effects, these events have rearranged institutional jurisdictions and responsibilities, often as a consequence of reforms, but also because such shocks bring new people into decision making. When the normal way of doing business is perceived to have failed, public confidence is shaken. New faces and new methods are often demanded. If the system is to survive, a fresh set of institutional routines and limits must form. We appear to be in such a period of transition, in which old alliances are being scrapped or reshaped to suit new demands. Perhaps one need only mention the 1972, 1976, and 1980 presidential elections to make the point: two overwhelming victories for Republican candidates in 1972 and 1980, and a victory for an unknown Democrat in 1976. Clearly the old alliances or coalitions are no longer reliable, even at election time.

Types of Formulation: The Methods

Many types of formulation can be identified, depending on the criteria used for classification. For example, one can form categories by subject matter: formulation of courses of action for economic problems, education problems, military problems, and so on. Each draws formulators from a different set of institutional units and groups. Different patterns of formulation develop because of the nature of the problems, the groups affected, and the institutional limits that have developed. Or one can classify formulation by the source of what we might call the "formulation population." That is, are the formulators drawn primarily from inside or outside government or do they come from both? Again, processes and behavior may differ. If the formulators are drawn from both inside and outside, does there appear to be one primary institutional base for formulation? As noted earlier, the executive is typically the major source of formulators inside government, but many notable cases of formulation in Congress can be cited.[8]

Rational and Subjective Approaches

Each of the above classifications requires considerable research to establish the patterns. From available studies we can say something useful about the *methods* and *styles* of formulation. Methods are the accepted means by which different people assemble a plan or proposal. Earlier I made a distinction between the rational planners and the more subjective reactors. Here I elaborate on how the two types do their work. Basically, I believe, they differ in the extent of their confidence in their ability to define problems and deal with them effectively. It is the difference between the planning specialist who knows the job can be done if the politicians will just get out of the way and the politicians who every day confront conflicting versions of the truth as offered by specialists. As one practitioner put it to me: "I have learned to live my life as a series of approximations."

This fundamental difference in approach is accompanied by variations in how the two types of formulators view external and internal issue relationships and judge human capacities for knowing what to do and how to analyze effects. These variations can be summarized as follows (recognizing, of course, that I have only identified model behaviors at opposite ends of a continuum):

1. External issue relationships: whether *integrative* or *sequential*. The integrative mode systematically links one issue with another. It may be all encompassing, as with the "planet earth" planners, or limited to other issues of the same genre (for example, linking energy with environmental issues). The sequential mode simply takes up one issue at a time, along with any associated issues that are obvious to the decision makers.

2. Internal issue relationships: whether *comprehensive* or *segmental*. The demand for comprehensiveness is predictable following a crisis, since it is assumed that the bad effects are the consequence of a failure to take a broader approach. Thus, for example, the Arab oil embargo in 1973 resulted in a demand for a comprehensive energy program, the recession of the early 1980s for a comprehensive economic program. The reference here is to comprehensiveness *within* an issue area (in the case of energy, for example, oil is to be considered in its relation to nuclear energy, coal, and so on). Those whose response tends to be segmental, on the other hand, are less troubled by the failure to be comprehensive; indeed, they doubt the capacity for broader analysis. As is discussed below, the demand for comprehensiveness (or integration, for that matter) is seldom accompanied by a clear vision of expected results.

3. Capacities for knowing what to do: whether data collection and analysis are *systematic* or *unsystematic*. How systematic one is in formulation depends in part on training and resources. But it may also reflect one's confidence in a working science. A member of Congress may have a great capacity for systematic policy analysis, yet wish to preserve a role for hunches, constituent mail, and impressions gained while campaigning back home.

4. Confidence in analyzing effects: whether *projective* or *reactive*. These categories distinguish between deciding what to do and judging the conse-

quences of an action. Those taking the projective approach are confident that a given plan can be analyzed for its impact on the problem, perhaps even on associated problems. Those relying on the reactive method are more skeptical. They rate a proposal more on its immediate consequences, and much less on estimates of future effects.

The model characteristics associated with the rationalist planner are thus integrative, comprehensive, systematic, and projective; those associated with the subjective reactor are sequential, segmental, unsystematic, and reactive. Of course, one seldom runs into a pure example of either type. The purpose of this model is simply to illuminate differences in behavior that may, in the practical world, influence policy products.

Formulating Comprehensive Proposals

Methods of formulation in response to crisis (referred to in item 2 of the list) are particularly important for studying policy making in the 1970s and 1980s. Crises in what might be referred to as the three E's—environment, energy, and economy—have provided ample experience for responding to demands for a total policy. Since each E potentially encompasses the other two, developing a comprehensive policy is a significant challenge. Yet the pressure exists to produce a "policy" when a crisis strikes. "The United States has no _____ policy" (fill in the blank with any one of the three E's). We are all familiar with this type of statement. The methods for developing such a policy are, however, less familiar. What is supposed to happen in order to produce a comprehensive proposal? At a minimum, the following elements must be addressed:

1. *The number of problems treated:* Will the proposal address all the problems within an issue area (all forms of pollution as well as the more positive aspects of the environment: parks, wilderness areas, quality of life, and so on)? Or will attention be directed to just a sample?

2. *The extent of the analysis:* Will the proposal treat all aspects of the problem or problems (for example, all the social, economic, physical, health, aesthetic, even political aspects of pollution)? Or will formulators treat only certain aspects?

3. *The estimation of effects:* Has the proposal been tested in all of its effects (primary, secondary, and beyond) on other problems and programs (the energy or labor costs of pollution solutions)? Or is testing limited to the more immediate effects within the issue area?[9]

These criteria suggest a wide range of possibilities, from a kind of super comprehensiveness to much more limited varieties that hardly extend beyond normal incremental policy making. It is instructive, I think, to apply these criteria to proposals that are promoted as being comprehensive; for example, the environmental programs of the 1970s, the Carter energy proposals, and the Reagan economic package. These efforts were certainly large scale by American standards, but they did not meet the criteria of the high end of the scale mentioned above. As a practical matter, a comprehensive proposal turns out to be a middling effort to sample problems, select aspects for analysis, and estimate some effects. Advice to "be comprehensive" often means only to do more than one might do otherwise. Although this may be good advice, following it is seldom likely to produce large change in the short run.

It is appropriate at this point to mention *formulation packages*. By constitutional mandate, the president "shall from time to time give to the Congress Information of the State of the Union, and recommend to their Consideration such Measures as he shall judge necessary and expedient. . . ." (Article II, Section 3). Here is a routine opportunity for making connections among proposals and programs. That opportunity is not always taken; often it results in no more than a list of what the president wants from Congress. Sometimes, however, a more comprehensive and integrated stocktaking occurs (typically when a president wishes to announce a new initiative).

Many major interest groups (for example, the AFL-CIO, U. S. Chamber of Commerce, American Farm Bureau Federation) also develop broad programs on various issues. The reason for mentioning these packages here is simply to point out that they represent a second formulation process. Proposals are developed for specific issues or problems—whether to treat continuing or new agenda items—and then priorities are set. It is this priority setting that constitutes a subsequent formulation. Decisions must be made as to which proposals are absolutely necessary and which can be sacrificed. Compromise points for each individual item are also identified.

Building support for the package is quite different from gathering it for individual items. Clearly much more effort must be directed toward justifying the relatedness of specific programs and identifying the more marginal items. The enormous complexity of this task frequently drives formulators to a salvaging operation for individual proposals. In other words, the comprehensive support-building effort may be short-lived. And yet there are instances when the president and others produce an integrated package—as with a set of economic proposals—that should, by their analysis, be enacted as a whole. Elaborate proposals of this type seldom survive the legitimation process intact.

Types of Formulation: The Styles

The *style* of formulation is the particular approach taken in preparing proposals. A style may be related to the formulator's training and experience or it may reflect the status of an issue in the government. Here are three examples:

1. *Routine formulation:* A repetitive and essentially changeless process of reformulating similar proposals within an issue area that is well established on the government agenda.

2. *Analogous formulation:* Treating a new problem by relying on what was done in developing proposals for similar problems in the past; that is, by searching for analogies.
3. *Creative formulation:* Treating each problem with an essentially unprecedented proposal, one that represents a break with past practice.

One expects routine and analogous formulation to occur more frequently than creative formulation. The weight of the familiar in ordinary decision making is considerable. It is understandable that having gotten satisfaction from government one would then opt for predictable increments. Likewise the "law of doing what is most comfortable" encourages those active in policy formulation to rely on their experience in facing new problems. Hence creativity may suffer along the route to final formulation of a proposal. Even if a creative proposal wins support, one can expect adjustments toward past practice during implementation.

Still, new approaches are tried. Daniel P. Moynihan describes a case of creative formulation in his account of how the Family Assistance Plan (a proposal to guarantee a minimum income for every family with children) was developed during the Nixon administration. As he points out:

■ One of the primary contentions of political science is that things don't change very much, or, rather, very fast. . . . The experience of Family Assistance, however, suggests that . . . an extraordinary, discontinuous, forward movement in social policy *did* occur, and in the very least promising of circumstances. Those who call for "fundamental social change" could . . . point to the events leading up to the proposal and near enactment of the Family Assistance Plan as evidence that "fundamental," rather than merely "incremental," social change *is* a realistic option for American society at this time.[10]

The Family Assistance Plan may also be used to illustrate the point that the product of creative formulation faces enormous difficulties in the legitimation process. Building support for the ordinary is demanding; building support for the unusual is downright taxing. Despite the early success of the plan (it was passed in the House of Representatives), the guaranteed income was not enacted into law.

Nelson W. Polsby has studied eight cases of policy innovation to determine whether definite characteristics are predictably associated with such breakthroughs. He examined three cases for post–World War II science (civilian control of atomic energy, the creation of the National Science Foundation, and the nuclear test ban treaty); two foreign policy cases (the Truman Doctrine, which provided aid to Greece and Turkey, and the creation of the Peace Corps); and three domestic policy cases (creation of the Council of Economic Advisers, medicare, and the development of the community action program as a part of the "war on poverty"). He found considerable variation in the conditions under which action was taken. He did spot a few instances of "acute" innovation, in which a new idea was developed rapidly, and a few others of "incubated" innovation, in which an idea was developed over a period of time.

He was not encouraged, however, to confirm a set of conditions for predicting innovation.

On the other hand, Polsby's effort tells us something about the general dynamics of innovation. He sees it "as a combination of two processes."

■ The first, the process of invention, causes policy options to come into existence. This is the domain of interest groups and their interests, of persons who specialize in acquiring and deploying knowledge about policies and their intellectual convictions, of persons who are aware of contextually applicable experiences of foreign nations, and of policy entrepreneurs, whose careers and ambitions are focused on the employment of their expertise and on the elaboration and adaptation of knowledge to problems. The second process is a process of systemic search, a process that senses and responds to problems, that harvests policy options and turns them to the purposes, both public and career-related, of politicians and public officials. . . . in the American political system search processes can be activated by exogenously generated crises and by constitutional routines, by bureaucratic needs and by political necessities. Describing political innovation in any particular instance thus entails describing how these two processes interact.[11]

A creative style of formulation fits Polsby's "process of invention." Its product is fed into a "process of systemic search" that is not always conducive to new ways of doing things. This makes it even more important to direct attention to instances of creative program enactment.

Thinking Ahead: Strategic Considerations in Formulation

Not all of the attention of formulators is focused on the problem and how to solve it. They must also think ahead to what is feasible in getting a course of action approved. And the closer formulators get to agreement among themselves about a suitable course of action, the more they must consider the requirements and conditions for approval. In the early stages of formulation many alternatives may be welcome. However, as discussion and evaluation pare down the alternatives and formulators prepare to offer a definite proposal, they must give thought to the attitudes, rules, and demands that circumscribe the behavior of legitimators. Strategic considerations are thus directed toward the legitimation process: building support for a proposed course of action, maintaining previous support, deciding where compromises can be made, calculating when and where to make the strongest play and when and where to retreat, and controlling information flow to advantage.

I have not discussed legitimation in detail as yet (see chapter 6). It is enough for now to offer one form of legitimation that allows us to proceed with the present discussion. For the time being, let us limit the concept to the case of majority building in a legislature. In other words, a course of action is legitimate when a majority in both houses of a legislature approve and the chief executive signs the measure.

Given the need to build a majority coalition of legislators for a particular course of action, formulators must consider all the factors involved in what sometimes is a complicated operation. Conditions may vary greatly. For example, the differences in majority building between the 73d and 89th Congresses, on the one hand, and the 72d, 86th, 93d, and 94th on the other, were very great. In the 73d (1933–1934) and the 89th (1965–1966), Presidents Franklin D. Roosevelt and Lyndon B. Johnson had huge margins in the House (196 and 155 seats, respectively) and the Senate (23 and 36 seats, respectively). Each man had won an overwhelming victory in the popular and electoral votes and could rely on this apparent popular appeal in building majorities in Congress. Under these circumstances, "what the president has formulated, the Congress legitimates." In both Congresses, the first session in particular resulted in a flood of legislation on social and economic problems—the greatest domestic policy output in our history.

In the 72d (1931–1932), 86th (1959–1960), and 91st (1969–1970) Congresses, however, majority building was not quite so simple. Of the three presidents involved, Herbert Hoover had the most frustrating conditions under which to operate. During the 72d Congress, the Democrats had taken control of the House of Representatives, while the Republicans maintained control of the Senate by only *one* seat. Since the Twentieth Amendment had not yet been passed, the second session of the 72d Congress took place *after* the 1932 elections. Both the House and Senate were full of "lame ducks," members defeated in the 1932 election but continuing to serve until the new Congress met in 1933. With all the pressures of virtual economic chaos in the nation, President Hoover, also defeated for reelection, faced insuperable odds in trying to build majorities for courses of action.

During the 86th Congress, a consistently popular president, Dwight D. Eisenhower, was serving his last two years in office. The Democrats controlled the Congress by the enormous margin of 129 seats in the House and 32 seats in the Senate. With the end of the Eisenhower administration in sight, they were intent on recapturing the White House in 1960. Again, the conditions called for very special strategies in building majorities, regardless of whether these were formulated primarily in the executive or elsewhere.

The 93d and 94th Congresses witnessed some of the weirdest political conditions of our history. In the 93d, President Richard M. Nixon was buoyed by an incredible landslide victory in the 1972 presidential elections, only to be toppled in 1974 by the Watergate crisis. With the downfall of President Nixon, and as a result of the earlier resignation of Vice-President Spiro T. Agnew, a congressionally approved vice-president assumed the presidency. Gerald R. Ford was the first vice-president to be selected by procedures outlined in the Twenty-fifth Amendment. With huge Democratic majorities elected to Congress in 1974, an unelected President Ford had to work with an initially confident, though essentially unled, opposition party.

The 97th Congress (1981–1982) should also be mentioned. In 1980 Ronald Reagan ousted an incumbent Democratic president, the first time this had happened since 1888, when Grover Cleveland lost to Benjamin Harrison. Although his victory in the Electoral College was of landslide proportions, his popular vote total was much more modest. Republicans also gained a majority in the Senate, while Democrats retained a majority in the House of Representatives. Like Hoover in 1931, President Reagan faced split party control of Congress. The situation was different, however. The Republican Party lost seats in the 1930 election; it gained seats in the 1980 election and therefore assumed an aggressive posture in the policy process.

Here then are dramatic cases of presidential–congressional conditions for policy making. Each required special strategies to supplement the ordinary efforts at majority building. I can do no more here than alert you to this possibility and encourage analysis of such conditions as important to understanding policy development and implementation within a particular issue area at a given time.

Formulation and Legitimation

I have so far avoided the question of where formulation ends and legitimation begins. For the purposes of this discussion, let us continue to define legitimation as the process of building majorities in legislatures. Certainly formulation and legitimation overlap; both are part of the overall policy process. One could also say that both functions are always present to some degree. *The important point, however, is that we don't really care where one ends and the other begins.* These are functional activities that may occur in regard to action on public problems. They do not have to be performed by separate individuals at different times in different institutions. To the extent that persons involved in formulating courses of action for public problems take into account the requirements for building a majority in a legislature, they are actors in the process of legitimation.

Any number of possibilities can be envisaged for combining these two important activities. I suggest four for purposes of discussion:

1. A perfect plan with an imperfect strategy
2. A perfect strategy with an imperfect plan
3. A perfect blend
4. An imperfect blend

In the first situation, the planners propose a course of action that is "perfect" in terms of dealing with the problem as they define it (and with all the values and preferences implicit in that definition). They are poor strategists, however, and do not take into account the essential conditions for building a majority in favor of their ideal plan; for example, the political conditions noted above as associated with different Congresses. Perhaps the plan will win approval on its own merits; more likely, however, it will fail. Professors Martin Meyerson and Edward C. Banfield have provided a superb case study of this situation in *Politics, Planning, and the Public Interest,* a book all students of public policy should read. In this instance, the Chicago Housing Authority—

the planners—had formulated a site-selection plan for public housing in Chicago in line with their definition of the problems to be attacked. Relatively little attention was paid to the hard realities of majority building in the Chicago City Council (whose approval was necessary). The results were disastrous. The council shredded the CHA's plan, and a long and bitter struggle ensued between the planners and the politicians; that is, between pure formulators and pure legitimators. As Meyerson and Banfield note:

■ The question . . . arises why the Council and the Authority engaged in a long struggle rather than in cooperation. . . .

The strategy of the Authority was to struggle rather than to bargain. Indeed, the Authority went somewhat out of its way to provoke the leaders of the Council; it did this by refusing to enter into even a *pro forma* discussion with the housing committee of the Council before the sites were formally submitted, by locating a large project in [Councilman] Duffy's ward without giving him any advance notice of it, and by taking a hostile tone in its public appearances before the Council.[12]

One can find any number of examples of the second situation, in which a proposal gains acceptance almost without opposition, and yet is totally inadequate to deal with the problem or problems to which it is directed. The poverty program, discussed later in this chapter, is one such example. For various reasons the Economic Opportunity Act of 1964 was an imperfect plan. Yet the political planning in getting a majority in Congress was almost faultless. Of course, in all cases, judgments about what is or is not perfect depend on one's preferences and the conditions at the time.

The third combination is intriguing: the perfect blend between plan and politics, between formulation and legitimation. In this case, all known factors are presumably taken into account. With the exception of the actual ratification of a proposal, which the law may require to occur within a legislature, formulation and legitimation are coincident functions. When one is complete, the other is as well. That is, policy actors have so thoroughly accounted for the conditions under which a majority must be constructed in a legislature that the task is completed along with the development of a course of action to solve a public problem. Surely this is the goal of many policy planners and strategists, but plans and politics are not always so compatible. I do not mean to imply that the perfect blend is a combination of perfect plans and perfect strategies. Rather it is a process of getting the best of both, given the circumstances at hand.

A perfect blend suggests by implication the possibility of an imperfect blend. Out of ignorance, miscalculation, or both, those engaged in formulating and legitimating a course of action may produce a bad plan and a worse strategy for gaining support. Though there are many examples, the 1977 energy proposals of the Carter administration are frequently cited as demonstrating the imperfect blend. The program was developed virtually in secret (see page 107). It contained provisions with little or no support beyond those who had conceived them. And President Carter unveiled the program before a television audience, going to Congress second. The reaction on Capitol Hill, even among the Democrats, was critical, to say the least. In fact, coming as it did early in the Carter administration, this imperfect blend of plan and politics had a seriously negative effect on the president's subsequent relations with Congress.

Formulation as a Total Policy Process

What has been described so far is a somewhat disorderly process by which proposals are presented to deal with public issues. In broadening the scope of formulation beyond planning we naturally include elements and activities that are less predictable. Yet these less predictable elements may dominate decision making. This situation is understandably frustrating for professional planners, who may find proposals they have developed over a five-year period treated on a par with the hastily drawn recommendations of a senator's personal staff or volunteers of a public interest group.

Such frustrations have led to efforts by planners to bolster their case. If proposals were irrefutably justified in terms of their effectiveness in achieving accepted goals, then other, less systematically drawn alternatives would presumably be rejected. During the 1960s a supreme effort was made to develop a system of program justification. This effort began in the Department of Defense and was referred to as the "planning-programming-budgeting system" (PPBS). "The system was based upon the limited rationality model of decision making in which multi-year plans are established and incremental decisions are used to adjust these plans."[13] The system was essentially an effort to force program planners and budget makers to think beyond immediate results and consider longer-range goals and effects; in other words, to break out of the pattern of justifying next year's proposals by inertia alone. In his order to use PPBS throughout the federal government, President Johnson claimed it would provide the following advantages:

1. Identify our national goals with precision and on a continuing basis
2. Choose among those goals the ones that are most urgent
3. Search for alternative means of reaching those goals most effectively at the least cost
4. Inform ourselves not merely on next year's costs, but on the second, and third, and subsequent years' costs of our programs
5. Measure the performance of our programs to insure a dollar's worth of service for each dollar spent[14]

PPBS was designed to reduce uncertainty, waste of resources, and misdirection in policy making through systematic analysis of the basic elements of that process: problems, goals, costs, allocations, appraisals. As one reviews PPBS in its pure form, it becomes evident that it is a *total policy process*. In theory, if everyone involved in policy making accepts the outcomes, then all functional activities take place within PPBS. In fact, of course, not everyone does accept the outcomes, and we can all agree that what comes out depends very much on what goes in. Given limited resources, people will debate what the goals are and where the resources ought to be allocated. This being the case, PPBS becomes one more strategy in what Aaron Wildavsky refers to as "policy politics." It can be an impressive strategy. That is, equipped with extensive computer-derived cost–benefit analyses of priorities among programs, a planner may overwhelm those who have the authority to legitimate one course of action over another. Former Secretary of Defense Robert McNamara was impressive in his performances before congressional committees, virtually inundating the members with quantitative data. But, as Professor Wildavsky warns, ". . . *a (if not the) distinguishing characteristic of systems analysis is that the objectives either are not known or are subject to change.*"[15] So, he concludes, a "perfect plan" becomes highly political because perfection is ultimately related to someone's analysis of goals to be achieved, priorities to be set, allocations to be made. While an effort like PPBS may increase efficiency by some measures of what that is, it is unlikely to do away with the policy process as we know it at the federal level.

■ A major task of the political system is to specify goals or objectives. It is impermissible to treat goals as if they were known in advance. "Goals" may well be the product of interaction among key participants rather than some *deus ex machina* or (to use Bentley's term) some "spook" that posits values in advance of our knowledge of them.[16]

Other efforts by planners to justify their proposals by setting them in broader context include what some refer to as the "what-if" approach. One variant is to ask, What if resources were available to meet all needs? This question presumably forces consideration of alternative needs, followed by justification of the choices made. The advantage, therefore, is in expanding the context for evaluating present programs. How are they doing compared to what might be done? "The disadvantage is that . . . requests may exceed the economic and political capabilities of the jurisdiction, so that the requests seem like fanciful wishlists."[17] Further, exercises like this and zero-based budgeting (see below) can become routine, bearing little relationship to original purposes.

Another what-if approach is to ask, What would happen if a program were discontinued? Called "zero-based budgeting" (ZBB), this method tries to force agency budget makers to justify the whole program from its root or base, not just next year's increment. The assumption is that if they go back to a zero base, political decision makers (presidents and their aides, the members of Congress) will be in a position to judge which programs are worth continuing. That is, the justification for an increase will be linked to the achievement of the broader social goals of the program.

As with other systems, ZBB is designed to strengthen the planning and evaluation components of decision making by increasing awareness of whether programs are working. The presumption is that those programs that have failed will be dropped and those that are struggling will be given less. Unfortunately, many of Wildavsky's worries about PPBS (see above) apply as well to the what-if approaches. It is just plain difficult to design a totally objective formulation process. Most programs have clienteles, which are unlikely to remain passive in the face of efforts to reduce or eliminate their benefits. Even if criteria are established for comparing programs at their zero base, one may expect the beneficiaries to search for support elsewhere, for example, in Congress or among the electorate. For our purposes, then, ZBB and other planning systems should be studied to learn how they alter the politics of the policy process. At this point I am moved to reiterate another of the initial realities: "No ideal policy system exists apart from the preferences of the architect of that system."

Three Cases of Formulation

It is time to introduce cases of formulation. I offer three. The "war on poverty" formulators were drawn primarily from the executive and from universities and private foundations. In the case of hospital cost containment, proposals by the executive were met with strong opposition and weak counterproposals by the health service industry. In the case of energy conservation and supply, both the president and Congress were active in formulation at different times. Thus, both the problems to be solved and the institutional bases for formulation differed in each of the three cases.

The War on Poverty: 1964[18]

■ . . . we have never lost sight of our goal: an America in which every citizen shares all the opportunities of his society . . .

We have come a long way toward this goal.

We still have a long way to go.

The distance which remains is the measure of the great unfinished work of our society.

To finish that work I have called for *a national war on poverty. Our objective: total victory.*

President Lyndon B. Johnson
Message on Poverty, March 16, 1964

This dramatic declaration signaled one of the most innovative and controversial policies in decades. The beneficiaries would be the poor of this nation. A first order of business was to determine who and where the poor were. To do that somebody had to decide what poverty was. The Council of Economic Advisers set an arbitrary standard of $3,000 for a family of four and declared that 20 percent of families were poor. That measure became controversial, and Mollie Orshansky of the Social Security Administration developed other measures, establishing several categories of poor and setting a "poverty threshold" for each.[19] Some rather sophisticated statistics on the poor of this nation gradually emerged.[20] But statistics are only one small part of defining the problems of poverty. By our definition of *public problem,* the people themselves are involved and the actual problems are many. As Anthony Downs observes, "Whether people *feel* poor or not depends to some extent on how their incomes compare with the incomes of other people around them."[21] He might have added, "Whether problems exist for them or not depends to a large extent on how they view the effects of low income."

The launching of a full-scale war on poverty had been preceded by skirmishes for several hundred years. There have always been poor people, and governments have long had some policy to treat them. Unfortunately, only very recently has that policy been in the least humane. A dominant theme in the United States has been, and still is to a great extent, that the poor are poor because of some flaw in their character. In the twentieth century, governments began to aid certain categories of poor: the aged, the blind, the retarded, dependent children.[22] And then suddenly even those with flawless characters were poor. The Great Depression had the effect of expanding the perception of poverty and giving policy makers some experience with the problems of the poor. A revolution in social welfare occurred in the United States with the passage of social security, housing, employment, and economic legislation. With the righting of the economy, those for whom economic depression was no new experience continued to suffer the indignities of poverty. The rest of the nation prospered.

Ultimately it was this contrast—the poverty amid affluence—that brought this issue area to the agenda of government. Despite the postwar economic success, a large group remained poor. By 1963 a large number of people in government and in the private sphere were occupied with treating symptoms. As James L. Sundquist describes it, programs in mental health, urban renewal, public welfare, and manpower retraining all pointed the way to a broad-scale effort to eliminate poverty.[23] The principal formulators included Presidents Kennedy and Johnson and persons drawn from the following organizations:

Council of Economic Advisers
Bureau of the Budget
Ford Foundation
President's Committee on Juvenile Delinquency and Youth Crimes
White House Staff
Departments of Labor; Health, Education, and Welfare; Agriculture; Commerce; Interior
Peace Corps
Small Business Administration
Housing and Home Finance Agency (now the Department of Housing and Urban Development)

In view of the enormity of what was being attempted in 1963 and 1964 and the number of people involved, it is absolutely incredible that a course of action could be formulated with such speed. At first, those involved in several programs treating the symptoms of poverty found themselves communicating frequently. President Kennedy's concern about Appalachia and other "pockets of poverty" made him receptive to a broad program. The Council of Economic Advisers, staffed largely by academicians, was free to devote research time to the development of proposals, and Professor Robert J. Lampman of the University of Wisconsin began to assemble data in early 1963. After the enactment of the 1963 tax cut, which was designed to stimulate the economy, all the conscious and unconscious efforts in behalf of a poverty program began to take on unity and direction. By October President Kennedy had become convinced that antipoverty measures should be included in the 1964 legislative program. The CEA proceeded full steam to assemble proposals, contacting many of the people who had previously been unwitting policy formulators.

On November 19, Kennedy asked Walter Heller, chairman of the Council of Economic Advisers, to have measures prepared for his review in a couple of weeks. The president then boarded the plane for Texas.

■ Budget Bureau, CEA, and White House staff were in the midst of a review of the departmental responses [to their request for proposals] when they were interrupted by the news from Dallas.
   President Johnson lost no time in restoring their momentum. At his first meeting with Heller, on November 23, Johnson said, "That's my kind of program. . . . Move full speed ahead." [24]

At this point, the "idea" unit, CEA, stepped back to let the Bureau of the Budget take the leadership in formulating definite proposals. After considerable frustration in discovering "a theme or rationale that would distinguish the new legislation," [25] the framers found the notion of community organizations, proposed by David Hackett and Richard W. Boone of the Juvenile Delinquency Committee. As Daniel P. Moynihan describes it:

■ In a subtle, not entirely clear process, the coordinated community approach to problems of the poor attracted great interest and ultimately powerful and crucial support in that nerve center, indeed superego, of the federal establishment [the Bureau of the Budget]. [26]

The community approach, eventually to be called "community action programs," had been tried, but not thoroughly tested, by the Juvenile Delinquency Committee and the Ford Foundation in their various projects. Despite lack of information about how it might work, "aid to community organizations was transformed from an incidental weapon in the war on poverty into the entire arsenal." [27]

Thus, by bits-and-pieces progress, the program was developing definite thrust by January 1964. The question of where to locate the problem was resolved in favor of establishing an independent agency. Many formulators were concerned that no department could provide the imagination needed for the poverty effort. Unless an independent agency were created, it was feared, funds would be used simply to bolster existing programs, all of which were inadequate.

Since a new agency was to be created, no unit existed to take the lead in developing a substantive program. The Bureau of the Budget performed its expected role of coordinating the early efforts, since it is charged with overseeing the development of the president's legislative program. But an idea of this magnitude needed somebody who was committed to it for its own sake, and not because of a general responsibility for coordinating all proposals. Sargent Shriver, brother-in-law of the late president and director of the Peace Corps, was selected as that "somebody." With his appointment, the poverty program had an energetic and influential advocate, one who had experience with local aid programs overseas through the Peace Corps.

Shriver took charge of the formulation system, establishing a task force to refine the proposals that would be submitted to Congress. All ideas were reviewed again; government, foundation, academic, and state and local officials were all consulted. Interestingly, *neither the poor nor the blacks had any role in the development of the program that was to affect them.*

■ ... it is worth noting that the American poor themselves did *not* participate in the process which led to the creation of the act.[28] At no time did any Negro have any role of any consequence in the drafting of the poverty program. Nor did any Negro have any role of any consequence in the drafting of the CAP guidelines.[29]

So it went. The formulation process was now in high gear. Shriver was appointed on February 1; by mid-March the legislation was ready for Congress. The community action idea was expanded beyond the initial experimental program; other programs, primarily directed toward job training, were added. Then, with virtually no consultation with members of Congress, the package was sent to the Hill for approval. Congress, controlled by large Democratic margins working in a post-assassination mood sympathetic to Kennedy programs, passed it overwhelmingly. Republican protests and strategies were buried in the whirlwind of publicity and support for unconditional war.

That which was to become so highly controversial later—the participation of the poor in community action programs—went almost unnoticed in the legislation. Moynihan, who was much involved in the construction of the program, reflects on this point.

■ Although memory too readily deceives, it may be of use to record here the impression that community action simply was not much on the minds of those who were most active in the Shriver task force. In retrospect, at least, it would seem to have assumed a kind of residual function. . . .

   . . . The community action title, which established the one portion of the program that would not be directly monitored from Washington, should provide for the "maximum feasible participation of the residents of the areas and the members of the groups" involved in the local programs. Subsequently this phrase was taken to sanction a specific theory of social change, and there were those present in Washington at the time who would have drafted just such language with precisely that object. But the record, such as can be had, and recollection indicates that it was intended to do no more than ensure that persons excluded from the political process in the South and elsewhere would nonetheless participate in the *benefits* of the community action programs of the new legislation.[30]

Congress was programmed for quick action. The hearings were stacked in favor: only nine of sixty-nine primary witnesses in the House were opposed. Chairman Adam Clayton Powell of the House Committee on Education and Labor declared in the face of Republican protests: "I am the chairman. I will run this committee as I desire."[31] The administration was successful in getting a Southern conservative as the House sponsor (Phil Landrum of Georgia), and the bill passed both houses virtually intact. The participation of the poor was not even discussed.

The poverty program is a textbook case of the executive as formulator. It also turns out to be a good case of flawless strategy in getting a course of action legitimated. Relative to other proposals, the Economic Opportunity Act of 1964 was innovative—a break with the past. One can see how events, perceptions, definitions of problems were all building toward the development of such a program. But the exceptional way in which the course of action was formulated caused complications in applying the policy to the problems. Administrators were given broad authority in the act, in part because no one was all that sure what ought to be done. The fact is that broad legislation was passed, a new agency created, and large sums appropriated, with only the vaguest definitions of the problems of poverty.

Controlling Hospital Costs

There are many ways to illustrate the rising cost of hospital care, all of them dramatic. As former Secretary of Health, Education, and Welfare Joseph A. Califano, Jr., observed, "Hospitals have become, over the years, many of them, quite obese. . . ."[32] Here are the facts and figures that were compiled to support President Carter's cost control program in 1977:

1. The cost of one day's stay in a hospital rose 1,000 percent between 1950 and 1976.
2. Hospital expenditures increased more than twice as much as the consumer price index between 1969 and 1978 (198 percent compared to 80 percent).
3. Expenditures are projected to exceed $180 billion in 1985 and $330 billion in 1990.[33]

Inflation, new and expensive technology, more patients, and more tests and treatment combined to contribute to this cost escalation. Growth has affected other services in the economy too, but, according to former secretary Califano, hospitals are structurally unsuited to developing more cost-effective methods.

"Hospitals are unlike any other segment of our economy. There is absolutely no competition among them."[34] He might also have said that the medical transaction in a hospital is wholly unlike other commercial transactions. Imagine that your local garage is a hospital. You bring your car in. The mechanic orders a series of tests without consulting you as to the cost. Perhaps a major overhaul (surgery) is judged to be required. The mechanic comes to this conclusion in consultation with other specialists; you are not normally involved in the decision. The work is completed and the car is returned to you. A third party—perhaps an insurance company or the government—pays the bill. You learn of the cost some weeks later, provided that you are able to decipher the statement. As you can see, there is very little incentive to reduce costs in this type of transaction. Ultimately the excesses of such a system are paid for indirectly (and not always by those who benefit) through increases in insurance premiums or taxes. Controlling these expenses is obviously a difficult challenge.

In the case of the war on poverty (see above) I noted that the major target group, the poor, was not represented on the Shriver task force. It is inconceivable that a major component of the health care system (with the possible exception of the patients) would not be represented by a parallel reform group. Certainly the doctors, hospital administrators, insurance companies, drug and equipment firms, and nurses are, compared to the poor, well organized and possessed of excellent access to decision making. As David Mechanic observes, this multiplicity of groups complicates policy making:

■ Medical care involves a variety of interest groups that tend to view priorities from their own particular perspectives and interests, and it is enormously difficult to achieve a consensus. Groups are usually reluctant to yield rights and privileges that they have already exercised, and will resist significant restructuring unless it appears that there is something in it for them. New priorities, if they are to be anything but slogans, must introduce innovations and change in a fashion that does not threaten too many of the groups involved.[35]

Perhaps nothing is more threatening than proposals designed to change the cost of something. After all, cost translates into salaries for some and profits for others. Therefore when the Carter administration decided to make "the rise in health care expenditures" a top priority, one could expect a reaction from the powerful health service industry.

Program formulation was naturally centered in the Department of Health, Education, and Welfare (HEW; since reorganized into two departments: Health and Human Services, and Education). Hospital and medical associations were not greatly involved in formulation. The timetable was short (the president wanted action in the first year of his administration) and the issue too complex. Given the congressional access of the health service industry, however, the president was unlikely to get the quick action he desired. On this issue one could not expect the smooth workings of a cozy little triangle.

Aaron Wildavsky has formulated the "law of medical money" by which "medical costs . . . rise to equal the sum of all private insurance and government subsidy."[36] It follows that "costs will be limited when either individuals or governments reduce the amount they put into medicine."[37] In essence, the HEW plan accepted the law of medical money and proposed to reduce the amount available to hospitals. The proposal set a cap on cost increases for inpatient services (up to 9 percent for the first year, less in subsequent years). In other words, hospitals (at least those included in the proposal) would be forced to live within a particular limit. They would not be permitted to exceed the revenue limits established by law. This proposal was offered to Congress on April 25, 1977, just three months after Carter's inauguration.

The hospital and medical professions were not long in responding. Predictably they focused first on the quality of medical care. Michael D. Bromberg of the Federation of American Hospitals (FAH) argued that HEW is "the last person you want making that decision as to how much health care is enough because they have a conflict of interest—they buy the care."[38] He argued that the administration's proposal is "rationing, pure and simple." J. Alexander McMahon, president of the American Hospital Association (AHA) predictably agreed with Bromberg: "The real victims of this bill are the sick and the injured."[39] The American Medical Association (AMA) also stressed the importance of the quality of health care as the first consideration. In addition, the medical and hospital groups were critical of legislation that placed the full burden of reducing costs on hospitals (though it is unquestioned that they would have opposed a broader attack on costs just as strongly).

The health service industry formulated its own proposal in response to that offered by the Carter administration. It was a voluntary effort organized primarily by the AHA, FAH, and AMA. The goal was a 2 percent reduction in the growth rate of expenditures for each of the first two years of the program. Goals were also set to restrain further hospital expansions (the Carter proposal had also addressed this issue).

Organized labor was also critical of the Carter proposal. Of particular concern to the AFL-CIO were (1) the failure to do anything about doctors' fees, (2) weak protections for unprofitable charity patients, and (3) most vital, the effects of reductions on the wages of lower-paid hospital workers. Clearly members of Congress had to take great care in resolving these serious conflicts in policy formulation.

That health policy issues are treated by two committees in each house did not simplify matters. Thus formulators had to take into account probable reactions, and possible counterproposals, in the following committees and subcommittees:

House:
    Committee on Interstate and Foreign Commerce (now called Energy and Commerce), Subcommittee on Health and Environment
    Committee on Ways and Means, Subcommittee on Health
Senate:
    Committee on Human Resources, Subcommittee on Health and Scientific Research
    Committee on Finance, Subcommittee on Health

One should not miss the lessons here. First note that there is no congressional committee on health, despite its importance as an issue on the agendas of government. Second, health policy proposals are therefore treated by groups with many other responsibilities. House Ways and Means and Senate Finance are the taxing committees; they have jurisdiction because much health care is financed through the social security tax. The House Commerce Committee, too, is one of the busiest on Capitol Hill. Third, one may expect that proposals before these committees will be thoroughly tested since many powerful groups have access to them (due to the many issues treated). Put otherwise, few health policy proposals can expect to have a free ride even at the subcommittee and committee stages.

As it turned out, another proposal did emerge from Congress. It was offered by Senator Herman Talmadge (D.–Georgia), then second-ranking Democrat on the Finance Committee. His proposal was designed to alter the whole payment structure for medicare and medicaid, changing from the fee-for-service system to so-called prospective reimbursement. By this latter system hospitals would be reimbursed by a preset, fixed-fee mechanism based on average costs.

The Carter administration was unsuccessful in enacting a cost containment bill. A great deal of time and effort was expended on this important issue between 1977 and 1980 but with no product. Bills passed both houses at one point or another but they were unsatisfactory to the White House. The result was a victory for the industry, which preferred no government action at all. Clearly the seriousness of the issue was not enough to insure successful formulation.

The Public Discovers Energy

President Carter found it difficult to project a sense of crisis in regard to hospital costs. As the car analogy for hospital costs suggests, elimination of direct payment by the consumer removes the potential for awareness of increasing costs. The situation was different for the large and complex energy issue area. A major crisis—the Arab oil embargo in the fall of 1973—had a striking impact on consumers. Whether or not they judged it to be a contrived crisis (and many did), the results were dramatic.

Energy: The Nixon and Ford Administrations

■ October 17, 1973, was energy Pearl Harbor day. Instead of dropping bombs, a handful of oil-rich Arab nations shut off a few valves and sent shock waves through the closely linked high-energy industrial civilization in the United States, Western Europe, and Japan.[40]

The long lines at gas stations and the threat of reduced residential heating, particularly in the Northeast, forced comprehension of national excesses in energy consumption. The price rises that followed taught us something else: that much of our prosperity, individually and as a nation, was based on the availability of cheap fuel. In 1973 the Arabs discovered a means for redistributing that prosperity.

■ Between 1973 and 1974 the Organization of Petroleum Exporting Countries (OPEC) increased the average export price of oil from $2.75 a barrel to $10 a barrel, thereby imposing a $75 billion "excise tax" on the oil-importing countries. Unprecedented in size and suddenness, this transfer of income sent a series of depressing shocks through the world economy. . . . The rapidity of the 1974 jump in oil prices . . . caused a simultaneous acceleration of inflation and loss of employment that the industrial countries proved unable to handle with the monetary and fiscal tools at their disposal.[41]

Here then was a major crisis with immediate personal effects because Americans had gotten used to higher energy consumption and because lots of jobs were at stake. Under the circumstances, energy problems bullied their way to the top of government agendas at all levels. The immediate crisis required the allocation of available petroleum, negotiation with the Arab states, and the lifting of certain restrictions on development of domestic resources. It was also necessary to plan future energy programs. It is this second effort that is briefly described here since it represents a case of formulating a comprehensive policy.

One must take account of the extraordinary political context in which energy proposals were formulated in 1974–1975. President Nixon was on his way out (resigning August 11, 1974), Gerald R. Ford would enter the White House with fewer political resources than almost any president in history, and the Democrats were to increase their numbers in the 1974 congressional elections to almost veto-proof proportions (nearly two-thirds in each house). Given these conditions, one could not expect a smooth and integrated formulation exercise. Rather, one could look for a disjointed and partisan process with participants drawn from both Congress and the executive, and the private and public spheres.

The awareness of shortages, of finite resources, called for a quite different philosophy and obviously promoted dramatic shifts in government policies. Thus, for example, a complete energy profile for the United States showed heavy reliance on a narrow and declining resource base. A study by the Energy Research and Development Administration (ERDA) showed that more than 75 percent of the energy consumed is drawn from the dwindling supplies of petroleum and natural gas, while the more abundant coal resources provide only 20 percent, and the source of greatest potential, uranium, provides about 2 percent.[42] Government policies have promoted this reliance, in part through tax breaks and leasing policies for the oil industry, and in part by failure to adopt an integrated national energy policy.

Program formulation in energy was characterized by participation of many departments, agencies, and committees; inadequate and unreliable information about the problems; premature announcement of broad proposals with impossible goals; and, as a consequence of the foregoing, little or no credibility for any one set of formulations. In short, the scene was one of confusion bordering on chaos. More analytically speaking, what we witnessed was not all that unfamiliar in American politics; it was our particular brand of crisis decision making made more dramatic by a major political upheaval.

The partisan division between Congress and the White House helped to explain the broad participation in formulation; for anything a Republican president could do, a Democratic Congress could do better. Thus, one cannot describe an organizationally tight process, as was possible with the poverty program. Rather, we witnessed a continuous process of formulation from several sources.

President Nixon sought to tighten the policy development process through a number of proposed organizational changes: in particular, the creation of a Federal Energy Administration, a Department of Energy and Natural Resources, an Energy Research and Development Administration, and a Nuclear Energy Commission. No action was taken in Congress on these proposals before the Arab boycott.

Following the boycott, a number of organizational changes were made. As a consequence, when President Ford began to pick up the pieces after President Nixon's resignation, he had a somewhat more coherent formulation network available for developing programmatic alternatives. The effort to centralize and coordinate energy policy making in the executive was not emulated in Congress, however. As indicated below, practically every committee sought to get a piece of the action. Here then were the principal executive units involved in program formulation in 1974 and 1975.

Executive Office of the President
    Council on Energy Resources (chaired by the Secretary of the Interior and including most of the secretaries and agency heads involved in energy-related programs)
Department of the Interior
    Several bureaus involved
Federal Energy Administration (FEA)
    New agency responsible for managing short-term fuel shortages
Energy Research and Development Administration (ERDA)
    New agency responsible for all research and development
Nuclear Regulatory Commission
    New agency encompassing the safety, licensing, and regulatory powers of the old Atomic Energy Commission

This structure was more rationally organized for program development. FEA was to be concerned with short-run allocations, ERDA with longer-term planning, and Interior with the management of resources, and the new council was to provide coordination. Although miracles do not occur as a result of reorganization, this structure nevertheless offered the president a greater potential for coherent formulation.

In Congress, on the other hand, practically *every* committee found that it had some claim to energy policy making. The leadership had no way to coordinate these diverse activities. As a consequence, a unified and integrated executive program was unlikely to be judged as such by any one congressional unit. The titles of the subcommittees speak for themselves. Whereas only three had *energy* in their titles in 1973, nine did in 1975. My count shows twenty-three committees and fifty-one subcommittees dealing with some aspect of energy by 1976. ERDA officials claimed that they were answerable to thirty-three committees, sixty-five subcommittees, and one panel—a total of ninety-nine units.[43]

This political and organizational context goes far toward explaining the lengthy and complex formulation activities during 1973–1975. We start with the president's energy message in April 1973, which emphasized supply. This message provided a comprehensive overview of problems and offered a number of individual programs for increasing resources and fuel imports, conserving energy, encouraging research and development, and developing international cooperation. In addition the president reintroduced his reorganization proposals.

The Arab embargo gave new urgency to programs already formulated by the executive. Though the president asked for energy powers and took a number of actions under existing authority, basically he reiterated the need to enact the program introduced earlier. He did attach a new name to his proposals: "Project Independence." While some emergency legislation was enacted, the bulk of the president's program remained in the proposal stage.

In 1974 energy policy formulation shifted to Congress. The president offered his proposals, and it was more than mere intransigence that kept Congress from acting. Many Democrats simply disagreed with the administration's approach. The principal source of congressional formulation was, as expected, the Interior committees. Congress passed an emergency energy bill in February that was based on a quite different view of the problem, including as it did broad authority for the president to ration gasoline, order conservation measures, and modify environmental standards, as well as providing a rollback on domestic crude oil prices. The bill was vetoed, leaving program development at a standstill.

Congress did take actions in 1974 that were to influence future formulation activities, however. Much of President Nixon's energy reorganization package was enacted (see above), and funds for research and development were increased. Thus, by 1975 the stage was set for another variation of program development. President Ford could rely on the new apparatus for developing a new set of energy proposals. Meanwhile, congressional Democrats were buoyed by victory at the polls in the 1974 congressional elections and were more determined than ever to counter with an energy program of their own.

In part as a result of these events, policy formulation in 1975 approached comic-opera proportions. An unelected president, serving out the term of the first chief executive to be forced to resign in disgrace, succeeded in taking the initiative despite his insecure political position. Any president has the constitutional advantage of presenting new proposals in the State of the Union Message. House Democrats sought to blunt this edge by announcing their economic and energy plans on January 13, two days before the president's message. President Ford countered by revealing the general thrust of his proposals in a television and radio address, also on January 13, thus upstaging the Democrats. As we will see, the opening act tended to characterize the whole play.

While we can't explore the details of the proposals offered in this essentially process-oriented description, we should note certain actions that came to have strategic importance. In the case of the president's plan, he sought to spur action on his legislative requests by making decisions already within his authority that would, he thought, force congressional action. Largely because the executive was developing a more integrated energy decision-making apparatus, the executive package was generally judged to be coherent and precise compared to that offered on January 13 by Speaker Carl Albert on behalf of the House Democrats.

But Congress was not done participating in the formulation of energy proposals. In addition to the scores of individual legislative proposals, three groups in particular offered energy packages. Two of these were quite innovative in effort, if abortive in outcome. A seven-member ad hoc committee in the Senate, led by Senator John O. Pastore (D.–Rhode Island), worked on an alternative economic and energy plan to present to the Senate Democratic Policy Committee and Caucus. They were assisted by Policy Committee staff. On the House side, a task force of the House Democratic Steering and Policy Committee headed by James Wright (D.–Texas) was instrumental in devising the initial counterproposals offered by the House Democrats on January 13. Thus the party structure in each house had established a mechanism for formulating an integrated set of proposals on major domestic issues. The two special committees met in February to mold their proposals and announced a joint plan on February 27.

The weakness of the party leadership structure was soon apparent as committee chairmen reacted to these proposals. In the Senate, Russell Long (D.–Louisiana), chairman of the Committee on Finance that would eventually act on the taxing proposals, said, "Let Pastore have his day. . . . I don't want to take issue with him. Some of these things we'll do and some we won't."[44] In the House, the Committee on Ways and Means, to which all tax proposals must go first, was formulating its own set of proposals. Chairman Al Ullman (D.–Oregon) had established eight task forces to review proposals he had initially developed, and on March 2 the Ways and Means Democrats offered their proposals. Earlier Ullman had characterized the Senate proposals as "a milk-toast program."[45] He considered it a mistake for the Wright task force to compromise with Pastore in a joint plan. Yet the Ullman plan was in turn criticized by other House and Senate Democrats.

This case is a classic illustration of the difficulties Congress has in producing unified programmatic alternatives to those offered by the executive. Special leadership initiatives are soon thwarted by the realities of congressional committee jurisdictions and internal party politics. Many Democratic leaders in Congress, both in the party and in committees, were intent on taking the formulation initiative away from the president in this important issue area in 1975. But the lack of coordinative mechanisms, or, put the other way, the premium placed on action by a decentralized and independent committee system, prevented any unified action.

Energy: The Carter Administration

In 1977 a new cast of characters entered the White House and introduced another style of formulation. President Carter made energy a top-priority issue for his administration. He was determined to produce a comprehensive energy proposal within ninety days. That time limit alone made it difficult to include all those many persons who could legitimately claim experience and expertise in this area. The president appointed James Schlesinger to head an energy task force with the responsibility for formulating an energy program. David H. Davis describes the process:

■ The NEP's [National Energy Program] genesis was remarkably closed *even within the executive branch.* Carter and Schlesinger were obsessed with secrecy. This secrecy allowed Carter to package a multitude of decisions about energy (many of which the Nixon and Ford administrations had considered) into a single, dramatic policy. Schlesinger's task force developed the NEP with minimal direct input from other government agencies and virtually none from congressional and business leaders. Only by forcefully demanding their rights to be consulted were the Treasury, the Office of Management and Budget, the Council of Economic Advisers, and the National Security Council allowed to participate in the final stage of the drafting.[46]

One would not expect much consultation between Republican presidents and a Democratic Congress. But Carter was a Democrat, and his party leaders (and committee chairmen) were critical of this method of developing a major domestic program. The president compounded the original error by presenting his program to the public in a television address before presenting it to Congress. Despite these problems, the House enacted the bulk of the president's program in three months—virtually a record for such a complex program. The story was very different in the Senate, however, where major energy forces concentrated their efforts to modify the president's program. That story takes one into the complexities of legitimation. It will suffice here to quote Senator Abraham Ribicoff (D.–Connecticut), who said at one point, "I am just wondering . . . if the President shouldn't admit that his energy program is a shambles."[47]

I selected the energy case primarily because it is a good example of the complications involved in trying to formulate a *comprehensive* proposal for an issue of such enormous scope. In particular, following a crisis it is difficult to contain participation in formulation. Where there are strong partisan divisions, as between Nixon, Ford, and Congress, it is very nearly inevitable that competing proposals will be developed. Conflict is intense under such conditions. Where an effort is made to insure coherence by limiting participation, as with Carter and Schlesinger, resentment builds into opposition. It is difficult to fashion coherent, comprehensive proposals in an open decision-making system.

Summary

No set of cases can possibly illustrate all the dynamics of formulation. Those offered here do show the variation in types of participants, political conditions, nature and scope of the issue, strategic considerations, government experience, and bases for compromise. They also illustrate points I particularly want emphasized. That is, first, formulation is not institution bound; second, it may result in one proposal or several; and third, it may proceed with several clear definitions of the problem or none. It is also worth stressing that formulators perform important linkage functions between problems and policies. They look in both directions at once. Moved to develop courses of action on public problems, they operate with a conception (sometimes very vague) of what those problems are, while looking ahead to the hard political realities of bargaining in the legitimation and application processes. And none of this is very tidy. If you got the impression that the process is spasmodic, spread over time, with episodic participation from persons with lots of other things to do, then the cases served the intended purpose.

Notes

1. Charles E. Lindblom, *The Policy-Making Process* (Englewood Cliffs, N. J.: Prentice-Hall, 1968), p. 13.
2. Herbert J. Gans, "Regional and Urban Planning," in *International Encyclopedia of the Social Sciences,* vol. 12, ed. David L. Sills (New York: Macmillan, 1968), p. 129.
3. Charles O. Jones and Dieter Matthes, "Policy Formation," in *Encyclopedia of Policy Studies,* ed. Stuart Nagel (New York: Marcel Dekker, 1982), p. 129.
4. Roger H. Davidson, "Breaking Up Those 'Cozy Triangles': An Impossible Dream?" in *Legislative Reform and Public Policy,* ed. Susan Welch and John G. Peters (New York: Praeger, 1977), p. 30.
5. Randall B. Ripley and Grace A. Franklin, *Congress, the Bureaucracy, and Public Policy,* rev. ed. (Homewood, Ill.: Dorsey Press, 1980), p. 8.
6. Don K. Price, *The Scientific Estate* (Cambridge, Mass.: Harvard University Press, 1965), pp. 42–43. For greater detail on the RAND Corporation, see Bruce L. R. Smith, *The RAND Corporation* (Cambridge, Mass.: Harvard University Press, 1966).
7. Charles V. Kidd, *American Universities and Federal Research* (Cambridge, Mass.: Harvard University Press, 1959), p. 206.
8. For examples, see David Price, *Who Makes the Laws?* (Cambridge, Mass.: Schenkman, 1972).
9. See Jones and Matthes, p. 131.
10. Daniel P. Moynihan, *The Politics of a Guaranteed Income* (New York: Random House, 1973), p. 7. Emphasis in original.

11. Nelson W. Polsby, *Political Innovation in America: The Politics of Policy Initiation* (New Haven, Conn.: Yale University Press, forthcoming), chap. 5, ms p. 32. Quoted by permission.
12. Martin Meyerson and Edward C. Banfield, *Politics, Planning and the Public Interest* (New York: Free Press, 1955), p. 256.
13. Robert D. Lee, Jr., and Ronald W. Johnson, *Public Budgeting Systems*, 2d ed. (Baltimore: University Park Press, 1977), p. 107.
14. U. S. Senate, Committee on Government Operations, Subcommittee on National Security and International Operations, *Planning-Programming Budgeting—Initial Memorandum* (Washington, D. C.: Government Printing Office, 1967), pp. 2–3. See also the December 1966 and March–April 1969 issues of the *Public Administration Review* for extensive analyses of PPBS.
15. Aaron Wildavsky, "The Political Economy of Efficiency," in *Political Science and Public Policy*, ed. Austin Ranney (Chicago: Markham, 1968), p. 65. Emphasis added.
16. Wildavsky, "The Political Economy of Efficiency," p. 80.
17. Lee and Johnson, p. 119.
18. The Economic Opportunity Act of 1964 has been analyzed more than practically any piece of legislation in the last twenty years. Fortunately, some of those who have written about it know the story first-hand—particularly James L. Sundquist and Daniel P. Moynihan. This section relies heavily on their books—Sundquist, *Politics and Policy* (Washington, D. C.: Brookings Institution, 1968); Moynihan, *Maximum Feasible Misunderstanding* (New York: Free Press, 1969)—and John C. Donovan, *The Politics of Poverty* (New York: Pegasus, 1967); John Bibby and Roger Davidson, *On Capitol Hill* (New York: Holt, Rinehart & Winston, 1967), chap. 7.
19. See *Social Security Bulletin*, January, July, 1965.
20. For a review of these, see Anthony Downs, *Who Are the Urban Poor?* (New York: Committee for Economic Development, 1968).
21. Downs, p. 8. Emphasis in original.
22. See Ben B. Seligman, *Permanent Poverty: An American Syndrome* (Chicago: Quadrangle Books, 1968), chap. 1, for a brief history of government policy on poverty.
23. Sundquist, *Politics and Policy*, pp. 115–134.
24. Sundquist, p. 137.
25. Sundquist, p. 138.
26. Moynihan, *Maximum Feasible Misunderstanding*, p. 77.
27. Sundquist, *Politics and Policy*, p. 138.
28. Donovan, *The Politics of Poverty*, pp. 31–32. Emphasis in original.
29. Moynihan, *Maximum Feasible Misunderstanding*, p. 98.
30. Moynihan, pp. 86–87. Emphasis in original.
31. Bibby and Davidson, *On Capitol Hill*, p. 241.
32. Quoted in *Health Policy: The Legislative Agenda* (Washington, D. C.: Congressional Quarterly, Inc., 1980), p. 20.
33. See *Health Policy*, pp. 19–20.
34. Quoted in *Congressional Quarterly Weekly Report*, April 30, 1977, 788.
35. David Mechanic, *Public Expectations and Health Care* (New York: Wiley, 1972), p. 6.
36. Aaron Wildavsky, *Speaking Truth to Power* (Boston: Little, Brown, 1979), p. 288.
37. Wildavsky, *Speaking Truth to Power*, p. 289.
38. *Health Policy*, p. 21.
39. *Health Policy*, p. 24.
40. S. David Freeman, *Energy: The New Era* (New York: Vintage Books, 1974), p. 3.
41. "Living with High Oil Prices," *The Brookings Bulletin* 12 (Fall 1975): 1.
42. U. S. Energy Research and Development Administration, *A National Plan for Energy Research, Development and Demonstration: Creating Energy Choices for the Future* (Washington, D. C.: Government Printing Office, 1975), p. I-1.
43. Cited in Davidson, "Breaking Up Those 'Cosy Triangles'", p. 34.
44. Quoted in *Congressional Quarterly Weekly Report*, February 22, 1975, 353.
45. Quoted in *Congressional Quarterly Weekly Report*, March 1, 1975, 426.
46. David H. Davis, "Pluralism and Energy: Carter's National Energy Plan," in *New Dimensions to Energy Policy*, ed. Robert Lawrence (Lexington, Mass.: Lexington Books, 1979), p. 192. Emphasis added.
47. Quoted in *Congressional Quarterly Weekly Report*, October 8, 1977.

Chapter Six

Legitimating Programs

Functional activities	Categorized in government	With a potential product
Legitimation: Agreement on means Identification of interests Communication Approval (various means)	Action in government	Program or decision

The verb *legitimate* can be defined as follows: "To make legitimate; to give legal force to. Hence, to authorize or justify." It is this end toward which the processes of formulation are directed. We may grant that there are side benefits from the mere participation in fashioning proposals (knowledge of the process, sensitivity to public problems, matching means to ends); still, the major payoff comes in getting official authorization to try out the plan. The processes of approval in our modern democratic society are justifiably complex, involving delegation of authority, reliance on expertise, changes in requirements, and intergovernmental variations (even within the same issue).

Legitimation must begin with a large measure of agreement about the means. In a stable political system the means of authorizing or approving can almost be taken for granted. Presumably every government strives for such stability. As indicated in chapter 1, however, the equilibrium of the American political system has experienced major threats in recent decades, threats that have directed attention to the fundamental means by which programs are approved. Thus the first topic to explore in this chapter is the underlying support for political institutions.

Agreement on Means

At least two forms of legitimation can be identified for any political system. The first is that which authorizes the basic political processes, including those designed to approve specific proposals for solving public problems. The second includes those specific processes by which government programs are authorized. The first will be referred to here as *legitimacy,* the second as *approval.*

Legitimacy is central to the existence of a political state. It involves authority, consent, obligation, support—indeed, the spectrum of governmental relationships with people and their problems. In her brilliant essays on obligation and consent, Hanna Pitkin questions why anyone should obey anyone else, including governmental officials. Under what conditions should one obey and who says what those conditions are? Should anyone have the last word?

■ Who is to say? I want to answer, each person who cares to, will say—not merely the one who acts, not merely his associates, not merely those in authority over him, not merely the detached historian or observer. No one has the last word because *there is no last word.* But in order to make that clear, one would have to say a great deal more about how language functions, and why we are persistently inclined to suppose that there must be a last word.[1]

The questions raised by Pitkin are fundamental. If she is right, however, that there is no last word, how can any system of government be legitimate? To say that there is no last word is, in effect, to say that legitimacy depends on various conditions. In practice, obligation becomes a very dynamic relationship between an individual and officialdom, one that is shaped by perceptions, values, information, hunches. Readers of this book no doubt vary in the extent to which they consider themselves obliged to accept authority. Circumstances may convince even the most law-abiding citizen to run a red light, exceed the speed limit, even fudge on a tax return! Each failure to obey may be rationalized. In so doing, however, you may or may not reject the legitimacy of the political system. That is, you may disobey for convenience, or because you can get away with it, or because you didn't know, and still accept that the rule broken is legitimate. Perhaps your actions are intended to point out that the rule in fact is not legitimate, though you may not reject the bases upon which the processes of legitimation are established. Or perhaps your actions are meant to reestablish a new order, totally rejecting the existing structure of legitimacy.

One measure of legitimacy is the support available for government and what it does. David Easton makes an important distinction between two types of support: specific and diffuse. "Specific support flows from the favorable attitudes and predisposition stimulated by outputs that are perceived by members to meet their demands as they arise or in anticipation."[2] Therefore, it is associated with what we have identified here as approval and will be treated subsequently. Diffuse support refers to "a reserve of favorable attitudes or good will that helps members to accept or tolerate outputs to which they are opposed or the effect of which they see as damaging to their wants."[3] Here then is a "reserve of support" which will carry government through good and bad times. Why should it exist? In large part because of a widespread trust in a particular government. Easton puts it this way:

■ The inculcation of a sense of legitimacy is probably the single most effective device for regulating the flow of diffuse support in favor both of the authorities and of the regime. A member [of society] may be willing to obey authorities and conform to the requirements of the regime for many different reasons. But the most stable support will derive from the conviction on the part of the member that it is right and proper for him to accept and obey the authorities and to abide by the requirements of the regime. It reflects the fact that in some vague or explicit way he sees these objects as conforming to his own moral principles, his own sense of what is right and proper in the political sphere.[4]

Legitimacy is obviously essential for a political system. It must exist before specific processes of approval can be effective, and its particular nature in any one system may well shape those processes. As Easton describes it, legitimacy is based on attitudes that are learned. He speaks of the "inculcation of a sense of legitimacy," and notes that "the most stable support will derive from the conviction" that one should obey. This suggests a number of interesting conclusions: that legitimacy can be managed in society; that incongruity among attitudes can cause complications; that, as Pitkin implies, legitimacy may be in the eye of the beholder; that legitimacy can be measured in a political system at any one point in time.

These conclusions, in turn, suggest a dynamic relationship between legitimacy of the system and approval of programs. For ultimately one's acceptance or rejection of government actions on specific problems may influence how one views the system. Short-run and intermittent disappointments may well be accepted; a consistent pattern of incongruity between expectations and output over time may threaten basic support for the system. This is particularly true when government itself is trying to manipulate legitimacy through the use of symbols. That is, the public may be *learning* to support a government through the flow of information and use of symbols by public officials. A new government program may be announced as consistent with or supportive of some accepted principle in society, for example, air pollution control with protection of the public health, federal aid to education with equality of opportunity, drug control with law and order. As Richard M. Merelman points out, however, there are risks attendant to any such efforts.

■ . . . care must be taken to maintain the association between particular symbols and the policies they legitimize. For example, policy makers can effectively associate the symbol, "rule of law," with the policy of integrating the schools, thereby instating perceptions of secondary and primary reinforcement to be gained from support of the policy. However, over time, as opposition rises or as circumstances change, "rule of law" may very well become separated in the public mind from the policy of school integration. The continuity between legitimacy symbol and its policy referent has broken down. Government must then absorb the costs of this separation.[5]

We can all think of examples of such discontinuities during the past decade or so. At one time America's wars could be supported by a veritable avalanche of symbols: American doughboys versus the despicable "Hun"; the righteous Marine versus the sly and treacherous "Jap"; a Kansas general leading the forces of good against Hitler's butchers. But the Korean and Vietnam struggles were not so easily characterized. We tried to identify the enemy as worldwide communism, but in Vietnam in particular the symbols never really took hold. As a result, questions about specific policies were broadened to include the whole decision-making apparatus. "Why are we there?" "Who is responsible for this mess?" "Why can't we just get the hell out?" "How can anyone be so dumb as to have gotten us in there in the first place?" Our policies and decision-making processes were affected by this fundamental questioning of the whole structure of government.

The civil rights movement of the early 1960s also represented a challenge to the basic means by which decisions are made and enforced. Blacks have known of the discontinuities between democratic principles and policies for scores of years. From their vantage point, the principles of political equality simply had a racial addendum: "If you're black, stand back." Their efforts during the 1960s were designed to make others aware of these gaps, sometimes in very dramatic fashion (as with the urban riots during that time). But black leadership was also challenging the legitimacy of a system structured to favor whites. Put another way, they were not content to accept new policies, they wanted new processes, different leaders, and greater access to decision making for themselves.

Then there were the remarkable events of the second Nixon administration: the president and vice-president forced to resign in dishonor, two attorneys general convicted of crimes (Richard G. Kleindienst pleading guilty to a misdemeanor charge for failing to testify fully before a Senate committee and John N. Mitchell for his involvement in Watergate), a secretary of commerce pleading guilty to illegal fund raising (unlawfully failing to report contributions), a secretary of the Treasury indicted but acquitted of accepting bribes, and countless presidential aides and campaign officials convicted and sent to prison. While not all of these resignations, indictments, and convictions were a direct result of Watergate, that event dominated American politics for 20 months and continues to influence decision making.

Congress also demonstrated its fallibility in the so-called Abscam scandal in 1980. In an extraordinary undercover operation by the Federal Bureau of Investigation, seven members of Congress—six from the House, one from the Senate—were caught taking bribes. All were convicted. Five of the seven were actually videotaped accepting money, and the tapes were shown on the evening news.

Not surprisingly, these many anxieties and disappointments have led to even greater cynicism than usual among American voters. Those believing that the government in Washington could be trusted "to do what is right only some of the time" increased from 22 percent in 1964 to 61 percent in 1974.[6] Trust and confidence in the executive branch dropped from 67 percent in 1972 to 45 percent in 1974.[7] Those responding that the government is doing a "good job" totaled just 8 percent in 1976, and that low figure was reduced to 4 percent in 1980![8] Yet even at the height of cynicism during the Watergate period, most Americans continued to express pride in their form of government.

This distinction between how people view government in particular and how they view government in general suggests that there may be several types and objects of legitimacy. David Easton argues precisely that. He points out that legitimacy may be ascribed to *political authorities*, "such as an elite, an administrative staff, or the whole undifferentiated set of persons through whom authority is exercised," or "to the norms and structure of a *regime*."[9] Clearly the two will not always enjoy equal amounts of legitimacy. Thus, for example, one can question the legitimacy of a president elected by a mere plurality of the popular vote, or even one who wins in a landslide but is guilty of nefarious campaign practices, without challenging, or even being very pessimistic about, the workings of democratic government. In fact, one of the most frequent reactions to the Nixon impeachment proceedings and eventual resignation was that it all demonstrated the strength, not the weakness, of the American political system. Easton may well be right in asserting that we have "a psychological need to find some leaders and structures in which to believe."[10]

This differentiation in the objects of legitimacy suggests that dips in public confidence and trust can be accommodated without resorting to major reform of political institutions. In fact, the evidence would warn against any such reaction since there remains a significant measure of support and pride even among those who demonstrate the least confidence. A change in leadership, programmatic shifts, an economic upturn, an international triumph—any one of these might reestablish confidence.

In summary, legitimacy is a dynamic attribute of any political system. This is particularly the case in democracies, where the people presumably have it within their collective power to confer or withhold legitimacy. Students of public policy cannot ignore this basic form of legitimation. If they begin their analysis without establishing the nature of legitimacy for institutions, decision makers, or the regime itself, they will have committed a fundamental error in research. For to neglect this phenomenon is to fail to consider and judge the context within which decisions occur.

It should also be noted, however, that measuring the legitimacy of government is no simple task. I have discussed indicators relied on by some: trust and confidence in government, public cynicism, pride or loyalty, views toward change. But I have also warned against hasty conclusions based on such measures. There is, perhaps, no more sensitive and complex interactive relationship between the people and their government than that involved in the conferral of legitimacy. While research may lead to an understanding of the decisional context legitimacy creates, it is probably too soon for research to permit confident predictions of events following even the more obvious shifts in public mood and confidence.

The Processes of Approval: Majority Building

The principal process of approval in American democracy is majority coalition building. Majority rule has long been a cornerstone of democratic theory. It is a practical way of getting from political equality and popular sovereignty to a working government. As Currin V. Shields observes:

■ The public desire served by the community should be satisfied to the greatest possible extent. In other words, the rules of the community should assure that the common purpose of the members is promoted as well as possible in the conduct of community affairs. How can this be achieved? The doctrine of majority rule is the Democrat's answer to this question.[11]

The doctrine then becomes a standard for measuring the product of policy making.

■ What is determined by a majority vote is "right" for the community. Authority exercised according to a decision arrived at by a democratic process is, then, legitimate. The legitimacy depends on how the authority is exercised. The test is, for the democrat, entirely procedural.[12]

It is true, of course, that the architects of the American constitutional system were not quite prepared to go all the way with majority rule. They developed a number of checks to curb majority tyranny. So concerned were these men with accumulated power that they opted for checks even on unanimities in public policy. In essence they argued that the mistakes made by not permitting quick action by large majorities are not as grave as those likely to be made when power is centered in a single group or institution. So while the legislature might sit as a representative body of the majority and should therefore be considered the primary institution of democracy, it too must be checked (see chapter 1).

Robert A. Dahl argues that the Founding Fathers were excessively concerned with majority tyranny. For him majority rule is a myth because there really is no majority. "If majority rule is mostly a myth, then majority tyranny is mostly a myth too." [13] He offers the concept "minorities rule," in which bargaining goes on between the legitimate groups in society that have access to decision making, and concludes that "on matters of specific policy the majority rarely rules."[14] Surely one cannot deny this proposition. On the other hand, any number of procedures have been established in American government to insure that decisions can be traced to a *numerical majority*. That is not to say that a majority of the citizenry is actively involved in making policy but rather that, at several points along the way to policy, numerical majorities are formed. The result is a system of layers of numerical majorities in elections, in referenda, in committee action, in roll-call voting, in court decisions. It is true, of course, that pluralities are sometimes accepted, but it is also true that those who rely on pluralities are likely to be limited in their exercise of authority and subject to criticism.

Who Is Involved?

Of the functional activities, that of legitimation is most closely identified in a democracy with a specific institution: the legislature. The legislature is carefully designed to represent the interests of people. It is logical, therefore, that efforts would be made to direct all policy proposals through the popularly elected institution for approval. Symbolically it is rationalized that a majority of legislator-representatives on any issue represents a majority of the citizenry. We all know that there are many problems with this as a description of reality, but it is also apparent that the political system must establish some processes of approval that are consistent with the symbols of democracy. So legislators will continue to be central figures in legitimation until someone can rationalize others performing that role in democracy.

At the same time they are seldom the only actors involved. Majorities may also be gathered through the efforts of bureaucrats, legislative liaison personnel, lobbyists, state and local officials, the president. Thus, I cannot provide a single answer as to who is involved. It obviously depends on what you find in studying any one public problem or issue area. Above all, do not restrict your analysis, assuming that *only* legislators participate simply because they are the ones who vote on the floor of the House and Senate.

Special consideration must be given to the role played by the president in legitimation. The Constitution (Article I, Section 7) includes a provision for presidential approval before a bill can become law. This simple requirement can greatly complicate the process of majority building by introducing a non-majoritarian element into legitimation. The president can thwart a majority in Congress, perhaps in the belief that majority does not truly reflect a majority in the nation. Of course, it is possible to override a presidential veto by constructing a two-thirds majority—no simple task! In order to avoid this circumstance, majority builders must consider the possibility of veto. The *threat* of veto, then, becomes as influential in legitimation as the veto itself.

Split-ticket voting in recent decades has provided some fascinating, if also frustrating, variations in legitimation politics. Republican presidents have served with Democratic Congresses during two periods, 1955–1961 and 1969–1977. President Ford showed that an unelected chief executive could use the veto effectively to thwart legislative majorities, even when the other party had nearly a two-thirds majority in each house. The 1980 election brought still more peculiar circumstances to presidential–congressional relations: a Republican president and Senate and a Democratic House of Representatives. With each of these variations one may expect significant changes in the populations and strategies associated with majority building.

Majority Building in Congress

It is useful to examine a major lawmaking body such as the Congress to increase one's understanding of legitimation. The legislative process in Congress is one of the most complicated parliamentary processes in the world. The few generalizations discussed below are meant merely to suggest some of the bases for analyzing legitimation in Congress. Also bear in mind that (1) legislators are not merely legitimators but perform other policy roles as well and that (2) other policy actors from other institutions also act as legitimators.

Collecting Knowledge

Building majorities begins with collecting knowledge about who favors what and why. Congress, like all legislatures, relies on many means for tapping the interests and knowledge of those associated with or affect by a proposal. Thus, for example, congressional committee hearings, staff research, diversified representation on committees, continuing contact with interest groups, research by congressional agencies (Congressional Research Service, Office of Technology Assessment, General Accounting Office), and requests for information from agencies and private research groups all contribute to a knowledge flow that is sometimes overwhelming. These activities perform the absolutely vital functions for a majority building of *identifying interests* and maintaining a flow of *communication*. Both are essential in allowing legislators to judge where compromise is necessary and possible. The continuing documentation of problems, interests, reactions, and systematic research serves many purposes in public policy making. As can be illustrated over and over again, effective working of the response network may only demonstrate why no majority is currently possible. Ten years later, however, a law may finally be enacted. Thus, the legitimation process of testing responses to determine where and how a majority might be built can contribute as well to defining the problem and formulating future proposals.

Other Characteristics of the Process

An important point to consider in studying majority building in Congress is that several majorities may have to be constructed. Separating the institutions, checking and balancing them to prevent tyranny, creating a specialized committee system—these and other features so characteristic of our political system provide various access points for special interests. At the same time, however, they offer appeal possibilities for those who lose along the way. It is seldom sufficient, therefore, to collect a majority at one point; it must be maintained throughout the intricate process of a bill becoming a law. Calculate the number of majorities that must be held for a *major* bill, beginning with subcommittee action in one house. I count a dozen just for authorizing a program, without counting amendments.

House
  Subcommittee
  Committee
  House Rules Committee
  Vote on the rule
  Vote in the Committee of the Whole

Vote on the bill in the House
Vote on recommital
Senate
  Subcommittee
  Committee
  Scheduling
  Vote on the bill
  Vote on reconsideration

Obviously amendments and appropriations can increase this number considerably so that a particularly complex piece of legislation requires fifty or sixty majorities—and may still not pass, or may be vetoed.

Of course these several majorities may overlap considerably in population. Once a majority is put together, it may be able to withstand several challenges. On the other hand, majorities for legislation may have different populations at every stage. Another point is that *different strategies may be needed to build majorities for the same proposal.* For example, getting a proposed course of action adopted in a standing committee may pose an entirely different problem from getting a rule from the House Committee on Rules; gaining approval in the populous and formal House typically requires different strategies from gaining approval in the smaller and more leisurely Senate.

In that same connection, different strategies may be required over time for building majorities in the process of legitimation in Congress. Most major policies are enacted over a period of years; in some cases it takes decades for the federal government to enter a particular issue area. During these periods committees change personnel and leadership, party leaders come and go, turnover occurs in the membership, procedural changes are made. For example, getting a majority in the House Committee on Rules proved very difficult for those who favored liberal proposals during the 1950s. With the important changes in the size and prerogatives of the committee during the period 1961–1965, however, the whole atmosphere changed. The committee was no longer a major stumbling block for the liberals.

A number of nonmajoritarian and extramajoritarian considerations must be taken into account in analyzing legitimation processes in Congress. I have already mentioned the president's role. For decades the standing committee chairmen had impressive power almost comparable to a presidential veto to thwart a majority by refusing to call a meeting of the committee; sending a bill to a subcommittee known to oppose it; delaying, denying, or obstructing hearings; or managing the timing of legislation to the least advantage for its proponents. While a majority might still work its will, the fear of reprisals and concern about precedents prevented any very frequent revolts. During the 1970s, however, the House in particular made a number of changes to curb the power of committee chairmen. In addition to modifying drastically the seniority rule by having committee leaders (chairmen and ranking minority members) subject to approval by party caucuses, each committee was required to establish rules and procedures to curb the arbitrary power of chairmen. These reform measures had dramatic impact in 1975 when three Democratic chairmen were turned out by the party caucus. Still, the chairmen and ranking minority members remain central figures in majority building. Whether they regain their previous status or not, the fact remains that the power of certain legislators over others introduces nonmajoritarian elements into the legislative process.

Next to the two-thirds majority required to override a veto, the infamous filibuster in the Senate is the best example of an extramajoritarian requirement for certain types of issues. For a long time in this nation, the legitimation process for civil rights legislation required a two-thirds majority in the Senate. When a motion is made to consider a bill, senators may begin lengthy speeches in opposition. A senator with enough stamina may speak forever, but cannot "speak more than twice upon any one question in debate on the same day without leave of the Senate." [15] Once several senators begin a round of endless speechmaking, the procedure for closing debate is cumbersome. Sixteen senators must sign a motion, and until 1975 two-thirds of the membership "present and voting" had to concur. In 1975 this figure was reduced slightly to three-fifths of the entire membership, except for rules changes (where two-thirds is still required). Until 1964 a minority in the Senate—the Southern Democrats—was virtually able to veto major civil rights legislation because of this procedure. Recent events have assisted in collecting the "extra" majority, however, and though the threat of filibuster is ever present, civil rights legislation is now easier to enact.

Another general point to consider in evaluating majority building in Congress is that bargaining is a central feature of all processes in that institution. Given the ubiquity of bargaining in Congress, it is almost certain that the outcome of majority building will be a program that is not absolutely satisfactory to anyone but is acceptable to many. This condition further suggests that persons making up a majority have various policy commitments. Support for a course of action may be offered because one really feels that a particular problem needs resolving, or because one determines that support in this instance will result in a quid pro quo, or because one expects to reap personal benefits of various kinds (a committee appointment, leadership post, additional staff), or because of a combination of these reasons. Obviously, the ideal situation is that of a majority actually concerned about the issue area and determined to do something about it. Even then, of course, bargaining characterizes behavior, since not everyone can be expected to view the specific problems in the same way or agree on what ought to be done to relieve needs.

Direct mention must also be made of the role of political parties in Congress. Parties function primarily to facilitate, but not guarantee, the development of majority coalitions. That is, the two parties organize the chambers, thereby establishing the machinery by which majorities can be constructed for specific proposals. That machinery—the caucus, committees of various types (policy and/or steering committees, committees-on-committees, research groups), a whip system, leaders of various types—can be used for legitimating a course of action, but traditionally has proved to be poorly designed for formulating courses of action.

Given this facilitative role of parties, one would not normally expect party leaders to be oriented toward the substance of policy. Rather, one would expect them to be more procedurally oriented: expert in the techniques of building majorities, possessing a fine sense of the possible in developing compromises, and aware of the intricacies of procedure on the House and Senate floors. Indeed, given expectations that party leaders will be more facilitative, those who inject themselves too much in program development and press too strongly for their preferences in policy substance will probably suffer heavy criticism.

The precise facilitative role of political parties differs between the majority and the minority and between the House and Senate. It is not necessary to go into detail on this point, which has been the subject of at least two books.[16] Suffice it to say that the majority party typically facilitates the construction of a majority in favor; the minority party often facilitates a majority against. Again, bargaining and compromise obviously characterize these activities. The need for political parties is greater in the House, due to its large size. Party is not insignificant in the Senate, but the greater informality reduces the need for elaborate organization and procedures.

Finally, it should be noted that legislative involvement in majority coalition building differs among issues. Thus, for example, Congress may only confirm a coalition built elsewhere, playing a minimal role in the creation of that support. Or the members may actively participate in developing a coalition—perhaps the more common role for legislators. An even stronger role is that of legislative leadership in building the majority—taking the initiative for getting the major interests and their representatives to compromise and coalesce. And a most interesting role is that of Congress seeking to satisfy what is assumed to be a majority among the public. Here then are four distinct institutional roles for Congress in legitimation. In each case Congress performs the legal task of authorizing the program. But, as I have stressed before, the actual participation of members in coalition building is not uniform.

Other Means of Approval

Though majority building in a legislature is generally acknowledged to be the principal form of program approval in a democratic system, there are many other means by which legitimate actions are taken by government. In recent years, two developments have influenced approval processes in government. On the one hand, the growth of distrust and cynicism about government has led to more direct involvement by groups in the policy process. The effectiveness of representative government itself appears to have been challenged, and the decline in voting turnout substantiates the claim that those elected lack legitimacy. On the other hand, increased complexity of government programs requires approval processes based on rational ordering of choices and professional expertise. Any such discretion must be traceable to authority granted by a legislative majority, but the result is often the creation of nonmajoritarian approval processes. Each of these developments deserves brief treatment.

Direct Participation

I have been an inveterate Congress watcher for twenty-five years. I like to spend time on Capitol Hill, talking to legislators and their staff, sitting in on congressional hearings and legislative markup sessions, observing the House and Senate in session, and just walking around, absorbing the atmosphere of the world's busiest legislative body. During this period there has been a quantum increase in activity. When I first started going to the Hill, one could walk into any committee hearing that was open (far fewer were open then) and take a seat. Now there are many more hearings, only a very few are closed, and one has to get there early to get in. Until recently, unless one had special access through a member or staff it was impossible to watch markup sessions or conference committees. Now the large majority of these meetings are open to the public. Turnout in elections may have decreased, but other forms of political participation appear to have increased considerably.

The effects of these developments on majority building are obvious. There is much more monitoring of who does what. Self-styled citizen groups like Common Cause or Ralph Nader's organization have been joined by the media to promote the openness of proceedings and publicize any violations. The result is more lobbying, not less. As described in chapter 1, the proliferation of citizen and single-issue groups is an important development in and of itself. But in addition, their involvement demands more activity from the more traditional groups. Thus, Capitol Hill comes to look like a kind of "town hall" of government.

Citizen participation as a form of legitimation has increased in other ways too. At one time citizen-based groups counted the passage of a law as the ultimate goal. Where Congress authorizes an agency to set standards, issue licenses, or make crucial decisions of other types, the law merely establishes a policy process that, in turn, includes means for approving decisions (see the air pollution case discussed below). To be effective, groups must then get actively involved in these second- or third-tier approval processes. Often the authorization of these processes will require opportunities for public involvement; for example, notice of public meetings or hearings on rules, standards, permits, or licenses.

Finally, one must record the increase in initiatives and referenda throughout the nation, but particularly in the West. The most famous recent example is California's Proposition 13, which was a property tax limitation measure. But there have been many more efforts to legislate outside the legislature in recent years. Commenting on the California situation, Eugene Lee notes:

■   . . . if every person is far from being his or her own legislature, it is equally
true that the initiative has become so deeply rooted in the political culture of
the state that no public figure in memory has suggested that it be eliminated—
or even substantially modified—and none is likely soon to do so. . . . The initiative's appeal for young and old, for liberal and conservative, is pervasive and
compelling. There is every reason to believe it will continue to be so.[17]

Approval Beyond Majority Building

The language of the Federal Water Pollution Control Act Amendments of
1972, Section 302, reads as follows:

■   (a) Whenever, *in the judgment of the Administrator,* discharges of pollutants
from a point source or group of point sources . . . would interfere with the
attainment or maintenance of that water quality in a specific portion of the
navigable waters which shall assure protection of public water supplies, agricultural and industrial uses, and propagation of a balanced population of shellfish,
fish and wildlife, and allow recreational activities in and on the water, *effluent
limitations . . . for such point source or sources shall be established which can
reasonably be expected to contribute to the attainment or maintenance of such
water quality.*
    (b) (1) Prior to establishment of any effluent limitation pursuant to subsection
(a) of this section, *the Administrator shall issue notice of intent to establish such
limitations and within ninety days of such notice hold a public hearing to determine the relationships of the economic and social costs of achieving any such
limitation or limitations.* (Emphasis added)

The administrator in this case is the top political appointee of the Environmental Protection Agency (EPA), which has jurisdiction over water pollution control. The italicized portions of this extract illustrate what Congress does many
times in lawmaking: it authorizes administrators to define problems and prepare solutions to those problems. In this case the EPA administrator must
determine when pollutants are harmful in the ways specified. Then he or she
must set limits to prevent these harmful effects, holding a public hearing on the
limits before implementing them.

This example of administrative discretion is but one of thousands. In fact,
the language cited above was a tiny part of the total statute—approximately
1/250th. How does an administrator or departmental secretary go about exercising this authority? Clearly expertise is required, and thus *professionalism*
may be the source of approval. The right to say yes or no—the final word—is
reserved for the expert. Increasingly, it seems, political decision makers are
turning to professionally trained specialists for authority. The expansion of
staff on Capitol Hill is notable in this regard, and the greater dependence on
consultants by the agencies is significant. When this reliance increases, responsibility is obscured since those providing the technical basis for decisions are
themselves quite distant from the political arena.

A commonly accepted means of approval within any bureaucracy is that associated with *hierarchy*. The presumably rational structure of organization by tiers offers a predictable flow of authority to the top. As Max Weber explained,

■ The principles of office hierarchy and of levels of graded authority mean a firmly ordered system of super- and subordination in which there is a supervision of the lower offices by the higher ones. Such a system offers the governed the possibility of appealing the decision of a lower office to its higher authority, in a definitely regulated manner. With the full development of the bureaucratic type, the office hierarchy is monocratically organized. The principle of hierarchical office authority is found in all bureaucratic structures.[18]

Thus, the EPA administrator cited above is in a position to use the bureaucratic structure, with all of its advantages of specialization, to accomplish assigned policy-making functions. Work may be assigned within the structure, but the final determination will be made by those at the top, a point that is presumably understood by subordinates. Of course, in reality, as Anthony Downs observes,

■ Officials near the top of the hierarchy have a greater breadth of information about affairs in the bureau than officials near the bottom, but the latter have more detailed knowledge about activities in their particular portions of the bureau. This implies that *no one ever knows everything about what is going on in any large organization.*[19]

In the example of administrative discretion for setting effluent limitations, the choice made by the administrator may well be structured by those with "detailed knowledge about activities in their particular portions of the bureau." Therefore the approval process for any one decision often involves a combination of professional and hierarchical means.

Paragraph (b) (1) of the Water Pollution Control Act introduces still another procedure for the EPA administrator to follow. A public hearing is required so as to judge economic and social costs. This is an example of the legal requirement to invite input from the community. It stems from suspicion about the capacity of bureaucracy to account for local effects of decisions. The administrator does not lose the authority to make the decision. The requirement simply is that the public (effectively, interested groups) have an opportunity to react. The rationale for this procedure is simple enough: the more authority assigned to agency heads, the more necessary it is in a democracy to provide opportunities for continuous input from affected publics. Rational or not, the result often is a lack of closure in the policy process.

It is useful at this point to refer to the discussion of total policy processes in chapter 5. By definition such methods as PPBS, management by objectives, and zero-based budgeting include approval processes, which are typically non-majoritarian.

Often *efficiency* is the criterion applied, that is, "meeting the objective at the

lowest cost or in obtaining the maximum amount of the objective for a specified amount of resources."[20] Approval is associated with a demonstration that
the choice meets the criteria of efficiency.

In summary, professionalism, hierarchical authority, and efficiency are all
common nonmajoritarian means of approval. With the growth in administrative discretion, these forms of approval require even greater study than in the
past.

Approval at All Stages

It is appropriate to pause here to make a more general point. Approval is
required at all stages in the policy process—in defining problems, determining
an agenda, formulating a proposal, implementing and evaluating a program. In
fact, each stage of action may be said to incorporate the previous activities as
well as some subsequent activities. For example, a proposal may require approval within a planning agency, a sort of pre-legitimation approval process.[21]
It can also be said that these approval processes are formed in accordance with
established principles. Legitimation quite naturally characterizes all governmental processes. Thus while there are forms of approval other than majority
building, and approval occurs throughout the policy process, it is essential to
acknowledge the special nature of legitimation that sanctions a program or
decision as authoritative for the system. It is that process that has been emphasized most in this chapter.

The Matter of the Revised Sequence

Table 2.1 (page 29) suggests a definite sequence for the various policy
activities. Logic might lead one to expect program development to occur as
follows: problem identification and definition $\rightarrow$ proposal formulation $\rightarrow$ program approval. In introducing table 2.1, however, I warned that the logical
sequence is not always followed in practice. Legitimation or approval may
precede formulation or even a very clear specification of the problem. Thus a
revised sequence requires brief mention and illustration.

Under what conditions might the revised sequence occur? We would expect
to see it associated with dramatic issues or periods when the public is highly
aroused and is pressing for government action of any kind. Thus, for example,
it seemed that broad public support developed for a more expansive federal
government following the assassination of President Kennedy. It is true that
several proposals were available to be submitted for approval; but President
Johnson was able to clear the domestic agenda during this period. Congress
appeared ready to support, even expand, almost any program that was submitted.

Even more dramatic was the anxiety to enact environmental regulations
during the 1960s and 1970s. A virtual explosion in concern for the environ-

ment occurred during the close of the 1960s. The normal process of temporizing policy proposals was abandoned in favor of program escalation. Air pollution was treated first, and the regulations were made more stringent at each stage along the way. The House of Representatives even seriously considered a bill that would have phased out the internal combustion engine if it did not meet tough standards.[22]

Policy escalation tends to occur in the revised sequence because elected decision makers seek to satisfy an indeterminate majority. No one knows quite what will suit the public. All that decision makers know for certain is that the public has been aroused and that an aroused public tends to be more attentive than normal to public policy. Table 6.1 compares the normal with the revised sequence, showing in each case the nature of the goal, process, and product for each policy activity. Observe that in the normal sequence a policy increment is the product of the second stage of approval. In the revised sequence, however, the second stage is formulation and its product is labeled "policy beyond capability." In the process of escalating proposals to satisfy a majority it is not unusual for policy makers to produce a program that cannot be implemented with current resources. Administrative, organizational, technological, and even political capabilities may be exceeded. If so, those charged with implementing the program are faced with a difficult challenge since they are supposed to administer a program that demands more resources than are presently available. This matter of the revised sequence will be treated again in chapter 8 and in chapter 10 (particularly in reference to so-called quadrant-4 decision making).

Three Cases of Getting Approval

I now offer three cases, two involving majority building in Congress and one associated with gaining approval for air pollution standards. The first describes the complicated and lengthy process of getting majority support for federal aid to education. Though it took place many years ago, it reveals particularly clearly what is necessary for a breakthrough in a difficult issue area. Next is a very recent case, that of an election year tax increase. Among other things, it illustrates the politics of mixed-party control in Washington, a condition that has occurred frequently in recent years (see chapter 5). The last case treats the problem of building support for administrative actions, problems that can contribute to revision of the policy process sequence.

Federal Aid Comes to Education: 1965

By the late 1960s the legitimation system for treating the vast numbers of problems in the education issue area had had decades to mature. Since the first land endowments were made to the states for educational purposes nearly two hundred years earlier, formulators had offered countless courses of action

TABLE 6.1 Comparing the normal and revised sequence in the policy process

	Normal sequence			Revised sequence		
	Expected Sequence of Activities					
Characteristics	1. Identification Formulation →	2. Approval →	3. Application	1. Approval →	2. Formulation →	3. Application
Goal	Articulation	Insured majority	Contextual change	Unspecified change	Satisfied majority	Determined limits
Process	Access/representation	Compromise/bargaining	Adaptation (mutual role taking)	Demonstration democracy	Escalation	Adaptation (mutual risk taking)
Product	Proposal	Policy increment	Rule (adjustment)	Indeterminate majority	Policy beyond capability	New basis for action

Source: Reprinted from Clean Air: *The Policies and Politics of Pollution Control,* by Charles O. Jones, by permission of the University of Pittsburgh Press. © 1975 by University of Pittsburgh Press. Modified version of Charts 2 and 15, pp. 16, 294.

to provide general aid to elementary and secondary schools. These efforts intensified in the period after World War II, culminating in the passage of the Elementary and Secondary Education Act in 1965.[23]

The many problems that make up the education issue area are some of the most intense in American domestic conflicts. The description by Frank J. Munger and Richard F. Fenno, Jr., is apt.

■ Even the briefest history of federal aid legislation makes clear one important fact, that the struggle over federal aid has not been a single conflict, but rather a multiplicity of controversies only loosely related to one another. The situation might be compared to a better-than-three-ring circus, although, in view of the tactics at times employed, a multiple barroom brawl might make a more apt analogy.[24]

Just developing a course of action adequate to meet the demands for classroom construction, teachers' salaries, teacher training, and curriculum development is complicated enough. But, in addition, several publics view the consequences of education policies at all levels in ways that are incompatible and directly conflicting.

To the blacks, education policies have been important in keeping them the underclass in American social life. They will examine any course of action carefully to determine whether it provides them with opportunities for advancement. Many whites, on the other hand, continue to believe in racial segregation. They see nothing but bad effects for them resulting from equal opportunity for both races within the same school building.

Many parochial school advocates, primarily the Roman Catholics, view any effort to correct the ills of public schools from their perspective as taxpayers also supporting a private school system. "Double taxation" is the cry among those who send their children to parochial schools while paying to maintain another school for their neighbors' children. Protestant and Jewish groups can be expected to oppose any proposal that either includes Catholic schools in aid benefits or allows Catholics to opt out of paying for the public schools. Since the public schools are for everyone, they believe everyone should pay. Any decision not to attend public schools is made freely and cannot release the individual family from its public responsibilities.

Other sets of eyes are also fixed on efforts to involve the federal government in the elementary and secondary schools. The specter of federal controls in "your neighborhood school," with coincident loss of influence by the "folks at home," is used by many groups to oppose any additional aid. Their influence is so great that even those who support extensive aid preface their remarks by paying lip service to local control. Munger and Fenno cite the example of Matthew Woll of the American Federation of Labor, who, in testifying before a Senate committee in 1945, stated: "We are unalterably opposed to any federal control of education or direction over the education process." He then introduced a set of resolutions urging that any federal aid to states be contingent on a series of standards for the length of the school year, integration of schools, distribution of funds, teachers' salaries, matching state appropriations, creation of an equitable state aid system, and teacher tenure.[25]

If some of these publics had only limited access to policy systems, one might expect little difficulty in legitimation. In fact, however, all have impressive access. Few conflicting perceptions and definitions were left out of the debate on federal aid to education in the 1950s and 1960s. Consider, for example, the membership of the House Committee on Education and Labor in 1961 (a particularly intense year for education policy). Though there was only one black on the committee, he was the chairman, Adam Clayton Powell (D.–New York), who had previously authored an amendment to deny federal aid to segregated schools. No legislation could expect approval without his support. Southern Democrats had unusually low representation on the committee but had strong bargaining positions in the Committee on Rules (chaired by Howard W. Smith, D.–Virginia) and in the Senate (with the filibuster).

Catholics had strong representation among the Democrats of the 1961 committee—seven of nineteen members. In addition, Catholics could count on support from certain other Democratic members from urban districts with large Catholic populations. And the "antifederal controls" viewpoint had many stalwarts on the committee—at least six on the Republican side. With such impressive access for all, majority building was difficult.

Participants in legitimation during the 1960s were drawn from a large number of institutions and groups, including the following:

Congress
   House Committee on Education and Labor
   House Committee on Rules
   Senate Committee on Labor and Public Welfare
   Senate Democratic Policy Committee
   Senate and House Party Leaders
Executive
   Office of Education, Department of Health, Education, and Welfare
   Bureau of the Budget
   White House Office
Private Groups
   National Education Association
   National Catholic Welfare Conference (later called the United States
      Catholic Conference)
   National Association for the Advancement of Colored People
   National Council of Churches
   American Federation of Teachers
   American Jewish Congress
   National Congress of Parents and Teachers Associations
   AFL-CIO

During the period 1961–1965, persons from these units searched for a compromise that would get the support of a majority in Congress. After so many years of working and reworking every aspect of every proposal, the prospects for general federal aid to elementary and secondary schools seemed dim.

Prospects appeared hopeless in 1962, partly because they had appeared so bright in 1960 and 1961. Federal aid bills actually passed both the House and Senate in 1960, an event unprecedented in the twentieth century. The two houses passed different versions, however, and the House Committee on Rules refused by a vote of seven to five to take actions allowing a conference with the Senate to iron out the differences.[26] Seven members of the Rules Committee thus presumed to override majorities in both the House and the Senate—a truly audacious action.

The near victory in 1960 was encouraging to proponents, and they expected to re-form the majorities necessary when the 87th Congress met in 1961. President Kennedy's strong support for legislation contrasted sharply with the ambiguous position of President Eisenhower on this issue. The expansion of the Rules Committee from twelve to fifteen seemed to remove that stumbling block. Passage of a general aid bill was virtually secured, or so many advocates thought. President Kennedy was a Roman Catholic, however, and, as the first of his faith to be elected president, had to lean over backwards to avoid favoring his church.

■ During the campaign he had repeatedly endorsed federal aid to education. . . . He had also emphasized that he favored such aid for public schools only and opposed granting funds to parochial schools. In his widely quoted speech to the Greater Houston Ministerial Association he had stated: "I believe in an America where the separation of church and state is absolute—where no church or church school is granted any public funds."[27]

Catholic leaders were disturbed by this statement. For them, 1961 was a crucial year. They, too, read all of the signs indicating passage of a general aid bill. *But if such legislation passed with no funds for parochial schools, a strong precedent would be set.* Unless they were included in this legislation, Catholics might never get government aid.

Building a majority suddenly became a much more complicated task. Many liberals who might ordinarily support an aid bill were Catholics, including the Democratic majority leaders in both the House and Senate, John W. McCormack of Massachusetts and Mike Mansfield of Montana. Catholics held the balance of power in the newly expanded Rules Committee. Thus parochial aid advocates were strong at many points where majorities had to be put together. Supporters of federal aid began the tedious process of trying to guarantee these majorities. Bargains were struck; compromises were the order of the day.

The Senate passed a bill with relatively little difficulty. In the House a delicate agreement had been worked out whereby some parochial school aid would be included in a different bill. In the end, however, the Catholics were fearful that their legislation would not survive. Two Catholics on the Rules Committee voted with the five Republicans and two Southern Democrats to delay the general aid bill until the parochial bill was reported out of the Committee on Education and Labor. Then one Catholic, James Delaney of New York, voted with the Republicans and Southern Democrats to table all education bills. The combination of Republicans and Southern Democrats had long dominated the Rules Committee and had been referred to as an "unholy alliance." "Now, one wit suggested, 'the unholy alliance has got religion.'"[28]

Pessimism reigned supreme after 1961. Practically every combination had been tried in offering courses of action. Legitimators were running out of strategies. In a sense, however, the fact that nobody got anything when all were so close to resolving age-old dilemmas spurred efforts to try again.

By 1965 the political climate had changed dramatically, with the result that conditions were even more conducive to the passage of legislation than in 1961. The tragic assassination of President Kennedy brought to the White House a Southern Protestant who was dedicated to enacting the Kennedy program. The largest Democratic majorities in nearly thirty years were elected with President Johnson in 1964, giving Northern Democrats greater force within their party. The Republican party made important leadership changes in the House (with younger, more positive members ousting conservative, old-guard leaders). Further changes were made to curb the power of the House Committee on Rules in 1963 and 1965. And the Civil Rights Act of 1964 had prohibited the use of federal funds for segregated public facilities, thus removing a major race issue from education aid.

Private groups were also making changes. After much painful reassessment, the National Education Association changed its stand against federal aid for parochial schools. Announcing its decision on December 16, 1964, the NEA, according to one spokesman, "recognized that if it took a rigid position on the church–state issue as an organization it would have been hamstrung politically."[29] The National Council of Churches joined NEA in its willingness to accept some form of support for church schools. Since the American Federation of Teachers was already more flexible on this issue, a basis for compromise was developing. For its part, the United States Catholic Conference had undergone an extensive review of its position after 1961. Some Catholics thought the organization had gone too far in 1961; indeed, not all church officials agreed that federal aid would be a good idea. In any event, the USCC was prepared to compromise in 1965.

With these important changes, passage of a federal aid bill seemed assured. Decades of experience in trying to build majorities in Congress had taught everyone extreme caution, however. The Commissioner of Education, Francis Keppel, was uniquely qualified to lead the last, careful expedition toward effective compromise. "Without exception the participants in these negotiations credit Keppel's work with producing a series of 'understandings' that developed into the basis for the church–state settlement. . . ."[30]

The formula for success in resolving the church–state issue was found in the Economic Opportunity Act of 1964. Why not aid the children instead of the schools? Specifically, aid was proposed for low-income school districts and could go for parochial as well as public school children. Aid was also provided for the purchase of books and the establishment of "supplementary educational centers" to serve both public and parochial schools. Linking aid to education with poverty was best summarized in this oft-quoted statement from the president's message: "Poverty has many roots but the tap root is ignorance."

Members of Congress prepared themselves for another round of hearings, executive sessions, rewritings, amendments. It is characteristic of Congress that fully 90 percent of its business is old business: expansion of existing programs, review of controversial proposals from the past, evaluation of ongoing policy, and so on. At least they had something new to consider in a time-worn issue area in 1965.

All major groups accepted the course of action proposed, though none was fully satisfied. So it is with compromises. Congress reflected this agreement by passing the bill in both houses by large margins. In fact, despite the years of bitter dispute, the legislative history of the Elementary and Secondary Education Act of 1965 was rather routine.

In the argument for passage, those leading the fight for legitimation asked that Congress "strike while the iron is hot," That is, since at that moment in history the major roadblock appeared resolved, some legislation should be enacted. "We will worry about altering the program at some future date." [31] This approach offers interesting lessons for understanding legitimation. It is a process of striking the bargains necessary to collect a majority, within the limits set by the values of the society. The most satisfactory course of action from one public's point of view (or definition of its problem) may have to be sacrificed to get policy. Bargaining occurs in the legitimation processes in Congress and later in the interpretations and applications of policy in the field. One member of Congress described very well what is involved in legitimation in discussing the 1965 act.

■ . . . we just had to make the hard choice and face the reality that in 1965 the issue was not good education policy versus bad. The question Congress had to settle in 1965 was whether there was ever to be federal aid to the elementary and secondary schools of this nation. *The 1965 bill, in all candor, does not make much sense educationally; but it makes a hell of a lot of sense legally, politically, and constitutionally.* [32]

From this vantage point the bill did not solve the problems of education, but a principle was legitimized. One could expect therefore that the substance of policy would be established over the next several decades.

Getting an Election Year Tax Increase: 1982

It is a maxim of American politics that there will be no tax increases in an election year. Why on earth would a group of legislator-politicians vote to tax their constituents just before returning home to seek reelection? In 1982, however, this maxim was broken. In fact, a tax *cut* was enacted in a nonelection year (1981) and a tax *increase* enacted in an election year. The majority-building politics associated with this latter effort were fascinating, requiring a strong bipartisan effort of congressional leaders and the president.

The story of the 1982 tax reform and increase is interesting for more than its precedent-shattering result. Though deficits were mounting, no one wanted the responsibility of fashioning a tax package. Having promoted supply-side economics, the Reagan administration was in a difficult position. It would seem a repudiation of the previous year's efforts (see chapter 7) to introduce a tax increase, and would be a dangerously divisive move within the president's own party. The Democrats were also very hesitant to take the responsibility for a tax hike. Thus it was that the Senate, with its longer terms, took the initiative in formulating a proposal. The principal work was done in the Senate Committee on Finance, chaired by Robert Dole (R.–Kansas). Dole was not up for reelection in 1982.

The Constitution is quite explicit in regard to the origination of revenue measures. Article I, Section 7, reads:

■   All Bills for raising Revenue shall originate in the House of Representatives; but the Senate may propose or concur with Amendments as on other Bills.

This provision is not as stringent as it might seem on first reading. The Senate is able to originate revenue legislation by amending House bills. But normally the House does act first, and the Senate amends the revenue measures that are sent over. With the Tax Equity and Fiscal Responsibility Act of 1982, however, the House *simply did not pass a bill at all.* The formalities were met by attaching this important and complex legislation to a minor revenue measure that had been passed by the House the previous year (and had not yet been acted on in the Senate). Strictly speaking, therefore, the House went into conference (that is, appointed a certain number of representatives to meet with senators) without having passed a major tax bill.

Figure 6.1 shows the sequence of action. What it does not show is the partisan maneuvering to avoid responsibility that took place. Party votes were the order of the day up until the last. In the Senate the initial committee vote was along party lines, eleven Republicans voting in favor, nine Democrats against. On the floor, forty-nine Republicans were joined by one Independent, Harry Byrd, Jr., of Virginia, in supporting the bill; forty-four Democrats and three Republicans voted against it. In the House, the motion to meet with the Senate in conference was preceded by a resolution challenging the constitutionality of the action. This resolution was tabled and the House voted to go to conference.

In addition to providing new taxes, the bill was an assault on certain traditional tax loopholes. It also included sizable cuts in expenditures. The whole package was estimated to total more than $98 billion in new revenues and more than $17 billion in budget reductions over a three-year period.

Many corporations and businesses were affected by the new taxes and the

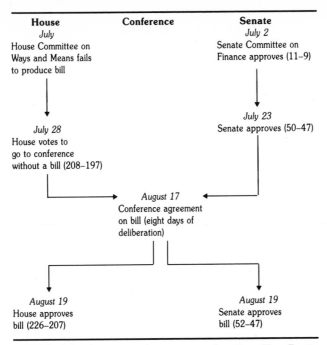

FIGURE 6.1   Sequence of congressional action: Tax Equity and Fiscal Responsibility Act of 1982

reforms, the result being furious lobbying. But the procedural situation was less advantageous than normal for lobbyists. Only one house had acted in the initial phases of the bill. Many amendments were introduced on the Senate side—a total of twenty-two were voted on by roll call (nine were adopted). But on the House side there was no real opportunity for amending. Therefore a great deal of effort was focused on the conference. Dale Tate describes the conference as follows:

■   Conference meetings on tax bills in recent years have tended to be held in one of several tiny, cramped rooms in the Capitol that are convenient to either the House or the Senate chamber.

This year things were different—sort of. Public meetings were held in the spacious and elegant Ways and Means hearing room. . . . There were plenty of seats for the press and for the hundreds of lobbyists, legislative analysts and the plain curious. . . .

The hearing room was capacious and comfortable, but conferees' decisions were hammered out elsewhere. Typically, the proceedings went like this:

The conference committee would gather in the hearing room, and one chamber's conferees would offer its proposals on one or another part of the bill. The other side would withdraw to consider the offer privately in caucus. Finally— often hours later—the conferees would troop back into the hearing room to announce their counteroffer. Then the process would start again.[33]

Thus, even though accommodations were provided for the many people vitally interested in the outcome, significant decisions were made out of public view.

When the bill emerged from conference a truly extraordinary bipartisan effort was made by the president and congressional leaders to insure passage of the bill in both houses. But the critical vote was to come in the House of Representatives, where a revolt was brewing among the Republicans. Led by Jack Kemp (R.–New York), many conservatives were opposed to any tax increase as inimical to the economic program that had been enacted the previous year. President Reagan made one of his patented television appearances in support of the bill and then worked closely with House Speaker Thomas P. O'Neill to deliver the votes needed for victory. The two had been adversaries the previous year (see chapter 7) but now were on the same side. Approval politics can make strange bedfellows on occasion.

■　　House Rules Committee Chairman Richard Bolling . . . called it a "unique coalition," unlike any he had seen since the Marshall Plan vote in the post–World War II days of bipartisanship.[34]

Speaker O'Neill said that the Republicans must come up with at least 100 votes in favor of the tax bill if he were to deliver a sufficient number of Democratic votes. At one point in the debate, O'Neill lectured the newly elected Republicans to support their president, noting that they wouldn't be there had it not been for Reagan. "The Democratic leader was plugging for the Republican president."[35]

In the end, 103 Republicans (54 percent) voted with 123 Democrats (51 percent) to pass the bill. The bill passed the Senate the same day. Three weeks later both houses voted to override the president's veto of a supplemental appropriations bill (requiring a two-thirds vote in both houses). The unusual alliance of the tax bill did not persist.

Approving a Standard: Beyond Majority Coalition Building

Cleaning the air in a complex industrial society like ours is a difficult and highly technical matter. Judging the most efficient means to accomplish the goal and balancing all the social and economic interests are demanding tasks, often requiring special expertise. Until the 1960s, air pollution control was strictly a state and local matter. The federal government provided support for research as early as 1955, but it wasn't until 1963 that a national clean air act was enacted. The first effort sought to encourage greater activity by state and local authorities (primarily through grants). But it also provided for federal action to abate pollution if it endangered "the health or welfare of persons in a State other than that in which the discharge or discharges . . . originate." Specific standards were not set, but an opening was created for direct federal involvement.

It did not take Congress and federal officials long to expand the role of the national government once the initial steps had been taken. The Air Quality Act of 1967 provided for the establishment of national air quality standards. Emphasis was still on state and local action, but under federal direction. Here is how it was supposed to work:

1. Air quality regions were to be created throughout the nation, based on jurisdictions, "urban–industrial concentrations," and "atmospheric areas."
2. Criteria based on the effects of certain levels of pollution were to be established.
3. Using those criteria, states would determine the standards to be met within the air quality regions and develop plans for meeting these standards.

The National Air Pollution Control Administration (NAPCA) in the Department of Health, Education, and Welfare was responsible for administering this act. The task proved quite beyond NAPCA's capabilities. The Subcommittee on Public Health and Welfare of the House Committee on Interstate and Foreign Commerce held hearings in 1969 on the progress being made. At that time regions had been established in only 20 urban areas. The acting head of the Public Health Service, Dr. Jesse L. Steinfeld, testified that 300 regions might ultimately be necessary for urban areas alone. Thus less than 7 percent of the areas had so far been designated. Upset with this limited progress, the subcommittee members demanded to know what was holding up the decisions. The NAPCA director, Dr. John Middleton, responded as follows:

■ Nothing is holding it up. The people are behind it, and what may seem to you to be holding it up is the desirability of having public participation and of having clear understanding on the part of the cities and counties and States of what is needed by way of a boundary. This interaction at the various governmental levels must take place, and before boundaries are set there must be the public hearing process. Getting the involvement of the official agencies and the public and trying to have the regions be meaningful in the sense of using the best political, social, and legislative levels, and having public hearings and consultations, that simply takes time.[36]

Progress has also been slow in developing criteria by which states, in turn, were supposed to set standards. In discussing criteria and standards, Dr. Steinfeld said: "*Over the next several years,* goals for reducing atmospheric levels of all pollutants injurious to public health and welfare will be established and concrete plans for reaching the goals will be worked out."[37] In summary, though NAPCA had been given impressive powers of approval in creating regions, establishing criteria, and ultimately in passing on standards set by the states, exercising these powers proved to be very complex. What Dr. Middleton described was an approval process involving *professionalism, hierarchy,* and *public participation.* Experts had to make judgments about the geographical and topographical settings of pollution in order to define regions. They also had to determine the effects of pollutants on public health and social life so as to establish broad criteria. While the law set specific deadlines, it was not possible for studies to be conducted in such a short time, given the resources available to NAPCA. Having the authority to approve is no guarantee that one has the capability to do what is necessary to approve.

Events were moving much more swiftly than NAPCA in 1970. The environmental movement was in full swing. Demonstrations, citizen groups, dramatic shifts in public support for government action—these and other developments led the president and Congress to reclaim the right of approval in establishing a national air pollution control system. The Clean Air Amendments of 1970 took a giant step in the direction of federal control in this field. An effort was made to reduce Dr. Steinfeld's estimate of "several years" for reaching goals to a few months. The new law began simply by declaring that any portion of a state not already included in a region "shall be an air quality control region." Thus by simple declaration Congress completed the task of designating regions. Of course, by this action all the painstaking work of NAPCA specialists was ignored.

There remained the problem of establishing criteria and setting standards. The new law gave the administrator of the newly organized EPA the authority to do both, and within the very short time span of 30 days after the enactment of the act. Again, Congress had demonstrated impatience with the time needed for professionals to approve such technically based decisions. They simply required that it be done.

The setting of a standard (which EPA did in the designated time) is by no means a guarantee that it will be met. As James E. Krier and Edmund Ursin note (in their study of automobile pollution control),

■ It is one thing . . . to reach a "scientific" conclusion about health effects in the absence of any "reliable" evidence . . . but quite another to make the "technical" or "engineering" judgment about how to reach an ambient goal once it is concluded that reaching that goal is important. The scientist might be understandably reluctant to judge how clean the air should be in the absence of good information about the judgment's implications, while the engineer steps in as a matter of course to venture judgment on the operational decision of how best to meet a given goal. . . . He especially does so when the legislature has charged that he must.[38]

In the case of the 1970 act, the actual implementation was to be the result of a state planning process in which EPA had final approval. But how were the states to go about meeting the new standards? What guidelines should they follow? The approval process for determining how the standards were to be met began very early, long before the states actually got down to planning. First a set of guidelines for the states had to be developed and approved. These guidelines were subjected to a review process within EPA that included invitations for comments from other agencies. They were then sent to the Office of Management and Budget (OMB), where, it was claimed, the Nixon administration exercised considerable influence in softening the requirements. "Exactly what happened during the process is not entirely known, but by the time the OMB finished its review, the guidelines had been changed drastically."[39]

Once the guidelines were established and distributed, the states had nine months in which to submit a plan, followed by four months of federal review, and two more months of state revision. In fact, the process took much longer, as the states and EPA entered into long and sometimes difficult negotiations before approval was forthcoming.

Much more could be included to show the complexities of approval processes of this kind. But the principal purpose is to illustrate what goes on *beyond majority coalition building*. Much in the law can be achieved only if resources and expertise are available. Even then it may take considerably longer than the law arbitrarily designates. This particular case also shows that Congress may grow impatient with the pace of professional or hierarchical approval and step in to move things along. In technical issue areas like air pollution control, however, declaring that a goal must be reached does not guarantee actual achievement. In 1970, Congress sought to force action, even going so far as to set standards in the case of motor vehicles. Once Congress has spoken, however, the other processes of approval again take over to work out the details. These less publicly visible processes tend to work at their own pace, and they respond to different values and criteria.

Summary

Legitimation produces an accepted base of action for alleviating human needs. But passing laws or creating standards does not, in itself, solve problems. Rather, a somewhat more coherent starting point is created. These widely diverse cases illustrate a number of points about the process by which this happens. First, majority building is not accomplished by simple dictation from party leaders or the president; as we have seen here, it reflects what may be occurring within an issue area. Complex and controversial matters do not conveniently subside in a democratic system. A second, concomitant point is simply that what goes on outside government may be critical in determining whether, how, and when a majority can be collected in Congress. With the education controversy, practically every major public or interest had the power to veto proposals that ignored or underrepresented its views.

Third, a congressional majority may support approval processes within program administration without losing control of legitimation. Yet, as shown in the air pollution standards case, no process automatically solves the problems associated with complex issues. Fourth, the time required for legitimating proposals varies greatly. Federal aid to education is, perhaps, the classic case at the snail's end of the continuum. The enactment of a huge tax increase in an election year was jet propelled by comparison.

Finally, to reiterate, what has been adopted must itself be interpreted in the context of the interests affected, the support available, the ever-changing conditions associated with an issue area. As government goes on to meet the problems, it has been provided with more or less specific guidelines. But no

amount of research, planning, experience, or resolution among diverse interests totally prepares the administrator for what he or she finds in the field. All
sorts of things turn up: more understanding of the problems, discovery of
related or totally new problems, inconsistencies in standards, unexpected side
effects, and so on. Typically such new knowledge brings the whole assemblage
of bureaucrats, executives, and group representatives right back to Congress
for further authorization, clarification, and occasionally even recision.

Notes

1. Hanna Pitkin, "Obligation and Consent—II," *American Political Science Review* 60 (March 1966):
   52. Emphasis added. See also Robert J. Pranger, "An Explanation for Why Final Political Authority Is Necessary," *American Political Science Review* 60 (December 1966): 994–997. In answer to
   the question of why we obey, Pranger says, "One obeys because of the personal repercussions of
   not obeying."
2. David Easton, *A Systems Analysis of Political Life* (New York: Wiley, 1965), p. 273.
3. Easton, p. 273.
4. Easton, p. 278.
5. Richard M. Merelman, "Learning and Legitimacy," *American Political Science Review* 60 (September 1966): 553.
6. Taken from Arthur H. Miller, "Political Issues and Trust in Government: 1964–1970," *American
   Political Science Review* 68 (September 1974): 953; and Michael J. Malbin, "Political Parties and
   1976," in *National Journal Reprints* (Washington, D. C.: National Journal, 1976), p. 10.
7. Taken from William Watts and Lloyd A. Free, *State of the Nation, 1974* (Washington, D. C.:
   Potomac Associates, 1974), pp. 71–80. Interestingly, during this period of declining confidence in
   the federal government, the public's respect for state and local government increased (at least as
   measured in this one study). Perhaps this supports the Easton view that we *need* to have confidence in government—if not in the national government, then in state and local governments.
8. Paul Abrahamson et al., *Change and Continuity in the 1980 Elections* (Washington, D. C.: Congressional Quarterly, Inc., 1982), p. 145.
9. Easton, *A Systems Analysis of Political Life*, p. 286. Emphasis added.
10. Easton, p. 309.
11. Currin V. Shields, *Democracy and Catholicism in America* (New York: McGraw-Hill, 1958), p. 244.
12. Shields, pp. 245–246.
13. Robert A. Dahl, *A Preface to Democratic Theory* (Chicago: University of Chicago Press, 1956), p.
    133.
14. Dahl, p. 124.
15. Rule XIX of the Standing Rules of the Senate.
16. Charles O. Jones, *The Minority Party in Congress* (Boston: Little, Brown, 1970) and Randall B.
    Ripley, *Majority Party Leadership in Congress* (Boston: Little, Brown, 1969).
17. In *Referendums: A Comparative Study of Practice and Theory*, ed. David Butler and Austin Ranney
    (Washington, D. C.: American Enterprise Institute, 1978), p. 120.
18. H. H. Gerth and C. Wright Mills, *From Max Weber: Essays in Sociology* (London: Routledge &
    Kegan Paul, 1948), p. 197.
19. Anthony Downs, *Inside Bureaucracy* (Boston: Little, Brown, 1967), p. 58. Emphasis added.
20. Aaron Wildavsky, *The Revolt Against the Masses* (New York: Basic Books, 1971), p. 184.
21. I am indebted to Charles Stubbart, then a graduate student at the University of Pittsburgh, for
    making this point. Professor Margaret Scranton demonstrates the significance of pre-legitimation
    approval processes in her important study of the Panama Canal treaties, "Changing United States
    Foreign Policy: Negotiating New Panama Canal Treaties, 1958–1978," unpublished Ph.D. disser-
    tation, University of Pittsburgh, 1979.
22. For details see Charles O. Jones, *Clean Air: The Policies and Politics of Pollution Control* (Pitts-
    burgh: University of Pittsburgh Press, 1975), chap. 7.
23. See Frank J. Munger and Richard F. Fenno, Jr., *National Politics and Federal Aid to Education*
    (Syracuse, N. Y.: Syracuse University Press, 1962) for a brief review of legislation in the past one

hundred years. Good literature by political scientists and journalists on the issue of federal aid to education is abundant. This case study relies heavily on Munger and Fenno; Eugene Eidenberg and Roy D. Morey, *An Act of Congress* (New York: Norton, 1969); Philip Meranto, *The Politics of Federal Aid to Education in 1965: A Study in Political Innovation* (Syracuse, N. Y.: Syracuse University Press, 1967); and Hugh D. Price, "Race, Religion, and the Rules Committee: The Kennedy Aid-to-Education Bills," in *The Uses of Power*, ed. Alan F. Westin (New York: Harcourt, Brace & World, 1962). See also Robert Bendiner, *Obstacle Course on Capitol Hill* (New York: McGraw-Hill, 1965).

24. Munger and Fenno, *National Politics and Federal Aid to Education*, p. 16.
25. Munger and Fenno, p. 49.
26. This power was taken from the Committee on Rules in 1965.
27. Price, *"Race, Religion, and the Rules Committee,"* p. 20.
28. Price, p. 63.
29. Quoted in Eidenberg and Morey, *An Act of Congress*, p. 64.
30. Eidenberg and Morey, p. 87.
31. Quoted in Eidenberg and Morey, p. 92.
32. Quoted in Eidenberg and Morey, p. 93. Emphasis added.
33. Dale Tate, "Legislative Legend-Making, Tax Bill Style," *Congressional Quarterly Weekly Report*, August 21, 1982, 2043.
34. *The Washington Post*, August 20, 1982, 1.
35. *The Washington Post*, August 20, 1982, 1. For other details on the tax increase see *Congressional Quarterly Weekly Report*, August 21, 1982, 2035–2046 and *The National Journal*, July 31, 1982, 1337–1338.
36. Quoted in Jones, *Clean Air*, p. 126.
37. Quoted in Jones, *Clean Air*, p. 127. Emphasis added.
38. James E. Krier and Edmund Ursin, *Pollution and Policy* (Berkeley: University of California Press, 1977), p. 130.
39. Richard J. Tobin, *The Social Gamble* (Lexington, Mass.: Lexington Books, 1979), p. 96.

Chapter Seven

Budgeting for Programs

Functional activities	Categorized in government	With a potential product
Budgeting: formulation legitimation	Action in government	Budget

The policy process is an endless game. The arenas change, players are replaced, new and old strategies are always available, and the game continues. In fact, several matches may occur simultaneously, even for the same set of issues. The budgetary process is perhaps the best illustration of this point. It is not enough to have a good idea for treating a public problem or even to be able to generate support for that idea. One must also get funding. Flushed with victory, our policy players must move on to yet another match. Leonard Freedman describes one of the more famous games, that associated with the Housing Act of 1949.

■ As the public housing forces celebrated their victory in July of 1949, they could not free themselves of an undertone of anxiety, for their 810,000 units had been approved with reluctance and only by the narrowest of margins.

Still, if some of them suspected that their victory might not be final, they could hardly have predicted the magnitude of the trouble that lay ahead. . . . Having at last attained their goal, they still would not be able to rest. On the contrary, the most arduous tribulations must yet be faced, and the battles which had been won must be refought under much less propitious circumstances than had prevailed in 1949.[1]

While, as Freedman notes, "the 1949 housing act did not . . . appear to place any significant power over public housing in the hands of the Appropriations Committees," the fact is that "authorization by Congress is one thing, appropriation another."[2] Thus, whereas the act authorized the construction of 810,000 public housing units over a period of six years, "two decades after the passage of the 1949 Act, only one-half of its authorized units had been built."[3] In reflecting on this record, Freedman noted:

■ . . . the Taft-Ellender-Wagner Act [Housing Act of 1949] . . . had been given
the most thorough scrutiny before it was accepted. Under most other systems
of representative government, the public housing program would surely have
been implemented in considerable measure at least, and then would have undergone an orderly process of modification and adjustment as defects showed
up. Its fate under the American system was very different.[4]

The London *Economist* illustrated the British perspective on such goings-on:
"Since the programme requires an annual appropriation, its opponents have
since had repeated opportunities of *replaying the match.*"[5]

In a sense I am now asking you to replay the match. Perhaps I could have
worked the budgeting decisions into the formulation and legitimation activities
previously discussed. I chose not to do so for several reasons. First, those
important program development activities require careful explication on their
own. The introduction of budgeting would have been confusing. Second, budgeting is a separate institutional process with its own timetable, structure, and
even vocabulary. Although policy making and budget making are interlaced
throughout government, their connection can be better understood by examining them separately. Third, budgeting is always important, but it has taken on
special significance at the national level in recent years.

A government must decide what it wants to do (authorization), how much it
wants to spend doing it (appropriation), and where to get the money (taxation).
Ideally these judgments would be well integrated, and activities in the three
areas would proceed in unison. Other political systems try to accomplish this
end. In the United States, however, the policy process is characterized by
separate channels of activity, although decision makers apparently worry
enough about the separation to make occasional changes (see below).

The Budget (and How It Grew)

In his classic study *The Politics of the Budgetary Process,* Aaron Wildavsky
concludes that "the budget lies at the heart of the political process."[6] It is a
statement of who won and who lost. It is an inventory of values, of what a
government judges to be worthy of attention. Wildavsky explains it as follows:

■   In the most general definition, budgeting is concerned with the translation of
financial resources into human purposes. A budget, therefore, may be characterized as a series of goals with price tags attached. Since funds are limited and
have to be divided in one way or another, the budget becomes a mechanism for
making choices among alternative expenditures.[7]

Small wonder that the budget commands a great deal of attention. It is one
of the few available documents that treat all government functions. *The United
States Budget in Brief,* published annually by the Government Printing Office,
provides both a useful summary of receipts and outlays and a statement of the
economic assumptions used to calculate budget estimates.

TABLE 7.1 Trends in budget outlays in
current and constant dollars,
1962–1982 (selected years)

Fiscal year	Current dollars	Percent change	Constant dollars (1972)	Percent change
1962	106.8	—	160.8	—
1967	157.6	+47.6	207.0	+28.7
1972	230.7	+46.4	230.7	+11.4
1977	400.5	+73.6	280.9	+21.8
1982	728.4	+81.9	338.7	+20.6

Source: Calculated from data in *The United States Budget in Brief: Fiscal Year 1984* (Washington, D.C.: Government Printing Office, 1983), p. 69.

Growth of the Budget

The budget has grown phenomenally in recent years. It was not until the 1960s that we had our first $100 billion federal budget (though we came close during World War II). Table 7.1 shows what has happened since then. We got the first $200 billion budget in 1971 and will no doubt see our first trillion-dollar budget in the 1980s. Note that the 1982 budget outlays were nearly twice those of 1977 (an 81.9 percent increase). The growth in current prices between 1962 and 1982 was nearly 600 percent.

Table 7.1 also shows the growth in terms of constant 1972 dollars. Even with this correction for inflation the increases are impressive: the budget more than doubled during the period. Another way to standardize the figures is to calculate the budget outlays as a percentage of the gross national product (GNP: the estimate of the total worth of all goods and services). This comparison provides some indication of government growth in relation to that of the economy. In 1962 budget outlays represented 19.5 percent of GNP; in 1982 they represented 24.0 percent of GNP, a sizable increase.

What explains these increases? In the past, wars accounted for the most dramatic growth in the government expenditures. In recent decades, however, nondefense budget outlays have grown more. Figure 7.1 shows the relatively flat curve for the defense share of the budget, which trends upward only at the very end of the period. In constant prices, defense outlays actually declined from the 1960s to the 1970s. Growth in nondefense outlays is comparatively dramatic, with the largest percentage going to payments to individuals (primarily pensions, but also to unemployment compensation and welfare payments). In 1962 defense outlays constituted 45.9 percent of the total; in 1982, they constituted 25.7 percent.

The rapid growth of so-called entitlement programs seems to explain much of the nondefense increase. As the name suggests, entitlements are benefits that are provided if one meets certain conditions. Examples are unemployment compensation, food stamps, medicare, and retirement income. Efforts to bal-

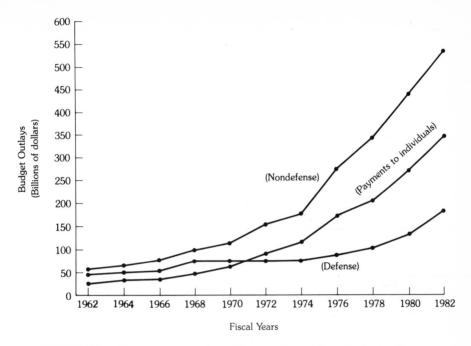

FIGURE 7.1 Comparative growth in defense and nondefense budget outlays, 1962–1982 (selected years, current prices). *(Source: The Budget in Brief: Fiscal Year 1984. Washington, D. C.: Government Printing Office, 1983, p. 69.)*

ance the budget are confounded by the difficulty of controlling these programs, or even of estimating how much they will cost. Thus, for example, when unemployment rises due to unforeseen economic troubles, outlays increase automatically (and government income is also reduced by loss of taxes from the unemployed). Such expenditures are therefore referred to as "uncontrollable." Entitlements constitute the largest category of uncontrollable outlays. "These open-end programs have grown from about 27 percent of the budget in fiscal 1967 to an estimated 48 percent in fiscal 1982, or from 5.5 percent of the gross national product to 11.0 percent."[8] The total of uncontrollable outlays is estimated to exceed 75 percent of the budget, a fact of profound significance for budget making. As Roger Davidson and Walter Oleszek observe: "Even if Congress adjourned on its very first day in session, the government is legally entitled to spend huge sums. . . . "[9]

Growth of Deficits

Of equal concern are the growing deficits. The gross federal debt exceeded $1 trillion in 1981 and is bound to escalate rapidly with the huge annual deficits (projected to exceed $200 billion annually in the mid-1980s). The estimates of debt in recent years have been wildly off the mark. In 1982 the estimate approached $100 billion (every effort was made to keep it below that mark), yet the actual deficit exceeded that figure by several billion. The explanation for these errors lies in the failure of economic assumptions to hold. Estimates of inflation, unemployment, and interest rates, all of which affect both revenue and outlays, have been wrong. A Brookings Institution study summarizes the situation as follows:

■   On the outlay side, the largest source of the higher spending was the disappointing economic performance, which raised outlays by $27.1 billion in 1980, $32.3 billion in 1981, and $25.9 billion in 1982. These enlarged outlays reflected increases caused by a combination of inflation, unemployment, and high interest rates. Policy changes also increased outlays significantly during 1980 and 1981, as did natural disasters and errors in estimation. . . . On the receipts side, growth in nominal incomes as a result of inflation raised tax receipts in 1980 and 1981. . . . For 1982, the delay in the tax cut from July 1 to October 1, 1981, and other changes made by Congress raised receipts by $11.2 billion, but this gain was more than offset by the $31 billion reduction in receipts resulting from the 1981–82 recession.[10]

Figure 7.2 displays the relation between budget authority and expenditures in any one year. The top of the chart shows the new authority requested, which normally includes huge amounts for ongoing programs whose authority has expired. The bottom of the chart shows the continuing buildup of unspent

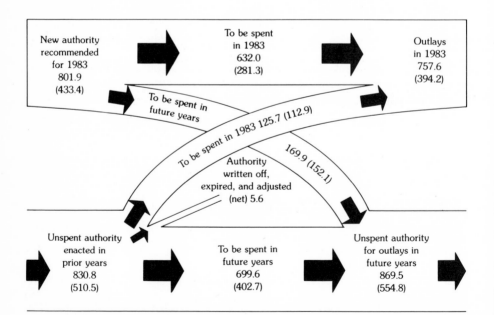

FIGURE 7.2   Relation of budget authority to outlays: 1984 budget. *(Source: The United States Budget in Brief, Fiscal Year, 1984. Washington, D. C.: Government Printing Office, 1983, p. 66. The figures in parentheses are those for the fiscal year 1977 budget.)*

authority that will continue to affect future budgets. The figures in parentheses are from the 1977 budget (the previous edition of this book was published in 1977). Note in particular the growth in unspent authority during these six years. Clearly that figure will soon exceed $1 trillion.

Wildavsky's claim that "the budget lies at the heart of the political process" is indisputable. Now, however, because of the remarkable growth in expenditures and deficits, the budget *is* the heart of the political process.[11] Among other developments, elected political leaders have discovered that they now have little to do with this growth. The budget has virtually taken on a life of its own. The policy struggles of the later part of the Carter administration and the early part of the Reagan administration appear to have been dominated by this fact, and by the efforts to regain control. In 1981, in particular, the budget (for fiscal year 1982) was front and center in national policy making (see below).

Making a Budget

In its most basic form a budget is a plan for raising and spending money. By this definition it is hard to demonstrate that the federal government had a budget before 1921.[12] Typically the departments and agencies dealt directly with Congress. By the early 1900s a "book of estimates" was being prepared by the secretary of the Treasury, but this was not really a budget as defined above. It was a compilation of spending requests from the departments and agencies along with revenue plans and estimates. In 1921 a budget and accounting act was passed that authorized the president to prepare a budget. By that time Congress had also concentrated appropriation power in appropriations committees (these committees were first established in 1865 but did not have consolidative control over all appropriations). Equally important were the two revenue committees—Ways and Means in the House, Finance in the Senate—which had also handled appropriations before 1865.

With these changes budget making was concentrated in the executive. A Bureau of the Budget was created within the executive, first located in the Department of the Treasury and later moved to the Executive Office of the President. Congress occasionally considered reforms to consolidate its work on the president's budget and actually provided for a legislative budget in the Legislative Reorganization Act of 1946 (a short-lived experiment). But for the most part it can be said that Congress did not have its own plan for raising and spending money. It reacted to what the president proposed, and then only in segments. The taxing proposals were treated by the revenue committees; the authorization of new programs by the substantive authorizing committees; and the spending by the appropriations committees. And, of course, all this was done in duplicate in the two houses.

The appropriations committees assumed considerable power during the 1950s and 1960s as protectors of the federal purse.[13] Authorizations must be followed by appropriations, and, as indicated earlier with the 1949 housing act, the appropriations committees were not always willing to provide the funds for programs. The authorizing committees regained a large measure of control in the late 1960s and 1970s, however, through the enactment of open-ended programs; that is, the entitlements. More than half of the budget was thereby removed from the control of the appropriations committees. As discussed above, the growth of these uncontrollable programs made it more difficult for the appropriations committees to hold down expenditures. Further, the revenue committees were subject to lobbying for tax breaks of various kinds, which contributed further to deficits but also cut into the authority of the appropriations committees; money one is not required to send to the government is just as real as money received through a government program.

Thus a reasonably coherent executive budget process (see below for details) produced a product that was literally shredded on Capitol Hill—torn apart and distributed to the relevant committees. Like Humpty Dumpty, it was never put back together again. There was no longer a budget as such. No one knew the full extent of budget authority until well into the next fiscal year (which, before 1976, ended on June 30). Agencies were forced to operate for months on continuing resolutions, that is, on the same budget authority as for the preceding fiscal year.

The last regular appropriation bill for FY 1968 was enacted on January 2, six months into the next fiscal year; for FY 1969 on October 17; for FY 1970 on March 5, eight months into the next fiscal year; for FY 1971 on January 11; for FY 1972 on March 8; and for FY 1973 on October 26. Often no single item was approved before the new fiscal year began. And for FY 1971 and again for FY 1973 certain departmental appropriations were never enacted (Transportation for FY 1971 and Labor and Health, Education, and Welfare for FY 1973).[14] These variations in procedures emphasize that budgeting is indeed a political process in its formulation, legitimation, and implementation stages.[15]

It took the challenge of an unacceptable Nixon budget and a series of presidential vetoes to spur reform action by Congress. Completing his radio address to the nation on the FY 1974 budget, President Nixon said: "It is time to get big government off your back and out of your pocket. I ask your support to hold government spending down, so that we can keep your taxes and your prices from going up."[16] The new budget proposed cuts or total elimination for more than 100 programs, leading Senator Walter F. Mondale (D.–Minnesota) to remark that if enacted, "this nation will have effectively repealed all of the major social legislation of the last 20 years." The clash between the president and Congress was more than an ordinary disagreement over this or that program. It was much more fundamental, in essence involving different philosophies of government. Speaker Carl Albert (D.–Oklahoma) vowed that Congress "will not permit the president to lay waste the great programs . . . which we have developed during the decades past."[17]

And yet, whereas Congress was capable of changing individual requests, it found itself quite incapable of dealing with the budget as a whole document. In fact, the president himself spoke of the need for congressional budgetary reform:

■ The cuts I have suggested in this year's budget did not come easily. Thus I can well understand that it may not be easy for the Congress to sustain them, as every special interest group lobbies with its own special congressional committees for its own special legislation. But the Congress should serve more than the special interest; its first allegiance must always be to the public interest. . . .

To overcome these problems, I urge prompt adoption by the Congress of an overall spending ceiling for each fiscal year. . . . Beyond the adoption of an annual ceiling, I also recommend that the Congress consider internal reforms which would establish a regular mechanism for deciding how to maintain the ceiling.[18]

The president had struck a sensitive nerve since congressional Democrats were painfully aware that however much they disagreed with the Nixon budget philosophy, they essentially had none of their own—and if they did, had only limited means for implementing it. A Joint Study Committee on Budget Control was established to make recommendations for change. After much investigation and deliberation Congress passed the Congressional Budget and Impoundment Control Act in June 1974, to take effect in 1976, with a test run in 1975. As a former assistant director of OMB noted, "To make it work, Congress and its individual members will have to act a hell of a lot differently than they do now."[19]

With the passage of the 1974 act, Congress announced its collective intention to produce its own plan—its own budget. To assist in this effort, three organizational units were created: a budget committee for each house and a Congressional Budget Office (CBO) to assist the committees in their work. New procedures were introduced that provided opportunities for the House and Senate to look at the big picture, to determine the relative growth of different government functions, and even to set priorities if they so desired. Budget formulation and legitimation were changed by these new procedures. Even now it is too soon to judge the full effect of the reform. But participation in budget-making activities has been significantly altered, and competitive executive and legislative processes have now been created.

Budget Formulation

The formulation and approval of a budget are routinized processes with rules and deadlines. This by no means implies that budgeting politics is cut-and-dried. But the production of a budget is a huge management problem, that requires standard operating procedures. It can be thought of as one of the most important display points in the policy process, where agreements reached elsewhere take concrete form and where the cost of these agreements can be compared and evaluated. Much of the previous discussion in this book reappears in the budget-making process.

Who participates in budget formulation? Within the executive, the Office of Management and Budget, under the guidance of the president and the president's closest aides, works with the various departments and agencies (each of which has a budget office). In Congress the principal participants are the members and staffs of the two budget committees, the CBO, the party leaders, and possibly other important committee chairmen (principally those from the money committees). This division between the executive and the legislature illustrates an important point. Before the passage of the 1974 act, one would not normally have bothered to identify congressional participants in budget formulation. Now they are very much involved. Their work comes together, or at least is associated, when Congress acts on the first budget resolution (see figure 7.5).

Executive Budget Formulation

Thus we have two budget formulation processes to consider. Within the executive, work at any one point proceeds on a minimum of three budgets: that being planned, that for which approval is sought, and that which is being implemented. The three are, of course, related. For example, at this writing it appears that the budget deficit will be much larger than predicted. Therefore the pressure is great for President Reagan's budget makers to close that gap in the future. The fiscal year is now defined as October 1 to September 30 (formerly it was July 1 to June 30). Changing these dates provided Congress with more time but the president still must present a budget within 15 days after Congress convenes. Figure 7.3 shows the timetable that is followed (or from which exceptions are made).

The executive budget formulation process is summarized in figure 7.4. Though the flow of decision making is clear, several observations can be made to clarify the dynamics of this process. First, although three decision-making units are identified as major participants in budget formulation—the agency, the Office of Management and Budget, and the president—they represent only the tip of the iceberg. For, with the agencies and the president in particular, budget decisions are normally the result of communication and consultation with other governmental units, supporting interests, agency clientele, trusted advisers, and possibly members of Congress and their staff. Therefore, given the emphasis of this book, the decisional steps noted in figure 7.4 are only the starting points for analysis of who is truly involved in formulating budget requests and final proposals.

In this same connection, a quick review of the figure shows the association of all budget and programmatic decisions. While this is an obvious relationship—that is, money is normally requested for specific purposes—the means for coordinating the two types of decisions are anything but obvious. As a result, the balancing and maintenance of programmatic goals within the agency, between agencies, and between the agency and OMB is a continuing and complex set of operations requiring the attention of decision makers at

Summary of Major Steps in the Budget Process

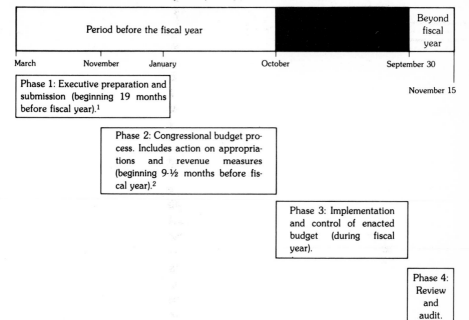

[1] The president's budget is transmitted to Congress within 15 days after Congress convenes.

[2] If appropriation action is not completed by September 30, Congress enacts temporary appropriation (i.e., continuing resolution).

FIGURE 7.3   The federal budget-making process. *(Source:* A Glossary of Terms Used in the Federal Budget. *Washington, D. C.: U. S. General Accounting Office, 1981, p. 7.)*

several levels. Things get even more difficult once the budget goes to Congress.

Another dynamic aspect of this formulation process that is suggested, but hardly made explicit, in the figure is the continuing effort by agencies to judge presidential priorities. Equally important is the effort by agencies to influence these top-level decisions. And, of course, no president can create a budget without information from bureaucrats and his own political appointees, who head the departments and agencies. If one reads figure 7.4 with this interaction in mind, the various steps are seen as a gradual unfolding of decisions based on or resulting from a two-way flow in influence and communication, with OMB acting as translation and communications center.

Also less graphic in the figure is that budget decisions have historical bases and, therefore, impact on the future as well. As the budget itself increases, representing the growth of governmental functions in society, these historical relationships become more significant. Beginning with the 1971 budget, five-year projections were included in the budget analysis so that decision makers might judge the commitments involved in enacting programs.

Finally, the figure clearly indicates the critical role played by the Office of

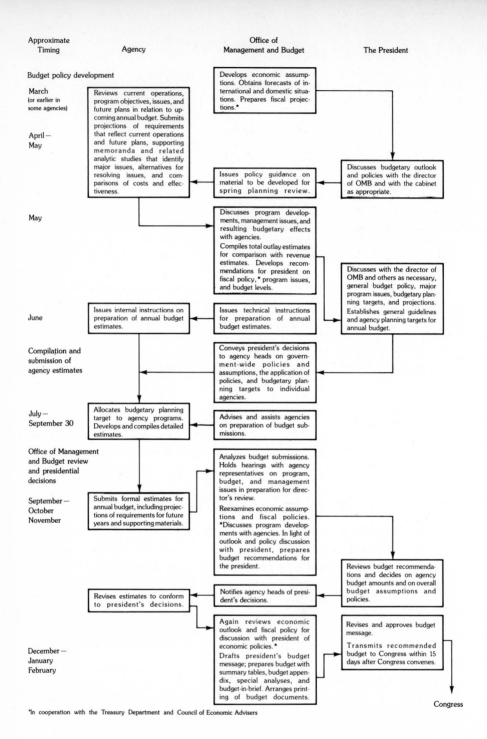

FIGURE 7.4 Formulation of the executive budget. *(Source:* A Glossary of Terms Used in the Federal Budget. *Washington, D. C.: U. S. General Accounting Office, 1981, pp. 8–9.)*

Management and Budget. Formerly called the Bureau of the Budget, this unit is located in the Executive Office of the President and performs several absolutely vital services for the president. The most obvious is well outlined in figure 7.4. The agency serves not only to transmit and translate presidential decisions to the agencies, but also to inform the president of agency programmatic goals. Inevitably OMB personnel themselves make vital decisions in performing this crucial intermediary role. They perform a similar role, once the budget has been approved, by controlling expenditures.

As a logical extension of its budgetary functions, OMB also acts as a clearing house for all legislative proposals flowing from the departments and agencies to Congress. Once again, it presumably tests these proposals against the programmatic priorities and interests of the president. A third function associated with OMB's privileged position of programmatic oversight is that of studying changes and advising agencies on organizational and management matters. This is an impressive list of functions, making service in OMB an interesting and challenging experience.

Since it too is populated with humans, not gods, OMB's actions vary both within the agency among budget examiners and with a change in directors. Aaron Wildavsky points out that:

- There are . . . always some people in [OMB] who identify more closely with an agency or program than do others, or who develop policy preferences independent of the president. They have a creative urge. . . . They see themselves as doing the right thing by pursuing policies in the public interest and they may convince themselves that the president would support them if only he had the time and inclination to go into the matter as deeply as they had. . . .

  Even within the same administration, different budget directors can have an impact of their own. . . . Some directors have much better relationships with the president than others; they get in to see him more often . . . ; he backs them up more frequently on appeals from the agencies.[20]

Further, OMB personnel must be sensitive to their own political position relative to those with whom they must deal; for example, the president and the White House staff, Congress, and the departments and agencies. They know that the wrong decisions on their part can result in loss of presidential confidence. But, as Wildavsky points out, they may face problems with Congress as well.

- The most serious obstacle to acceptance of [OMB] leadership is that Congress determines appropriations. Everyone knows that agencies make end-runs around [OMB] to gain support from Congress. If they do so too often, [OMB] finds that its currency has depreciated. Hence [OMB] frequently accepts consistent congressional action as a guide. A close eye is kept on congressional action for the preceding year before an agency's total is set for the next one. Failure to do so might leave [OMB] with a record of defeat that jeopardizes its effectiveness in other areas.[21]

In summary, whereas a routine with scheduled decision points can be identified for budget formulation, students of public policy will want to inquire beyond these points to explore the interactions among those contributing the advice, information, and conclusions that form the basis of budget construction.

Congressional Budget Formulation

How can a two-house legislature of 535 representatives formulate a budget? Answer: With difficulty. As described above, Congress found that it could not intelligently respond to presidential initiatives with which it disagreed. The institution needed some means for taking a comprehensive look at the budget, and relying on its own resources to do so. Dennis S. Ippolito puts it this way:

■   The 1974 budget act did not transform internal congressional politics, nor was it likely to do so. It did provide Congress with the potential for altering the balance of influence between the president and Congress.[22]

Thus Congress backed into a kind of formulation activity because of its concern that it was unable to respond to executive budget making. The activity itself does not resemble the detailed work with the agencies as shown in figure 7.4. Rather, it involves the work of the budget committees, their staffs, and the Congressional Budget Office in trying to produce spending targets. The formulation-like work culminates in a concurrent resolution that is supposed to be enacted by May 15 each year.

Figure 7.5 shows the full process by which Congress acts on the budget. The work by the budget committees (and CBO) before May 15 is included here as budget formulation. Note that the principal stimulus to this activity is still the president's budget (along with a so-called current services estimate, that is, estimates of budget authority and outlays if continued at the present level of government services). But Congress also tries to do something up front, so to speak, and on its own. The budget committees hold hearings on the president's economic assumptions, spending priorities, and program initiatives. They also receive estimates of new budget authority from the authorization and appropriations committees. Meanwhile, CBO is hard at work preparing a report that reacts to executive action and reviews alternatives. The total task is massive, particularly considering that it occurs within two houses, neither of which is well designed to produce well integrated and comprehensive proposals. Allen Schick describes the process as follows:

■   A budget resolution appears to be a rather simple measure. In printed form, it is usually only two pages long. Each resolution is formatted into the five fiscal aggregates prescribed by the Budget Act (total revenues, total new budget authority, total outlays, the budget surplus or deficit, and the public debt) and budget authority and outlay allocations for 19 functional categories. Yet drawing up a budget resolution can be a complex undertaking. Each resolution requires more than 40 separate, but arithmetically consistent, decisions. The functional parts have to add up to the spending totals; the budget authority allocated to each function must be coordinated with estimated outlays; the

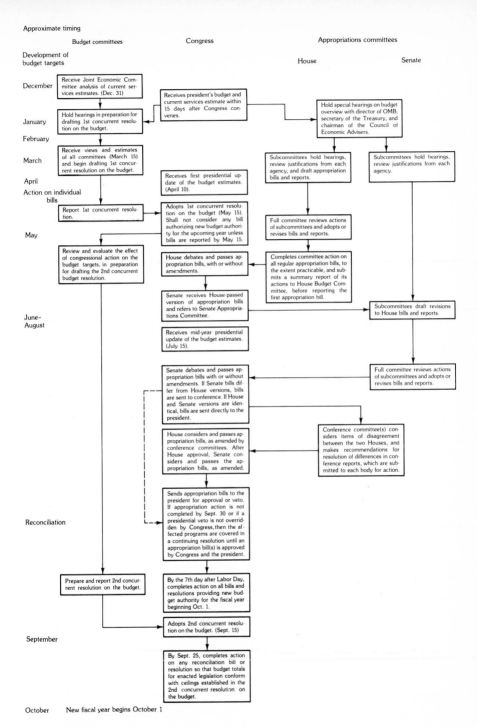

FIGURE 7.5 The congressional budget process. *(Source: A Glossary of Terms Used in the Federal Budget. Washington, D. C.: U. S. General Accounting Office, 1981, pp. 10–11.)*

difference between total revenues and outlays must equal the projected deficit.[23]

As one would expect, this work takes place in an atmosphere of high politics. Budgets are about "who gets what, when, how." That has not changed with the new process, but the politics has been rearranged. In a sense, Congress has brought priority setting out of the closet. Before the budget act, those in the know could identify a process by which budgetary preferences were declared and choices were made. Many of the same preferences still exist. However, now there are more visible and formal stages for declaring priorities. One still needs an interpreter since the nineteen functional categories in the budget resolutions do not coincide with actual committee or subcommittee jurisdictions; but at least one has a place to start. Further, the earlier start of the reconciliation process (see figure 7.5) provides a concrete translation of goals into committee targets that was not so readily available in the past.

What happens to budget formulation in Congress when political conditions are unstable, for example, when the president is of one party and Congress is controlled by the other? This situation has occurred often in recent years. The Ford and Reagan presidencies evidenced very unstable politics, and even in the Carter presidency there was conflict between executive and congressional priorities. Schick notes that the one constant is the effort to get the budget resolution passed in both houses. "In so doing, [the budget committees] will have to seek accommodation to the dominant political interests in their respective chambers."[24] Getting accommodation when it is difficult, if not impossible, to spot "dominant political interests" can produce exactly the kind of stalemate that has been observed in recent years.

In summary, the executive budget formulation process is long and complex but provides means for authoritative resolution of conflicts; in the end the president can say yes or no and make it stick long enough to deliver a budget document to the Congress. The congressional budget formulation process is not so lengthy and is complicated by Congress's need to accommodate its own decentralized structure. Congress cannot change its internal politics. It is, however, trying to provide a means by which it can identify and apply these politics in a more orderly fashion.

Budget Legitimation

A budget approval process exists in both the executive and Congress. In the executive the process is typically associated with the standard hierarchy of presidential approval and acquiescence. Though the departments and agencies win and lose in this process, and the president has become one of the more temporary public officials in Washington, still it is the president who must ultimately have the authority to say yes or no. Each year the budget is associated with whoever is in the White House. At this writing we are coping with "the Reagan budget." Of course, in reality much of the budget is predetermined by obligations already in effect (see discussion earlier in this chapter). Thus, it is important to realize that budget commitments are made in approving substantive policy programs—commitments that more or less bind subsequent presidents and congresses. In part, the realization of just how many such commitments have been made has led to the complicated budget politics of the mid-1980s.

As a consequence of these developments, the formal processes of presidential and congressional approval are more marginal than one might at first imagine. Today, more than at any previous period in our history, programmatic imperatives drive the budget.

With these caveats in mind, we consider the approval processes in the new congressional budget system. I have already observed that budget makers in Congress are sensitive to the need to accommodate various political interests. In so doing, of course, they act as legitimaters. Getting a budget resolution approved is an important legitimation activity, requiring majority support in both houses. As indicated in figure 7.5, however, the battle has hardly begun at that point. The budgetary targets have to be realized by the authorizing, taxing, and appropriating committees in each house. Until 1980 these committees did their work during the summer, presumably bearing in mind the targets set in the first budget resolution. More bluntly, the budget committees might very well be successful in cutting expenditures, but their resolutions were not law. Only if they were successful in convincing the other committees to act would their actions be effective.

Following actions by the other committees, a second budget resolution is to be introduced and passed by September 15 (see figure 7.5). If what the committees have produced is out of line with this resolution, a so-called *reconciliation* process is provided for. The purpose is just as the name suggests: a settling or harmonizing between the adjusted budget targets and the authorized expenditures reported by the standing committees. The effectiveness of the new process could be measured easily enough, for example, by determining whether the budget committees were able to make their numbers stick or whether they simply adjusted their figures to coincide with those produced by the other committees. Allen Schick's conclusion is that the budget makers in Congress have had "marginal—though potentially significant—influence on budgetary outcomes."[25] He observes that:

■ The Budget Committees have had limited success in protecting Congress from itself. Congress has, in fact, passed just about all the legislation it has wanted, though not always in the preferred form.[26]

Lance LeLoup goes so far as to say that "it would be difficult to make a case that the budget would have looked significantly different without the procedural changes in Congress." He judges that

■ . . . although budget priorities are more clearly expressed by Congress, the preferences of members have not changed radically since before 1975. The major issues in the budget reform movement were, in fact, as much procedural as they were policy issues.[27]

Even if the members had changed their policy preferences, however, it is not altogether certain that the new system would have registered these changes. Decision making on specific budget items remained disaggregated. The crucial reconciliation process came very late, after commitments had already been made. As Schick observes, "It was unreasonable to expect the House and Senate to reopen appropriations issues that had been decided only weeks earlier or to take away funds that were about to be spent."[28]

Beginning in 1980, reconciliation was moved up to follow passage of the first budget resolution. This change was crucial and involved much more than simply the timing of process. It meant that the budget committees could seek to enforce the resolution as limits on the committees. Schick explains:

■   The shift from the second to the first resolution is much more than a matter of timing; it also changes the focus of reconciliation. Rather than targeting reconciliation on actions taken during the current session, Congress now uses it to change legislation enacted in previous years. Although reconciliation was originally expected to deal mostly with appropriations, it is now aimed principally at the substantive legislation. While reconciliation was once conceived as a means of ensuring that new legislation is in accord with the budget, it has become an instrument for forcing action on matters that Congress might otherwise disregard. Rather than merely being a means of changing existing law, reconciliation promises to become a process by which Congress makes and enforces a consistent and comprehensive budget policy for the U. S. government.[29]

What Schick has described is a process of very high-level decision making. It forces all committees to become more involved in the development and passage of the first budget resolution. It then makes the work of the committees much more visible and establishes a mechanism for measuring this work against the standards of the budget resolution. The process of approval is dramatically altered by this change. Participation in majority building for the first budget resolution is greatly expanded, possibly resulting in delay. Effective reconciliation at this earlier stage may also attract a president who is intent on reducing the rate of budget growth. In summary, the new reconciliation procedure presents a direct challenge to normal majority-building politics in Congress. It forces cross-issue and therefore cross-committee analysis of legislation and does so at an early stage. This threatens the autonomy of the committees and subcommittees and the interests they represent. They must now get support prior to acting on legislative and appropriations requests. Advance approval is necessary if priorities are to be set. The new procedure introduces a set of political dynamics different from that associated with the old, complex system of quid pro quos.

It is not certain that the new procedures will continue. Budget reform is once again in the air. Representative Morris K. Udall (D.–Arizona) complains that "We don't have time to legislate." Senator Patrick Leahy (D.–Vermont) says that "We've become elected line-item bureaucrats."[30] The work on the FY 1983 budget missed every deadline. It may well be that the approval processes have become so interwoven and complicated that they simply cannot function. Changes will no doubt be made, because dissatisfaction is presently very high.

In summary, approving a budget at either end of Pennsylvania Avenue has become a difficult and trying process. Given the realities of budget growth noted earlier, frustration was inevitable. The new congressional processes merely provide greater focus for those frustrations by aggregating them.

The Fiscal Year 1982 Budget

President Ronald Reagan's first budget was enacted in 1981 for the fiscal year 1982. He was determined to have a profound impact on the government's role in the economy, having promised to cut taxes, cut domestic expenditures, and increase defense expenditures. To everyone's surprise the Republicans captured control of the Senate in 1980 and increased their numbers in the House by 33 (the largest Republican gain in a presidential election since 1920). Conditions were excellent for the president to get his way on Capitol Hill in spite of what many judged to be a radical economic program. The new budget process, particularly early reconciliation, served his purposes very well.

Formulation

In our political system outgoing presidents leave budgets behind for their successors. As is evident in figure 7.3, work on the budget precedes an election by many months, and the requirement is that the budget be presented shortly after Congress convenes. President Carter offered his last budget on January 15; President-elect Reagan was inaugurated on January 20. The Carter budget was basically in line with current services, with new proposals essentially balanced by cuts. Reagan's new director of the Office of Management and Budget, David Stockman, reacted to Carter's budget with a statement that revealed the intentions of the new administration. He judged that the Carter budget called for "more of the same." "We have a budget that's obviously out of control."[31]

Stockman and his assistants worked feverishly during the next seven weeks to prepare a new budget. William Greider's famous account of these efforts in *The Atlantic Monthly* describes the initial shock as follows:

■ In early January, Stockman and his staff were assembling dozens of position papers on program reductions and studying the internal forecasts for the federal budget and the national economy. The initial figures were frightening— "absolutely shocking."[32]

The initial analysis demonstrated that astronomical cuts in nondefense programs would be required to balance the budget if the president were to keep
his promise to cut taxes and increase defense spending. The projected deficits
were "from $82 billion in 1982 to $116 billion in 1984. Even Stockman
blinked." [33]

The short-run solution was to change the economic assumptions upon which
such dire projections were based. Even then huge cuts in the proposed Carter
budget were required if a tax reduction program was to be enacted. Table 7.2
compares the two budgets. Note that despite a $44 billion cut in outlays, the
proposed Reagan budget results in a much larger deficit. The reason is found
in the second column: a significant reduction in revenues—$61.5 billion. If it
were not for the Reagan cuts in outlays, the projected deficit, given the revenue loss, would have been $89 billion—just in the range that made Stockman
blink. (The actual deficit far exceeded even this larger figure.)

Budget formulation within the executive was a hectic affair. First, there was
little time (less than two months) in which to produce this revolutionary budget. Second, two of Reagan's promises, to cut taxes and increase defense
expenditures, made it extremely difficult to accomplish a third, to balance the
budget. The president also declared several social benefit programs (primarily
pension programs) exempt from budget cuts. Finally, Stockman had to work
with a new cabinet and new White House aides.

Stockman actually turned the timing and cabinet inexperience to his favor.
A budget working group was organized that was fully committed to the president's goal of cutting most non-pension-related domestic programs. A cabinet
official then had to review the relevant cuts before the group. Greider quotes
Stockman on this procedure:

■ "Each meeting will involve only the relevant Cabinet member and his aides
   with four or five strong keepers of the central agenda," Stockman explained at
   one point. "So on Monday, when we go into the decision on synfuels programs,
   it will be [Energy Secretary James B.] Edwards defending them against six guys
   saying that, by God, we've got to cut these back or we're not going to have a
   savings program that will add up."

Greider then summarizes the process and how it worked:

■ In general, the system worked. Stockman's agency did in a few weeks what
   normally consumes months; the process was made easier because the normal
   opposition forces had no time to marshal either their arguments or their constituents and because the President was fully in tune with Stockman. After the
   budget working group reached a decision, it would be taken to Reagan in the
   form of a memorandum, on which he could register his approval by checking a
   little box. "Once he checks it," Stockman said, "I put it in my safe and I go
   ahead and I don't let it come back up again." [34]

This "top-down" rather than "bottom-up" budgeting was necessary under the
circumstances. But it carried great risks once the whole program arrived on

TABLE 7.2 The Carter and Reagan
budgets for fiscal year 1982
(in billions of dollars)

	Outlays	Revenues	Deficit
Carter budget	739.3	711.8	27.5
Reagan budget	695.3	650.3	45.0
Differences	−44.0	−61.5	+17.5

Source: Congressional Quarterly Weekly Report,
March 14, 1981, 443.

Capitol Hill, where appeals to restore funds that had been cut could be expected.

Congressional budget formulation was more dependent than usual on what the president did. The Republicans were basically unified behind the president. Furthermore, the president's party held a majority in the Senate, an advantage not available to other recent Republican presidents since Eisenhower's first Congress (1953–1954), when the Republicans had a majority in both houses. As Allen Schick concludes, " . . . the key to presidential success was held in the Senate, not in the House, and by Republicans, not by Democrats."[35] The Democrats had Carter's budget as an alternative, but it was of little value given Reagan's landslide victory and the fact that his budget promised to be truly extraordinary (making the Carter budget less relevant). Therefore the House Democrats more or less had to wait and then react to the president's budget. Budget Committee Chairman James Jones (D.–Oklahoma) was the principal formulator, and he was faced with a difficult balancing act that would "restore some funds to social programs, to keep the liberals happy," project "a smaller deficit than Stockman's, to appear more responsible in fiscal terms," and leave the defense budget intact so as not to "offend the southerners."[36]

Approval

Getting approval for the FY 1982 budget was a long and very complex process requiring at least one book-length description. It will probably never again happen in quite this way. Much of the story is evident in the sequence of action and the party breakdown on key votes. Table 7.3 provides the basic information, but it does not begin to tell the story of one of the most remarkable presidential–congressional budget battles ever.

The administration relied on its advantage in the Senate, where the majority Republicans, skillfully led by Howard Baker (R.–Tennessee), achieved extraordinary unity. Note in table 7.3 that on only two Senate votes did the Republicans lose more than two of their numbers. This feat was particularly impressive given that past "budget resolutions were devoid of party label." As Schick observes, "Senate Republicans abandoned bipartisanship in 1981, preferring to make their deals with the White House rather than with Democratic colleagues."[37]

TABLE 7.3 Budget approval in 1981

	Sequence of major action	Vote	Party division	
February 18	President delivers economic message and introduces tax cut plan	—	—	
March 10	President's budget presented	—	—	
April 2	Senate adopts budget reconciliation instructions	88–10	R:	51–1
			D:	37–9
May 7	House adopts Gramm-Latta substitute (budget targets)	253–176	R:	190–0
			D:	63–176
May 12	Senate adopts House resolution with amendments	78–20	R:	50–2
			D:	28–18
May 14	House–Senate conference agrees	—	—	
May 20	House approves conference report (budget targets)	244–155	R:	167–8
			D:	77–147
May 21	Senate approves conference report (budget targets)	76–20	R:	49–2
			D:	27–18
June 25	Senate adopts budget reconciliation	80–15	R:	52–0
			D:	28–15
June 26	House adopts Gramm-Latta substitute (budget reconciliation)	217–211	R:	188–2
			D:	29–209
July 29	House adopts Conable substitute (tax cuts)	238–195	R:	190–1
			D:	48–194
July 29	Senate adopts Finance Committee substitute (tax cuts)	89–11	R:	52–1
			D:	37–10
July 31	House approves conference report (budget reconciliation)	Voice vote	—	
July 31	Senate approves conference report (budget reconciliation)	80–14	R:	49–1
			D:	31–13
August 3	Senate approves conference report (tax cuts)	67–8	R:	41–1
			D:	26–7
August 4	House approves conference report (tax cuts)	282–95	R:	169–1
			D:	113–94
September 24	President requests additional budget cuts	—	—	
November 22	House approves conference report (continuing appropriations)	205–194	R:	10–166
			D:	195–28
November 22	Senate approves conference report (continuing appropriations)	46–39	R:	44–6
			D:	2–33
November 23	President vetoes continuing appropriations	—	—	
November 23	House approves continuing appropriations	367–26	R:	170–6
			D:	197–20
November 23	Senate approves continuing appropriations	88–1	R:	50–0
			D:	38–1

Source: Votes taken from various issues of the Congressional Quarterly Weekly Reports, 1981.

The Democrats had a 243 to 192 majority in the House, but Republican unity combined with the votes of the so-called Boll Weevils—Southern Democrats defecting to vote with the president—gave the White House the margin of victory. Again the key to success was a unified Republican party. The percentage of Republicans supporting the president on the votes included in table 7.3 was, in sequence, 100, 95, 99, 99, 99, 94, and 97. House Republicans worked directly with the Boll Weevils to fashion substitute budget packages for those offered by the House Committee on the Budget (the Gramm-Latta substitutes). This alliance commanded the House floor despite the Democratic majority.

President Reagan was not idle in this extraordinary majority-building exercise: he was a willing lobbyist for his own program. Before crucial votes Reagan went on television to boost the program. In addition, he worked directly with congressional leaders and his own liaison staff to pressure members of both houses. The House Republican whip, Trent Lott of Mississippi, observed, "I've got the best whip organization because Ronald Reagan is in it." The president even went to Capitol Hill "to cheer on the House Republican caucus." His lobbying team organized interest group support in telephone campaigns with members. It was a total effort and, according to White House Chief of Staff James Baker, "the president blew them away." [38]

Later in the session the president called for additional cuts (see table 7.3). Budget planners realized that budget growth and tax cuts would in fact produce huge deficits. It proved difficult to call upon members of Congress to sacrifice still more. Senator Jake Garn (R.–Utah) asked, "How many times can you cut the same piece of pie?" [39] Appropriations politics became very complicated late in the session. The president insisted on further cuts and the appropriations committees found it difficult to resolve the issues. Continuing resolutions were necessary just to keep the government operating. Those resolutions, too, became the subject of intense debate between the White House and Congress. Reagan was understandably concerned that these resolutions might be a way around his intended cuts, since continuing resolutions typically provide appropriations at current levels of spending. The president vetoed one such resolution as not being within his guidelines, and the government was forced to reduce its services for one day (an event treated in the media as a "shut down of the government"). A resolution more to his liking was enacted almost immediately.

In his analysis of "how the budget was won and lost" in 1981, Allen Schick concludes that this case tells us a lot about the future. He judges that the same forces that controlled events in 1981 will continue to drive budgetary politics in subsequent years.

■ Regardless of the medium-term performance of the economy, recovery will not come fast enough to help the president in his next round of budget battles. The signs point to another large package of savings in the fiscal 1983 budget and fresh confrontations with Congress. On the basis of last year's performance and the president's political talents and resources, one should be wary of betting against him the next time. But the odds now are against a replay of 1981 in 1982.

Republicans and Democrats are weary of budgetary conflict; the more intractable the problems seem to be, the less they want to tackle them. They are tired of having their broader legislative interests crowded out by never-ending budget crises, and they do not want to have every issue denominated in budgetary terms. Members are resentful of the concentration of power and of legislative activity forced by the 1981 reconciliation procedures, and they do not want this to become a recurring feature of the legislative process.[40]

Weary or not, members of Congress are bound to face continuing problems in managing the budget. The 1982 battle was different from that of 1981, as Schick predicted, but it was no less intense.

Summary

I began this chapter by emphasizing that budgeting is like "replaying the match." In so doing, I connected policy programs with specific funding decisions in formulation and approval. Another fundamental point, however, emerges from this chapter. Budgeting has come to be a policy issue in and of itself, separate from, yet a direct consequence of, the many individual spending and taxing decisions. The Reagan budgets surely represent the epitome of this trend. The process formerly was one of collecting specific decisions into a document referred to as "the budget." The executive typically sought to integrate these decisions, but Congress then disaggregated them. Now the new congressional budget process requires a more comprehensive outlook. Presently it is not working well. As Schick notes, the members themselves are uncomfortable having "every issue denominated in budgetary terms." These significant changes make budget making even more important than in the past, thus requiring greater attention by students of the policy process.

Notes

1. Leonard Freedman, *Public Housing: The Politics of Poverty* (New York: Holt, Rinehart & Winston, 1969), pp. 19–20.
2. Freedman, pp. 20–21.
3. Robert Taggart III, *Low-Income Housing: A Critique of Federal Aid* (Baltimore: Johns Hopkins University Press, 1970), p. 5.
4. Freedman, *Public Housing*, p. 56.
5. As quoted in Freedman, p. 20. Emphasis added.
6. Aaron Wildavsky, *The Politics of the Budgetary Process*, 3d ed. (Boston: Little, Brown, 1979), p. 5.
7. Wildavsky, *The Politics of the Budgetary Process*, pp. 1–2.
8. Joseph A. Pechman, ed., *Setting National Priorities: The 1982 Budget* (Washington, D. C.: Brookings Institution, 1981), p. 46.
9. Roger Davidson and Walter Oleszek, *Congress and Its Members* (Washington, D. C.: Congressional Quarterly, Inc., 1981), p. 329.

10. Joseph A. Pechman, ed., *Setting National Priorities: The 1983 Budget* (Washington, D. C.: Brookings Institution, 1982), pp. 30–31.
11. For Wildavsky's analysis of budget growth, its implications and correction, see his *How To Limit Government Spending* (Berkeley: University of California Press, 1980).
12. For a brief history of budget making, or lack thereof, see Dennis S. Ippolito, *Congressional Spending* (Ithaca, N. Y.: Cornell University Press, 1981), chap. 2.
13. See the classic work by Richard F. Fenno, Jr., *The Power of the Purse: Appropriations Politics in Congress* (Boston: Little, Brown, 1966).
14. Figures supplied in U. S. Senate, Committee on Government Operations, *Congressional Budget Reform*, July 1974, p. 4.
15. For a detailed discussion of these procedures see Louis Fisher, *Presidential Spending Power* (Princeton: Princeton University Press, 1975).
16. *Congressional Quarterly Weekly Report*, February 3, 1973, 234.
17. Both the Mondale and Albert statements are cited in *Congressional Quarterly Weekly Report*, February 3, 1973, 175.
18. *Congressional Quarterly Weekly Report*, February 24, 1973, 397.
19. Quoted in *Congressional Quarterly Weekly Report*, September 7, 1974, 2415.
20. Wildavsky, *The Politics of the Budgetary Process*, pp. 36–37.
21. Wildavsky, *The Politics of the Budgetary Process*, p. 41.
22. Ippolito, *Congressional Spending* , pp. 73–74.
23. Allen Schick, *Congress and Money: Budgeting, Spending, and Taxing* (Washington, D. C.: Urban Institute, 1980), p. 221.
24. Schick, *Congress and Money*, p. 306.
25. Schick, *Congress and Money*, p. 356.
26. Schick, *Congress and Money*, p. 412.
27. Lance LeLoup, *The Fiscal Congress: Legislative Control of the Budget* (Westport, Conn.: Greenwood Press, 1980), p. 157.
28. Allen Schick, *Reconciliation and the Congressional Budget Process* (Washington, D. C.: American Enterprise Institute, 1981), p. 5.
29. Schick, *Reconciliation*, p. 8.
30. Quoted in *The Washington Post*, December 12, 1982, C4.
31. Quoted in *Congressional Quarterly Weekly Report*, January 17, 1981, 123.
32. William Greider, "The Education of David Stockman," *The Atlantic Monthly*, December 1981, 32.
33. Greider, p. 32.
34. Greider, p. 33.
35. Allen Schick, "How the Budget Was Won and Lost," in *President and Congress: Assessing Reagan's First Year*, ed. Norman J. Ornstein (Washington, D. C.: American Enterprise Institute, 1982), p. 16.
36. Greider, *The Education of David Stockman*, p. 38.
37. Schick, "How the Budget Was Won and Lost," p. 17.
38. All quotes in the paragraph from *Congressional Quarterly Weekly Report*, August 1, 1981, 1372.
39. Quoted in *Reagan's First Year* (Washington, D. C.: Congressional Quarterly, 1982), p. 38.
40. Schick, "How the Budget Was Won and Lost," pp. 41–42.

Chapter Eight

Implementing Programs

Functional activities	Categorized in government	With a potential product
Implementation: organization interpretation application	Government to problems	Varies (service, payments, facilities controls)

In his provocative book *The Implementation Game,* Eugene Bardach states:

■   It is hard enough to design public policies and programs that look good on paper. It is harder still to formulate them in words and slogans that resonate pleasingly in the ears of political leaders and the constituencies to which they are responsive. And it is excruciatingly hard to implement them in a way that pleases anyone at all, including the supposed beneficiaries or clients.[1]

Bardach illustrates the difficulties in getting agreements in the policy process and, more important for present purposes, in putting agreements into effect. It is to the latter that we now turn: the problem of actually getting the job done, of moving from the agreement on goals to the process of achieving goals.

This shift represents one of the more popularly accepted breaks in the policy process: that from politics to administration. It is important, therefore, to recognize that no such clear delineation exists in the real world of public policy. As Bardach suggests: the process of compromise associated with approving a program seldom resolves all the issues to everyone's satisfaction.

Thus the creation of a program is itself an event that may stimulate the emergence of a mini–policy process. Problems may have to be defined, options identified, and agreements reached. One must not confuse an analytical or conceptual framework (the map) for what happens in real political life (taking a trip).

What Is Implementation?

Like so many of the policy activities treated in this book, *implementation* is easy to understand in the abstract. "Getting the job done" and "doing it" are common short-hand definitions of the term. But "doing it" is not always so simple. "It" may not be a well-defined object; "doing" may require more people, money, and organizational skill than are available. Under these circumstances, implementation is a process of getting additional resources so as to figure out what is to be done.

Implementation is highly interactive with prior policy activities. In their study of the implementation of a federal program in Oakland, California, Jeffrey L. Pressman and Aaron B. Wildavsky strike exactly the right chord in defining implementation:

■   Implementation may be viewed as a process of *interaction* between the setting of goals and the actions geared to achieving them. . . .

Program implementation thus becomes a seamless web. . . .

Implementation, then, is the ability to forge subsequent links in the causal chain connecting actions to objectives. . . .[2]

These interactive elements are vital to the whole concept of implementation. But as Bardach points out (see opening quotation), they surely complicate the process. Previous actions (problem definition, formulation, legitimation) may not be conclusive in any sense. Many unresolved dilemmas and conflicts carry over, contributing to the dynamic and interactive quality of implementation. In fact, program goals may be truly revealed or substantially altered in the process of implementation. Walter Williams puts it this way:

■ The most pressing implementation problem is that of moving from a decision to operations in such a way that *what is put into place bears a reasonable resemblance to the decision and is functioning well in its institutional environment.* The past contains few clearer messages than that of the difficulty of bridging the gap between policy decisions and workable field operations.[3]

Williams's statement raises the question of what a program or decision really is. His analysis is consistent with that of Pressman and Wildavsky in proposing that a program or decision may be only a hunch or proposition about solving a public problem. Further, this estimate about what will work may itself be an amalgam of estimates resulting from a process of bargaining and compromise (see chapter 6). Implementers are then faced with the task of validating the proposition.

■ A program consists of governmental action initiated in order to secure objectives whose attainment is problematical. A program exists when the initial conditions—the "if" stage of the policy hypothesis—have been met. The word "program" signifies the conversion of a hypothesis into governmental action. The initial premises of the hypothesis have been authorized. The degree to which the predicted consequences (the "then" stage) take place we will call implementation.[4]

Having provided the proper interactive context for program implementation, we can now offer a more concrete definition. Let us say simply that implementation is that *set of activities directed toward putting a program into effect.* Three activities, in particular, are significant:[5]

1. *Organization:* The establishment or rearrangement of resources, units, and methods for putting a program into effect
2. *Interpretation:* The translation of program language (often contained in a statute) into acceptable and feasible plans and directives
3. *Application:* The routine provision of services, payments, or other agreed-upon program objectives or instruments

---

The Challenge of Implementation

Before turning to a direct discussion of these subactivities of implementation it is useful to stress the sizable challenges facing implementers. Consider the effect of several of the initial realities at this stage of the policy process.

Problems and demands are constantly being defined and redefined in the policy process.

Policy makers sometimes define problems for people who have not defined problems for themselves.

Programs requiring intergovernmental and public participation invite variable interpretations of purpose.

Inconsistent interpretations of program purpose are often not resolved.

Programs may be implemented without provisions for learning about failure.

Programs often reflect an attainable consensus rather than a substantive conviction.

Many programs are developed and implemented without the problems ever having been clearly defined.

Imagine that you have taken a job in Washington (or any other seat of government) as an "administrator" or "executive." You expect to administer or execute, just as your title suggests. The realities listed above suggest, however, that you may well need to adjust your expectations to an ambiguous decision-making environment. At least when it comes to significant issues, the process of putting a program into effect is seldom done by the book. You must frequently take risks in judging what to do next. Even doing nothing may be risky for your reputation as an administrator and for the political position of your agency.

Randall B. Ripley and Grace A. Franklin propose other realities consistent with those identified here:

1. No one is in charge of implementation.
2. Domestic programs virtually never achieve all that is expected of them.

The first of these is the stark recognition that programs are absorbed into an expanding labyrinth of agencies located at various levels of government. As Ripley and Franklin observe, "In a very real sense there is no single government . . . to promote, oversee, or conduct implementation. Rather, there are many governments and, in some cases, government is often indistinguishable from nongovernment."[6] The second item is an addendum to Bardach's realistic statements quoted at the beginning of this chapter.

We will return to this matter of the many governments involved in implementation. For now, however, I simply want to emphasize the emergence of a vast intergovernmental network of implementers and the challenge it represents for putting a program into effect. The growth in the national domestic agenda has resulted in a quantum increase in federal programs, a large majority of which are administered at the state and local levels. In a more hierarchically organized system one might expect this increase in activity to result in greatly expanded national power. One might even predict the absorption of lower levels of government into a nationally directed implementation system. But our system is not hierarchically organized; in fact it is not altogether clear what the organizing principle is, if indeed one exists. Carl Van Horn, in his study of domestic federal programs, concluded that "the image of virtually unbounded federal power, of an uncontrollable federal juggernaut" is a gross exaggeration. He advises that one must consider the contributions of the state and local governments as well as of interest groups.

■ The policy's standards and resources circumscribe state and local action, but public policy happens, succeeds or flops, in thousands of state and local governments and private agencies. Anyone who seeks to influence or understand policy implementation must therefore set his sights on the day-to-day activities at the local level.[7]

Equally challenging to understand and cope with is the growth in administrative discretion permitted by the law. Again, this is a subject of direct interest later in this chapter ("Interpretation," pages 178–180). I flag it here because neither the scope nor the implications of such awesome delegations of authority are well understood. Further, as noted in chapter 7, broad delegation of authority can lead to the creation of full policy processes within administrative structures. In essence, legislatures may authorize an agency to define problems, propose and approve solutions, and then administer these solutions. Conceptually such developments do not trouble us since the emphasis here is on policy activities rather than specific institutions As a practical matter, however, it can be confusing to discover a complete policy process within something called an "administrative agency."

Who Is Involved in Implementation?

In his study of mental health reform in California (*The Implementation Game*), Bardach described the implementation process as that of "strategic interaction among numerous special interests all pursuing their own goals, which might or might not be compatible with the goals of the policy mandate."[8] The number of persons potentially involved in implementation is typically limited only by the extent of awareness of possible effects and the resources available. As with the other policy activities discussed, participation is by no means limited to those persons identified with the institution most associated with the policy activity in question. In considering program implementation it is thus important to bear in mind that:

1. Many others besides bureaucrats may be involved, for example, legislators, judges, private citizens.
2. Bureaucrats themselves are involved in functional activities other than implementation.

The first point may need more clarification than the second simply because one is not used to thinking about legislators, judges, or private citizens as putting programs into effect. Representatives and senators are overloaded with "casework," however. This term refers to the activities in congressional offices that are directed toward coping with the problems of individual constituents. Frequently the "case" results from applying a federal program, and it often is resolved by a congressional staff member pressing an agency for favorable action. Legislators are frequently consulted regarding the administration of policy in their particular areas of expertise, and they are also involved in appointments and other personnel matters of administration. Bardach provides a strong example of a state legislator and staff "actively and continually" involved "in what would normally be considered administrative matters."

■ They intervened at the level of the individual counties, in the Conference of Local Mental Health Directors, in the Department of Mental Hygiene, in the Department of Social Welfare, and in the Human Relations Agency. . . . Much of this activity . . . was initiated by complaints received from parties attempting to enlist their support for battles they were in danger of losing in their own local arenas. In no way is this sort of activity unusual for a legislator, except in this case perhaps by virtue of its scope and intensity.[9]

Judges also deal with cases and apply policy. The role of the court in policy making is typically seen in the dramatic pronouncements regarding constitutional interpretation, particularly those striking down a national statute as unconstitutional. Such cases are the exception, however. As Professor Glendon Schubert observes:

■ By far the larger function of the national courts, certainly in terms of the number of decisions and perhaps in terms of impact upon the American polity

as well, lies not in "constitutional interpretation" but in the judicial interpretation of national statutes, administrative regulations and decisions, judicial regulations (such as the procedural rules for the national courts), and judicial decisions.[10]

Judges may be involved in straightforward administrative tasks; for example,
naturalization of aliens, approval of passport applications, bankruptcy proceedings, and parole cases are the most common items for federal courts. But
judges are involved in implementation in other ways as well. Civil and criminal
cases result from the application of policy. Many of these are excluded from
our analysis because they primarily involve private problems. When publics are
affected, however, judges perform a type of administrative function. Professor
Samuel Krislov suggests that the first major function of courts is to provide "a
means for securing compliance with public policies, such as those proclaimed
by legislatures."[11] Much of the docket of the Supreme Court is the result of
Department of Justice decisions seeking compliance with the law. In a contest
between you and the government, judges may have the last word in interpreting policy for application (one of the most important aspects of administration).
Of course, it is quite possible that you have challenged the constitutional basis
of the policy, in which case the court is asked to perform another vital policy
function, that of evaluation or appraisal.

The participation of private groups in applying policy takes many forms.
Groups may cooperate with government agencies in applying policy. From the
first, the poverty program relied on citizens' groups in applying the broad
policy of the Economic Opportunity Act of 1964. The American Farm Bureau
Federation, now the most powerful farm group, was actually created as a
result of the administration of farm policy. The Smith-Lever Act of 1914 was
designed to improve farm methods through the county-agent system. Essential
to the success of this policy was the development of an effective means of
communicating with farmers. Encouraged by the Department of Agriculture,
farm bureaus were established to assist in communication. The national federation eventually developed as a private group, still retaining its semiofficial
status in some areas.

Groups may have representatives in administrative positions. A change of
administrations frequently finds representatives from one set of interests leaving, another set coming in. In other instances, groups take it upon themselves
to participate in applying policy to problems whether the government wants
them to or not. For example, civil rights groups have not waited for an invita-
tion to participate in seeing to it that the legislation passed during the 1960s is
applied. Veterans' groups insure that their clientele is aware of the benefits
they have helped to promote in federal policy. And environmental groups have
been very active in implementing the many federal, state, and local programs
in the 1970s and 1980s.

I can do no more than illustrate the varieties of participation. In their work
on implementation, Ripley and Franklin identify significant differences among

types of programs in terms of who participates and how they participate. "Implementation . . . involves a highly politicized set of interactions and inter-relationships on the part of many actors."[12] The principal lesson here is in the form of a warning not to limit one's scope in identifying these actors.

Implementation Activities: An Overview

We now consider the three primary activities typically associated with program implementation: organization, interpretation, and application. The first of these requires the most extensive treatment because it is important to discuss the concept of bureaucracy and its form in the American setting.

Organization

In a lively essay on "organized life," Brian Chapman concludes:

■   Bureaucracy is like sin: we all know something about it, but only those who practice it enjoy it. Ordinary people tend to be against both, and experts on the subjects tend to become obsessed, so that some see bureaucracy everywhere, as fanatical clerics see sin up every back alley. If you hold that all sex is sin, you simply mean you wish you had never been born; if you believe all bureaucracies are degenerate you are simply registering a protest against modern society.[13]

"Public policies are rarely self-executing."[14] Organization is essential for "getting the job done." Organization in government has become synonymous with the term *bureaucracy*, and bureaucracy has become synonymous with evil, if not sin. Yet, as Chapman argues, fear and loathing of bureaucracy often represent rejection of the intricacies of modern social life. For as public problems become more complex, so do governmental responses. It is therefore important to understand, rather than condemn, the ways in which government organizes to get the job done.

In the first edition of his classic work *Constitutional Government and Politics*, Carl J. Friedrich treats the bureaucracy first among the institutions as "the core of modern government."[15] While this insight may not be extraordinary, seldom do political scholars acknowledge it in organizing their work. More often than not, institutional analyses begin with the executive, then the legislature, the courts, and finally the bureaucracy. Yet Friedrich is so right: a complex of bureaucratic mazes is what makes our modern government so vastly different from what it was 100 years ago.

What is a bureaucracy? No response would be complete without reference to the writings of Max Weber, who viewed the bureaucracy as the means for accomplishing the difficult and demanding tasks of modern government. According to H. H. Gerth and C. Wright Mills, who translated the German scholar's works, bureaucracy, for Weber, established the "routines of workaday life."[16] Weber contrasted bureaucracy with charismatic leadership or personality, the former representing the everyday life of institutions and the latter representing the unusual. Gerth and Mills summarize the comparison as follows:

■ ... mass *versus* personality, the "routine" *versus* the "creative" entrepreneur, the conventions of ordinary people *versus* the inner freedom of pioneering and exceptional man, institutional rules *versus* the spontaneous individual, the drudgery and boredom of ordinary existence *versus* the imaginative flight of genius.[17]

Thus, it was in effecting the rational order of things that bureaucracy played its most important role for Weber. In this view bureaucracy is not expected to produce great creativity or policy innovation. Here is the way Weber himself defined the bureaucratic role:

■ There is the principle of fixed and official jurisdictional areas, which are generally ordered by rules, that is, by laws or administrative regulations.
   1. The regular activities required for the purposes of the bureaucratically governed structure are distributed in a fixed way as official duties.
   2. The authority to give the commands required for the discharge of these duties is distributed in a stable way and is strictly delimited by rules concerning the coercive means, physical, sacerdotal, or otherwise, which may be placed at the disposal of officials.
   3. Methodical provision is made for the regular and continuous fulfillment of these duties and for the execution of the corresponding rights; only persons who have the generally regulated qualifications to serve are employed.
   In public and lawful government these three elements constitute "bureaucratic authority."[18]

Here then is modern governmental machinery, putting into effect the rules, laws, or regulations. In its ideal form, this institution offers "technical superiority" by providing "precision, speed, unambiguity, knowledge of the files, continuity, discretion, unity, strict subordination, reduction of friction and of material and personal costs."[19] Note that *these advantages accrue when bureaucracy is functioning as it should*, according to Weber. It is quite possible that the machinery will not achieve these advantages. All Weber sought to do was to identify a set of functional activities and an organizational form for effecting these activities. By no means was he arguing that anything called "bureaucracy" produced the advantages noted above.

Nor was Weber insensitive to the political role of the bureaucracy. He pointed out that:

■ Once it is fully established, bureaucracy is among those social structures which are the hardest to destroy. Bureaucracy is *the* means of carrying "community action" over into rationally ordered "societal events." Therefore, as an instrument for "societalizing" relations of power, bureaucracy has been and is a power instrument of the first order—for the one who controls the bureaucratic apparatus.[20]

There are several clues in this important statement as to why Weber's ideal bureaucratic system seldom is realized, particularly in democracies. First, being "fully established" presumably means meeting the criteria set down by Weber. Yet in a democracy, meeting the conditions of fixed jurisdictional areas, specialization, hierarchy, and so on, is complicated by innumerable political pressures. Therefore bureaucracy is never really "fully established." Even a partially established bureaucracy, however, is difficult to destroy. Second, "carrying 'community action' over into rationally ordered 'societal events' " is a highly complex and politically sensitive operation involving the sort of implementation activities identified above: organization, interpretation, and application. Each of these activities requires that bureaucrats maintain communication with those who make the laws and those who must obey them. In other words, Weber has, in this second sentence, described a process seemingly identical with what Pressman and Wildavsky identify as implementation. As we have stressed, however, implementation is a dynamic process that may vary considerably among issues, thus raising doubts about a particular idealized version applicable everywhere under all circumstances. Third, Weber's accurate, almost axiomatic, statement that bureaucracy is "a power instrument of the first order—for the one who controls the bureaucratic apparatus" must be assessed in light of the probability that no single person or group will be in control in a pluralistic state. Indeed, there is unlikely to be a single bureaucratic apparatus.

Where does this analysis leave us in assessing the role of the bureaucracy? It suggests that while Weber may have identified certain ideal characteristics against which bureaucracies are measured, real-life government bureaus are highly dependent units, which must monitor the intentions of the rule makers and the demands of their clientele. And this conclusion supports the generalization, stated earlier, that bureaucrats are inevitably drawn into activities beyond the simple application of rules or standards to public problems and conflicts. The role of bureaucracy then is much more politically dynamic than is that conjured up by Weber's "machine" imagery.

The view of bureaucracy as a political institution stresses its need for support. It is not enough to promise efficiency; agencies need to nurture their constituencies every bit as much as legislators. Francis E. Rourke stresses this theme in his analysis of the bureaucratic policy system.

■ The power of government agencies can be looked upon as resting essentially on political support. Agencies have power when they command the allegiance of fervent and substantial constituencies. . . .

A first and fundamental source of power for administrative agencies in American society is their ability to attract outside support. Strength in a constituency is no less an asset for an American administrator than it is for a politician, and some agencies have succeeded in building outside support as formidable as that of any political organization. The lack of such support severely circumscribes the ability of an agency to achieve its goals, and may even threaten its survival as an organization.[21]

Different agencies require different strategies to get or maintain support. Some administer highly attractive and popular programs and can therefore depend on broad public support. Despite all their problems in the recent decade, social security programs continue to have impressive public backing. Similarly, a strong defense is supportable even in difficult economic times. Thus the Social Security Administration and the Department of Defense have definite advantages in bureaucratic politics. Less fortunate are those agencies that must administer the more marginal programs, such as foreign aid and support for the arts, and those that are highly conflictual, such as pollution control and public jobs programs. (Table 3.1 suggests areas that are favored in the 1980s.)

Not surprisingly, the need for support often leads to bureaucratic expansion, even imperialism of a sort. That is, a new and aggressive agency may seek to increase its jurisdiction by accommodating new programs, poaching on the territory of another agency, or taking over the responsibilities of a weaker agency. Matthew Holden, Jr., judges that this imperialism may be quite rational for the agency and for the whole bureaucratic system.

■   The administrative world in reality is a place of confusion and uncertainty, with false signals strewn about like dandelion seeds in an open meadow. Bureaucratic imperialism is a part of the process of clarification. Decisionmakers need some guides to the needs, preferences, ambitions and hopes of the various and constantly changing constituencies. Competition between agencies, engendered by competition between constituencies, is a vital part of the process of clarification.[22]

Holden is not proposing that competition among clienteles and agencies guarantees clarification. He asserts only that the motivation "of the administrative politician . . . is to maintain sufficient power for his agency."[23] That drive helps explain the conduct of bureaucratic infighting and should therefore contribute to a realistic appraisal of the role of bureaucracy in the policy process.

It is important to understand, among other things, that organization itself has impact in the policy process. The original purpose of organizing may be to implement a program. But as Weber and others clearly suggest, this purpose may be supplemented by other motivations, for example, expansion for its own sake (or for the sake of increasing one's power) or perhaps simply survival. These supplemental motivations may even dominate. James S. Fleming reports on his experience in the Public Health Service, specifically commenting on how bureaucrats use social science research.

■   What I found was what, in hindsight, I should have found: bureaucrats use social science for bureaucratic purposes (not necessarily for the purposes of democracy or humanity, or even to help solve public problems). Bureaucrats (the ones I worked with) didn't know much about social science, but they did know that the jargon and methodology of social science provided a certain measure of legitimacy and certainty (or the image of certainty) which they needed to advance bureaucratic causes—e.g., pleasing the boss, getting evaluation proposals (and therefore money) through the central evaluation office in the Department (usually headed by methodologists), controlling the consultants (who often present themselves as methodological priests), showing agency success, building agency support, competing with other agencies, controlling the field offices, and all the other things bureaucrats do to advance their cause and habits.[24]

Fleming has identified many of the supplemental motivations that are likely to drive an organization. Many, perhaps all, are compatible with program goals. Yet, as Fleming clearly suggests, the immediate needs of persons working in an organization may overshadow program goals. One cannot ignore the realities of personal and group behavior in studying program implementation.

Organization of the Federal Bureaucracy

The federal bureaucracy is composed of a wide variety of organizations, as any trip through the *U. S. Government Organizational Manual* graphically illustrates. First there are the cabinet-level departments, which presumably reflect and administer the most significant government functions. Since departmental secretaries are members of the president's cabinet, one might assume that they are in a favorable position for getting support. In fact, of course, presidents vary greatly in their use of the cabinet and in their relationships with individual departmental secretaries. Further, certain departments can be rather tightly organized and administered (for example, Treasury, Labor, Commerce), whereas others are no more than conglomerates of individual bureaus, some of which may have independent sources of power with either the president or Congress (for example, Defense, Energy, Health and Human Services). Departmental budgets vary dramatically, by as much as a factor of one-hundred. The size of the budget does not necessarily indicate importance, however. The Department of State typically has the smallest budget, but most would agree that it has enormous responsibilities. The cabinet-level departments at this writing are (with dates of creation):

Agriculture (1862)
Commerce (1913)
Defense (1947)
Education (1979)
Energy (1977)
Health and Human Services
(as Health, Education,
and Welfare in 1953;
redesignated in 1979)
Housing and Urban Development
(1965)
Interior (1849)
Justice (1870)
Labor (1913)
State (1789)
Transportation (1966)
Treasury (1789)

Second are the myriad agencies, many of which have major responsibilities and sometimes larger budgets than a department. They do not have cabinet status, though an agency head may be designated a member of the cabinet by the president. They may eventually become departments, however. The Departments of Energy, Health and Human Services, Housing and Urban Development, and Transportation are all examples of agencies (or groups of agencies) that were elevated to a higher status. The more important agencies are:

Community Services Administration (CSA)
Environmental Protection Agency (EPA)
General Services Administration (GSA)
National Aeronautics and Space Administration (NASA)
National Labor Relations Board (NLRB)
National Science Foundation (NSF)
Office of Personnel Management (OPM)
Selective Service System
Small Business Administration (SBA)
United States Arms Control and Disarmament Agency
Veterans Administration (VA)
United States Information Agency (USIA)

As the titles of these units indicate, they vary in terms of their organizational structure (agency, administration, board, commission, foundation), leadership, and scope of responsibility. They also serve very different types of clientele and thus face enormously varying problems in building and maintaining political support. For example, GSA and OPM are essentially "in-government" service agencies—GSA for buildings, property, and supplies; OPM for personnel management; NASA works with and spawns technologically oriented industries; NSF relates to the universities and private research organizations. Each has special problems in its dealings with Congress, the president, its "constituents," and the general public.

Third are the regulatory commissions, whose independent status derives from the long terms of the commissioners and their protection from arbitrary control of the president. These units are charged with regulating practices that Congress has determined require control, though it must be noted that regulatory authority is given as well to other agencies (e.g., EPA) or units within departments (like the Food and Drug Administration in Health and Human Services). The regulatory agencies currently are:

Civil Aeronautics Board (CAB)
Federal Communications Commission (FCC)
Federal Election Commission (FEC)
Federal Energy Regulatory Commission (FERC)
Federal Maritime Commission (FMC)
Federal Reserve Board (the "Fed")
Federal Trade Commission (FTC)
Interstate Commerce Commission (ICC)
Nuclear Regulatory Commission (NRC)
Securities and Exchange Commission (SEC)

Fourth are several government corporations established to carry out specific functions that presumably bear some relationship to ordinary business operations. The most recent example is the Postal Service, which was reorganized from a cabinet-level department into a government corporation. Other examples are the Tennessee Valley Authority, the Federal Deposit Insurance Corporation, the Reconstruction Finance Corporation of the 1930s, and the Overseas Private Investment Corporation.

Any number of other types of boards, commissions, councils, offices, companies, foundations, institutions, and authorities populate the executive branch of government and are involved in some manner of implementation. But special mention must be made of the units within the Executive Office of the President. Though typically engaged in formulation activities, these instrumentalities help the president oversee and coordinate the implementation of programs. Perhaps more than with the other agencies, their responsibilities span the functions identified here, primarily due to their location in the hierarchy. Some of these units are more permanent than others. Since they are close to the White House, reorganizations may occur to suit particular presidential preferences and styles. Among the more permanent of these units are the following (listed by the title used in the Reagan administration):

Central Intelligence Agency (CIA)
Council of Economic Advisers (CEA)
Council on Environmental Quality (CEQ)
Council on Wage and Price Stability (CWPS)
National Security Council (NSC)
Office of Management and Budget (OMB)
Office of Science and Technology (OST)
Office of the U. S. Trade Representative

The great variety of organizations suggests that the location of a program can make a great deal of difference in its implementation. Knowing this, promoters of a particular program may try to create a new agency, get the program located in an agency or department known to be sympathetic, or perhaps seek reorganization of an existing agency scheduled to get a program. Victory in the legislative halls may be short-lived if the program goes to the wrong place in the bureaucracy. At any one point the following situations may exist:

1. *An old-line agency continues to administer increments of policy as these are legitimated over time.* No major shift in the structure or status of the agency has occurred. (Countless examples.)

2. *A new agency is created within an existing parent department.* The policy to be administered represents a relatively new area of concern, but the decision is made to include it within the jurisdiction of an existing department or division. (Example: Rural Development in the Department of Agriculture.)

3. *An existing agency is upgraded in status.* Policy developments in an issue area or several related issue areas are interpreted to require departmental status for the administrative units. (Examples: creation of the Departments of Energy and Housing and Urban Development.)

4. *No agency exists.* The policy to be administered represents a relatively new area of concern, and the decision is made to create a new agency (perhaps for strategic reasons). (Examples: Office of Economic Opportunity—since dissolved, National Aeronautics and Space Administration, Environmental Protection Agency.)

5. *An old-line agency determines, or it is determined for such an agency, that policy developments dictate a reorganization to adjust to shifts in administrative activities.* (Example: reorganization of defense-related agencies, leading to their unification in the Department of Defense.)

Many other possibilities exist for creating or rearranging departments, agencies, bureaus, and divisions. The point is that implementation of policy may vary depending on the particular stage of agency development. Anthony Downs suggests that "every bureau is initially dominated by either advocates or zealots."[25] The Office of Economic Opportunity, which administered the poverty program (the agency has since been dissolved), and the Peace Corps are good examples.

With maturation comes increased efficiency, greater knowledge, and more formalized procedures. Downs proposes the "law of increasing conservatism": "All organizations tend to become more conservative as they get older, unless they experience periods of rapid growth [for example, expansion of number of agencies; item 2 in the preceding list] or internal turnover [for example, reorganization of an agency; item 5]."[26] Such developments affect individual administrative actors. The pressure to become more conservative increases as an organization ages. An organization's way of protecting itself affects the application of policy, the participation of other actors outside the agency, the interpretations of policy by agency bureaucrats, and perhaps the perceptions agency bureaucrats have of public problems to which the program is directed.

These two brief sections on organization have moved from a discussion of the inevitability of bureaucracy in complex society to an overview of federal bureaucratic organization and a review of how the variation in organization may affect program implementation. It would be difficult to overstate the importance of bureaucracy. It has enormous advantages in the policy process: control of information, expert knowledge, a "departmental ideology."[27] It would be wrong, however, to portray the bureaucracy as a monolith or to suggest that it is somehow impervious to outside pressures. The bureaucracy tends to reflect the politics of the country, which in the United States is highly pluralistic. No one controls the bureaucracy sufficiently to permit it to take charge of American politics. As Douglas Yates argues, "the structure of public bureaucracies is characterized by interest-group behavior, fragmentation, and conflict and competition."[28] These characteristics should lead us to expect a variable role for organization and bureaucracy among policy programs.

Interpretation

The guiding question for the implementer is, What do I do now? A program has been approved, words are on paper (often in "legalese"), and an organization is in place. It is now time to give practical meaning to the words, to declare what they will mean in regard to specific cases and real problems. George C. Edwards states that:

■   The first requirement for effective policy implementation is that those who are to implement a decision *must know what they are supposed to do.* . . .

    If policies are to be implemented properly, implementation directives must not only be received, but they must also be clear. If they are not, implementors will be confused about what they should do, and they will have discretion to impose their own views on the implementation of policies, views that may be different from those of their superiors.[29]

Effective program implementation is likely to be rare if clarity is a prerequisite. It appears to be an unwritten law that the more complex the social issue, the more ambiguous the social policy. And, as Edwards notes, ambiguity may lead to discretion for implementers, though they will not necessarily use it to expand their authority. Instead, they may use it to avoid particularly difficult issues.

The central point is that lawmaking does not conclude the policy process even if we have what Theodore J. Lowi calls the "rule of law."[30] A clear standard must also be applied, which involves, at a minimum, a process by which implementers learn what the standard is and develop means for applying it. Where the standard is not clear, however, implementers are faced with heavier responsibilities. Whether and how they assume these responsibilities depends on a multitude of conditions. Surely among the most important of these is the implementers' estimate of the available resources. Among these resources *political support* rates highly. Thus, for example, one observes different behavior in implementing environmental regulations in the Carter administration than in the Reagan administration. The laws have not changed that much, but the interpretations of these laws in terms of practical application have changed considerably.

That the implementer must respond to the question, What do I do now? disturbs many people. It guarantees frustration for the tidy mind seeking closure in the policy process. It is not surprising, therefore, that formulas for good administration or effective implementation are developed. Typically these formulas emphasize clarity, precision, consistency, priority setting, adequate resources, and the like. The study of public administration is replete with these guides to efficient management.

The more contemporary analyses of implementation (Bardach, Edwards, Hargrove, Hofferbert, Mazmanian and Sabatier, Pressman and Wildavsky, Ripley and Franklin, Van Horn) explain the sometimes dramatic differences in implementation behavior in terms of variability of social, political, legal, and organizational conditions. Of these scholars, Mazmanian and Sabatier offer the most elaborate set of variables.[31]

1. Those associated with the tractability of the problem: "Totally apart from the difficulties associated with the implementation of government programs, some social problems are simply much easier to deal with than others."[32] Variables include technical difficulties, diversity of target group behavior, target group size, behavioral change required.

2. Those associated with the extent to which the statute will structure implementation: " . . . original policy makers can substantially affect the attainment of legal objectives by utilizing the levers at their disposal to coherently structure the implementation process."[33] Variables include clear and consistent objectives, adequate causal theory (how b will follow from a), sufficient start-up funds, integration among implementing agents and agencies, stipulation of decision rules, commitment to statutory objectives, formal access by outsiders.

3. Nonstatutory variables affecting implementation: "The policy outputs of implementing agencies are essentially a function of the interaction between legal structure and political process."[34] Variables include socioeconomic conditions and technology, public support, attitudes and resources of clienteles, support from above, commitment and skills of implementing officials.

This list offers a useful inventory of factors that help explain the differences in the perceived success of implementers in carrying out a program. Mazmanian and Sabatier use these factors in studying several policy areas and, as expected, find dramatically varying results.[35] There may be a best way to implement, but there is no uniform method by which implementation occurs.

The policy process relies heavily on the communication of words and their meaning. Interpretation—"What did they mean by that?"—is crucial to understanding what goes on at every stage of decision making. It is stressed here because we often assume that laws, decisions, directives, and orders are definitive. Often they are not, and greater attention must therefore be given to the ways in which implementers interpret their responsibilities. This analysis should include an inquiry into the sources of interpretation. To whom does the implementer turn? Who is judged to be authoritative? These questions lead to explorations of the amount of discretion implementers think they have. The answers may also help to explain the *delay* that Bardach identifies as the "one attribute of the implementation process that *everyone* would agree was symptomatic of 'pathology'."

■ Implementation takes a long time, much longer than most of the program sponsors had hoped it would take and longer even than the law's hypothetical "reasonable man" might have expected. . . . If certain outcomes are going to be achieved eventually, why not earlier rather than later? ask the policy designers and advocates.[36]

The answer lies largely in the risks, complexities, and uncertainties of trying to decide what to do.

Another important reason to explore the what, how, and who of interpretation is that such study inevitably focuses attention on the expectations of implementers and others for a policy program. This type of inquiry drives one to the very core of policy substance, to the question of what policy makers thought might happen when a program was approved and implemented. One may find, of course, that they had very little in mind, that approving the program was itself a symbolic act. That finding, too, is very important for understanding subsequent activity. Erwin C. Hargrove speaks of "the missing link" in his fine review of the study of implementation.[37] It is my view that the study of interpretation at the point of implementation will supply many of these linkages.

Application: Doing the Job

Application simply refers to doing the job. It includes "providing goods and services" (Ripley and Franklin) as well as other programmatic objectives (for example, regulation and defense). There are volumes of literature on this topic (under the rubric of *public administration* or *policy implementation*). Here I simply encourage you to adopt the same interactive approach that is emphasized elsewhere in this book. Application too is inexorably linked to other activities. It is a dynamic process because it is connected to other policy activities by the human linkages of people trying to do their jobs.

Metaphors are very helpful as tools for forcing one to consider alternative conceptions of politics and administration. Eugene Bardach uses "the idea of 'games' " as "a master metaphor that directs attention and stimulates insight" in studying implementation.[38] By their nature, games involve rules, players, strategies, winners, losers; their use as a metaphor undermines the idea that there is only one way to accomplish a particular goal. I know of no game in which victory can be achieved by only one strategy. One need not rely on a master metaphor, however, to achieve the current goal. It may be enough simply to remind oneself constantly that politics is everywhere, even invading activities whose participants earn their living by denying its influence.

Adjustments in either organization or interpretation during program application are not at all unusual. A politically feasible interpretation of authority may turn out to be impractical in the field. Application is often a dynamic process in which the implementer or enforcer is guided generally by program directives or standards and specifically by actual circumstances. For example, meeting the national ambient air quality standards for carbon monoxide, hydrocarbons, photochemical oxidants, and oxides of nitrogen required that cities alter their patterns of automobile transportation. Proposals to this end had to be submitted to the states, which in turn were required to send plans to EPA in Washington for approval. A part of the plan for the city of Pittsburgh included a rush-hour ban on passenger cars carrying fewer than three persons from one of the busiest outbound parkway ramps in the central city. Enforcement of the ban was announced on a Thursday (to go into effect on the following Wednesday), the Pennsylvania Department of Transportation was swamped with complaints from the public on Friday, and the ban was postponed for 90 days on Saturday (with EPA approval). Adjustments to reality are not often so abrupt but they occur on a daily basis in government.

Murray Edelman, in *The Symbolic Uses of Politics*, is particularly instructive on this matter of accommodating even unambiguous laws to the circumstances at hand. He uses the example of speed limits, pointing out that behavior is adapted to the assumption that "most speeders will not be caught or fined."

■ . . . drivers speed when the chance of being caught is slight or considered worth taking. Policemen stop some but not all violators, and let some of these off with a warning. As long as the game is played in this way, both drivers and policemen accept the order of things fairly contentedly. . . . Similarly, employers accept health, safety, child labor, and minimum wage laws on the assumption that inspectors will appear at the plant only once in a while, and that if they are caught in violations on *these* occasions, a fine may have to be paid.[39]

Edelman further illustrates what may happen when the law is too strenuously enforced with the case of a certain Officer Muller, who ticketed state and city officials' cars parked in a nonparking zone near city hall in Chicago. "The conscientious Mr. Muller was assigned to a remote beat."[40] Clearly judgment is as much valued in applying legal remedies to the problem as is an accurate understanding of the remedies. While rules may not strictly be made to be broken, they are typically made to be prudently applied.

We all can cite cases similar to that of Officer Muller. Normally we use them to illustrate favoritism in the system. Edelman tells us that such adjustments are common and therefore to be expected in all administrations. He describes the process of accommodation as "mutual role-taking."

■ . . . so far as the great bulk of law enforcement is concerned "rules" are established through mutual role-taking; by looking at the consequences of possible acts from the point of view of the tempted individual and from the point of view of the impact of his acts upon the untempted. The result is a set of unchallenged rules implicitly permitting evasions and explicitly fixing penalties. Administrators are thereby able to avoid the sanctions of politically powerful groups by accepting their premises as valid; while at the same time they justify this behavior in the verbal formulas provided in the rules.[41]

And further:

■ Politics always involve conflicts. For the individual decision maker group conflict means ambivalence, and ambivalence can be described in behavioral terms as the concomitant of taking of incompatible roles. . . . Enforcers and "enforced" alike assume both the role of the potential violator and the role of his victim. Out of their responses to such mutual role-taking come the rules as actually acted out; the specification of the loopholes, penalties, and rewards that reflect an acceptable adjustment of these incompatible roles.[42]

This analysis surely describes an active and ever-changing process and thus is well suited to the emphasis of this book. It not only assigns a low probability to literal application or enforcement of the law but suggests that those making such an effort may well face problems within their organization. This interpretation is at variance with the more traditional concepts of public administration and scientific management, which stress the establishment of policy goals to be effectively and efficiently implemented by an objective civil service.

The Intergovernmental Partnership

"When the federal government has a domestic policy job to do, it increasingly relies on an intergovernmental grant to do it."[43] This statement by Donald F. Kettl has profound significance for understanding developments in program implementation. The intergovernmental network for administering federal domestic programs proliferated between the immediate post–World War II period and the 1980s. Growth in federal grants has been phenomenal—from a few billion dollars annually in the 1950s to $100 billion annually in the 1980s. Deil S. Wright makes the following comparisons:

■   In 1950 federal aid was less than 9% of all federal domestic outlays and climbed to over 18% in 1965. By 1970 it exceeded 20%, above which it has remained through the 1970s and into the 1980s. Federal aid was barely above 10% of state/local expenditures in 1950 and 1955, but it jumped to nearly 15% by 1965. Steady rises moved the proportion to nearly one-fifth by 1970 and to more than 23% in 1975. In 1977–1981 it exceeded 25%.[44]

Much of this dramatic growth occurred as a result of the Great Society programs enacted during the 1960s. Richard H. Leach describes what happened:

■   More new programs involving appropriations of federal aid were initiated by the 85th through the 89th Congresses (1957–1966) than by all the previous sessions of Congress since the beginning of the Republic. The 89th Congress (1965–1966) alone passed no fewer than 136 major domestic bills, including seventeen new resource development programs, seventeen new educational programs, twenty-one new health programs, fifteen new economic development programs, twelve new programs on city problems, and four for manpower training. By 1969, there were all told fifty different programs for vocational and job training, thirty-five programs for housing, sixty-two for community facilities, and twenty-eight for recreation, as well as countless others in a great variety of fields.[45]

It comes as no surprise, I am sure, that federal money influenced the organization, interpretation, and application activities of state and local officials. As Wright notes, "To say that state and local officials must pay attention to actions in Washington, D.C., is an understatement; what happens there is part of the daily operating reality and routine for thousands of these officials."[46] These developments instruct us to look beyond Washington for the implementers of federal domestic programs.[47]

We are also well advised to trace populations of implementers by issue area.

There is no one implementation system. Terry Sanford, former governor of North Carolina, refers to picket-fence federalism. "The lines of authority, the concerns and interests, the flow of the money, and the direction of the programs run straight down like a number of pickets stuck into the ground."[48] Once again we are instructed to pay attention to the issues and the programs as a way of understanding how the institutions work. That is, whether it be public housing, vocational education, agriculture, urban renewal, pollution control, welfare, highways, or whatever, we should search for the connections among federal, state, and local officials (as well as the ties between them and private persons) that are important in putting the program into effect. Thus, for example, when state and local housing officials hear of a new federal program in their area, they know their lives are about to change again. Many are as attentive to what goes on in Washington as to what goes on in their more immediate governments. Figure 8.1 graphically displays picket-fence federalism.

Morton Grodzins has described all of this as "marble-cake federalism," in which there is a high degree of mixing and sharing of governmental functions.[49] While few would disagree with Grodzins, the nature of this intergovernmental sharing nevertheless varies over time with the growth and change in programs and means for implementing them. Deil S. Wright has studied these

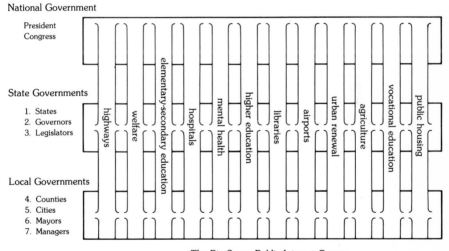

National Government

President
Congress

State Governments

1. States
2. Governors
3. Legislators

Local Governments

4. Counties
5. Cities
6. Mayors
7. Managers

highways · welfare · elementary-secondary education · hospitals · mental health · higher education · libraries · airports · urban renewal · agriculture · vocational education · public housing

The Big Seven Public Interest Groups

1. Council of State Governments
2. National Governors Association
3. National Conference of State Legislatures
4. National Association of County Officials
5. National League of Cities
6. U.S. Conference of Mayors
7. International City Management Association

FIGURE 8.1   Picket-fence federalism: a schematic representation. *(Source: Wright, 1982.)*

variations, and his conclusions are offered in table 8.1. The trends identified here must be studied in conjunction with the growth of federal aid and involvement cited earlier. Note in particular the growth of various types of grants in the post–World War II period and how these grants tend to focus or channel intergovernmental relations during the concentrated phase, proliferate with "a superficial appearance of fusion" during the creative phase, fragment during an uncertain and tense competitive phase, and simply get overloaded during the calculative phase. It is entirely possible that the last phase will result in remedies that reduce the federal role in the future. Certainly that is the intention of the Reagan administration.[50]

The purpose of including Wright's phases of intergovernmental relations is merely to illustrate the variation over time in the participation and configuration of domestic program implementation. Students interested in pursuing details should read Wright's important book *Understanding Intergovernmental Relations*. There is one further point that should be emphasized, however, in relying on these phases for further exploration of program implementation. Wright warns that "the phases are less like repetitive linear phenomena and more like developmental geological rock strata."[51]

■   Thus, like successive, somewhat porous strata that have been superimposed on each other . . . no phase ends at an exact point. . . . Each phase is continu-

TABLE 8.1   Phases of intergovernmental relations (IGR)

Phase descriptor	Main problems	Participants' perceptions	IGR mechanisms	Federalism metaphor	Approximate climax period
Conflict	Defining boundaries Proper spheres	Antagonistic Adversary Exclusivity	Statutes Courts Regulations	Layer-cake federalism	Nineteenth century–1930s
Cooperative	Economic distress International threat	Collaboration Complementary Mutuality Supportive	National planning Formula grants Tax credits	Marble-cake federalism	1930s–1950s
Concentrated	Service needs Physical development	Professionalism Objectivity Neutrality Functionalism	Categorical grants Service standards	Water taps (focused or channeled)	1940s–1960s
Creative	Urban–metropolitan Disadvantaged clients	National goals Great society Grantsmanship	Program planning Project grants Participation	Flowering (proliferated and fused)	1950s–1960s
Competitive	Coordination Program effectiveness Delivery systems Citizen access	Disagreement Tension Rivalry	Grant consolidation Revenue sharing Reorganization	Picket-fence (fragmented)	1960s–1970s
Calculative	Accountability Bankruptcy Constraints Dependency Federal role Public confidence	Gamesmanship Fungibility Overload	General aid entitlements Bypassing Loans Crosscutting regulations	Façade (confrontational)	1970s–1980s

Source: Wright (1982).

ously present in greater or lesser measure, bearing the weight, so to speak, of the overlying strata . . .; each produces carryover effects much wider than the climax periods indicated in Table [8.1]. . . . The task of an IGR analyst is like that of a geologist—to drill or probe the several strata and from the samples make inferences about the substructure of the terrain.[52]

Comprehending the scope and nature of domestic program implementation is difficult in the extreme. The growth in complexity of intergovernmental contact and dependency contributes to this difficulty. If we want to understand how the domestic policy process works, we have to acknowledge these developments and choose our topics accordingly. What this brief section advises is that most domestic program implementation includes participants from all three levels of government and that the mix of problems, perceptions, and mechanisms varies over time.

Two Cases of Implementation

An abundant literature on policy implementation has been published since the last edition of this book (see the Bibliography). Many of these works include cases to describe various aspects of implementation. I have therefore selected just two cases to illustrate the problems of organizing, interpreting, and applying federal programs. First is a brief examination of how an existing agency is restructured to administer a quantum jump in federal responsibility for education. Second is a case of modern "bundling." In an effort to reduce the federal role somewhat, block grants have been developed that provide for greater discretion at the state and local levels. One such program, the Community Development Block Grants, is described.

From Washington to the Classroom

The Elementary and Secondary Education Act of 1965 (ESEA) declared that:

■ In recognition of the special educational needs of children of low-income families and the impact that concentrations of low-income families have on the ability of local educational agencies to support adequate educational programs, the Congress hereby declares it to be the policy of the United States to provide financial assistance . . . to local educational agencies serving areas with concentrations of children from low-income families to expand and improve their educational programs by various means (including preschool programs) which contribute particularly to meeting the special educational needs of educationally deprived children. (Title I, Sec. 201, Elementary and Secondary Education Act of 1965.)

Here was a deceptively simple goal: aid children who need special help. But, of course, those associated with formulating and adopting this legislation understood its broader implications. With school consolidation in recent decades, few, if any, school districts in the nation failed to qualify for program benefits. For the fact is that while the rich/poor distinction between school districts remains, it is considerably less sharp than it used to be. Thus, here was a program that required the development and maintenance of contact and communication between Washington, the 50 states, and nearly 25,000 school districts. Further, since the act carried only a one-year authorization, administrators had to act fast to justify an extension. "The federal aid advocates had won a stunning victory, but they knew full well that they would have to renew the battle again the following session [of Congress]."[53] Finally, there was little or no organizational memory available to direct this massive operation. The U. S. Office of Education (USOE) had been a relatively obscure unit in the Department of Health, Education, and Welfare (HEW); and many, if not most, school districts "had no previous experience in carrying out federally connected projects of any kind."[54]

Whole books have been written on this subject. Consequently the most we can do is illustrate a few of the more difficult problems of implementation. Three topics in particular are emphasized here: the reorganization of the Office of Education, the myriad intergovernmental connections that had to be established, and the early efforts to interpret and apply the law.

"The job of administering Public Law 89-10 [ESEA] fell to an agency with a long and pedestrian past."[55] In their full treatment of ESEA, Stephen K. Bailey and Edith K. Mosher list the many problems of the Office of Education as an organizational unit before its reorganization: atomization and specialization (powerful "guilds of professionals" running the place), superannuated personnel and personnel systems (an average age of over 50 among the professional staff), archaic financial and management information systems, an unrationalized bureau and field structure (it had "'growed' like Topsy"), anomie within the executive branch, and a constant fear of the charge of federal control.[56]

Anticipating the passage of a comprehensive federal aid to education program, the commissioner of education, Francis Keppel, well understood the need to retool this clumsy and outmoded structure. Occupied himself with the legislative battles necessary to pass ESEA, Keppel obtained the services of one Henry Loomis as deputy commissioner and charged him with the responsibility of reorganizing the office. Described as a "no-nonsense type," Loomis "began what was probably one of the most extraordinary, bruising, controversial, if in some ways effective, administrative operations in the recent annals of the federal government."[57] The strategy was simple in concept, but required extraordinary skill in execution. A special task force (not drawn from HEW) was appointed to study the organizational insufficiencies of USOE, and its recommendations were effected in a very short period of time. The theory behind this move was that outside help was necessary in rationalizing and supporting the changes, and that carefully paced implementation of reforms over time only invited resistance from the many fiefdoms in USOE. "Quick and dirty" was thus the chosen method. The results were stunning, if a little traumatic. Bailey and Mosher describe it as follows:

■ . . . less than two weeks after submission of the report, the reorganization *was effected.* The speed of action and the fact that the plan was shattering to *all* vested interests produced a reaction of numbed, bewildered, bitter acquiescence. . . . The anguish can only be imagined. The ensuing, if temporary, administrative chaos was shattering. For days and weeks, people could not find each other's offices—sometimes not even their own. Telephone extensions connected appropriate parties only by coincidence. A large number of key positions in the new order were, vacant or were occupied by acting directors who were frequently demoralized by status ambiguity and eventual status loss. . . . And all of this came at a time of maximum work load.[58]

It should be noted further that HEW itself was undergoing important personnel and policy shifts.

But organizational accommodation in Washington was only part of the story. Education has traditionally been a state and local concern, and state departments of education, local school boards, and other local policy and administrative apparatus exist to develop and implement policy in this sphere. Now the "feds" were to be heavily involved too, with the dollar bill as their calling card. Though the national government had, in the past, provided various types of special support, here was the first attempt to fashion a federal-state-local education policy system. Title I of ESEA was the principal stimulus for this development in its provisions for aid to low-income children. The intergovernmental distribution of responsibility for this program was as follows:

The United States Office of Education

1. Develops and disseminates regulations, guidelines, and other materials regarding the approval of Title I projects.
2. Reviews and assesses the progress under Title I throughout the nation.

State education agencies

1. Approve proposed local projects in accordance with federal regulations and guidelines.
2. Assist local educational agencies in the development of projects.
3. Submit state evaluative reports to USOE.

Local education agencies

1. Identify the educationally deprived children in the areas where there are high concentrations of low-income families and determine their special educational needs.
2. Develop and implement approved projects to fulfill the intent of Title I.[59]

The trained eye can spot mountains of paper with each set of responsibilities. An experienced observer would also see any number of possibilities for tension among the various levels of government in this distribution of responsibilities. An elaborate system of interdependency was created that was bound to result in conflict. As federal funding increased, it became clear that no one layer could accomplish its goals without the others. As Frederick M. Wirt and Michael W. Kirst point out, federal and state governments depend on local governments to run the schools, and the locals depend on federal and state financial aid.[60] Further, any number of private, citizen, and professional groups were involved in applying this policy, including groups representing low-income families.

I have stressed throughout this text that laws passed are not laws universally understood or enforced. Not surprisingly, many educators throughout the nation were ill informed about the specifics of ESEA. After all, they were engaged on a daily basis in running the schools. "Congressional consideration of ESEA had progressed so rapidly that few state and local school authorities understood the Act's specific recommendations or its thrust toward certain basic educational changes."[61] The net result was an uncertain agency undergoing drastic reorganization administering a massive new program to a well-established clientele, some of whom were uninformed on federal policy, most of whom were wary of federal intentions. ESEA was to be accomplished in this context.

Bailey and Mosher conclude that the process of implementation

■ involved an administrative dialectic—a series of promulgations from USOE which were preceded, accompanied, and followed by inputs and feedbacks from affected clientele. The process was cumbersome, and involved both underprescriptions and overprescriptions from Washington.[62]

This description fits well with the generalizations set forth in this chapter that stress the interactive and dynamic qualities of implementation. It properly ignores the neat flow-chart process of administration wherein an agency simply implements legislative intent. Bailey and Mosher are, in essence, describing a process of interpretation, estimation, and adjustment.

In their study of implementing economic development policy, Pressman and Wildavsky stress that many decision points are involved in implementing any major program. They conclude that "the probability of agreement by every participant on each decision point must be exceedingly high for there to be any chance at all that a program will be brought to completion."[63] The many tasks associated with just getting money to qualified school districts involved countless decision points. At the federal level, the initial tasks—those required just to get the process underway—were as follows:

1. The development of standards and procedures for the funding and control of authorizations;
2. The construction of ground rules and guidelines for educational programming and project design;
3. The preparation and analysis of reports and other informational and administrative data.[64]

Many of these actions were taken in consultation with state and local officials. "Just as the drafting of ESEA involved a delicate balance of intergovernmental interests, so the development of ground rules became a matter of vital concern to all the affected groups."[65] But though guidelines are essential, they too require interpretation and adjustment if a comprehensive federal program is to be adapted to the social, economic, and political diversity represented by the 50 states. Thus the many decision points associated with preparing the basis for program implementation were multiplied many more times as local school districts actually developed plans to spend the money. All this activity consumed several months and millions of hours of work at all levels of government. As David B. Truman correctly concludes, "The administration of a statute is, properly speaking, an extension of the legislative process."[66]

With the passage of ESEA, one of the last remaining exclusive state and local responsibilities had settled within the national decision-making orbit. Norman C. Thomas has observed: "It has often been asserted that 'education is a local responsibility, a state function, and a national concern.'"[67] After ESEA "there was no longer serious debate over the propriety of a major federal role in education."[68] Little wonder, then, that the initial stages of implementation were complex and often confused. A new intergovernmental decisional system was in the making. Bailey and Mosher cite David B. Truman's view that administrators are forced "to seek . . . a means of converting the controversial into the routine."[69] In the case of ESEA, educational officials were handed "an adjustment, among conflicting interests" (Truman's definition of a mandate in this setting) that no one knew for certain would last.

One important organizational development in 1979 surely contributed to the continuance of a strong federal role in education: A Department of Education was created. It even survived the early threats by the Reagan administration to disband it.

New Grants for Old

The preceding case illustrates the so-called categorical grant: federal funds available for a specific purpose, to be allocated and spent under specific conditions. Such programs were heavily criticized in the 1970s for preempting state and local decision making. The federal government was charged with setting state and local priorities and then managing the handling of these priorities. President Nixon was determined to make changes. In his 1971 State of the Union Message he proposed a "new federalism" to reduce federal control but maintain federal aid. State and local governments were to receive relatively unrestricted grants based on a formula that accounted for population, tax effort, and certain other factors related to need. This program, referred to as "general revenue sharing," received broad support in Congress.

A second type of proposal was not as immediately popular. Grants referred to as "special revenue sharing" would be allocated within certain broad areas; for example, urban development, education, transportation, and job training. State and local governments would be permitted discretion in spending within these areas. No federal approval was required for plans, and matching funds were not required (as was typical for categorical grants).

President Nixon's special revenue sharing proposals were not approved.

Many members of Congress were unwilling to grant such wide discretion to state and local governments. Donald F. Kettl explains the negative reaction as follows:

■ They [the state and local governments] might . . . ignore the needs of the poor and minorities and concentrate the money instead on the privileged. Furthermore, without federal supervision, mismanagement or perhaps even fraud might weaken the programs.[70]

At the same time there was widespread dissatisfaction with the manner in which aid programs were being administered. As is typical in the American political system, a compromise was developed. The "block grant" consolidated several programs within a general area (for example, job training or law enforcement) and allowed more latitude in using the money, but provided for limited federal review of plans.

■ The federal agencies administering the programs were charged with setting broad guidelines to govern the programs' mechanics, and the subnational government bore the responsibility for executing the projects. The federal job was to establish a set of rules neither so restrictive as to rob subnational governments of their new discretion nor so loose as to allow evasion of national program goals.[71]

One such program was in the area of urban development. The Housing and Community Development Act of 1974 established Community Development Block Grants (CDBG), which consolidated ten existing categorical grants.[72] There were federal requirements, but far fewer than in the previous programs. "The . . . primary objective, as stated in the statute, was the creation of 'viable urban communities by providing decent housing and a suitable living environment for persons of low and moderate income.'"[73] CDBG was reauthorized in 1977 and again in 1980.

The implementation of CDBG programs illustrates many of the basic problems associated with federalism. By this concept, a political system seeks to centralize without losing the advantages of decentralization. Federalism guarantees continual conflict and compromise between the national and subnational governments. Thus any one program (like CDBG) inevitably is in the process of adjustment—just the kind of ambiguity, uncertainty, and change we have come to expect in major national domestic politics.

How and when was the CDBG program organized, interpreted, and applied? The simple answer seems to be: continually and all over the place. It was in the nature of the greater latitude provided to lower-level governments that ways of getting the job done would vary. At the most general level, implementation involved elected officials, administrators, and citizen groups at the local level, and the Department of Housing and Urban Development (HUD) at the national level. Participation in particular programs was determined by local conditions. "Compared to their participation during the categorical era, elected officials [at the local level] have taken a greater part in community development programs under CDBG."[74] Perhaps this follows from the greater discretion involved, which permits officials to satisfy political goals. But the main point is that greater local discretion makes central control much more difficult. Either one trusts the locals to do what is right or it is necessary to recreate mechanisms to regulate their behavior.

Kettl found that the four cities he studied in Connecticut were "overloaded" in their attempts to implement the CDBG program. They were put in the position of having to organize to meet the demand, interpret their authority, and apply difficult policy choices. Here is some of what Kettl has to say on each subject:

■ 1. *Organizing to meet the demand*

CDBG stimulated huge new demands for federal money. The program's advance advertising was as a no-strings revenue sharing program, and this created a grab-bag mentality from which CDBG never advanced. . . . Local officials, especially in the first years of the program, were deluged with far more demands for projects than local officials could hope to satisfy.

■ 2. *Interpreting authority*

Despite HUD's increasing regulation of the program, local officials still had far broader discretion in how to use the money than they did in the categoricals. They could decide which functional areas would receive how much money. which geographical areas would receive the most attention, and . . . which projects would be funded. . . . No longer could they say, "We have to do it this way because the feds make us" or "Your part of the city cannot be included because of federal regulations."

■ 3. *Applying the decisions*

For local officials, these administrative chores were imposing. Each city funded many projects, sometimes over 100 in each year, and administrators had to supervise and account for each project. Because of HUD's principle of supporting local discretion, the agency gave little technical assistance. Building local administrative strength to meet these needs was a slow and uneasy process.[75]

The CDBG program illustrates, among other things, that doing business differently isn't all that easy. The grant of authority can be more burdensome than might be expected. Not surprisingly, the intergovernmental relationships changed from what they were when the programs were categorical in nature and continued to change as the program matured. Kettl and Carl Van Horn, in their separate studies, agree that implementation under the block grant method led to changes in community development standards. Kettl noted a shift from redistributive programs (aid to the poor) to distributive services (more general public improvements). Van Horn noted an "emphasis on physical development and deemphasis on social services." The two more or less agree on the reasons why this shift occurred.

■ *Kettl*: City governments are organizations in the business of distributing basic services: garbage collection, fire protection, road repair, and policy protection.[76]

■   *Van Horn*: The attitudes of local elected officials and their response to the politics of community development led to projects designed to capture broad-based political support.[77]

Very simply put: if local officials are given discretion to implement a federal program, they will do it in a way that will benefit them politically. Organization, interpretation, and application will proceed accordingly, whether or not they produce the policy desired by federal officials.

These developments led to a reevaluation by HUD, resulting in what Kettl refers to as "creeping categorization." Here is how it happened:

■   The program as enacted by Congress contained a great deal of unclear and ambiguous language. In releasing its first regulations on the program, HUD, trying to act in the spirit of the New Federalism, used most of the act's language. A host of questions predictably arose. How thoroughly should HUD's area offices review local applications? Was the purchase of Little League baseball uniforms an eligible expenditure? What did "maximum feasible priority" of the needs of the poor mean? . . . The questions . . . led to more than 100 pages of regulations in the *Federal Register* during the program's first two years. Each new . . . regulation had a dual effect: it increased the red tape associated with the program, and it drew at least a small measure of discretion back to HUD from the cities.[78]

Program implementation through block grants represents a compromise approach between the narrower categorical grant, with its many strings attached, and the freedom of general revenue sharing. Thus it is not totally satisfying either to those who want to effect national change or to those who want the federal government to supply money but no controls. Partly for these reasons, a program like CDBG illustrates particularly clearly the dynamics of intergovernmental program implementation. Whatever else we learn, we surely are advised not to oversimplify the problem of implementing federal intentions at the local level.

Summary

With implementation we watch policy actors move toward the problems of society, presumably equipped to relieve certain of people's needs. It is a simple matter, of course, when a hungry man asks for food and those with authority, and the resources, say, "Give the man food." We have seen that the goals and directives of programs are seldom so unambiguous. Nor are implementing organizations designed for such swift and purposeful action. Rather, major federal programs are multifaceted, subject to varying interpretations, competitive with other programs at various levels of government, administered by a labyrinth of organizational units throughout government, and, therefore, the object of considerable negotiation. The two cases presented here offer a limited sample of these characteristics, demonstrating in particular the organizational and interpretational problems associated with improving education and developing urban communities.

Notes

1. Eugene Bardach, *The Implementation Game* (Cambridge, Mass.: MIT Press, 1977), p. 3.
2. Jeffrey L. Pressman and Aaron Wildavsky, *Implementation*, 2d ed. (Berkeley: University of California Press, 1979), p. xxi. Emphasis added.
3. Walter Williams, "Special Issue on Implementation: Editor's Comments," *Policy Analysis* 1 (Summer 1975): 451. Emphasis added.
4. Pressman and Wildavsky, *Implementation*, 2d ed., pp. xx–xxi. See also Erwin C. Hargrove, *The Missing Link: The Study of the Implementation of Social Policy* (Washington, D. C.: Urban Institute, 1975), pp. 1–3.
5. Others use different labels but appear to be describing essentially the same phenomena. See, for example, Randall B. Ripley and Grace Franklin, *Bureaucracy and Policy Implementation* (Homewood, Ill.: Dorsey Press, 1982), p. 5; George C. Edwards III, *Implementing Public Policy* (Washington, D. C.: Congressional Quarterly, Inc., 1980), pp. 9–14; and Daniel A. Mazmanian and Paul A. Sabatier, *Implementation and Public Policy* (Glenview, Ill.: Scott, Foresman, 1983), pp. 35–41.
6. Ripley and Franklin, *Bureaucracy and Public Policy*, p. 2.
7. Carl Van Horn, *Policy Implementation in the Federal System* (Lexington, Mass.: Lexington Books, 1979), pp. 163–164.
8. Bardach, *The Implementing Game*, p. 9.
9. Bardach, p. 17.
10. Glendon Schubert, *Judicial Policy-Making* (Glenview, Ill.: Scott, Foresman, 1965), p. 60.
11. Samuel Krislov, *The Supreme Court in the Political Process* (New York: Macmillan, 1965), p. 34.
12. Ripley and Franklin, *Bureaucracy and Public Policy*, p. 187. The authors find distinctive patterns among the following types of policy programs: distributive, competitive and protective regulation, redistributive. See also similar distinctions made by Kenneth J. Meier in *Politics and the Bureaucracy* (Monterey, Calif.: Brooks/Cole, 1979), chap. 4.
13. Brian Chapman, "Facts of Organized Life," *Manchester Guardian Weekly*, January 26, 1961, 20.
14. Edwards, *Implementing Public Policy*, p. 1.
15. Carl J. Friedrich, *Constitutional Government and Politics* (New York: Harper, 1937), chap. 2. Friedrich notes that: "The cradle of modern government has been variously recognized in the kingdoms of France and England, in the Italian city state, in the Roman Catholic Church, and even in the Sicilian realm of the brilliant Emperor Frederich II. All of these claims are based upon one aspect common to these several political bodies: the possession of a bureaucracy, a body of servants devoted to prince, civilta or church" (p. 20).
16. H. H. Gerth and C. Wright Mills, *From Max Weber: Essays in Sociology* (London: Routledge & Kegan Paul, 1948), p. 52.
17. Gerth and Mills, p. 53.
18. Gerth and Mills, p. 196.
19. Again quoting Weber—Gerth and Mills, p. 214.
20. Gerth and Mills, p. 228. Emphasis in original.
21. Francis E. Rourke, *Bureaucracy, Politics, and Public Policy* (Boston: Little, Brown, 1969), pp. 1, 11.
22. Matthew Holden, Jr., "'Imperialism' in Bureaucracy," reprinted in *Bureaucratic Power in National Politics*, 2d ed., ed. Francis E. Rourke (Boston: Little, Brown, 1972), p. 211.
23. Holden, p. 212.
24. Personal communication from Professor Fleming. Quoted by permission.
25. Anthony Downs, *Inside Bureaucracy* (Boston: Little, Brown, 1967), p. 8.
26. Downs, p. 20.
27. Advantages cited by B. Guy Peters, *The Politics of Bureaucracy: A Comparative Perspective* (New York: Longman, 1978), p. 32.
28. Douglas Yates, *Bureaucratic Democracy* (Cambridge, Mass.: Harvard University Press, 1982), p. 100. See also Hugh Heclo's fascinating analysis in *A Government of Strangers* (Washington, D. C.: Brookings Institution, 1977).
29. Edwards, *Implementing Public Policy*, p. 17. Emphasis added.
30. Theodore J. Lowi, *The End of Liberalism*, 2d ed. (New York: Norton, 1979), p. 92.

31. Mazmanian and Sabatier, *Implementation and Public Policy,* chap. 2. See also each of the other works cited in this paragraph.
32. Mazmanian and Sabatier, p. 21.
33. Mazmanian and Sabatier, p. 25.
34. Mazmanian and Sabatier, p. 30.
35. See their detailed analysis of the conditions across five policy areas, pp. 273–274.
36. Bardach, *The Implementation Game,* p. 180.
37. Hargrove, *The Missing Link,* chap. 5.
38. Bardach, p. 56.
39. Murray Edelman, *The Symbolic Uses of Politics* (Urbana, Ill.: University of Illinois Press, 1964), p. 45. Emphasis in original.
40. Edelman, p. 45.
41. Edelman, p. 48.
42. Edelman, p. 51.
43. Donald F. Kettl, "Regulating the Cities," *Publius* 11 (Spring 1981): 111.
44. Deil S. Wright, *Understanding Intergovernmental Relations* (Monterey, Calif.: Brooks/Cole, 1982), pp. 92–93.
45. Richard H. Leach, *American Federalism* (New York: Norton, 1970), p. 168.
46. Wright, *Understanding Intergovernmental Relations,* pp. 93–94. It should be noted that the relationship is not simply dictated by Washington. State and local governments lobby for grants and negotiate for advantages in implementation. See Robert D. Thomas, "Intergovernmental Coordination in the Implementation of National Air and Water Pollution Policies," in *Public Policy Making in a Federal System,* ed. Charles O. Jones and Robert D. Thomas (Beverly Hills, Calif.: Sage Publications, 1976), chap. 6.
47. In *The American Partnership* Daniel J. Elazar shows that the three levels also cooperated to a considerable extent in the nineteenth century.
48. Terry Sanford, *Storm over the States* (New York: McGraw-Hill, 1967), p. 80.
49. Morton Grodzins, *The American System* (Chicago: Rand McNally, 1966).
50. For a review of Reagan's proposals see Timothy J. Conlan and David B. Walker, "Reagan's New Federalism: Design, Debate and Discord," *Intergovernmental Perspective* 8 (Winter 1983): 6–22.
51. Wright, *Understanding Intergovernmental Relations,* p. 77.
52. Wright, p. 44.
53. Eugene Eidenberg and Roy D. Morey, *An Act of Congress* (New York: Norton, 1969), p. 176.
54. Stephen K. Bailey and Edith K. Mosher, *ESEA: The Office of Education Administers a Law* (Syracuse: Syracuse University Press, 1968), p. 101. It should be noted that my account of the implementation of ESEA draws heavily on the scholarship of Bailey and Mosher.
55. Bailey and Mosher, p. 72.
56. Bailey and Mosher, pp. 72–75.
57. Bailey and Mosher, p. 77.
58. Bailey and Mosher, p. 89. Emphasis in original.
59. As summarized in Frederick M. Wirt and Michael W. Kirst, *The Political Web of American Schools* (Boston: Little, Brown, 1972), pp. 154–155.
60. Wirt and Kirst, p. 158.
61. Bailey and Mosher, *ESEA,* p. 99.
62. Bailey and Mosher, p. 159.
63. Jeffrey L. Pressman and Aaron B. Wildavsky, *Implementation* (Berkeley: University of California Press, 1973), p. 107.
64. As summarized in Bailey and Mosher, *ESEA,* p. 102.
65. Bailey and Mosher, p. 109.
66. David B. Truman, *The Governmental Process* (New York: Knopf, 1951), p. 439.
67. Norman C. Thomas, *Education in National Politics* (New York: David McKay, 1975), p. 19.
68. Thomas, p. 34.
69. Truman, *The Governmental Process,* p. 444.
70. Donald F. Kettl, *Managing Community Development in the New Federalism* (New York: Praeger, 1980), p. 8.
71. Kettl, "Regulating the Cities," pp. 111–112.
72. For details see *Congress and the Nation,* vol. IV (Washington, D. C.: Congressional Quarterly, Inc., 1977), pp. 480–481.
73. Van Horn, *Policy Implementation in the Federal System,* p. 106.

74. Van Horn, p. 111.
75. The quotations are from Kettl, *Managing Community Development*, pp. 134, 135. Kettl provides accounts of how each of the cities in his study (New Haven, New London, Bridgeport, and Norwich) developed and administered projects.
76. Kettl, *Managing Community Development*, p. 139.
77. Van Horn, *Policy Implementation in the Federal System*, p. 122.
78. Kettl, *Managing Community Development*, pp. 132–133.

Chapter Nine

Evaluating Programs

Functional activities	Categorized in government	With a potential product
Evaluation: specification measurement analysis recommendations	*Program to government*	*Varies (justification, adjustment, and so on)*

In recent years a program was developed in California to support more comprehensive treatment of skid row alcoholics. This laudable effort encouraged greater coordination and team effort among those involved in serving and rehabilitating such people. As a part of the program, a clinic was attached to one large mission already located in the heart of a major metropolitan skid row. The mission was managed by a religious organization; the clinic employed an interdisciplinary team of professionals (supported by different state and local agencies). In an effort to judge its effectiveness, two researchers spent twenty-seven months observing the mission/clinic and collecting other data from questionnaires and interviews. They concluded that severe organizational, personnel, and technological problems led to failure.

■ In fact, the final conclusion to be drawn from this case history is that the planning and coordinating strategy responsible for creating the clinic actually contributed to the skid row alcoholism problem.[1]

Do police patrols prevent crime? Certainly many city departments have assumed so for decades. In 1972 the Kansas City, Missouri, Police Department undertook a study to find out. An experimental fifteen-beat area was designated: five reactive beats with no patrols (only response to calls for service), five control beats with the normal level of patrols, and five proactive beats, in which patrols were increased by a factor of two to three. Data were then collected from ten surveys and questionnaires (administered to citizens, officers, businessmen, and observers), four types of interviews and recorded observations, and six different forms of regularly collected departmental data (on crime, traffic, arrests, and so on). In summary, the government program to be tested (preventive police patrols) was clearly specified, an experimental design was formulated and put into effect, and mountains of relevant data were carefully developed and analyzed. Here was a model case of systematic evaluation research. What were the results?

■ The essential finding . . . is that decreasing or increasing routine preventive patrol within the range tested in this experiment had no effect on crime, citizen fear of crime, community attitudes toward the police on the delivery of police service, police response time, or traffic accidents.[2]

The Growth of Evaluation Research

This chapter is about the process of learning whether government programs are worth doing. The two cases cited above are example of many systematic studies that have been conducted in recent years to determine whether programs are working as expected. Such studies on a mass scale are relatively new, particularly for testing the effects of social programs. A report on federal evaluation policy published in 1970 stated:

■ The most impressive finding about the evaluation of social programs in the federal government is that substantial work in this field has been almost nonexistent.

Few significant studies have been undertaken. Most of those carried out have been poorly conceived. Many small studies around the country have been carried out with such lack of uniformity of design and objective that the results rarely are comparable or responsive to the questions facing policy makers.[3]

The first edition of this book was published in 1970, and at that time it was difficult to find sufficient material for a separate chapter on evaluation. The problem now is just the reverse. We have been inundated with studies, reports, and how-to-do-it books and manuals. Public policy evaluation research is a growth industry. Journals devoted exclusively to policy evaluation have been created. Courses on the subject are now offered in colleges and universities. A professional association—the Evaluation Research Society—has been formed. I have a catalog from one publisher listing thirty-seven books with *evaluation, evaluating,* or *evaluative* in the titles. To say the least, "evaluation research is a robust area of activity devoted to collecting, analyzing, and interpreting information on the need, implementation, and impact" of public policy.[4]

What explains this growth? Peter Rossi and his coauthors attribute it in part to the work of social scientists who have promoted the policy sciences.

■ But . . . it is the politician, planner, and the foundation executive who exercise the leadership in the evaluation research field. It is persons of power and influence, not academicians, who are the evaluation research lobby and who are responsible primarily for the widespread growth of the evaluation endeavor.[5]

This answers the question of who promoted the growth; it does not explain their motives. The most logical explanations for expanded evaluation research lie in budgetary politics. First is the quantum increase in the proportion of the budget allocated to social programs (see figure 7.1). It was predictable that "persons of power and influence" would begin to ask, Is it worth doing? when the federal government began to spend hundreds of billions of dollars on domestic programs. Second is the inevitable conflict that accompanies the increase in claims on the budget. Those who have had large shares in the past object to dividing these shares with other claimants. Decision makers may be able to resolve these conflicts by expanding the pie (that is, increasing revenues or deficits so as to provide for new claimants without having to take from old claimants). When the mood is to balance the budget, cut expenditures, and reduce taxes, however, decision makers are forced to make judgments about which programs deserve support. Evaluation research is a natural ally under these circumstances, and its use is often highly political.

Associated reasons for the increase in program evaluation include the sizable increase in what Richard A. Brody refers to as "politics one-on-one" and the greater mistrust of government exhibited by the general public. *Politics one-on-one* identifies the phenomenal growth in direct participation by groups and individuals in all aspects of the policy process (see chapter 1). Groups that have lobbied for a particular program are then moved to determine whether the program is, in fact, having the intended effect. For example, the political problems of the Environmental Protection Agency in 1983 were the consequence of such worries. Many environmentalists were concerned that EPA was not administering the hazardous waste control program to achieve the desired results. Accompanying and supporting this increased policy participation is the greater suspicion by the public and the media that government is not doing its job well. All these developments contribute to a mood that has encouraged public officials to support more program evaluation.

What Is Evaluation?

The meaning of *evaluation* is revealed by the way it has been categorized in government: that is, "program to government." Individual programs are, in a sense, returned to government for review and judgment of their worth. Carol H. Weiss observes:

■   Evaluation is an elastic word that stretches to cover judgments of many
     kinds. . . . What all the uses of the word have in common is the notion of
     judging merit. Someone is examining and weighing a phenomenon (a person, a
     thing, an idea) against some explicit or implicit yardstick.[6]

For this book in particular we need to include *process* along with program as a phenomenon to be judged. Thus, evaluation is *judging the merit of government processes and programs.*

The word *evaluation* is frequently used to mean evaluation research. That will not be done here. *Evaluation* is defined above. It is a more inclusive term, referring to all the many forms of appraisal that take place within a political system, including those by politicians, journalists, citizens, judges, bureaucrats, and so on. *Evaluation research* refers to the more recent social scientific efforts at systematic data collection and analysis (such as those in the skid row and preventive patrol cases cited earlier).[7] This research is typically aimed at specific programs. The several methods that may be employed are discussed in this chapter.

It is important to make this distinction, because it is evaluation research that has developed as a growth industry. Government officials have been judging the merit of their efforts for centuries, as have others. Elections, budget-making, investigations, State of the Union Messages—these and other familiar activities all have evaluative aspects. The idea of estimating whether this or that program merits continued support was not born with the development of more rigorous research techniques in the 1970s.

The subactivities identified here—specification, measurement, analysis, and recommendation—characterize all forms of evaluation. What differs is the degree of effort to be precise, scientific, or systematic. *Specification* is the most important of these subactivities. It refers to the identification of the goals or criteria by which a program or process is to be evaluated; for example, the rehabilitation of skid row alcoholics or reduced crime where the police regularly patrol. Specification is therefore the trigger activity for evaluation; it is the means by which "merit" is to be judged.

Measurement simply refers to the collection of information relevant to the object of evaluation. It may be very precise (for example, a vehicle count to determine highway use) or imprecise and impressionistic (for example, a legislator's casual visit with nursing home patients to check on improvements resulting from a new federal program). *Analysis* is the absorption and use of the information collected in order to draw conclusions. Here too one finds significant differences in method and style, ranging from powerful quantitative techniques for comparative analysis of costs and benefits to highly impressionistic and experiential methods. Finally, *recommendation* is the determination of what should be done next, including such options as letting well enough alone, doing even more of the same, making major or minor adjustments, or possibly terminating the program. Recommendations can take the form of oral orders or lengthy written reports.

In summary, evaluation is an activity designed to judge the merits of government programs or processes. It varies in the specification of criteria, the techniques of measurement, the methods of analysis, and the forms of recommendation. Above all, it must be stressed that evaluation takes many forms. It occurs at many levels of government and outside government, and involves people with different training, experience, and aptitudes. The results are frequently political even when they are produced scientifically. A final point is that the time dimension for evaluation may also vary dramatically. It may occur in a matter of minutes, when a public official is called upon to make a judgment and then act on that judgment, or it may be the result of months, even years, of careful research and study.

Purposes of Evaluation

In chapter 1, I quoted from and listed several studies that were very harsh in judging government programs. In reading such works as Pressman and Wildavsky's *Implementation* and Meehan's *The Quality of Federal Policymaking: Programmed Failure in Public Housing,* one is led to inquire, Why do failing programs survive? How are they able to continue despite overwhelming evidence that they are not accomplishing stated goals? In part the reasons are lodged in the physical properties of bureaucratic motion. An inertia is created when several levels of administrative units are finally meshed and operating to implement a program. It takes an extraordinary external force to stop or even redirect this movement.

Furthermore, it is unlikely that a program will be terminated if those administering it don't know it is failing. Alice M. Rivlin asks, "Can we find out what works?"[8] It is not certain that we can. Perhaps the most disconcerting finding by Pressman and Wildavsky in their study of economic development programs is that:

■   Inability to learn is fatal. . . . A major criticism that can be made of the EDA public works program in Oakland is that it closed off the possibilities of learning. Far from being a model from which the organization could learn success, it was not even an experiment from which the organization could learn from failure.[9]

But there are other reasons for continuing programs that are judged to have failed. The key to understanding may be rooted in *specification,* that is, the criteria by which results are tested. It is, of course, typical to rely on the stated goals of the substantive progam in question for judging results: more and improved housing, better mental health care, more hiring of minorities, physical renewal of slum areas, and so on. There are also other goals that may be equally important to those involved with the program. At a minimum the following purposes of evaluation can be identified:

1. *Political evaluation:* Does the program distribute benefits to all states and congressional districts? Can it be interpreted as having contributed to reelection? To media support? To campaign contributions?
2. *Organizational evaluation:* Does the program generate support for the implementing agencies? Do the benefits for the agency outweigh the costs? Is it likely to lead to further expansion of the agency?
3. *Substantive evaluation:* Does the program accomplish its stated goals (in the law or as expressed in subsequent specification)? What impact does the program have on the problems to which it is directed?

By identifiying different purposes of evaluation we can see how a program that fails by one set of criteria may be successful by another set. In fact, it is entirely possible that a politically or organizationally successful program may not even be evaluated by substantive criteria, or if it is, that the results may be ignored. For the professional evaluator who finds substantive failure in a program with strong political and organizational support the problems are obvious. It is not pleasant to be the messenger under these circumstances.

The same actual methods—systematic and scientific, casual and impressionistic, or some mixture—may be used to achieve all three purposes of evaluation. As it happens, however, the more scientific methods of evaluation research tend to be used in substantive and organizational evaluation, the more impressionistic methods in political evaluation. In fact, it is probably considered unethical by some to use the science of evaluation for political purposes, this despite the acknowledgment by most scholars of evaluation research that the two (science and politics) do get joined. Laura I. Langbein observes that "while evaluation research uses the methods of social science to determine whether programs are successful, experience suggests that the boundary between the scientific and the political is neither clear nor immutable."[10] And David Nachmias quotes one observer as stating that "evaluations can influence fine-grain program decisions, and that's about it. For any of the big policy decisions, research is marginal. These yea/nay decisions are made on the basis of political tea leaves."[11]

The Politics of Evaluation

All the topics discussed so far lead inexorably to politics, as befits the purpose of this book. Aaron Wildavsky illustrates the dilemmas created by the demand for substantive program evaluation by asking us to imagine a self-evaluating organization.

■ It would continuously monitor its own activities so as to determine whether it was meeting its goals or even whether these goals should continue to prevail. When evaluation suggested that a change in goals or programs to achieve them was desirable, these proposals would be taken seriously by top decision makers. They would institute the necessary changes; they would have no vested interest in continuation of current activities. Instead they would steadily pursue new alternatives to better serve the latest desired outcomes.[12]

What Wildavsky has described is an organization constantly at war with itself. "Organizational structure implies stability while the process of evaluation suggests change." The evaluators are the "agents of change acting in favor of programs as yet unborn and clienteles that are unknown."[13] This process of adjustment is a political process.

Recall the statement used as the title of chapter 1: "The causes of policy failure are, at root, political." The causes of policy evaluation, too, are political. Someone must judge it important to do in the first place, resources have to be committed to accomplish it, methods for doing the work must be selected. Somebody wins and somebody loses even before the results are announced. "Policy evaluation is . . . frequently the arm of politics, not just the judge or spectator."[14]

When the results are in hand, however, politics begins in earnest. As Carol Weiss, a leading student of evaluation processes, observes:

■ Evaluation has always had explicitly political overtones. It is designed to yield conclusions about the worth of programs and, in doing so, is intended to affect the allocation of resources. The rationale of evaluation research is that it provides evidence on which to base decisions about maintaining, institutionalizing, and expanding successful programs and modifying or abandoning unsuccessful ones.[15]

Knowing this, it is easy to see the importance of controlling the evaluation process and the strength of the temptation to influence the outcome if one's agency or program were being reviewed.

Another important point is that the politics of evaluation is no longer small-town stuff. With the growth of federal domestic programs, there has been a natural tendency for greater routinization and standardization. Weiss says:

■ Programs may actually be no more standardized in form, content, and structure than they ever were, but they are funded from a common pot and bear a common name: "community action program," "Head Start," "model cities," "legal services," "neighborhood service centers," "Title I of the Elementary and Secondary Education Act," "maternal and child health program," and so forth.[16]

Consequently, evaluations are huge enterprises with potentially massive effects, a characteristic that reinforces the importance of an agency managing the "who, what, when, and how" of program evaluation.

Donald T. Campbell proposes another important political dimension to evaluation. In discussing social reforms, he points out that many policy makers become committed to such an extent that objective evaluation is impossible. Indeed, "if the political and administrative system has committed itself in advance to the correctness and efficacy of its reforms, it cannot tolerate learning of failure."[17] It might also be said that such commitments also provide protective lenses through which decision makers view program evaluations. Those findings that are supportive filter through; those that are critical do not.

In trying to comprehend the politics of this endeavor it may be helpful to assume that evaluation in whatever form is an exercise in *justification*. That is, the motivation for evaluating a program is to justify present efforts by existing personnel. In this view, evaluations become an important means of support. Those that fail to justify the program receive little, if any, credence or publicity if political or organizational support for the program is strong. Even congressional committee involvement in evaluation can be viewed in this way. The process of reauthorization and oversight is typically a process of justification. Members of the administration present supporting evidence drawn from their formal or informal evaluations. Members of Congress either accept the evidence, offer support of their own for programs to which they are committed, or provide weak opposition by drawing on independent evaluations (for example, their own unsystematic study, staff reports, General Accounting Office evaluations). The style may even be adversarial, but the process is one of justification. It may take a major agenda shift due to a crisis to change this process (as with the budget crisis of the 1980s, when even popular programs were threatened).

This is not to say, of course, that evaluation may not result in strong criticism and significant change. Not all programs can be justified, even by those administering them. What I am proposing rather is that students will find it generally useful to study evaluation in this way, understanding that evaluation as justification does not inevitably mean that a program will expand or even continue (though most surely will). It might also be noted that an extensive and highly visible evaluation may result in important programmatic and organizational changes but, nevertheless, continued expansion of an agency.

Getting Started

It is useful in discussing the actual process of evaluation to remind ourselves of a few of the relevant initial realities. The statements listed in chapter 2 under the heading "Programs" reiterate the difficulties associated with getting a program evaluation underway.[18] David Nachmias advises us:

■ Program objectives are not known with certainty, nor are they unanimously accepted by the policymakers. Even the cost and effectiveness of programs are sometimes controversial.

And further:

■ . . . the problems of public policy are likely to be "squishy" problems, that is, they may have no definite formulation and no rule of thumb to tell the researcher when he or she has found a solution. . . . Moreover, goals may not be static, but may change in accordance with changes in the policymakers' perceptions of the societal problems or with the political climate.[19]

Uncertain objectives for coping with "squishy problems" does not sound like the perfect basis for judging the merits of a program. Can a program even be administered when its objectives are unclear? Apparently it happens all the time. A study by the Urban Institute found:

■ Most of the programs examined lacked adequately defined criteria of program effectiveness. This lack stems partially from the fact that the typical federal program has multiple objectives and partially from difficulties in defining objectives in measurable terms, particularly when the authorizing legislation is very general. But the widespread absence of evaluation criteria stems mainly from two things—the failure of program managers to think through their objectives, and the failure by evaluators to insist on the guidance they need to define evaluation criteria.[20]

Here is a double indictment: poorly defined objectives and little effort by evaluators to determine objectives. Despite these problems, evaluations are increasingly required by law. Presumably this demand will eventually result in perfected means for determining the effectiveness of programs. In the meantime, however, many studies fail before they even begin due to insufficient specification of what is to be measured.

Peter H. Rossi argues that the task of evaluation will never be simple. During the days of the New Deal programs, he points out, estimates of progress were possible because the problems were principally economic in nature. Programs were directed to getting people jobs and income, and the results were easily measured. The present social welfare programs are more difficult to weigh, however, because they are "designed to bring about changes in individuals and in institutions. . . ."

■ The goals set for [these] programs were difficult to state with either specificity or clarity. Thus the preambles to enabling legislation tended to refer to very broad objectives—for example, improving the quality of life in urban neighborhoods, or providing better health care for disadvantaged neighborhoods, or improving the quality of education to poor children, etc. These are objectives for which we do not yet have indicators on which there would be broad consensus.[21]

And yet these programs are enormously significant, representing as they do a major shift in government responsibility toward greater concern with and involvement in social life. The complexity of the task itself makes unlikely the crisp identification of objectives. Once the program is established, however, it must be administered in some fashion, whether or not its goals are articulated or well understood. The challenge for policy implementers in all of this is considerable. As Rossi wisely observes, "It is hard enough to change individuals, but it is even harder [shall we say hopeless?] to change individuals to an unspecified state."[22]

Those who study evaluation in government tell us that it falters at a very basic point: the establishment of well-stated criteria. This failure does not necessarily interrupt the process of evaluation, which proceeds because there are political and other reasons for making judgments and/or because such analysis is required by law. What is recommended here is that students try to determine what criteria are involved in making judgments about programs, whether these judgments are made in the political arenas or in systematic evaluation. Edward A. Suchman concludes, "the process of evaluating is highly complex and subjective."[23] The trick for students of the policy process is to unravel the complexities and identify the intrinsic subjectivities.

Doing Evaluations: Many Forms

We turn now to a sort of catalog of the forms or types of evaluations. I divide these into two broad categories: (1) the traditional, ongoing, less systematic methods of appraisal; (2) the newer, more systematic and scientific methods associated with evaluation research.

Traditional Forms

There are many ongoing forms of activity in and alongside government that have been judging the merits of programs for decades. To illustrate, specific reference will be made to congressional oversight, the budget process, the auditing function, presidential commissions, and evaluations by those outside government.

Congressional Oversight

A leading student of legislative oversight, Morris S. Ogul, points out:

■ There is a large gap between the oversight the law calls for and the oversight actually performed. . . . One reason for the gap between expectations and behavior lies in the nature of the expectation. The plain but seldom acknowledged fact is that this task . . . is simply impossible to perform. No amount of congressional dedication and energy, no conceivable boost in committee budgets will enable the Congress to carry out its oversight obligations in a comprehensive and systematic manner.[24]

Here is a realistic account of what is supposed to be one of the most institutionalized evaluation processes. In essence, Ogul argues that oversight proceeds as an unsystematic sampling method in which a few programs may be selected for review. Certainly this is the most that the committees with oversight responsibility can hope to accomplish. The Legislative Reorganization Act of 1946 charges the Senate and House oversight committees with the staggering tasks of:

1. Studying the operation of government activities at all levels with a view to determining its economy and efficiency
2. Evaluating the effects of laws enacted to reorganize the legislative and executive branches of the government
3. Studying intergovernmental relationships. . . .[25]

While the committees do conduct many investigations, they can never conduct the type of comprehensive analyses called for by this act.

Where, then, does one look for evaluation? Institutionalized congressional evaluation is essentially a state of mind that leads to discontinuous surveillance as programs are developed, funded, and adjusted over time. Carol Goss wisely describes it as:

■ . . . a continuous process which occurs when a committee considers new legislation concerning a program, when it is engaged in specific review activities, and
when agency-relevant business is conducted at other times. The one activity
blends into the other as the cumulative experience of the executive agency-
congressional committee relationship bears on the policy problems at hand.[26]

Thus Ogul and others advise us to look to the full set of congressional–
executive relations for an understanding of how Congress "oversees" and
evaluates programs and their implementation. That search leads to authorizations, wherein programs are initially legitimated; appropriations; reauthoriza-
tions; and even to casework, where members are fed information about how
well a program is accomplishing its objectives.

The Budgeting Process

The annual budgeting process also provides routine opportunities for evaluation. This is not to say that any very systematic evaluation will in fact occur,
but the theory and practice of budgeting invite "judging the merits" of programs. The agency must justify its current activities and support any new
projects with the understanding that they will compete eventually with requests from elsewhere. The Office of Management and Budget must comparatively analyze agency requests and measure these by presidential priorities.
And, of course, Congress has traditionally demanded justifications in its appropriations process. Its 1974 budgetary reform even sought to establish priorities that might serve as a basis for assessing the executive budget (see chapter 7).

In chapter 5 I referred to efforts to create total policy processes; in particular
the planning-programming-budgeting system (PPBS) and zero-based budgeting
(ZBB). These systems grow out of the need some people feel for more rational
budgeting procedures. They obviously contain strong evaluative components,
since they depend on clarifying goals and measuring performance. The experience of PPBS outside the defense area is particularly instructive for students of
program evaluation. Once again we run up against the problems of judging
what a program's objectives are, determining which programs are best, and
analyzing whether a particular goal might better be accomplished by other
means. Aaron Wildavsky, perhaps the most outspoken critic of PPBS, summarizes the difficulties.

■ All the obstacles previously mentioned, such as lack of talent, theory, and data,
may be summed up in a single sentence: no one knows how to do program
budgeting. Another way of putting it would be to say that many know what
program budgeting should be like in general, but no one knows what it should
be like in any particular case. Program budgeting cannot be stated in operational terms. There is no agreement on what the words mean, let alone an
ability to show another person what should be done. The reason for the difficulty is that telling an agency to adopt program budgeting means telling it to
find better policies and there is no formula for doing that. One can (and should)
talk about measuring effectiveness, estimating costs, and comparing alterna-

tives, but that is a far cry from being able to take the creative leap of formulating a better policy.[27]

The Auditing Process

The flip side of budgeting is, of course, auditing. The General Accounting Office (GAO), which reports to Congress, has the responsibility for overseeing government auditing. By its nature the audit is evaluative; that is, it determines whether funds are expended in accordance with the purposes stated in law. Much of this process is defined by standard accounting procedures, of course. Still, it was a perfectly natural development that GAO should be called upon by Congress to study program effectiveness. In 1966 special requests for such studies constituted just 8 percent of the work load of a professional staff of 2,400; in 1977 requests were estimated at 34 percent of the work load of a professional staff of 3,800.[28] Congressional committees increasingly rely on the studies for recommending changes in the statutes that authorize programs.

Presidential Commissions

A less regularized yet traditional technique for evaluation is the presidential commission. These groups are typically multimember, limited to a particular issue area, lacking in power to implement their findings or recommendations, and composed in part of persons from the private sphere.[29] Some focus more on the substance of problems, others on government organization; some seek to develop policy proposals, others seek to evaluate policy. Regardless of their specific charge, however, many of the following were drawn inexorably into evaluation of existing policy and administration.

Commission on Organization of the Executive Branch of the Government (Hoover Commission)
President's Water Resources Policy Commission
President's Commission on Higher Education
Commission on Intergovernmental Relations (Kestnbaum Commission)
Commission on Foreign Economic Policy (Randall Commission)
President's Committee on Government Housing Policies and Programs
President's Commission on Law Enforcement and Administration of Justice
National Advisory Commission on Civil Disorders (Kerner Commission)
President's Committee on Juvenile Delinquency and Youth Crime
National Commission on the Causes and Prevention of Violence
President's Commission on School Finance
President's Commission on Federal Statistics
National Commission on Social Security Reform

As with congressional oversight, but in contrast to PPBS, the idea behind an evaluation commission is that it is important to have review and analysis outside the bureaucracy itself. The information needs for evaluation don't change, however, just because a presidential commission is appointed. Often, therefore, the commission must rely on agencies for information, or it may be dominated by the members who are public servants, or the commission staff (not infrequently drawn from the civil service) may become more influential in decisions than anyone intended.

The result is that most commissions have little immediate impact on policy. While they face many of the same problems in evaluation that congressional committees face, most are ad hoc and therefore do not have the continuing role in other functional activities of policy that legislators have. Thus, the one-shot review depends for success on career policy actors. The optimum conditions for impact by a presidential evaluation commission would appear to be:

1. A report coincident with other supporting events
2. Commission members from public service who are in important positions of authority in government and are committed to the recommendations
3. Commission staff who return to positions in government in which they will influence the acceptance of recommendations
4. A report that supports the president's policy preferences in the issue area under consideration

Outside Evaluations

Frequently the most dramatic evaluations of government policy come from outside government: from the press, television, individuals, private groups, scholars. Identification of public problems and evaluation of public policy are time-honored functions of the press. In addition to the almost daily evaluation in the nation's great newspapers, many magazines devote several articles in every issue to judging existing policy. Notable among these currently are the *Washington Monthly*, the *New Republic*, the *National Review*, *Commentary*, *The Progressive*, *Society*, and *The Public Interest*. Sometimes articles from these and weekly newsmagazines trigger congressional investigations or publicize ongoing investigations.

Television journalism has had a major impact in the post–World War II period (though the precise impact has had little systematic study). The many special news programs on air and water pollution, urban crises, the poverty program, migrant workers, hunger, and unemployment have publicized the inadequacies of existing domestic policies. And though the effect is difficult to measure, surely the on-the-spot coverage of the Vietnam War, the many Middle East conflicts, and the hostage crisis in Iran, contributed to criticism of American policies.

Certain individuals also contribute important appraisals of existing policy, either in their role as scholars, free-lance writers, or, as in the case of Ralph Nader, as self-appointed overseers of government action. Nader emerged in the 1960s as a sort of "watchdog" for the consumer. Politicians and bureaucrats have come to know Mr. Nader and his task groups very well as he has delved into meat and fish inspection, mine safety, auto safety, regulation of trade, mental health, air and water pollution, pensions, nursing homes, and the general consumer protection policies of the federal government.

Interest groups obviously remain alert to the effect of policy on problems of direct concern to them. Many maintain rather extensive research units to evaluate policy, notably the American Medical Association, the Chamber of Commerce, the AFL-CIO, the National Association of Manufacturers, the American Farm Bureau Association, the National Education Association, the NAACP, and the Urban Coalition. Of the independent research organizations, the Brookings Institution and the American Enterprise Institute (AEI) are among the best known. Brookings scholars annually produce an analysis of the budget that has become an important policy document in Washington. Hardly a major foreign, defense, or domestic issue has been ignored by the Brookings staff over the years. They have produced a library of significant policy literature. AEI, too, has been very active on policy issues and has gained stature in the Washington community in recent years. It publishes a magazine called *Regulation* that contains many articles evaluating regulatory policies. The scores of studies and forums on major public issues also have a continuing impact. Many other policy institutes have been created in the last two decades to guarantee that no policy program will be ignored: The Urban Institute, Institute for Policy Studies, Institute for Public Policy Research, Roosevelt Center for American Policy Studies. A check of the District of Columbia phone book shows 92 center listings and 105 institute listings (as the first word in the name; many others exist where the word is last in the name). Clearly a lot of policy watching is going on.

Here then is a combination of governmental and private activities that, although they are not all explicitly and by design evaluatory, constitute a set of judgments on the merits of government programs. This is the very essence of the first use of the term *evaluation:* as a functional activity occurring in all political systems. Whether or not one explicitly and consciously includes an evaluative component in public policy, people will make judgments in a democratic system, and these tend to be collected to form a basis for further decisions.

Scientific Forms

We turn now to what Edward A. Suchman refers to as "the specific use of the scientific method for the purpose of making an evaluation."[30] Stimulated by legal requirements for program evaluation and the funds to do the work, evaluation research has evolved into a significant enterprise. The basic methods are those of any scientific research effort. Suchman cites the following six steps for evaluative research:

1. Identification of the goals to be evaluated
2. Analysis of the problems with which the activity must cope

3. Description and standardization of the activity
4. Measurement of the degree of change that takes place
5. Determination of whether the observed change is due to the activity or to some other cause
6. Some indication of the durability of the effects[31]

He also identifies several of the questions that must be answered if program objectives—presumably the directing force of evaluation—are to be made operational for research purposes.

1. *What* is the nature of the content of the objective?
2. *Who* is the target of the program?
3. *When* is the desired change to take place?
4. Are the objectives *unitary* or *multiple*?
5. What is the desired *magnitude* of effect?
6. *How* is the objective to be attained?[32]

The importance of the problem definition activity is obvious from this list. Failure to define the problem makes it difficult to set clear objectives and therefore impossible to conduct evaluation research. That does not mean, of course, that people will not try. Congress can and does require evaluation studies whether or not programmatic objectives have been clearly specified. And so something called "program evaluation" is carried out, typically with poor results.

As the preceding discussion suggests, description of methods seldom coincides with description of realities. Yet one can hardly proceed any other way. Evaluation research must be developed as though it really could be carried out—as though conditions would always favor an objective and systematic analysis. The effect for present purposes is a variant on the "rules-are-made-to-be-broken" theme. That is, just as with many legislative procedures, compromises have to be made in order to get the job done. Further, the job to be done may itself be at variance with what is publicly stated, in part because certain goals are not publicly acceptable or because people differ on the goals to be achieved. I stress this point to illustrate that even the scientific method may be incorporated into the functional charade that frequently characterizes a human policy process.

The discussion of the specific forms of evaluation research is divided into two segments. First, the various types of stages of the research are identified—the matter of *where the research is done;* second, the designs that are relied on by evaluation scientists are introduced—the matter of *how the research is done.*

Where the Research Is Done

There appears to be general agreement that there are three types of evaluation research: *program monitoring or process studies, impact assessment studies,* and *economic efficiency or cost-effectiveness studies.*[33] Rossi et al. specify the following questions for each of these types of studies (which, of course, may be combined in one large study for any one program):

1. *Program monitoring/process*

Is the program reaching the persons, households, or other target units to which it is addressed?

Is the program providing the resources, services, or other benefits that were intended in the program design?

2. *Impact assessment*

Is the program effective in achieving its intended goals?

Can the results of the program be explained by some alternative process that does not include the program?

Is the program having some effects that were not intended?

3. *Economic efficiency/cost effectiveness*

What are the costs to deliver services and benefits to program participants?

Is the program an efficient use of resources compared with alternative use of the resources?[34]

These foci and questions reflect a logical progression from reaching the targets to achieving the goals to measuring the costs. Rossi and his colleagues add a type of evaluation study that others do not include, that of program planning and development.

■ Evaluation at the planning stage may include the following: first, how much of a problem there may be and where it is located. . . . Second, there is the issue of how participants should be defined in operational terms. . . . Third, is whether the proposed intervention is a suitable way of remedying the problem at which it is directed.[35]

This stage takes evaluation back into what is identified in chapter 8 as "interpretation." The need for this stage is understandable given the dependence of evaluation research on the identification of goals, criteria, and targets. It is thus worth including here as a reiteration of the significance of goal setting for triggering proper evaluation.

How the Research Is Done

The methods of research differ for each of the four types of evaluation study (the standard three plus the program planning research added by Rossi et al.). The methods for program planning are similar to those relied on in problem definition: social surveys, elite interviews, community forums, analysis of social indicators and/or census data. Research methods for program monitoring would include direct observation; study of records and reports; spot checking; and interviews with administrators, both those delivering the service and those receiving the service. Comparative analysis among sites may be particularly useful.

Moving down the list to economic efficiency or cost-effectiveness studies, we find standard and therefore accepted means for collecting and analyzing data. This is not to say that the data themselves are always easy to generate in the desired form. It is not always so simple to translate benefits into dollar amounts. But the methods themselves are well known. Rossi et al. describe the goals of this research:

■   A comprehensive *cost-benefit* analysis requires estimates of the benefits of a program, both tangible and intangible, and the costs of undertaking the program, both direct and indirect. Once specified, the benefits and costs are then translated into a common measure, usually (but not necessarily) a monetary unit. The benefits and costs can then be compared, generally by computing either a benefit-to-cost ratio (benefits divided by costs), the net benefits (benefits minus costs), or some other value . . . for summarizing the results of the analysis.[36]

Of course, since a benefit is a type of impact, this type of analysis depends on impact assessment studies. "The information on the probable differences in impact of particular programs is . . . combined with data on the costs of implementing them in order to make cost-effectiveness comparisons."[37]

I have left the most difficult problem for last: that of how to conduct impact assessment studies. Is the program effective in achieving its intended goals? That is something more than the $64,000 question. How does one find out? Weiss catalogs three experimental options, each of which further employs any number of standard techniques of data analysis. First is the *experimental design,* in which a systematic effort is made to select an experimental and control group (see the preventive police patrol case discussed earlier).

■   Out of the target population, units (people, work teams, precincts, classrooms, cities) are randomly chosen to be in either the group that gets the program or the "control group" that does not. Measures are taken of the relevant criterion variable . . . before the program starts and after it ends. Differences are computed, and the program is deemed a success if the experimental group has improved more than the control group.[38]

The problems in carrying out this design are legion. It is one thing to conduct experiments in the laboratory or in a relatively short time period in a controllable environment. It is quite another to pursue this method in the dynamics of ongoing social life, where the experiment itself is but one of many competing forces. Still, advances are being made with this approach and imaginative adaptations have produced some interesting results.[39]

Second are the *quasi-experimental designs,* less conscious efforts to "protect against the effects of extraneous variables. . . ."[40] Weiss wisely observes that this means not simply "sloppy experiments" but rather an acknowledgment of what can and cannot be controlled. Techniques include time-series analysis (measurements before, during, and after implementation of a program) or use of a so-called nonequivalent control group (individuals with similar characteristics but not strictly a control group). The advantages of this method are obvious. Without abandoning systematic research methods, one has a more flexible and feasible instrument for evaluating effects.

Third are the *nonexperimental designs*, of which the three most common are "before-and-after study of a single program, after-only study of program participants, or after-only study of participants and [a comparison group]."[41] By definition, these studies are less rigorous but they may still provide insight into the operation and effects of a program. And, in fact, such a design may be necessary as a first step toward a more scientific study.

Why conduct nonexperimental designs? Weiss notes two important reasons beyond the obvious one of feasibility: (1) They may provide "a preliminary look at the effectiveness of a program," and (2) there may be no other choice. The second point is worth expanding on since it involves political considerations.

■ Many government agencies tend to demand one-time ex post facto investigations; they are responding to political pressures and short-term needs, and they want quick results. The system of competitive contracting for evaluation leaves the major decisions in their hands. . . . the agency develops a "request for proposal" (RFP) for evaluation of its program. . . . Research organizations are invited to submit applications . . . and after review, one applicant organization is selected.[42]

In this system, the evaluator must accept the conditions as specified in the RFP, and the agency is left with whatever is possible given the constraints identified. In short, the nonexperimental design may be the best that can be produced in this situation.[43]

While there are many question marks concerning the current status of evaluative research, there seems little doubt that we will witness many future developments in this sphere. It is presently characterized by the kind of faddishness that often eventually produces routine processes. We may look forward, then, to further testing of evaluative research design and methods, particularly if Rivlin's judgment is accepted that "the federal government should follow a systematic experimentation strategy in seeking to improve the effectiveness of social action programs."[44] Her observations on this point are worth fuller exposition.

■ The process will not be easy or quick or cheap. Nor can one look forward to an end to it. It would be a mistake to adopt systematic experimentation in the hope that it would "tell us what works." The phrase suggests that there is some all-time optimum way of organizing social services and that we are going to find it and then quit. Clearly the world is not like this. What works for one place or one generation will not work for another. The process of developing new methods, trying them out, modifying them, trying again, will have to be continuous. But unless we begin searching for improvements and experimenting with them in a systematic way, it is hard to see how we will make much progress in increasing the effectiveness of our social services.[45]

Thus systematic evaluative methods too must be judged in the context of the continuous and incremental adjustment toward elusive goals that are often themselves in the process of being redefined.

Policy Cycles

In the remarks quoted above, Rivlin refers to a continuous process by which methods are tested, modified, tested again, and so on. The same might be said about the policy process overall, at least as portrayed in this book. This observation leads us to consider cycles of policy; that is, the ongoing patterns of accommodation in which various institutional actors play various roles in accomplishing the functional activities of the policy process. *Policy cycles* is not the best term for what I want to discuss because it implies more neatness of pattern than I mean to suggest. I do, however, want to build on the notion of a "round of events or phenomena that recur regularly and in the same sequence" (a dictionary definition of *cycle*).

In his discussion of the appraising function in decision making, Harold D. Lasswell limits the function to the making of factual statements about the causes and effects of public policy. He notes that "strictly speaking, no applications, prescriptions, or recommendations are part of it."[46] That is a narrower concept of the evaluating function than has been used here. I assume definite output as a result of evaluation. The whole purpose of evaluation is to judge programs as they are applied to problems; to determine whether objectives are being realized and, if so, which ones.

The specific output of evaluation may take several forms, often depending on who has evaluated, how, and why. Thus, for example, if evaluators are intent on justifying a program and find any evidence to that end, then *support* for the program and the methods of implementation may be the result. On the other hand, evaluators may identify the need for minor adjustment in either program or procedures. Perhaps the corrective will take the form of a reorganization, a personnel action of some kind (reassignment, removal, reprimand), or a reinterpretation or clarification of program intent.

If evaluators conclude that the program is simply not doing the job, then more extensive change may be required, again depending on what is to be achieved and whether change can, in fact, be effected. It may be that administrators have enough authority to reformulate and reorganize. Or perhaps they will have to seek new authorization, in which case majority coalition building may once again be involved.

Another variation in output is that associated with the discovery that the existing program is based on an erroneous interpretation of the problem. In this case policy makers may have defined the problem vastly differently from those most affected. Perhaps policy makers assumed that physical conditions in slum areas constituted the real problem for slum dwellers. Clearing of slums and construction of large public housing units would alleviate this need. Thorough evaluation (which in fact has hardly occurred even today) might well reveal, however, that slum dwellers view their problems quite differently. Actual physical conditions may be less important in the short run than job opportunities, transportation to employment sites, or educational opportunities. Clearing the slums will not alleviate these needs. Alleviation of these needs, however, may result in improved physical conditions in the slums. Minor procedural adjustments in policy will not make a difference in this case. What evaluators may call for is a completely new policy approach (though, in assessing the probability and form of change, you should recall the earlier discussion of bureaucratic commitment to existing programs).

Another possibility is that new problems are discovered in the process of evaluating certain programs. The output in this case affects agenda setting, as new demands are brought to the attention of government decision makers. Evaluation results in a spin-off of another cycle. These various situations of possible output from evaluation suggest different types of policy cycles, or "rounds of events." First is the very simple and frequently occurring cycle of support.

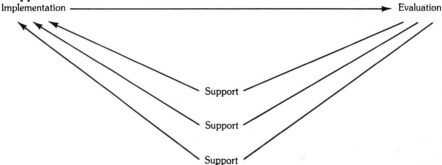

Second is the incremental adjustment cycle, occurring within the functional activities of implementation and evaluation.

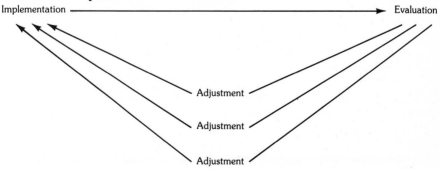

The third type of cycle is more complex. It may involve other functional activities beyond implementation and evaluation and two or more revolutions. I suggest two of many possible variations. The first involves programmatic shifts, either within existing authority or where new authority is required. The second captures those cases in which the problem is redefined or new problems are identified.

Program Changes

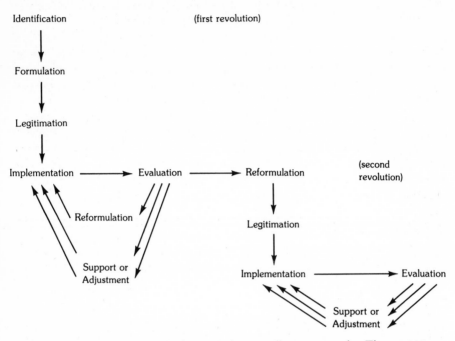

It goes without saying that these cycles are illustrative only. The variations are virtually limitless. The point is not to identify all combinations but to encourage you to discover the patterns appropriate to public policies being studied.

Two Cases of Evaluation

There are abundant case materials in the burgeoning literature on evaluation. One need only choose the topic and the probability is that there will be a case study available. Two of the most famous evaluations are those associated with the National Income Transfer (NIT) experiment and Head Start. NIT was sponsored by the Office of Economic Opportunity (OEO, since dissolved) as a test of the feasibility of the negative income tax or family payment plan (as a substitute for welfare programs). Peter H. Rossi and Katharine Lyall show how the study got tangled up in the politics of the Nixon administration. Preliminary data were released under pressure from the administration because of their support for a family payment plan. As Rossi and Lyall conclude:

■   It is apparent that the political conditions that make it possible to conduct field experiments are the *same* political conditions that make it likely that a related proposal will appear on the agenda. Hence, the NIT Experiment, which

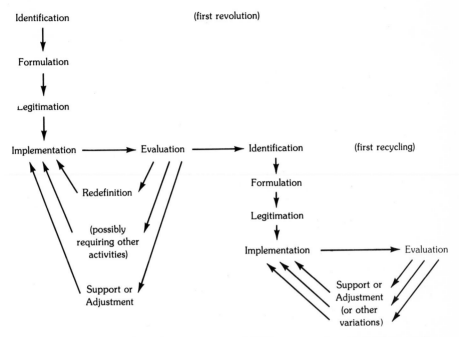

Redefinition or Discovery of Problems

Identification   (first revolution)

Formulation

Legitimation

Implementation ⟶ Evaluation ⟶ Identification   (first recycling)

Redefinition   Formulation

(possibly   Legitimation
requiring other
activities)   Implementation ⟶ Evaluation

Support or   Support or
Adjustment   Adjustment
(or other
variations)

was seen by the OEO administrators and NIT personnel as providing results relevant for a distant future, turned out to be badly timed for consideration as relevant to the FAP [Family Assistance Plan] proposal.[47]

The NIT case illustrates the fundamental point that the politics of the policy process does not wait patiently for the results of scientific testing and analysis.

Head Start is a program for preschool children from low-income families, an effort to give them a "head start" in the educational system. This program consistently has had strong political support. It was particularly interesting, therefore, to observe the reactions to an evaluation of the effects of the program. The study results produced something less than a ringing endorsement of the program.

■   ... although this study indicates that full-year Head Start appears to be a more effective compensatory educational program than summer Head Start, its benefits cannot be described as satisfactory. Therefore we strongly recommend that large-scale efforts and substantial resources continue to be devoted to the search for more effective programs, procedures, and techniques....[48]

Head Start flourished despite the report; it met the test of political evaluation and later the test of organizational evaluation (once it was moved from OEO to the Department of Health, Education, and Welfare).

The two cases offered here illustrate the two broad types of evaluation I have stressed throughout: (1) the less systematic and more political appraisal that occurs with any major government program and (2) the more systematic administrative effort to measure the effects of a program. The public housing program is an example of the first; the community mental health program is an example of the second. The cases also illustrate the crucial importance of political support, not just in the early stages of enactment but also in the later stages, when the program has been implemented for some years and needs sufficient backing for improvements.

Public Housing Meets the Housing Public

Massive mobilization of resources for the war effort in the early 1940s interrupted the normal course of economic affairs. One of the many effects was to create a housing shortage at war's end. With millions of servicemen returning to civilian life, replenishing the nation's housing supply became a major priority. What better time, then, to set a national housing goal? The Housing Act of 1949 (a major amendment to the Housing Act of 1937) did just that, and in the boldest of terms:

■ The Congress hereby declares that the general welfare and security of the Nation and the health and living standards of its people require housing production and related community development sufficient to remedy the serious housing shortage, the elimination of substandard and other inadequate housing through the clearing of slums and blighted areas, and the realization as soon as feasible of the goal of a decent home and suitable living environment for every American family. . . .

Policy Statement in the Housing Act of 1949

To this end, the act authorized federal support for 810,000 housing units for low-income families to be built locally over a period of six years. This came to be known as the public housing program and its history has been marked with struggle. In part, the conflict can be attributed to a growing lack of support among the housing public. By definition, the low-income housing program would positively touch only a small portion of the total housing public. While a social welfare program can survive without strong support, it has difficulty accomplishing grand goals without that backing. And the Housing Act of 1949 had set a noble goal.

The political evaluation of the public housing program, then, was not likely to ignore the reactions of the large and powerful housing public, including the construction industry, real estate dealers, bankers, and the huge middle- and upper-income groups that did not directly benefit from the program. In fact, the decision-making units involved in the continuous political monitoring of the program were much more likely to reflect these affluent and active interests than the poorly articulated housing interests of the low-access poor. Further, since implementing the national public housing program involved all layers of government (national, state, local), there was an overlapping network of assessment, which, though it never killed the program, produced enough uncertainty to prevent steady progress.

The population for the more political evaluation of the public housing program was drawn primarily from the following units:

National government

Executive:

Department of Housing and Urban Development (formerly Housing and Home Finance Agency)
Department of Commerce (notably the Bureau of the Census)
Office of Management and Budget (formerly the Bureau of the Budget)
Council of Economic Advisers
White House Office (special advisers to the president)

Congress:

House Committee on Banking, Finance and Urban Affairs; Subcommittee on Housing and Community Development
House Committee on Appropriations; Subcommittee on Housing and Urban Development—Independent Agencies
Senate Committee on Banking, Housing, and Urban Affairs; Subcommittee on Housing and Urban Affairs
Senate Committee on Appropriations; Subcommittee on Housing and Urban Development—Independent Agencies

State and local governments

Local housing authorities
Other public and quasi-public local bodies (for example, planning agencies)
Local governing units (for example, city councils, county commissions)
State legislatures
State departments of community affairs (a relatively recent organizational unit in some states)

Private groups

Real estate, construction, business, labor, banking, architect, civil rights, neighborhood, citizen groups
The press

Several points should be emphasized in reviewing this imposing list. First, we are speaking of an evaluation process occurring over a period of three decades. During that time many organizational changes occurred. Thus, for example, the program was at one time administered in Washington by a specific agency—the Public Housing Administration—located within the Housing and Home Finance Agency (later the Department of Housing and Urban Development). Reorganizations now make it difficult to locate the program per se within the executive. Second, not all of these units are continuously involved in evaluating the public housing program. Rather, the list represents *sources of potential participants.* A review of the period will show individuals circumstantially and episodically involved in judging the program. Third, and perhaps most obvious, these units have not been engaged in producing formal evaluation reports that then serve as a basis for comprehensive interaction and decision making. Rather, we are identifying a network within which individual and often segmented evaluation-type activities take place. This characterization also suggests that specification, measurement, and analysis are not well programmed. Finally, these various units clearly have different types of authority that may affect whether and how they get involved in evaluation in the first place, as well as determining what actions they might take as a result of their assessments. This difference is perhaps most clearly illustrated with the congressional committees. Whereas the House Committee on Banking, Finance and Urban Affairs can authorize an extension of the public housing program, the House Committee on Appropriations can refuse to provide the money for it. Both must make judgments about the program, often relying on similar information but reacting to different pressures.

Given this description, it is not surprising that the public housing program has not fared too well. It proved extremely difficult to get funding for the 810,000 units originally authorized. In fact, this program is a classic case of the proposition that authorization does not necessarily lead to appropriation. The Public Housing Administration in the 1950s had the authority to support the construction of public housing units at the local level; it just did not have the funds to do so! In 1951 a ceiling of 50,000 units was set on contracts for new housing in appropriations bills, 85,000 below the annual authorization in the 1949 act. In 1952 the ceiling was set at 35,000, in 1953 at 20,000, and in 1954 no funds at all were appropriated for new starts. As a result of these restrictions, less than one-fourth of the units authorized by the 1949 act were completed at the end of the six years.

Meanwhile, implementation of the public housing program and general analysis of the nation's housing problems were resulting in other types of programs. These efforts were either directed at a special group in the society (for example, the elderly) or were designed to assist low-income groups between the poverty level and the lowest levels of the middle-income bracket (as with rent supplements and interest subsidies).[49] In addition, other government programs contributed to the housing problem by supporting urban renewal projects and highway construction. Further, the middle-income and high-access groups in the society were solving their post–World War II housing problems. Private housing starts increased dramatically during the first five years after the war, dipped, and then leveled off at a high mark. Public housing surged slightly, fell off in the mid-1950s, and then leveled off at a modest amount.

A poorly organized clientele, solution of housing problems for well-organized publics, attractiveness of other programs (particularly urban renewal), negative feedback—all combined to prevent the emergence of a policy cycle of support leading to incremental growth of the public housing program. Those adjustments that were made *reduced* the program. Far from realizing growth, it was all the public housing program could do to maintain itself. As Catherine Bauer Wurster described it:

■ Public housing, after more than two decades, still drags along in a kind of limbo, continuously controversial, not dead but never more than half alive. . . . No obituary is yet in order for the U.S. Housing Act of 1937 [as amended by the Housing Act of 1949]. . . . It is more a case of premature ossification.[50]

By contrast, urban renewal enjoyed considerable positive feedback. A definite policy cycle of support with upward increments emerged after 1949. In 1954, when the public housing program was being emasculated, urban renewal was extended. Though the uncertain public housing program continued to exist—administered by the Public Housing Administration through countless local agencies—"the slum clearance provisions of the Housing Act of 1937 [were] slowly transformed into a large-scale program to redevelop the central city."[51] The effect of a successful urban renewal program, administered by a different agency in the Housing and Home Finance Agency, the Urban Renewal Administration, was to increase the need for an expanded public housing program. One of the most severe critics of urban renewal, Martin Anderson, calculated that between 1950 and 1960 urban renewal projects destroyed 126,000 homes, 101,000 of which were substandard. Since the public housing program atrophied during the same decade, the effect was devastating. Anderson estimates that 28,000 housing units were built, most of them in high-rent apartments. His conclusions?

■ More homes were destroyed than were built.
Those destroyed were predominantly low-rent homes.
Those built were predominantly high-rent homes.
Housing conditions were made worse for those whose housing conditions were least good.
Housing conditions were improved for those whose housing conditions were best.[52]

These two intimately related programs were applied by different populations but evaluated by many of the same people. The significance of support, organization, and resources during these stages is highlighted by this contrast. Scott Greer summarizes:

■ The LPAs [local authorities] move toward a program of downtown development and the upgrading of residential districts nearby because this is effective propaganda of the deed. They produce the positive response of relevant publics, including the political officials of the central city and the downtown businessmen. As it succeeds in this sense, it tends to set the precedent for other programs, in this and other cities. In the center of the city many persons can see the program's effects; and they are influential persons. Tall towers and green malls have a disproportionate intellectual appeal because of their esthetic effect. Meanwhile, most of the substandard homes, neighborhoods, and districts may remain exactly what they were before—substandard.[53]

There is thus considerable doubt that local units would have been anxious to apply the program, even if public housing had been expanded during the 1950s. The fact is that when public housing was introduced to the housing public, it simply was not well received. And, however arcane the evaluation system might appear, it did reflect these negative signals.

The black ghetto riots of the 1960s rekindled interest in low-income housing programs. As they watched the cities burn, those in positions of influence and authority concluded that they might have a stake in slum *improvement* as well as slum *clearance*. Even the public housing program benefited. Almost as many units were constructed in the period 1965–1970 as had been built in the previous decade. Some lessons in the unsystematic political evaluations of this program in the past, however, suggest that it will continue to face problems in the future. A program that must depend on street rioting for support is not likely to fare well in the long run.

In his extensive analysis of public housing programs in St. Louis, Eugene Meehan identifies the several changes that were made in housing programs for low-income families during the 1960s and 1970s. The overriding change was a shift toward more private development, through so-called "turnkey" housing (developed by private interests and sold to a public agency) and leasing of privately owned facilities. The modifications were apparently an attempt to reduce the number of complaints rather than to achieve clearly specified goals. Meehan concludes:

■   Various modifications have been made in the original public housing program over the years, usually in an effort to eliminate observable deficiencies or to respond at least to major complaints. Unfortunately, such changes have all too rarely been grounded in careful study of past experiences or parallel operations; most commonly, they have been ad hoc improvisations that rely on current fads in social science or administration, ignoring appropriateness or performance.[54]

In assessing the program's performance Meehan relies on a dramatic medical analogy.

■ The best available analogy is to a physician starting out to perform a simple appendectomy, making a mistake at the beginning that was corrigible but lethal if not corrected; ignoring the mistake and inflicting yet more damage on the body in a series of futile and misdirected efforts to remove the appendix; then, after trying belatedly and at great cost to repair the original mistake, abandoning the operation in despair, leaving the patient to die under sedation—and going on to the next patient.[55]

No analysis of public housing programs would be complete without reference to the massive Pruitt-Igoe project in St. Louis. Begun in 1953, the project at one time housed 12,000 people. It was, perhaps, the most spectacular failure in the national public housing program.

■ Within 18 months of its opening, small children had fallen from its upper windows, assaults became commonplace and vandals attacked and stripped vacant apartments abandoned by terrorized residents.

Entire buildings became vacant as crime spread throughout the projects. Frozen pipes burst in winter, flooding apartments of those families that remained. . . .

Those who remained in those final years were subjected almost nightly to gun battles between drug-running gangs fighting to establish their "territories" in the vacant, deteriorating buildings.[56]

In May 1974, the last of the Pruitt-Igoe residents moved out and a seven-foot-high fence sealed off the sixty-seven-acre area. By mid-1976 the project was no more: all the buildings were demolished, and the site looked like London cleaned up after the blitz.[57]

Not every project has met the fate of Pruitt-Igoe. But it does not take very many such cases to elicit a negative reaction in an unsystematic, impressionistic evaluation network. As noted earlier, this more political evaluation is not necessarily either objective or comprehensive. Rather, it proceeds under the pressure of those with resources and access, a group that has not included the presumed beneficiaries of public housing.[58]

To summarize, here was a program for which evaluation criteria were available, both in general terms ("a decent home and suitable living environment for every American family") and in specific, quantitative goals (810,000 housing units in six years). Yet as the program was implemented, other, less public criteria were obviously being applied in a seemingly amorphous evaluation process controlled, if at all, by those unsympathetic to or disinterested in the original goals. An important lesson to be drawn from this case is that the clientele group for a particular policy must be strong enough (or develop the organizational strength) to influence the evaluation of that policy. I have stressed throughout that the poor in this society have trouble organizing to gain access to any of the decision-making processes (from problem definition to evaluation). As a consequence, and as is illustrated here, programs designed for their benefit meld into an environment that is unlikely to be supportive in the long run. Thus, a further lesson would appear to be that unless programs of this type provide means by which those affected can organize and speak for themselves—that is, provide meaningful reactions pro and con—they will remain essentially gratuitous: mere patronizing concessions of the more affluent majority.

Eugene Meehan puts all of this in context in discussing the "normative dimension." He proposes that "laws unsupported by norms will fail." What he is really saying is that intricate social programs that are somehow dropped on agencies without proper backing are difficult to implement, impossible to evaluate, and likely to fail.

■ When the social institutions responsible for making policy must create programs out of an interplay of conflicting and competing interests, the results will necessarily reflect the inadequacies and inconsistencies that characterize society as a whole. Such factors limit the life expectancy and potential for accomplishment of any policy proposal. It is both futile and irresponsible to ask a public agency, whether a school, a police force, or a local housing authority, to solve a problem that society at large has not yet resolved in its fundamental norms.

In that context, the public housing program was a victim of society's inability or unwillingness to come to grips with the problem of dealing with the poor and the powerless.[59]

The Many Faces of Evaluation in Mental Health Policy

In an essay presumably directed to evaluating the national mental health program, Dr. Stanley F. Yolles, former director of the National Institute of Mental Health, pointed out:

■ At its best, public policy in the United States is a reflection of the will of the people. At our best, we can serve that will by learning as much as we can about why man behaves as he does and by suggesting methods of intervention to change the way people act, think, work, and live. If we succeed, we need not worry about evaluating the national health program. The people of the United States will do it for us.[60]

Through this bit of convoluted logic, Dr. Yolles essentially dismisses the need for evaluation as long as "we" do "our" job and democracy is allowed to work its will. That evaluation is necessary just to determine whether the job itself is appropriate apparently was not considered by Yolles. The statement does, however, illustrate one of the many faces of evaluation. In this view, programs are developed and implemented in accordance with prevailing professional goals and values. This process somehow reflects the will of the people, who in turn will evaluate its products favorably (or so the statement seems to imply).

I begin with this statement not because it represents a misguided minority view, but rather because it tends to dominate much of the thinking among professional staff in government agencies. Essentially it is a rationale for doing what you have been trained to do—a not uncommon tendency in all endeavors. The statement also warns us that evaluations conducted within agencies or by committed professionals are likely to justify what is. Critical internal reviews leading to significant change in organization, procedures, or purposes are likely to be rare.

Two levels of evaluation will be described here: that within the national policy-making apparatus and that at the local level, where services are delivered. The primary focus of attention is the Community Mental Health Centers program, first authorized in the Mental Retardation Facilities and Community Mental Health Centers Construction Act of 1963. The discussion illustrates the variety of the more systematic evaluations that can occur and, by inference, suggests that evaluation, like all policy processes, depends very much on the initial assumptions, breadth and depth of analysis, political and organizational context, and, of course, programmatic commitment.

Before proceeding, it is useful to distinguish among several kinds of questions that might serve as the basis for evaluation. Paul Binner distinguishes among such questions as: What is being done by this program?; How much is being done?; How much is being accomplished?; and Are the accomplishments of the program worthwhile?[61] The first two questions simply ask for descriptive data with no particular attention to the ends to be achieved. Many so-called evaluations are of this type. The third question asks about goal achievement. Is what is being done accomplishing anything—that is, in the direction of program purposes? The last question raises the more fundamental point of whether the purposes themselves are useful.

Binner also distinguishes between program and procedural evaluations. This is essentially a distinction between goals and methods for achieving them.

■ The program evaluation model is concerned primarily with progress toward a goal and requires a clear enough conception of the goals to provide milestones that indicate relative distances from it. The procedure evaluation model is primarily concerned with establishing cause-and-effect relationships between procedures and their outcomes. As such, the two answer related but different questions and the answer to one does not necessarily provide the answer to the other.[62]

We will see in the first instance described below that program and procedural evaluations did result in quite different sets of proposals. We will also see that, just as with public housing, the context of evaluation is important. In this case, however, an active and supportive clientele was able to resist critical, independent evaluations of their program.

Evaluation from the Top

The Community Mental Health Centers (CMHC) program has met one of the principal tests for congressional support; that is, it distributed facilities throughout the nation, potentially a little something for every congressional district. Perpetuity is not necessarily guaranteed for such programs (the poverty program also spread largesse liberally among constituencies), but they begin with a definite advantage. Marc Fried identified another edge for the program, a further advantage in meeting the challenge of critical evaluations: it simply sounded like a good idea. Those familiar with the "snake pit" image of state mental hospitals were attracted to what appeared to be a more humane method for treating the mentally ill.

■ The vast and rapid impact of community mental health programs suggests that the spread of interest was as much ideological as it was a realistic response to realistic gaps in services. Thus, we are confronted with a movement rather than with a theory or empirical data or methods. We remain uncertain about what has been wrong with previous approaches to mental health and illness, except at the grossest level, and we are unclear about the range of options opened up by a new conception of the relationship between communities and professional mental health services and facilities.[63]

So what serves as an advantage in resisting threats from the outside also makes an objective internal evaluation more difficult. Fried observes that evaluation of services has traditionally been informal and unsystematic. Therefore, "In view of our deep reluctance to confront problems of service evaluation . . . it is hardly surprising that the development of community mental health programs and centers has far outstripped our capacity to assess their benefits and deficiencies."[64]

Here then was a generally supportive environment for the extension and expansion of the community mental health program. At the same time, however, the Nixon administration was formulating a philosophical approach to the proper role of the federal government in domestic policy issues. Dubbed the "new federalism," this approach placed a great deal of stress on state and local decision making, with national financial support through general revenue sharing. The expiration of the CMHC Act in 1973 and the prospect of a national health insurance program (possibly including mental health) were sufficient stimuli for a full-scale policy evaluation of community mental health.

Two analyses were produced, one by the National Institute of Mental Health (NIMH) working with the staff of the secretary of Health, Education, and Welfare (HEW), and one independently by those in the office of the HEW secretary who were sympathetic to the new federalism concept. Not unexpectedly, the reports came to quite different conclusions. Joseph L. Falkson, a participant in the second evaluation, describes the NIMH effort as reducing the scope of the study by "bringing it down from the big question . . . to a series of limited, safe questions, the answers to any of which would not prove inimical to its [NIMH's] interests."[65] The result then was supportive. The document itself was huge and simply directed attention to individual programs without comparative analysis or comprehensive evaluation of whether the accomplishments were worthwhile (see Binner's question above).

■ It covered virtually every program service area run by NIMH. Its pages were flooded with data. Each separate section on programs conveyed a series of . . . budgetary options (i.e., how many more projects could be set up under alternative levels of funding). The message came through loud and clear: NIMH is doing a fine job, except for its continuing financial problems. More money for its programs will prove highly beneficial to society.[66]

The second study began with a different set of specifications, those drawn from the framework of the new federalism. According to Falkson, this led to a set of large questions that the community mental health fraternity was unlikely ever to face directly.

1. Should CMHCs be permanently subsidized by the federal government? If not, how long should grant subsidies be retained for a given project?
2. If permanent federal subsidy should prove necessary, which allocative tools available to the federal government would best serve to finance CMHCs (for example, insurance premiums covering primary mental health services,

continued reliance on federal grants, or allocations to the states as part of a health revenue sharing program)?
3. How effective have CMHCs been in (a) ameliorating mental illness and promoting mental health, and (b) distributing mental health services to the poor and to others in need but not receiving services?[67]

These questions obviously broadened the evaluation. While equally subjective in nature ("Should CMHCs be permanently subsidized . . . ?" sets the boundaries for analysis just as surely as does "How can we do even better than we already are?"), the questions made the normative framework of the second study quite explicit, thereby permitting specification of the kinds of data required. The group studied the distribution of benefits among the states and concluded:

■ While project grants have expanded the absolute supply of services, they have tended to reinforce preexisting maldistributive tendencies of the private sector by flowing more to resource-dense than resource-scarce areas.[68]

Five options were offered as a result of this analysis, ranging from permanent federal support to CMHCs to a phasing out of CMHC grants and funding through health insurance. According to Falkson, the group hoped that the last option would ultimately prevail.

To make a long story short, the Nixon administration recommended still another option: the *immediate* end to the CMHC program. Congress was not impressed with this choice, however. It proposed an extension of the program, merely changing the labels to suit the circumstances. The president was presented with the Health Revenue Sharing and Health Services Act of 1974. Falkson argued that "health revenue sharing was a euphemism . . . which could not hide the categorical nature of the legislation."[69] President Ford vetoed the legislation; Congress passed it again in 1975; President Ford vetoed it again, and Congress overrode the second veto.

Falkson concluded that "the New Federalist mental health services policy options were lost in an atmosphere of ideological commitment and the evangelical rhetoric of the community mental health lobby."[70] Marc Fried's conclusions about the "movement" (see above) appear to find support in this statement. But one might note further that ideology combined with practical constituency benefits presents a particularly tough adversary for those supporting a contrary view. As Falkson realistically observes, this second evaluation report "could not have prevailed through the cogency of its logic alone."[71]

Evaluation Below

However complex the evaluation of programs might be in terms of the "big questions" asked by decision makers in Washington, the process becomes incomprehensibly muddled when state and local administration is added. As Wholey et al. note:

■ The evaluation of federal social programs is complicated by the fact that most are administered by state and local governments or other public agencies. . . . A long tradition of local autonomy and the lack of precedents for federal monitoring of local efforts . . . often leads to reluctance on the part of federal managers to insist on evaluation of such programs, even when the federal input is substantial.[72]

Given the increasing pressure to evaluate, often in the form of a congressional mandate, review exercises must be carried out. As noted above, Carol Weiss, among others, has identified several designs for systematic evaluation (experimental, quasi-experimental, nonexperimental designs, etc.), but any such efforts require a common methodology and comparable resources if they are to facilitate comparative analysis and be additive for comprehensive program evaluation. While efforts are being made in these directions, the present state of "evaluation below" is primitive.[73]

Even if the methods and resources favor systematic evaluation, however, there are organizational problems involved in guaranteeing useful results. Bruce A. Rocheleau studied fourteen mental health organizations in Florida in order to judge the extent to which they might accommodate any form of evaluation of their work. He interviewed clinicians, directors, and evaluators and found support of general evaluations of programs, but considerable opposition to evaluations of individuals who implement the programs. Yet "all groups were agreed that the performance of the individual clinician is a key to the success of the programs and to the overall quality of service provided by the organization."[74] In a sense, therefore, the local psychology of evaluation was to depersonalize it as much as possible in order to protect those actually doing the job.

Rocheleau also found that evaluation was viewed as a means for insuring organizational survival and security. His interviews revealed the following functions that might be served:

■ 1. Evaluation as a defensive strategy in anticipation of future requirements for . . . accountability by funding agencies and other bodies. . . .
2. Evaluation as a means of providing justification of the worth of the mental health services to the community.
3. Evaluation as a method of securing grants and other resources for the organization. . . .
4. The use of evaluation staff to carry out "nonevaluative" activities necessary or useful to the organization's survival.[75]

Finally, Rocheleau considers the in-house evaluator to be highly sensitized to his or her organization's social life. He stressed the need for evaluators to have more than one source of authority and found relatively high turnover in this most difficult and demanding position. Evaluators "placed a high priority on obtaining the trust and respect of operational personnel," which often led them to "activities and pursuits quite different from those they had originally planned" (for example, simple descriptive data collection).[76]

It is clearly difficult for internal evaluators to fight their organization's ethos. As Carol H. Weiss concludes, "Organizations tend to find the status quo a contentedly feasible state."[77] Thus evaluations below do not look too different from in-house evaluations above. What this brief excursion into evaluation by local mental health organizations suggests, however, is that they possess a capacity to accommodate to, even anticipate, demands to justify their existence. Because of this capacity they can conduct evaluations on their own terms. This suggests that any effort to appraise the evaluation function outside its organizational and political context leads to misunderstanding.

Summary

In reflecting on his experience at the Public Health Service, James S. Fleming observed:

■   To me the whole experience in the bureaucracy was summarized by a . . . woman I worked with who was depressed by her work, but trapped by the income and status. She was depressed, she said, because she had seen "what the bureaucracy does to the individual." "You can work in this building [Public Health Service] all your life," she said, "and not know there are sick people outside."[78]

This statement well illustrates the difficulty of connecting public policy to public problems. Program implementation presumably brings the government to the problem, but not everyone is directly involved in the delivery. Thus the ultimate programmatic goal is frequently not perceived by many whose activities may be vital to implementation.

Evaluation presumably brings the program back to government for study. The principal questions to be answered are: What are the effects of the program? and Are these effects desirable? To say the least, answering these questions is made difficult if one doesn't even know that "there are sick people outside." In other words, it is certainly difficult to judge whether "it" was worth doing if one doesn't know what "it" refers to.

This chapter has concentrated on the activities, purposes, politics, and methods of program evaluation. I have made special effort to delineate the traditional forms by which judgments are made about ongoing programs and the recent scientific techniques of evaluation research. The latter are associated with a new profession, one with its own journals, handbooks, language, society. Creating a profession does not immediately solve the many complex problems that are characteristic of effective program evaluation. These problems, too, are rooted in politics. It is normally the case that the findings of the new evaluators are fed into the processes by which politicians decide what to do next, if anything. Therefore a more comprehensive view of evaluation has been stressed, rather than one limited to the science of measuring programmatic impacts. In a book on the politics of the policy process, I judge it fitting to emphasize the broader context of evaluation. Therefore even in the second case discussed (community mental health), the more political aspects of evalua-tion studies are stressed. Studies of methods for treating alcoholics, preventive police patrols, income transfer payments, preschool education, and the like are important in their own right. How the studies are used in the policy process and how this knowledge may influence evaluation research (as described in the second case) are of even greater significance for the purposes of this book.

Notes

1. Lincoln J. Fry and Jon Miller, "Responding to Skid Row Alcoholism: Self-Defeating Arrangements in an Innovative Treatment Program," in *Readings in Evaluation Research*, 2d ed., ed. Francis G. Caro (New York: Russell Sage Foundation, 1977), p. 308.
2. George L. Kelling et al., "The Kansas City Preventive Patrol Experiment: A Summary," in Caro, *Readings in Evaluation Research*, p. 331.
3. Joseph S. Wholey et al., *Federal Evaluation Policy* (Washington, D.C.: Urban Institute, 1970), p. 15.
4. Peter Rossi et al., *Evaluation: A Systematic Approach* (Beverly Hills, Calif.: Sage Publications, 1979), p. 15.
5. Rossi et al., p. 28.
6. Carol H. Weiss, *Evaluation Research* (Englewood Cliffs, N.J.: Prentice-Hall, 1972), p. 1.
7. Edward A. Suchman makes exactly the distinction relied on here in *Evaluation Research* (New York: Russell Sage Foundation, 1967), p. 31.
8. Alice M. Rivlin, *Systematic Thinking for Social Action* (Washington, D. C.: Brookings Institution, 1971), chap. 5.
9. Jeffrey L. Pressman and Aaron Wildavsky, *Implementation*, 2d ed. (Berkeley: University of California Press, 1979), p. 127.
10. Laura I. Langbein, *Discovering Whether Programs Work* (Santa Monica, Calif.: Goodyear, 1980), p. 5.
11. David Nachmias, ed., *The Practice of Policy Evaluation* (New York: St. Martin's Press, 1980), p. 17.
12. Aaron Wildavsky, "The Self-Evaluating Organization," in Nachmias, pp. 441–442.
13. Wildavsky, "The Self-Evaluating Organization," pp. 442, 443.
14. Fred M. Frohock, *Public Policy: Scope and Logic* (Englewood Cliffs, N. J.: Prentice-Hall, 1979), p. 184.
15. Carol H. Weiss, "The Politicization of Evaluation Research," *Journal of Social Issues* 26, no. 4 (Autumn 1970): 58. See also Carol H. Weiss, "Where Politics and Evaluation Research Meet," *Evaluation* 1, no. 3 (1973): 37–45.
16. Weiss, "The Politicization of Evaluation Research," p. 58.
17. Donald T. Campbell, "Reforms as Experiments," *American Psychologist* 24, no. 4 (April 1969): 410.
18. See also Frohock, *Public Policy: Scope and Logic*, chap. 6, for a realistic appraisal of problems, politics, the public interest, and evaluation.
19. Nachmias, *The Practice of Policy Evaluation*, p. 17.
20. Wholey et al., *Federal Evaluation Policy*, p. 28.
21. Peter H. Rossi, "Testing for Success and Failure in Social Action," in *Evaluating Social Programs*, ed. Peter H. Rossi and Walter Williams (New York: Seminar Press, 1972), pp. 17–18.
22. Rossi, "Testing for Success and Failure in Social Action," p. 18. My addition in brackets.
23. Suchman, *Evaluation Research*, p. 11.
24. Morris S. Ogul, "Legislative Oversight of Bureaucracy," in U. S. Congress, House of Representa-tives, Select Committee on Committees, *Committee Organization in the House*, 93rd Cong., 1st Sess., 1973, vol. 2, pp. 701–702.
25. U. S. Congress, Senate, *A Compilation of the Legislative Reorganization Act of 1946*, Document No. 71, 83d Cong., 1st Sess., 1953, p. 16.
26. Carol Goss, "Congressional Committee Oversight: The Case of the Office of Saline Water," unpublished M.A. thesis, University of Arizona, 1968, p. 8.

27. Aaron Wildavsky, "Rescuing Policy Analysis from PPBS," *Public Administration Review* 29 (March–April 1969): 193.
28. Cited in Joseph Pois, "The General Accounting Office as a Congressional Resource," in U. S. Congress, Senate, Commission on the Operation of the Senate, *Congressional Support Agencies*, 94th Cong., 2d Sess., 1976, p. 34.
29. See Daniel Bell, "Government by Commission," *The Public Interest* 1 (Spring 1966): 3–9; and Thomas R. Wolanin, *Presidential Advisory Commissions* (Madison, Wis.: University of Wisconsin Press, 1975).
30. Suchman, *Evaluation Research*, p. 31.
31. Suchman, p. 31.
32. Suchman, pp. 39–41. Emphasis in original.
33. Nachmias, *The Practice of Policy Evaluation*, pp. 4–14; Rossi et al., *Evaluation: A Systematic Approach*, pp. 32–51.
34. Rossi et al., p. 33.
35. Rossi et al., p. 37.
36. Rossi et al., p. 247.
37. Nachmias, *The Practice of Policy Evaluation*, p. 13.
38. Weiss, *Evaluation Research*, p. 61. See also the extended review of these designs in Langbein, *Discovering Whether Programs Work*, chaps. 6–9.
39. See in particular Campbell's discussion in "Reforms as Experiments," *American Psychologist* 24, no. 4 (April 1969): 409–429.
40. Weiss, *Evaluation Research*, p. 67.
41. Weiss, p. 73.
42. Weiss, p. 74.
43. For cases illustrating various types of evaluation research see Caro, *Readings in Evaluation Research*, Part IV; and Nachmias, *The Practice of Policy Evaluation*, chaps. 1–8.
44. Rivlin, *Systematic Thinking for Social Action*, p. 118.
45. Rivlin, p. 119.
46. Harold D. Lasswell, "The Decision Process: Seven Categories of Functional Analysis," reprinted in *Politics and Social Life*, ed. Nelson W. Polsby et al. (Boston: Houghton Mifflin, 1963), p. 102.
47. Peter H. Rossi and Katharine C. Lyall, "The External Politics of the National Income Transfer Experiment," in *Readings in Evaluation Research*, 2d ed., ed. Francis G. Caro (New York: Russell Sage Foundation, 1977), p. 293. The larger study from which this selection is taken is Peter H. Rossi and Katharine C. Lyall, *Reforming Public Welfare: A Critique of the Negative Income Tax Experiment* (New York: Russell Sage Foundation, 1976).
48. Victor Cicarelli, "The Impact of Head Start: Executive Summary," in Caro, *Readings in Evaluation Research*, p. 347.
49. See Robert Taggart III, *Low-Income Housing: A Critique of Federal Aid* (Baltimore: Johns Hopkins University Press, 1970), pp. 18–20, for a review of these programs.
50. Catherine Bauer Wurster, "The Dreary Deadlock of Public Housing," in *Urban Housing*, ed. William L. C. Wheaton et al. (New York: Free Press, 1966), p. 246.
51. Scott Greer, *Urban Renewal and American Cities* (Indianapolis: Bobbs-Merrill, 1965), p. 32.
52. Martin Anderson, "The Federal Bulldozer," in *Urban Renewal*, ed. James Q. Wilson (Cambridge, Mass.: MIT Press, 1967), p. 495.
53. Greer, *Urban Renewal and American Cities*, p. 34. The reasons for urban renewal's failure to produce better housing for the poor, despite the intention of the law, are too complex to discuss here. Suffice it to say that urban renewal specializes in knocking down housing units and replacing them primarily with government buildings, shopping centers, office buildings, malls, and high-rent apartments.
54. Eugene J. Meehan, *The Quality of Federal Policymaking: Programmed Failure in Public Housing* (Columbia, Mo.: University of Missouri Press, 1979), p. 41.
55. Meehan, p. 198.
56. *The Christian Science Monitor*, May 30, 1974.
57. See Meehan, *The Quality of Federal Policymaking*, p. 134 ff., for pictures of the Pruitt-Igoe project from the beginning to the end.
58. Of course, all projects have some positive effects. Thus, for example, Meehan points out that "as a make-work program for the construction industry it [Pruitt-Igoe] was an outstanding success since it produced minimum facilities for the least time at maximum cost." p. 202.
59. Meehan, pp. 198–199.

60. Stanley F. Yolles, "The Comprehensive National Mental Health Program: An Evaluation," in *Comprehensive Mental Health*, ed. Leigh M. Roberts et al. (Madison, Wis.: University of Wisconsin Press, 1968), p. 287.
61. Paul Binner, "Program Evaluation," in *The Administration of Mental Health Services*, ed. Saul Feldman (Springfield, Ill.: Charles C Thomas, 1973), p. 345.
62. Binner, p. 349.
63. Marc Fried, "Evaluation and Relativity of Reality," in Roberts et al., *Comprehensive Mental Health*, p. 42.
64. Fried, p. 42.
65. Joseph L. Falkson, "Minor Skirmish in a Monumental Struggle: HEW's Analysis of Mental Health Services," *Policy Analysis* 2 (Winter 1976): 106.
66. Falkson, p. 106.
67. Falkson, p. 107.
68. Falkson, p. 112. For a critical review of other outside evaluation studies contracted for by NIMH, see Franklin D. Chu and Sharland Trotter, *The Madness Establishment* (New York: Grossman, 1974), pp. 110–120.
69. Falkson, p. 116.
70. Falkson, p. 118.
71. Falkson, p. 119.
72. Wholey et al., *Federal Evaluation Policy*, p. 73.
73. See Rivlin, *Systematic Thinking for Social Action*, ch. 1.
74. Bruce A. Rocheleau, "The Organizational Context of Evaluation Research," in *Public Policy Making in a Federal System*, ed. Charles O. Jones and Robert D. Thomas (Beverly Hills, Calif.: Sage Publications, 1976), p. 245.
75. Rocheleau, p. 248.
76. Rocheleau, p. 254. See also Scott Greer and Ann L. Greer, "Governance by Citizens' Boards: The Case of Community Mental Health Centers," in Nachmias, *The Practice of Policy Evaluation*, pp. 352–375.
77. Weiss, *Evaluation Research*, p. 114.
78. Personal communication from Professor Fleming, September 10, 1982. Quoted by permission.

Chapter Ten

Conclusion as Prelude

Functional activities	Categorized in government	With a potential product
Resolution/ termination	Problem resolution or change	Solution or change

As will soon become apparent, this is a last chapter that isn't absolutely essential as far as the framework of study is concerned. For, in fact, much of what is to be discussed here is implicit in the explication of other functional activities. In particular, it should be apparent that one seldom has a sense of closure in studying the policy process. I have judged that an explicit discussion of this point is useful, however, and in addition I wish to draw your attention to other matters that seem properly placed in a concluding chapter. First, then, I discuss the nature of resolution and termination as functional activities in the policy process. Second, I offer a set of categories for decision making and policy. Third, I introduce some difficult problems in what one might call "the morality of choice." And finally I recap the framework in more elaborate form.

Resolution for Whom?

In his discussion of policy analysis, Robert Eyestone points out:

■ Policy questions are questions of differing values, and policy decisions are the result of some kind of settlement among people whose preferences are somewhat different. A choice usually satisfies some people more than others because it comes closer to what they wanted than to the wishes of others.[1]

One of the major lessons of this book is that public problems aren't comprehensively or universally "solved." In fact, the term *solution*, which has a ring of finality to it, is so highly relative that its more common usage is distorted. This explains the reliance on *resolution*, a word that literally refers to an "act or process of resolving, or reducing to simpler form." Specifically, resolution is viewed here as *a process in which public problems undergo change.* This definition encourages study of the effects of various government programs. Solutions, as such, are not presumed to result from government action on public problems.

There are any number of practical justifications for this approach. First and foremost, for some of the following reasons it is impossible simply to hold the problem and its environment constant:

1. Events interfere to alter people's perceptions of their needs.
2. Other problems emerge for some people that are of a higher priority than those for which a program has been developed.
3. Pressures from some sources are reduced or dispersed.
4. Private actions relieve needs, often influencing how people define problems and react to programs.
5. Programs themselves have unanticipated outcomes that may influence the definitions of problems.
6. ". . . objectives in any public policy are multiple, ambiguous and conflicting."[2]

This list is a small sample of the factors that constitute the dynamic social world into which government programs are introduced. The most we can do is identify the effects of particular programs and decisions through observation (for example, 100 new housing units, 120 fewer substandard housing units), inference (for example, reduced rioting, less press attention), and more or less systematic measurements (for example, surveys, field research, experimentation).

Second, even if the world were more static, with few changes occurring between the perception of problems and the implementation of programs, determining when and whether a solution was at hand would be difficult. What measures would be relied on? What criteria would be used to determine when a particular public's needs were being met? What of the case in which problems are defined for others (who are unable to define problems for themselves or are uninterested in doing so)? Nor can we forget such complicating "initial realities" as "Policy makers are not faced with a *given* problem" and "Many programs are developed and implemented without the problems ever having been clearly defined" (see chapter 2). I have already discussed many of these problems as they apply to evaluation. Policy actors normally do no more than keep the channels open for feedback and make imprecise judgments about customer satisfaction. While members of Congress pay attention to their mail and executives are sensitive to the need for public support for programs, very little conscious effort is made to determine whether problems are actually "solved."

Third, whether or not the policy environment remains static, it is difficult to know what other outcomes might have been realized had a different program been developed and implemented. Social change achieved in one way may or may not be similarly achieved by others. Alice M. Rivlin illustrates this point in discussing the popular Head Start program:

■ After the fact, an evaluation attempted to uncover whether the program had had an *average* effect, discernible in test scores at the first and second grade levels. But the program was not designed to answer the really important and interesting questions: Were some approaches more successful than others? Were some more successful with particular types of children?[3]

A similar point is made in a study of the effects of the 55 mph speed limit. While the limit was judged to be effective and efficient, in and of itself, it was by no means certain that this was the best way of promoting conservation and highway safety. "It is quite possible that other policies, aimed directly at these goals, would be more effective."[4]

These cases introduce two important concepts, effectiveness and efficiency, that require careful testing. Yehezkel Dror defines effectiveness as the "extent to which direct goals are achieved" and efficiency as a "cost-benefit ratio." Clearly, an effective program can be inefficient if costs are ignored, and an efficient program can be ineffective if the scale of benefits is ignored.[5] Just to reach the point of measuring requires a capacity to determine goals, costs, and benefits (both what and whose they are). A government report put it this way:

■ The basic requirement for productivity measurement in an organization is that both its outputs and its inputs be measurable. Valid measurement of the end-product output may be more or less difficult in various organizations and in some instances, especially where the nature, quality, and purpose of output undergo rapid change, or where the output is otherwise undefinable or nonhomogeneous, it may be practically impossible.[6]

If goals, costs, benefits, inputs, and outputs are determinable at all, then one is faced with the multiplicity of interpretations and changes over time. Further, as stressed in the discussion of the purposes of evaluation (see chapter 9), sometimes effectiveness, efficiency, and productivity are measured by political and organizational, not programmatic, criteria. As Fremont J. Lyden and his colleagues observe:

■ The process of goal definition should not be taken for granted. Operating goals are not self-evident in an organization's official goal statement. And real, or operative, goals must be ascertained for development of an effective design for the operation of the organization, and realistic criteria for measuring organizational accomplishment.[7]

"Most problems are not solved by government, though many are acted on there." This reality (see chapter 2) allows for those problems that are solved in government (by someone's criteria). More importantly, however, it advises the student to concentrate analysis on who wants what done and what is in fact done, rather than on what is solved.

Termination as a Process

■   The difficulties involved in policy innovation have been the object of much attention. But this interest has rarely extended to issues raised by the other side of the policy coin—what happens when a policy is discontinued.[8]

■   With due respect to those who have described implementation as "the missing link" in policy analysis, it is clear that public policy termination has been much less attended, much less linked to policy analysis.[9]

It is certainly true that few scholars have concentrated on program termination as a separate policy activity deserving of study. But therein lies a lesson. The word itself—*termination*—sounds so very final, even abrupt. And much of what happens in government doesn't seem to end quite that way. Scholars are not necessarily attracted to the study of something that doesn't happen very often.

Still, changes occur constantly, creating a motion not unlike that of the sea. The direction of a current is not always evident, least of all from offshore, yet the observer is aware of being carried away from certain features of the landscape and toward others. It is also very difficult to identify the conclusion of sea undulations, or waves; yet they must end somewhere.

The point is that study of the ending cannot be disconnected from study of the many preceding actions. Furthermore, an ending may come decrementally, in bits and pieces, just as programmatic growth may come incrementally. Termination therefore should be viewed typically as a process, not a single, sudden act of closure. So defined, the concept becomes integrated with and dependent on the other activities in the policy process.

Peter deLeon employs the "termination as process" approach. He finds the dictionary definition "too restrictive."

■   The March of Dimes did not conclude its operations with the discovery of the Salk polio vaccine, nor did the U. S. Army Horse Cavalry canter off into the sunset with the advent of the mechanized army. To include these sorts of phenomena, we need to appreciate the concept of "partial termination," in which specific government functions, programs, policies, or organizations significantly redirect their activities so as to remain operant. . . .[10]

Thus *fading* and *melding* are appropriate images for termination as that concept is used here.

Gradualness in termination is explained by what has gone on before in the policy process. Support obviously is required for programs to gain approval in the first place. Intelligent and practical implementation and evaluation are directed toward maintaining that support and increasing it if possible. It may take as much time and as many resources to delegitimate an operating program as it took to legitimate the same program. deLeon identifies six obstacles to policy termination that elaborate on this point:

1. *Intellectual reluctance:* Those involved in and committed to a project will

resist bringing it to an end. Few people want to hear about failure or a major change.

2. *Institutional permanence:* ". . . organizations are deliberately designed to endure."

3. *Dynamic conservatism:* Organizations are dynamic, not static, and will make defensive adjustments.

4. *Antitermination coalitions:* Benefiting groups "are particularly successful when they form coalitions to block threatened termination acts."

5. *Legal obstacles:* Arbitrary acts of dissolution are frequently prevented by law.

6. *High start-up costs:* This obstacle refers to the inertia that is characteristic of an ongoing program. ". . . the analyst who recommends termination must be quite certain of his evaluation measures and the efficacy of his proposed alternatives."[11]

Some terminations are easier than others, of course. Anthony Downs explains:

■ The older a bureau is, the less likely it is to die. This is true because its leaders become more willing to shift major purposes in order to keep the bureau alive [deLeon's "dynamic conservatism"].

The best time to "kill" a bureau is as soon as possible after it comes into existence.[12]

The implication of this is that not many bureaus will be killed. Herbert Kaufman asked, *Are Government Organizations Immortal?* His response was quite positive. Nearly 85 percent of the government organizations he studied (148 of the 175 agencies in his sample) survived from 1924 through 1973.[13] The Office of Economic Opportunity (OEO) is a classic example of an organization that was able to survive long after its support had waned. It was surely one of the weakest federal agencies, but it survived well into the Nixon administration, even beyond President Nixon's efforts to disband it. And when it was finally terminated as an agency, many of its programs survived in other agencies.

The OEO example suggests an important distinction between terminating an *agency* and terminating a *program.* The former will be more difficult since an agency typically administers a bundle of programs and can therefore command support from diverse groups, which may coalesce to help the agency survive. One strategy for terminating an agency, then, is to distribute its programs elsewhere, as was done with OEO. Even an agency weakened by lack of a function, however, can resist. The Subversives Activities Control Board existed long after its functions had all but disappeared. Charged with the responsibility of maintaining a list of Communist-associated organizations, the board was successful in listing only eight in its twenty-two-year lifetime (others listed were negated by the courts). Even at the board's death an effort was made in Congress to expand its functions and change its name (always a good antitermination strategy) to the Federal Internal Security Board.

Programs are more vulnerable, though termination for them may also be a process of dispersal. President Carter's effort to terminate the breeder reactor demonstration plant on the Clinch River in Tennessee demonstrates the resilience of a program that has congressional support.[14] Carter's effort began in 1977; the plant is still being funded at this writing. President Reagan had more luck in terminating programs, due primarily to his overwhelming victory in 1980, Republican control of the Senate for the first time in twenty-six years, and an apparent agenda shift toward support for reduction of government. It should also be noted, however, that certain bold Reagan termination promises—notably to dissolve the departments of Education and Energy—were not fulfilled.

Frustration with the failure to stop programs and disband agencies has led to demands for institutional reform. In part, the increased emphasis on program evaluation is a consequence of bafflement by decision makers to redirect government resources when they conclude that these resources are misspent or wasted. The discussion in chapter 9 shows that program evaluation, too, is typically integrated into the network of support for an agency or program. It is not a magic formula for sorting out failure from success. With this understanding, however, evaluation can become an effective tool in the termination process.

One of the more blunt proposals for facilitating termination is the so-called sunset law. By this method, agencies or programs have a designated life span of a certain number of years. At the end of that time they are automatically terminated, thus forcing decision makers to recreate them if they are really needed. Unfortunately, this procedure does not solve the basic problems associated with termination. In fact, it may even worsen them in some cases, for example, by giving an agency or program a guaranteed life regardless of its effectiveness and by setting a day certain for an agency to build support for its survival.

Thus, as with the other policy activities, the politics of termination is inexorably linked to what has gone on before. It is a subject that deserves more attention and is likely to receive it as long as budget deficits send decision makers scurrying to make cuts. Clearly we know much more about how to get government going than we do about how to get it stopped.

Types of Decision Making

In their book *A Strategy of Decision,* David Braybooke and Charles E. Lindblom rely on two important dimensions—understanding and change—in identifying four types of decision making. Primarily Lindblom's formulation, this set of categories is most suggestive for policy study (see figure 10.1). Lindblom argues persuasively that most democratic decision making fits within the third quadrant. The 1960s in particular, however, provided us with examples of fourth quadrant decision making, and the other quadrants are worth further pondering as well. Given his principal judgment and interest, Lindblom is considerably more explicit in describing the conditions for the third quadrant than for the other three. Therefore, in accepting the utility and potential of this framework, I was motivated to conceptualize further.

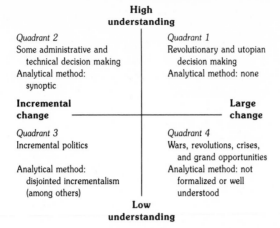

Figure 10.1   Lindblom's four quadrants of decision making. *(Source: Bray-brooke and Lindblom, 1963, p. 78.)*

Figure 10.2 displays my modifications of Lindblom's work. Several points need clarification. First, consider the two dimensions for classifying decision making: the vertical dimension is labeled *estimated capacities;* the horizontal dimension is labeled *intended change.* In dealing with estimates and intentions I have sought to finesse the difficult problem of measuring impact. That is, I shift the emphasis up front, so to speak, asking what policy actors want to accomplish and whether they believe they have the resources to accomplish it.

Estimated capacities refers to the bundle of resources presumably required for effective policy making. These resources incorporate what Lindblom refers to as "understanding" but also include the administrative, informational, communication, and political resources. Taken together, these estimates indicate whether those involved think they presently have the capability to do the job. Of course, any very systematic analysis of decision-making styles requires study of the variation among these many types of resources.

Intended change directs attention to the scope of a policy proposal or program. What do policy actors think will happen as a result of approval and implementation of the decision or program? Do they have grand hopes for effecting large social change? Or do they expect only minor shifts? The notion is that policy actors differ in what they intend to happen as a result of a particular policy action. Some have bold expectations for dramatic social change (behavioral, institutional, physical); others expect only modest increments. We can expect these estimates and intentions to influence decision-making styles.

Four modes or styles of decision making are identified in figure 10.2 and are discussed below. First, however, it is essential to point out that the quadrants are, in fact, collections of an inestimable number of variations of decision making. The two dimensions are, after all, continua. Thus literally hundreds of

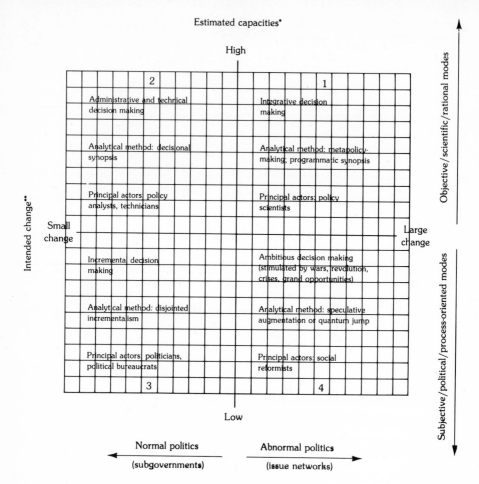

Figure 10.2 — text content within figure:

Estimated capacities*

High

Objective / scientific / rational modes

2

1

Administrative and technical
decision making

Integrative decision
making

Analytical method: decisional
synopsis

Analytical method: metapolicy-
making; programmatic synopsis

Principal actors: policy
analysts, technicians

Principal actors: policy
scientists

Intended change**

Small
change

Large
change

Incremental decision
making

Ambitious decision making
(stimulated by wars, revolution,
crises, grand opportunities)

Analytical method: disjointed
incrementalism

Analytical method: speculative
augmentation or quantum jump

Principal actors: politicians,
political bureaucrats

Principal actors: social
reformists

3

4

Low

Subjective / political / process-oriented modes

Normal politics
(subgovernments)

Abnormal politics
(issue networks)

*Including knowledge, administrative, political capacities
**Evidenced in goal statements and measured against existing policy

Figure 10.2 Four modes of decision making. *Variations on a theme of Charles E. Lindblom*

intersections might be identified in a comprehensive survey of programs and decisions. I have therefore superimposed a grid on the figure to suggest the many additional variations that are possible. Each of the illustrations provided below varies somewhat in its place in the figure; for example, the poverty program was bolder in conception than the clean air program, though both are examples of efforts to have laws lead social change (referred to as "speculative augmentation" in quadrant 4).

Quadrant 1: Integrative Decision Making

I will examine the characteristics and conditions associated with each quadrant, illustrating each with familiar government programs. Lindblom has little to say about quadrant 1, perhaps because he has elevated it beyond the ordinary business of government. As modified in figure 10.2, however, quadrant-1 behavior appears to characterize those who believe they are able to understand what the problem is and how it can be solved. Further, they expect their actions to have significant effects. These attitudes and behaviors seem to be characteristic of the so-called comprehensive rationalists (see table 2.2). Thus I have labeled this mode of decision making "integrative," that is, presuming to achieve rational and integrated public policy and, therefore, effect large social change.

The analytical methods used may be either on the grandest scale—metapolicy making—or merely comprehensive within a single large issue. *Metapolicy making* is defined by Yehezkel Dror as "policymaking on how to make policy."[15] Thus it deals with core issues of how the system itself will be structured—rather comprehensive matters. *Programmatic synopsis* refers to comprehensive analysis within the issue being treated. That may sound modest enough, but the fact is that most issues are not treated comprehensively in the sense that all effects of all options are examined.

What are the facilitating conditions for integrative decision making? They include the following:

1. An issue susceptible to imaginative goals
2. Public interest and support
3. A highly trained scientific and technical corps
4. Uncommitted, flexible budget
5. Limited issue development (the full costs are not realized)
6. Limited public awareness of eventual effects (essentially a corollary of condition 5)

The outstanding example in recent decades of a program that met these conditions is the moon exploration program. President Kennedy declared on May 25, 1961, "I believe we should go to the moon." He meant it literally: the United States should make a landing on the moon. It was a fanciful goal, requiring extraordinary resources. "Congress approved his requests, almost without a murmur."[16] Nuclear power development also met these conditions, at least in the early stages. A confident corps of scientists promised virtually cost-free energy once nuclear plants were fully developed. This case, however, also illustrates a point emphasized below: that there may well be significant shifts in decision making from one quadrant to another. By the 1980s nuclear power development was characterized by incrementalism, perhaps even decrementalism.

Quadrant 2: Administrative and Technical Decision Making

In this quadrant, decision makers have confidence in their capacities to do the job. But the job they perceive is relatively small scale. These people tend to be the technicians described in table 2.2. They are skilled in administrative or technical work and are not susceptible to fanciful goals. The principal analytical method is that of "decisional synopsis." That is, the method attempts to be complete within the limited scope of a decision. The technicians presumably know how to assess the impacts within a narrow base.

The conditions facilitating this style of decision making include:

1. Growth of a technically competent staff
2. Limited public attention to the decision
3. Limited involvement by elected decision makers
4. Growth in research capability
5. Adaptability of discretionary authority to analytic techniques
6. Separable programmatic decisions

In essence, these conditions describe the many routine decisions that are characteristic of implementing and maintaining specialized aspects of a policy program. The examples are innumerable: developing and applying an environmental standard, building a highway, providing a service, and so on.

Quadrant 3: Incremental Decision Making

The third quadrant is the most familiar, due primarily to Lindblom's descriptions and analysis. Note where it fits on the two dimensions: the estimate of capacities is low, the intentions are modest. These are decision makers who accept the limitations of their condition and work with them.

■ . . . their investigations are concerned with the margins at which it is contemplated that social states might be changed from that existing. They are focused on incremental alteration of existing social states.[17]

The method employed is "disjointed incrementalism," a term invented by Lindblom to characterize decision making "through small or incremental moves on particular problems rather than through a comprehensive reform program."[18] It is "endless," taking "the form of an indefinite sequence of policy moves," and it is "exploratory."

■ . . . policy-making proceeds through a sequence of approximations. A policy is directed at a problem; it is tried, altered, tried in its altered form, altered again, and so forth. . . . incremental policies follow one upon the other in the solution to a given problem.[19]

The conditions facilitating incrementalism are those characteristic of the pluralistic politics of this country:

1. Balanced strength and access of affected groups
2. Conflicting technical knowledge (regarding both the problem and its solution)
3. Growing significance of the issue (enough for gaining agenda status but not sufficient to result in a crisis)
4. Adaptability of the issue to compromise proposals

5. Involvement by elected decision makers at a crucial point
6. Limited public attention to the issue

Taken together, these conditions force policy making through "a sequence of approximations." The lack of knowledge of what to do next and the strength of competing groups make compromise and exploration almost certain. Once the ice is broken and a program is on the books, policy moves are continuous, often as routines. In fact, decision makers are unlikely to challenge the basic premises upon which the program is based; rather, it just continues, with marginal changes.

As expected, there are countless examples of incrementalist programs. One can almost select at random from major domestic programs and hit upon one with the characteristics cited above. One outstanding case, however, is social security. Martha Derthick describes it as follows:

■ Policy choices for social security can be summed up in two maxims: a little bit more is always a good thing; anything less is inconceivable. There is always forward movement along a familiar, if not actually predestined, path. Sometimes there are delays. . . . Sometimes there are temporary deviations. . . . Eventually, though, the insurance program advances and displaces any alternative. Expenditures and tax rates rise steadily and, under the statute, are planned to rise still more in the future. The product of the incremental, inertial process is a mammoth program approaching nearly $100 billion a year in volume of expenditure and apparently immune to the least reduction even if decreasingly immune to criticism. The result of the many steps, each small in itself yet in practice irreversible, is a massive shift of resources to the public sector.[20]

The latter half of this statement illustrates how incrementalism can lead to large commitments or even large change. It was the growing awareness of the scale of social security commitments that led to a crisis atmosphere in the early 1980s. A bipartisan National Commission on Social Security Reform was appointed by President Reagan in 1981 to prepare a plan. This extraordinary procedure was necessary because normal politics would not accommodate the conflicts involved in making changes. As Derthick suggests above, the inertia of incrementalism is hard to resist.

Quadrant 4: Ambitious Decision Making

We turn now to perhaps the most interesting of the four quadrants, that in which estimated capacities remain low but an opportunity to act presents itself to those intending large change in policy. This opportunity may come in the form of war or revolution, but such events are of course rare. More likely as stimuli for ambitious decision making are crises, massive expressions of public opinion on an issue, or possibly landslide elections. Whatever the cause, a policy breakthrough is achieved despite the acknowledged limitations of knowledge, communication, political support, and administrative skills. The analytical method employed in this quadrant is that of "speculative augmentation," perhaps even a quantum jump in policy. *Speculative* refers to the style of knowledge use, *augmentation* to the nature of policy change. Thus the style of decision making is judged to be "ambitious" and the product tends to be a *marginal program.*

The facilitating conditions for speculative augmentation are as follows:

1. Extraordinary public awareness of the issue
2. Overriding crisis or grand opportunity to act
3. Broad perception of the issue among elected decision makers
4. Effective neutralization of moderating interests (technicians, bureaucrats, conservatives)
5. Availability of experimental techniques
6. Awareness of support from outside government (among the media and the general public)

Many of these conditions were met in the 1960s and 1970s, when we witnessed a veritable explosion of public participation in decision making. An anxiety developed to act, and to ignore the restrictions that so often modify or halt innovative efforts. Writing in 1969, David Easton captured much of the spirit of quadrant 4:

■ We need to accept the validity of addressing ourselves directly to the problems of the day to obtain quick, short-run answers with the tools and generalizations currently available, however inadequate they may be. We can no longer take the ideal scientific stance of behavioralism that because of the limitations of our understanding, application is premature and must await future basic research. Application is always premature, information is always incomplete, choices are never the best possible. Certainly the fact that you are aware of these limitations of man should not cause your withdrawal from social and political processes. "To know is to bear the responsibility for acting and to act is to engage in reshaping society." [21]

There are many outstanding examples of ambitious decision making during the 1960s and 1970s: the social programs of the Great Society, the regulatory programs during the Nixon administration. Perhaps the most obvious example among social programs is the Economic Opportunity Act of 1964—the poverty program. Part of the design of this program was to discover what needed to be known in order to solve the problems of poverty. In other words, the limitations of knowledge and know-how were built into the very purpose of the act. From the start the poverty program was acknowledged to be beyond existing capabilities. [22]

Another good example of policy beyond capabilities is the Clean Air Amendments of 1970. Impatient with the progress being made in air quality improvement, environmental groups pressed for a policy breakthrough. New, tough standards were set for both stationary and moving sources of pollution. It was generally acknowledged that the standards could not be met within existing technology. [23]

In both these cases, efforts to implement were characterized by accommodations to the realities of political and social life. The ambitiousness of the original intentions was never realized. Subsequent decision making was thus of the quadrant 2 or 3 variety. As with nuclear power development, we witness *a shift over time in decision-making style within an issue*. This shift may occur as a consequence of a learning process by which decision makers identify the dimensions of an issue. What seems resolvable if government can only lead the technology is later discovered to be much more complex. Accommodations are then made, and the innovative policy program begins to look like the classic incremental model, with one important difference. The program is racheted down, not up.

Summary

The four types of decision making discussed in this chapter provide a means for distinguishing among government decisions and programs. Each of the two dimensions, estimated capacities and intended change, acts as a dividing line between broadly different approaches to policy making. Quadrants 1 and 2 are on the high side of estimated capacities and tend to be more objective, scientific, and rational. Quadrants 3 and 4 are on the low side and tend to be more subjective, political, and process oriented (see figure 10.2). Likewise there are broad differences between the quadrants along the "intended change" continuum. Quadrants 1 and 4 tend to require abnormal politics, in which highly visible issues command broad public interest. Hugh Heclo refers to "issue networks" to describe the increased participation and public interest of this brand of politics. Quadrants 2 and 3 tend to reflect what we have come to think of as the normal politics of subgovernments, or so-called cozy little triangles.

These variations clearly illustrate that the policy process differs significantly among issues. But it may also differ within an issue through the various stages of decision making, from problem definition to program evaluation and termination. For example, what begins as ambitious decision making in the planning and approval stages may settle down to administrative or incremental decision making in the implementation stage (see discussion of quadrant-4 cases above). Ambitiousness may emerge again in program evaluation if it is learned that the original plans are not being fulfilled. The turmoil in 1983 over the Environmental Protection Agency appears to be a case in point. Ambitious plans for environmental cleanup were not being realized; highly public investigations were therefore launched to expose EPA's failures and to reiterate the commitments of the original quadrant-4 decision making.

Types of Policy Effects

We come now to one of the more difficult matters of policy study, that of the effects or impacts of policy actions. We encountered this issue in the discussion of program evaluation. It is worth treating again here.

The Apollo "man on the moon" project of the National Aeronautics and Space Administration (NASA) represented a huge commitment of national resources (more than $25 billion during the period 1965–1970). What were the effects? What needs were met? What problems were solved? One thinks immediately of national pride, international goodwill, sectional economic gain (in Florida and Texas), technological breakthroughs, and so on, but these represent only the most obvious, first-order effects, which in many cases are no more than the promotional efforts of NASA and its supporters. More difficult to determine are the secondary and tertiary, intended and unintended effects and consequences of having pursued a particular government program. Policy *intentions or goals* are not normally synonymous with policy *effects*. Furthermore, Lindblom points out that analysts typically "identify situations or ills from which to move *away* rather than goals *toward* which to move."

■ Even short-term goals are defined largely in terms of reducing some observed ill rather than in terms of a known objective of another sort. . . . Policy aims at suppressing vice even though virtue cannot be defined, let alone concretized as a goal; at attending to mental illness even though we are not sure what attitudes and behavior are most healthy; at curbing the expansion of the Soviet Union even though we do not know what positive foreign policy objectives to set against the Kremlin's; at reducing the governmental inefficiencies even though we do not know what maximum level of competence we can reasonably expect. . . .[24]

This set of observations further illustrates the complexity of identifying and measuring policy effect, suggesting as it does the need to analyze a full range of changes and movements resulting from a government program. For in studying outcomes one is faced with the fact that some are expected, others are not; some are manifest, others are latent; some are short run, others long run; some are easily identifiable, others are not; some propagate, others terminate; some are fed back into the government, others are either fed into other institutions or simply absorbed "out there." These differences once again emphasize the need to specify the basis for any one classification of policy effects. Though all too common an exercise, it is not enough merely to create categories and label the entries "policy" or "policy effects" or "policy outcomes." Whatever we learn must be specified in terms of the questions we sought to answer, the time frame within which our research was conducted, and the institutional units studied.

Perhaps the most frequently cited public policy categories are those developed by Theodore J. Lowi: distribution, regulation, and redistribution. In what sense are these "public policies?" The discussion of the term *policy* in chapter 2 advises that such a question must be asked in order to delineate the focus of study. In this case Lowi responds by defining policies "in terms of their impact or expected impact on the society."[25] He speaks of three types of policy impacts noted above: *distributive, regulatory,* and *redistributive.* By *distributive* he refers to the effects of programs that give somebody something. The land distribution program of the federal government during the nineteenth century is a classic example, but many subsidy programs would also qualify. By *regulatory* he refers to those government standards and controls that seek to influence our behavior. Typically these regulations develop in response to practices that are deemed unacceptable for some reason (for example, polluting the environment, price fixing, endangering the public health). *Redistributive* is not quite so simple since, as Lowi points out, "in the long run, all governmental policies may be considered redistributive . . . some people pay in taxes more than they receive in services."[26] What he means to convey, however, is that some programs more than others take from one group and give to another. It is a matter of degree, of course, and an important determinant in distinguishing *distributive* from *redistributive* appears to be the extent of group involvement and conflict in policy development and implementation. The less a group contributes and the more it gets from government, the more redistributive the policy. Randall B. Ripley and Grace A. Franklin also suggest that it is a matter of intention; that "redistributive policy involves a *conscious* attempt by the government to manipulate the allocation of wealth, property, rights, or some other value among broad classes or groups in society."[27]

Robert H. Salisbury has extended Lowi's categories to include self-regulation—a necessary addition. Obviously, self-regulation also involves limits on what certain people may do, but the group itself is authorized to set these limits (for example, professional licensing of lawyers, physicians, and engineers). Salisbury also distinguishes between policy that is primarily allocative and policy that is primarily structural. Allocative policies, as the term implies, are those that confer benefits (distributive and redistributive). Structural policies, on the other hand, create units and guidelines for future allocations.[28] It is the distinction between whether, for instance, the law specifically allocates money to a group for some purpose (for example, veterans through the GI Bill of Rights) or whether some unit of government is given authority by law to allocate resources under certain circumstances (for example, secretary of agriculture in raising price supports).

Ripley and Franklin have begun the arduous task of identifying the manifold characteristics of the Lowi "policy types." They specify how certain broad features and core relationships differ among the three. Further, they assume the existence and importance of "subgovernments" in policy development and implementation, stressing the cross-institutional nature of most government decision making. Subgovernments emerge as collections of actors directing their attentions and efforts to particular issues. These actors are drawn from various institutional units: agencies, committees, interest groups. They interact frequently around the subject matter; for example, agriculture, veterans' benefits, medicare, minimum wage.

It is neither possible nor necessary to repeat the details of this fine effort to encourage students of public policy to venture from the more institution-bound analysis. It is sufficient for present purposes to note that Ripley and Franklin find different patterns of relationships among various institutional units for programs with distributive, regulative, and redistributive effects. These relationships are generalized in figure 10.3.

One of the more obvious conclusions from reviewing these charts is that they represent a global mapping of relationships. Research will likely show variation within as well as among these three types of policies.

The effort by Ripley and Franklin also supports a point frequently made in

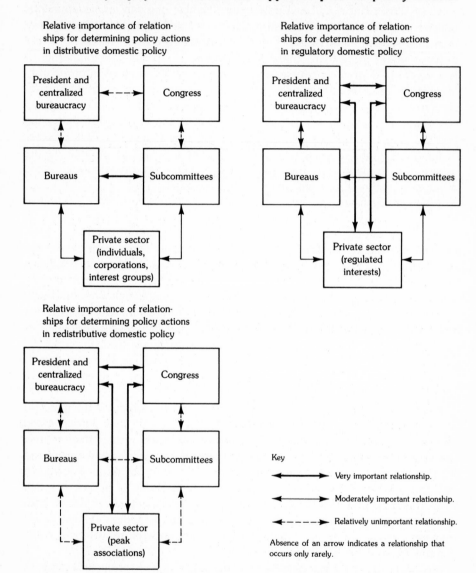

Figure 10.3 Institutional relationships among different policies. *(Source: Ripley and Franklin, 1976, pp. 167–168.)*

these pages. Exploring policy effects, like studying any other feature or output, inevitably draws one back to consider events and how they are variously interpreted as needs, problems, issues. In short, what comes out is related to what goes in.

Some attention must be paid to the question of who is affected. Often the discussion of policy effects is conducted at a very high level, suggesting general societal impacts. But most programs are directed to some group. Thus we need to think of the various impacts (distributive, redistributive, regulatory, and so on) as affecting different populations—those targeted and those who may also benefit or suffer. This sort of thinking leads one to the following populations:

1. *Target population:* Those to whom the program is specifically directed, either to benefit (for example, recipients of welfare aid or a tax break) or to control behavior (for example, a regulatory program)
2. *Associated population:* Those aligned with or affected by the target population who may benefit or suffer (for example, the supermarkets with the food stamp program or the labor unions with a stringent air pollution control program)
3. *Resource population:* Those who are taxed or otherwise called upon to support the program
4. *Governmental population:* Those who are involved in promoting, implementing, and evaluating the program

Complete analysis of policy effects requires study of the many possible effects (primary, secondary, tertiary; anticipated, unanticipated; social, economic, political) on these several populations. Once this is done, conclusions can be developed about whether a program that is *intended* to be distributive, regulatory, or redistributive actually turns out to have those effects on this or that population.

The Morality of Choice

What should come out of the policy process? What effects are we seeking? And how should these favored outcomes be achieved? One measure of our national choices is, of course, the budget. At the writing of the first edition of this book (1970), the budget dollar was still heavily committed to national defense (more than forty-one cents, with thirteen cents going to Vietnam), and the amount allocated to human resources (education, health, income security programs) was increasing steadily. At the writing of the second edition (1977), national defense accounted for approximately twenty-five cents and human resource programs more than fifty cents of the budget dollar. At the present writing (the fiscal 1984 budget), the Reagan administration has proposed significant increases in national defense expenditures (to approach thirty cents of the budget dollar in 1984) and cuts in most domestic programs. A debate

raged in 1983 over the efforts of the Reagan administration to reverse spending trends of recent decades. Who is right? The answer depends on who is
drawing conclusions and the values used to judge what is right. There are
those who argue that the principal function of the national government is to
provide a stout defense so that the citizenry can realize its potential. Human
resources programs in this view are not only unnecessary, but are actually
dysfunctional for the realization of a diverse and dynamic society. Others
argue that large defense expenditures do no more than guarantee immorality.
Preparation for war, they believe, leads to war. Governments should serve
those whom society has not rewarded. In this view, equality is not a passive
process in which individuals are merely guaranteed freedom from interference.
It is an active process in which serious attention and sizable resources are
directed toward adjusting imbalances in society.

In fact, the morality of choice in a democratic system appears to depend on
maintaining such diverse views, thus complicating the smooth flow of public
policy. Abraham Kaplan points out that "an absolutistic morality cannot take
hold on democratic politics, for politics in a democracy is essentially pluralistic,
tolerant, compromising." [29] Democratic public choice then cannot avoid certain
human limitations; indeed, as E. E. Schattschneider and others argue, it is
founded and structured on the human condition.

■ Democracy is based on a profound insight into human nature, the realization
that all men are sinful, all are imperfect, all are prejudiced, and none knows the
whole truth. That is why we need liberty and why we have an obligation to hear
all men. Liberty gives us a chance to learn from other people, to become aware
of our own limitations, and to correct our bias. Even when we disagree with
other people we like to think that they speak from good motives, and while we
realize that all men are limited, we do not let ourselves imagine that any man is
bad. *Democracy is a political system for people who are not too sure that they
are right.*[30]

This conclusion should not be interpreted as downgrading the intelligence of
democrats. Quite the reverse. Democratic public choice carries with it a heavy
burden of community awareness and knowledge. Scientific inquiry and understanding are not only to be encouraged in democracy, they are essential for the
operation and survival of that form of government. As T. V. Smith aptly
observed: ". . . democracy succeeds in proportion as it discovers a form of
education calculated to get at the bases of physical and social living and then
makes this education accessible to all its citizens." [31] In this view, the morality
of choice is corrupted when the citizenry fails to engage in or support inquiry
and/or refuses to acknowledge or integrate its results. No small social experiment this! And the temptations to abandon the effort are many. For the
ultimate challenge is to realize a humane, but human, government; to achieve
social justice without determining and enforcing absolute values.

It is important to point out, of course, that whereas democracy cannot
countenance an absolutistic morality, it must sustain, even protect, moralists.

And, in fact, Kaplan finds Americans susceptible to moralization that "sentimentalizes the people," on the one hand, and pragmatism that seeks to make democracy effective on the other. The inevitable conflicts keep politics interesting, if slightly unsettling to the tidy mind. Kaplan's comments, written in the late 1950s, are remarkably contemporary.

■ The American morality of power is under continuous tension between our moralization and our vulgar pragmatism. The uneasy equilibrium between what we think of as "idealism" and "realism" periodically gives way to the one tendency or the other. Like a character in Dostoevski, we hang suspended between bursts of religious ecstasy and drunken debauchery. Power is to be used by men of conscience and integrity for the common good, and its exercise guided always by the ideals of justice and humanitarianism, sympathy and fair play. At the same time, power is intrinsically immoral, corrupting those who have it, and in its very nature destroying the freedom of those subjected to it. Politics, in short, we regard as a succession of necessary evils; we play with words to make virtues of these necessities, rather than apply our energies to reconstituting either the facts that make them necessary or the valuations that make them evil.[32]

The 1960s and 1970s were characterized by high moralism—and for good reason. Civil rights and environmental insults, the tragedies of Vietnam and Watergate, had the combined effect of increasing cynicism, if not destroying the underlying support for the system. Our pragmatically oriented decision makers had to join in the broad philosophical and moral debate about what had gone wrong. While this form of discourse has its place and can, in fact, influence the future course of events, a major lesson derived from this book is that big decisions effecting large social change are infrequent. Translating the conclusions of grand national debates into effective policy development and implementation is no simple matter. Typically decision makers are faced with proximate choices and limited, often conflicting, information, rather than a linear decision path from a consensus on ultimate values and goals. And "political morality," according to Kaplan, "lies in the everyday shaping of policy, not merely in the heroic stand at a time of crisis."[33]

None of this is to downgrade the role of criticism and national debates, or to suggest that they have no function or impact. Indeed, the criticism of American foreign and domestic policies in Vietnam and the moral fervor expressed over presidential excesses in Watergate and related matters surely influenced American politics and policy making. But unless such dramatic expressions of public outrage cause revolution, they tend to result more in turning corners, making adjustments, and preventing the next increment. Even where large change is intended, the programs designed to achieve it are fitted within an organizational and programmatic setting that may resist sudden movement.

What should come out? is a basic question that will, and should, require extensive discussion among students of public policy. I think it is important (1) to consider the problems of applying absolute moral principles in a democratic policy process, (2) to evaluate one's own values and policy biases, and (3) to acknowledge the fact that most choices in the policy process are highly constrained. These recommendations are designed to improve understanding of the policy process. They are not meant to dissuade anyone from critically analyzing American public policies and how they are developed. Criticism is essential in politics and social life. Constructive criticism is better than negative criticism, but negative criticism is better than no criticism.

In this connection, one should be forewarned that the study of how things really work can sometimes blunt critical drive. Several things can happen. One may become enamored with the process as a result of studying it, seeing a reasonable function for everything that goes on, "understanding" every bit-and-piece decision that is made. Or one finds the process so complicated, so lengthy, and so unmanageable that all reform seems hopeless. Since every aspect of the overall process is so extraordinarily intricate, another possibility is that one never has enough information to evaluate and criticize. Students of

TABLE 10.1   The policy process: a recapitulation

Functional activities	Categorized in government	With a potential policy product
Problem identification		
Perception	Problems to	Problem
Definition	government	Demand
Aggregation		Access
Organization		Priorities
Representation		
Agenda setting		
Proposal formulation		
Research	Action in	Proposal or plan
Review	government	
Projection		
Selection		
Program legitimation		
Agreement on means	Action in	Program or
Identification of	government	decision
interests		
Communication		
Approval		
Program budgeting		
Formulation	Action in	Budget
Legitimation	government	
Program implementation		
Organization	Government to	Varies (service,
Interpretation	problem	payments, facili-
Application		ties, controls)
Program evaluation		
Specification	Program to	Varies (justification,
Measurement	government	adjustment)
Analysis		
Recommendations		
Problem resolution/	Problem resolution	Solution or change
program termination	or change	

public policy should guard against all of these. We can't afford to have our scholars "neutralized" in politics.

Conclusion as Prelude

It is altogether appropriate to the principal theme of this book that it close without ending. The policy process is ongoing. Once an issue is acknowledged to require action, seldom will that issue disappear from the government agenda, though its status may change. Adjustments are made constantly in a politics of continuance. The mixes of people, methods, resources, proposals, and support differ greatly among issues and programs. That is what makes the policy process so fascinating.

As a final illustration, table 10.1 recapitulates the several stages of the policy process, as formulated within each of the chapters.

Notes

1. Robert Eyestone, *Political Economy* (Chicago: Markham, 1972), p. 80.
2. Martin Rein, *Social Science and Public Policy* (New York: Penguin, 1976), p. 21.
3. Alice M. Rivlin, *Systematic Thinking for Social Action* (Washington, D. C.: Brookings Institution, 1971), p. 85. Emphasis in original.
4. Charles T. Clotfelter and John C. Hahn, "Assessing the National 55 M.P.H. Speed Limit," in *The Practice of Policy Evaluation,* ed. David Nachmias (New York: St. Martin's Press, 1980), pp. 408–409.
5. Yehezkel Dror, *Ventures in Policy Sciences* (New York: Elsevier, 1971), p. 2.
6. Bureau of the Budget, *Measuring Productivity* (Washington, D. C.: Government Printing Office, 1964), p. 17.
7. Fremont J. Lyden et al., eds., *Policies, Decisions and Organization* (New York: Appleton-Century-Crofts, 1969), p. 137.
8. James M. Cameron, "Ideology and Policy Termination: Restructuring California's Mental Health System," in *The Policy Cycle,* ed. Judith V. May and Aaron Wildavsky (Beverly Hills, Calif.: Sage Publications, 1978), p. 301.
9. Peter deLeon, "A Theory of Policy Termination," in May and Wildavsky, *The Policy Cycle,* p. 279. See also R. P. Biller, "On Tolerating Policy and Organizational Termination: Design Considerations," *Policy Sciences* 7 (June 1976), and Gary Brewer, "Termination: Hard Choices—Harder Questions," *Public Administration Review* 38 (May/June 1978).
10. deLeon, "A Theory of Policy Termination," p. 280.
11. deLeon, pp. 286–293. The specific quotes are taken from pp. 288, 290, and 292, respectively.
12. Anthony Downs, *Inside Bureaucracy* (Boston: Little, Brown, 1967), p. 20.
13. Herbert Kaufman, *Are Government Organizations Immortal?* (Washington, D. C.: Brookings Institution, 1976), p. 34.
14. For details see *Congress and the Nation,* vol. V (Washington, D. C.: Congressional Quarterly, Inc., 1981), pp. 522–523.
15. Yehezkel Dror, *Public Policymaking Reexamined* (San Francisco: Chandler, 1968), p. 160.
16. John M. Logsdon, *The Decision to Go to the Moon* (Cambridge: MIT Press, 1970), p. 129.
17. David Braybrooke and Charles E. Lindblom, *A Strategy of Decision* (New York: Free Press, 1963), p. 84.
18. Braybrooke and Lindblom, p. 71.
19. Braybrooke and Lindblom, p. 73.
20. Martha Derthick, *Policymaking for Social Security* (Washington, D. C.: Brookings Institution, 1979), p. 412.

21. David Easton, "The New Revolution in Political Science," *American Political Science Review* 63 (December 1969): 1055–1056, 1052.
22. See John D. Donovan, *The Politics of Poverty* (New York: Pegasus, 1967).
23. See Charles O. Jones, *Clean Air: The Policies and Politics of Pollution Control* (Pittsburgh: University of Pittsburgh Press, 1975).
24. Braybrooke and Lindblom, *A Strategy of Decision*, p. 102.
25. Theodore J. Lowi, "American Business, Public Policy Case Studies, and Political Theory," *World Politics* 16 (July 1964): 689.
26. Lowi, p. 690.
27. Randall B. Ripley and Grace A. Franklin, *Congress, the Bureaucracy, and Public Policy* (Homewood, Ill.: Dorsey Press, 1976), p. 18. Emphasis added.
28. See Robert H. Salisbury, "The Analysis of Public Policy: A Search for Theories and Roles," in *Political Science and Public Policy,* ed. Austin Ranney (Chicago: Markham, 1968), pp. 151–175.
29. Abraham Kaplan, *American Ethics and Public Policy* (New York: Oxford University Press, 1963), p. 50.
30. E. E. Schattschneider, *Two Hundred Million Americans in Search of a Government* (New York: Holt, Rinehart & Winston, 1969), p. 53. Emphasis added.
31. T. V. Smith, *The Democratic Way of Life* (Chicago: University of Chicago Press, 1926), p. 192.
32. Kaplan, *American Ethics and Public Policy,* p. 77.
33. Kaplan, p. 103.

Bibliography

Compiling a complete bibliography on the politics of the policy process is something more than difficult—it is impossible. The topic is too large, including as it does so much of social, economic, and political life. The best one can do is offer a sample of the many rich sources that are available. After directing the reader to journal, newspaper, and documentary sources, I provide listings of books in several categories: general works on public policy, general works on political institutions, selected analyses of domestic issue areas, and selected studies of the policy process.

Certain journals, magazines, and newspapers are particularly rich in material relevant to the study of public policy. *Social Forces, Urban Affairs Quarterly, Journal of Policy Analysis and Management, The Public Interest, Policy Studies Journal, Policy Studies Review, Policy Sciences, Policy Review, Publius, Public Administration Review, Growth and Change,* and the several new policy evaluation journals have a number of relevant articles in every issue. The *Annals* of the American Academy of Political and Social Science, *The American Behavioral Scientist, Society,* and *Law and Contemporary Problems* frequently devote whole issues to particular policy areas. Other more popular journals, such as *Commentary, The New Republic, The National Review, Regulation,* and *The Nation,* are designed to provide intelligent analysis of contemporary public problems. Among the national newspapers, the *New York Times,* the *Christian Science Monitor,* the *Wall Street Journal,* and the *Washington Post* provide the best coverage and analysis of issues and the policy process. The *American Political Science Review* and the various regional political science journals— *Polity* (Northeast), *Journal of Politics* (South), *American Journal of Political Science* (Midwest), and *Western Political Quarterly*—have occasional articles of major interest, as do such specialized journals as the *Legislative Studies Quarterly, Congress and the Presidency,* and the *Presidential Studies Quarterly.*

One should also draw upon the many publications of the Congressional Quarterly, Inc. The *Weekly Reports,* the *Almanacs, Congress and the Nation,* the *Washington Information Directory, Politics in America, Federal Regulatory*

Directory, and the many special reports are invaluable sources. Also useful are the *Editorial Research Reports* devoted to specific issue areas. A similar publication, the *National Journal,* provides additional analysis of the national scene, with particularly fine analyses of specific issues.

Another important source is the fantastic array of government documents. No other country in the world has so many documentary sources. The place to begin is one of the many useful indexes. The *Monthly Catalog of U. S. Government Publications* takes a bit of getting used to, but the effort will be rewarded. The Congressional Information Service (CIS) provides an index to most congressional documents and is very simple to use. Among the congressional documents that are particularly rich source materials are the following: committee hearings and reports, special staff studies, calendars, the *Congressional Record,* and the *Journals.* The *Federal Register,* presidential papers, annual reports of departments and agencies, reports of presidential commissions, and the budget are all useful executive documents. The *Statistical Abstract of the United States* is a must for the student of public policy.

Students will find that few issues are left untouched in these documentary sources. It is highly recommended that all public policy students take the time to familiarize themselves with government documents. They should welcome a project that encourages their use since the professional payoff for the future lawyer, congressional staffer, bureaucrat, researcher, journalist, and so on, is very great.

I turn now to a listing of selected books that are valuable source materials for understanding the nature and functioning of the policy process.

General Works on Public Policy: Theory, Framework, Analysis

Agger, Robert E., Goldrich, Daniel, and Swanson, Bert E. *The Rulers and the Ruled.* New York: Wiley, 1964.

Agnew, John A. *Innovation Research and Public Policy.* Syracuse, N.Y.: Syracuse University Press, 1980.

Anderson, James E. *Public Policy-Making.* New York: Praeger, 1979.

Bauer, Raymond A., and Gergen, Kenneth J., eds. *The Study of Policy Formation.* New York: Free Press, 1968.

Braybrooke, David, and Lindblom, Charles E. *A Strategy of Decision.* New York: Free Press, 1963.

Browne, William P. *Politics, Programs, and Bureaucrats.* Port Washington, N.Y.: Kennikat Press, 1980.

Caputo, David A. *Politics and Public Policy in America.* Philadelphia: Lippincott, 1974.

———, ed. *The Politics of Policy Making in America.* San Francisco: W. H. Freeman, 1977.

Carey, Raymond, and Posavac, Emil. *Program Evaluation: Methods and Case Studies.* Englewood Cliffs, N.J.: Prentice-Hall, 1980.

Caro, Francis G., ed. *Readings in Evaluation Research.* 2d ed. New York: Russell Sage Foundation, 1977.

Charlesworth, James C., ed. *Contemporary Political Analysis.* New York: Free Press, 1967.

Cobb, Roger W., and Elder, Charles D. *Participation in American Politics: The Dynamics of Agenda-Building.* Boston: Allyn & Bacon, 1972.

Coleman, James S. *Policy Research in the Social Sciences.* Norristown, N. J.: General Learning Press, 1972.

Dahl, Robert A. *Modern Political Analysis.* Englewood Cliffs, N.J.: Prentice-Hall, 1963.

————. *A Preface to Democratic Theory.* Chicago: University of Chicago Press, 1956.

————. *Who Governs?* New Haven, Conn.: Yale University Press, 1961.

————, and Lindblom, Charles E. *Politics, Economics, and Welfare.* New York: Harper & Row, 1953.

————. *Polyarchy.* New Haven, Conn.: Yale University Press, 1971.

Davies, James. *Human Nature in Politics.* New York: Wiley, 1963.

Deutsch, Karl W. *The Nerves of Government.* New York: Free Press, 1963.

Dewey, John. *The Public and Its Problems.* New York: Holt, Rinehart & Winston, 1927.

Dolbeare, Kenneth, ed. *Public Policy Evaluation.* Beverly Hills, Calif.: Sage Publications, 1975.

Donovan, John C. *The Policy Makers.* New York: Pegasus, 1970.

Downs, Anthony. *An Economic Theory of Democracy.* New York: Harper & Row, 1957.

Dror, Yehezkel. *Design for Policy Sciences.* New York: Elsevier, 1971.

————. *Public Policymaking Reexamined.* San Francisco: Chandler, 1968.

————. *Ventures in Policy Sciences.* New York: Elsevier, 1971.

Dunn, William N. *Public Policy Analysis: An Introduction.* Englewood Cliffs, N. J.: Prentice-Hall, 1981.

Dye, Thomas R. *Understanding Public Policy.* Englewood Cliffs, N. J.: Prentice-Hall, 1981.

Easton, David. *A Framework for Political Analysis.* Englewood Cliffs, N. J.: Prentice-Hall, 1965.

————. *A Systems Analysis of Political Life.* New York: Wiley, 1965.

Edelman, Murray. *The Symbolic Uses of Politics.* Urbana, Ill.: University of Illinois Press, 1964.

Edwards, George C., III. *Implementation and Public Policy.* Washington, D. C.: Congressional Quarterly, Inc., 1980.

————, and Sharkansky, Ira. *The Policy Predicament.* San Francisco: W. H. Freeman, 1978.

Etzioni, Amitai. *The Active Society.* New York: Free Press, 1968.

Eulau, Heinz, and Prewitt, Kenneth. *Labyrinths of Democracy.* Indianapolis: Bobbs-Merrill, 1973.

Eyestone, Robert. *Political Economy.* Chicago: Markham, 1972.

————. *The Threads of Public Policy.* Indianapolis: Bobbs-Merrill, 1971.

Freeman, J. Leiper. *The Political Process.* New York: Random House, 1955.

Frohock, Fred M. *Public Policy: Scope and Logic.* Englewood Cliffs, N. J.: Prentice-Hall, 1979.

Galbraith, John K. *Economics and the Public Purpose.* Boston: Houghton Mifflin, 1973.

Gaus, John M. *Reflections on Public Administration.* University, Ala.: University of Alabama Press, 1947.

Gerston, Larry N. *Making Public Policy.* Glenview, Ill.: Scott, Foresman, 1983.

Gerth, H. H., and Mills, C. Wright. *From Max Weber: Essays in Sociology.* London: Routledge & Kegan Paul, 1948.

Gohagan, John K. *Quantitative Analysis for Public Policy.* New York: McGraw-Hill, 1980.

Gramlich, Edward M. *Benefit-Cost Analysis of Government Programs.* Englewood Cliffs, N. J.: Prentice-Hall, 1981.

Greenberg, Edward S. *Serving the Few: Corporate Capitalism and the Bias of Government Policy.* New York: Wiley, 1974.

Greenberger, Martin, Crenson, Matthew A., and Crissey, Brian L. *Models in the Policy Process.* New York: Russell Sage Foundation, 1976.

Greenstein, Fred I., and Polsby, Nelson W., eds. *The Handbook of Political Science.* Reading, Mass.: Addison-Wesley, 1975.

Grodzins, Morton. *The American System.* Chicago: Rand McNally, 1966.

Gwyn, William B., and Edwards, George C., III. *Perspectives on Public Policymaking.* New Orleans: Tulane University, 1975.

Hargrove, Erwin C. *The Missing Link.* Washington, D. C.: Urban Institute, 1975.

Heclo, Hugh. *Modern Social Politics in Britain and Sweden.* New Haven, Conn.: Yale University Press, 1974.

Hennessy, Bernard C. *Public Opinion.* Belmont, Calif.: Wadsworth, 1970.

Hofferbert, Richard I. *The Study of Public Policy.* Indianapolis: Bobbs-Merrill, 1974.

Holden, Matthew, Jr., and Dresang, Dennis L., eds. *What Government Does.* Beverly Hills, Calif.: Sage Publications, 1975.

Hoos, Ida R. *Systems Analysis in Public Policy: A Critique.* Berkeley: University of California Press, 1972.

House, Peter W. *The Art of Public Policy Analysis.* Beverly Hills, Calif.: Sage Publications, 1982.

Ilchman, Warren F., and Uphoff, Norman T. *The Political Economy of Change.* Berkeley: University of California Press, 1971.

Jones, Charles O., and Thomas, Robert D., eds. *Public Policy Making in a Federal System.* Beverly Hills, Calif.: Sage Publications, 1976.

Kaplan, Abraham. *American Ethics and Public Policy.* New York: Oxford University Press, 1963.

Key, V. O., Jr. *Public Opinion and American Democracy.* New York: Knopf, 1961.

Lasswell, Harold D. *A Pre-View of Policy Sciences.* New York: Elsevier, 1971.

———. *The Future of Political Science.* New York: Atherton, 1963.

———. *Politics: Who Gets What, When, How.* New York: Meridian Books, 1958.

———, and Kaplan, Abraham. *Power and Society.* New Haven, Conn.: Yale University Press, 1950.

Lerner, Daniel, and Lasswell, Harold D., eds. *The Policy Sciences.* Stanford, Calif.: Stanford University Press, 1951.

Lindblom, Charles E. *The Intelligence of Democracy.* New York: Free Press, 1965.

———. *The Policy-Making Process.* Englewood Cliffs, N. J.: Prentice-Hall, 1968.

———. *Politics and Markets.* New York: Basic Books, 1977.

———, and Cohen, David K. *Usable Knowledge: Social Science and Social Problem Solving.* New Haven, Conn.: Yale University Press, 1979.

Lineberry, Robert L. *American Public Policy.* New York: Harper & Row, 1977.

Lowi, Theodore. *The End of Liberalism.* 2d ed. New York: Norton, 1979.

———. *The Politics of Disorder.* New York: Basic Books, 1971.

Lynn, Laurence E., Jr., ed. *Knowledge and Policy.* Washington, D. C.: National Academy of Sciences, 1978.

MacRae, Duncan, Jr. *The Social Function of Social Science.* New Haven, Conn.: Yale University Press, 1976.

———, and Wilde, James A. *Policy Analysis for Public Decisions.* Monterey, Calif.: Brooks/Cole, 1979.

May, Judith V., and Wildavsky, Aaron, eds. *The Policy Cycle.* Beverly Hills, Calif.: Sage Publications, 1978.

Mazmanian, Daniel A., and Sabatier, Paul A. *Implementation and Public Policy.* Glenview, Ill.: Scott, Foresman, 1983.

McConnell, Grant. *Private Power and American Democracy.* New York: Knopf, 1966.

Meehan, Eugene J. *The Theory and Method of Political Analysis.* Homewood, Ill.: Dorsey Press, 1965.

Meyers, William R. *The Evaluation Enterprise.* San Francisco: Jossey-Bass, 1981.

Mitchell, Joyce, and Mitchell, William C. *Political Analysis and Public Policy.* Chicago: Rand McNally, 1969.

Mitchell, William C. *The American Polity.* New York: Free Press, 1962.

Murphy, Jerome T. *Getting the Facts: A Fieldwork Guide for Evaluators and Policy Analysts.* Santa Monica, Calif.: Goodyear, 1980.

Nachmias, David, ed. *The Practice of Policy Evaluation.* New York: St. Martin's Press, 1980.

Nagel, Stuart, ed. *Encyclopedia of Policy Studies.* New York: Marcel Dekker, 1982.

————. *The Legal Process from a Behavioral Perspective.* Homewood, Ill.: Dorsey Press, 1969.

————, ed. *Policy Studies in America and Elsewhere.* Lexington, Mass.: Lexington Books, 1975.

Parenti, Michael. *Democracy for the Few.* New York: St. Martin's Press, 1974.

Paul, Ellen F., and Russo, Philip A., Jr. *Public Policy.* Chatham, N. J.: Chatham House, 1982.

Pitkin, Hanna F. *The Concept of Representation.* Berkeley: University of California Press, 1967.

Polsby, Nelson W., Dentler, Robert A., and Smith, Paul A., eds. *Politics and Social Life.* Boston: Houghton Mifflin, 1963.

Presthus, Robert. *Elites in the Policy Process.* London: Cambridge University Press, 1974.

Price, Don K. *The Scientific Estate.* Cambridge, Mass.: Harvard University Press, 1965.

Raiffa, Howard. *Decision Analysis: Introduction to Making Choices Under Uncertainty.* Reading, Mass.: Addison-Wesley, 1968.

Ranney, Austin, ed. *Political Science and Public Policy.* Chicago: Markham, 1968.

Reagan, Michael D. *The Managed Economy.* New York: Oxford University Press, 1963.

Redford, Emmette S. *Democracy in the Administrative State.* New York: Oxford University Press, 1969.

Rein, Martin. *Social Science and Public Policy.* New York: Penguin, 1976.

Riker, William. *The Theory of Political Coalitions.* New Haven, Conn.: Yale University Press, 1962.

Rivlin, Alice M. *Systematic Thinking for Social Action.* Washington, D. C.: Brookings Institution, 1971.

Rogers, Harrell R., Jr., and Bullock, Charles S., III. *Law and Social Change.* New York: McGraw-Hill, 1972.

Rose, Arnold M. *The Power Structure.* New York: Oxford University Press, 1967.

Rose, Richard. *What Is Government?* Englewood Cliffs, N. J.: Prentice-Hall, 1978.

Rossi, Peter H., and Williams, Walter, eds. *Evaluating Social Programs.* New York: Seminar Press, 1972.

Rossi, Peter, Freeman, Howard E., and Wright, Sonia. *Evaluation: A Systematic Approach.* Beverly Hills, Calif.: Sage Publications, 1979.

Schattschneider, E. E. *The Semisovereign People.* New York: Holt, Rinehart & Winston, 1960.

————. *Two Hundred Million Americans in Search of a Government.* New York: Holt, Rinehart & Winston, 1969.

Schneier, Edward V., ed. *Policy-Making in American Government.* New York: Basic Books, 1969.

Schulman, Paul R. *Large-Scale Policy Making.* New York: Elsevier, 1980.

Scott, Robert A., and Shore, Arnold R. *Why Sociology Does Not Apply.* New York: Elsevier, 1979.

Smith, T. Alexander. *The Comparative Policy Process.* Santa Barbara, Calif.: ABC-CLIO, 1975.

Straayer, John A., and Wrinkle, Robert D. *American Government, Policy, and Non-Decision.* Columbus, Ohio: Merrill, 1972.

Starling, Grover. *The Politics and Economics of Public Policy.* Homewood, Ill.: Dorsey Press, 1979.

Suchman, Edward. *Evaluative Research.* New York: Russell Sage Foundation, 1967.

Thayer, Frederick C. *An End to Hierarchy! An End to Competition!* New York: New Viewpoints, 1973.

Tullock, Gordon, and Wagner, Richard E. *Policy Analysis and Deductive Reasoning.* Lexington, Mass.: Lexington Books, 1978.

Truman, David B. *The Governmental Process.* New York: Knopf, 1951.

Van Dyke, Vernon. *Political Science: A Philosophical Analysis.* Stanford, Calif.: Stanford University Press, 1960.

Wade, Larry L. *The Elements of Public Policy.* Columbus, Ohio: Merrill, 1972.

————, and Curry, R. L., Jr. *A Logic of Public Policy.* Belmont, Calif.: Wadsworth, 1970.

Weiss, Carol H. *Evaluation Research.* Englewood Cliffs, N. J.: Prentice-Hall, 1972.

Williams, Walter L. *Social Policy Analyses and Research.* New York: Elsevier, 1971.

Wilson, James Q. *Political Organizations.* New York: Basic Books, 1973.

Young, Roland, ed. *Approaches to the Study of Politics.* Evanston, Ill.: Northwestern University Press, 1958.

General Works on Political Institutions

Abraham, Henry J. *The Judicial Process.* New York: Oxford University Press, 1980.

Altshuler, Alan, ed. *The Politics of the Federal Bureaucracy.* New York: Dodd, Mead, 1968.

Barber, James D. *The Presidential Character.* Englewood Cliffs, N. J.: Prentice-Hall, 1972.

Benveniste, Guy. *Bureaucracy.* San Francisco: Boyd & Fraser, 1977.

Bernstein, Marver H. *The Job of the Federal Executive.* Washington, D. C.: Brookings Institution, 1958.

————. *Regulating Business by Independent Commission.* Princeton, N. J.: Princeton University Press, 1955.

Berry, Jeffrey M. *Lobbying for the People.* Princeton, N. J.: Princeton University Press, 1977.

Break, George F. *Financing Government in a Federal System.* Washington, D. C.: Brookings Institution, 1982.

Brewer, Garry D. *Politicians, Bureaucrats, and the Consultant.* New York: Basic Books, 1973.

Burns, James M. *Presidential Government.* Boston: Houghton Mifflin, 1973.

————. *Leadership.* New York: Harper & Row, 1978.

Cater, Douglass. *The Fourth Branch of Government.* Boston: Houghton Mifflin, 1959.

————. *Power in Washington.* New York: Random House, 1964.

Ceaser, James W. *Reforming the Reforms.* Cambridge, Mass.: Ballinger, 1982.

Cronin, Thomas E., and Greenberg, Sanford D., eds. *The Presidential Advisory System.* New York: Harper & Row, 1969.

Davis, James W., Jr. *The National Executive Branch.* New York: Free Press, 1970.

Davis, Kenneth C. *Discretionary Justice.* Baton Rouge, La.: Louisiana State University Press, 1970.

Dodd, Lawrence C., and Oppenheimer, Bruce I., eds. *Congress Reconsidered.* Washington, D. C.: Congressional Quarterly, Inc., 1981.

Dodd, Lawrence C., and Schott, Richard L. *Congress and the Administrative State.* New York: Wiley, 1979.

Downs, Anthony. *Inside Bureaucracy.* Boston: Little, Brown, 1967.

Elazar, Daniel J. *The American Partnership.* Chicago: University of Chicago Press, 1962.

Fenno, Richard F., Jr. *Congressmen in Committees.* Boston: Little, Brown, 1973.

————. *The President's Cabinet.* Cambridge, Mass.: Harvard University Press, 1959.

Froman, Lewis A., Jr. *The Congressional Process.* Boston: Little, Brown, 1967.

Gawthrop, Louis. *Bureaucratic Behavior in the Executive Branch.* New York: Free Press, 1969.

Gross, Bertram. *The Legislative Struggle.* New York: McGraw-Hill, 1953.

Grossman, Joel B., and Wells, Richard S. *Constitutional Law and Judicial Policy Making.* New York: Wiley, 1980.

Heclo, Hugh. *A Government of Strangers.* Washington, D. C.: Brookings Institution, 1977.

Herring, E. Pendleton. *Group Representation before Congress.* Baltimore: Johns Hopkins University Press, 1929.

————. *The Politics of Democracy.* New York: Holt, Rinehart & Winston, 1940.

Hinckley, Barbara. *Stability and Change in Congress.* New York: Harper & Row, 1983.

Horn, Stephen. *Unused Power: The Work of the Senate Committee on Appropriations.* Washington, D. C.: Brookings Institution, 1970.

Hyneman, Charles. *Bureaucracy in a Democracy.* New York: Harper & Row, 1950.

Jacob, Charles E. *Policy and Bureaucracy.* Princeton, N. J.: Van Nostrand, 1966.

Jacob, Herbert, and Vines, Kenneth N., eds. *Politics in the American States.* Boston: Little, Brown, 1982.

Jewell, Malcolm E., and Patterson, Samuel C. *The Legislative Process in the United States.* New York: Random House, 1977.

Jones, Charles O. *The United States Congress.* Homewood, Ill.: Dorsey Press, 1982.

Kaufman, Herbert. *The Administrative Behavior of Federal Bureau Chiefs.* Washington, D. C.: Brookings Institution, 1981.

————. *Are Government Organizations Immortal?* Washington, D. C.: Brookings Institution, 1976.

Keefe, William J. *Parties, Politics and Public Policy.* New York: Holt, Rinehart & Winston, 1980.

————, and Ogul, Morris S. *The American Legislative Process.* Englewood Cliffs, N. J.: Prentice-Hall, 1981.

King, Anthony, ed. *The New American Political System.* Washington, D. C.: American Enterprise Institute, 1978.

————. *Both Ends of the Avenue.* Washington, D. C.: American Enterprise Institute, 1983.

Kingdon, John W. *Congressmen's Voting Decisions.* New York: Harper & Row, 1973.

Koenig, Louis W. *The Chief Executive.* New York: Harcourt Brace Jovanovich, 1975.

Kohlmeier, Louis J. *The Regulators.* New York: Harper & Row, 1969.

Kozak, David C., and Macartney, John D., eds. *Congress and Public Policy.* Homewood, Ill.: Dorsey Press, 1982.

Krislov, Samuel. *The Supreme Court in the Political Process.* New York: Macmillan, 1965.

Leach, Richard H. *American Federalism.* New York: Norton, 1970.

Light, Paul C. *The President's Agenda: Domestic Policy Choice from Kennedy to Carter.* Baltimore: Johns Hopkins University Press, 1982.

Mainzer, Lewis C. *Political Bureaucracy.* Chicago: Scott, Foresman, 1973.

Manley, John F. *The Politics of Finance.* Boston: Little, Brown, 1970.

Mann, Thomas E., and Ornstein, Norman J., eds. *The New Congress.* Washington, D. C.: American Enterprise Institute, 1981.

Martin, Roscoe. *The Cities and the Federal System.* New York: Atherton, 1965.

Matthews, Donald R. *U. S. Senators and Their World.* Chapel Hill, N. C.: University of North Carolina Press, 1960.

Mayhew, David R. *Congress: The Electoral Connection.* New Haven, Conn.: Yale University Press, 1974.

Meier, Kenneth J. *Politics and the Bureaucracy.* Monterey, Calif.: Brooks/Cole, 1979.

Milbrath, Lester W. *The Washington Lobbyists.* Chicago: Rand McNally, 1963.

Monsen, R. Joseph, Jr., and Cannon, Mark W. *The Makers of Public Policy.* New York: McGraw-Hill, 1965.

Nachmias, David, and Rosenbloom, David H. *Bureaucratic Government USA.* New York: St. Martin's Press, 1980.

Neustadt, Richard E. *Presidential Power.* New York: Wiley, 1960.

Ornstein, Norman J., ed. *President and Congress: Assessing Reagan's First Year.* Washington, D. C.: American Enterprise Institute, 1982.

————, Mann, Thomas E., Malbin, Michael J., and Bibby, John F. *Vital Statistics on Congress, 1982.* Washington, D. C.: American Enterprise Institute, 1982.

Ott, David J., and Ott, Attiat F. *Federal Budget Policy.* Washington, D. C.: Brookings Institution, 1969.

Peabody, Robert L., and Polsby, Nelson W., eds. *New Perspectives on the House of Representatives.* Chicago: Rand McNally, 1963.

Peltason, Jack. *The Federal Courts in the Political Process.* New York: Random House, 1955.

Peters, B. Guy. *The Politics of Bureaucracy: A Comparative Perspective.* New York: Longman, 1978.

Polsby, Nelson W. *Congress and the Presidency.* Englewood Cliffs, N. J.: Prentice-Hall, 1976.

————. *Consequences of Party Reform.* New York: Oxford University Press, 1983.

Pressman, Jeffrey L. *House vs. Senate: Conflict in the Appropriations Process.* New Haven, Conn.: Yale University Press, 1966.

Price, David. *Who Makes the Laws?* Cambridge, Mass.: Schenkman, 1972.

Reagan, Michael D., and Sanzone, John G. *The New Federalism.* New York: Oxford University Press, 1981.

Rieselbach, Leroy N. *Congressional Politics.* New York: McGraw-Hill, 1973.

————, ed. *People vs. Government: The Responsiveness of American Institutions.* Bloomington, Ind.: Indiana University Press, 1975.

Ripley, Randall B. *Congress: Process and Policy.* New York: Norton, 1983.

Ripley, Randall B., and Franklin, Grace A. *Bureaucracy and Policy Implementation.* Homewood, Ill.: Dorsey Press, 1982.

————. *Congress, the Bureaucracy, and Public Policy.* Homewood, Ill.: Dorsey Press, 1976, 1980.

Rourke, Francis E. *Bureaucracy, Politics and Public Policy.* Boston: Little, Brown, 1976.

Schooler, S. Dean. *Science, Scientists, and Public Policy.* New York: Free Press, 1971.

Schubert, Glendon. *Judicial Policy-Making.* Chicago: Scott, Foresman, 1965.

Shapiro, Martin. *Law and Politics in the Supreme Court.* New York: Free Press, 1964.

Smith, Bruce L. R. *The RAND Corporation.* Cambridge, Mass.: Harvard University Press, 1966.

Smith, T. V. *The Democratic Way of Life.* Chicago: University of Chicago Press, 1926.

Sorensen, Theodore C. *Decision-Making in the White House.* New York: Columbia University Press, 1963.

Sundquist, James L. *Making Federalism Work.* Washington, D. C.: Brookings Institution, 1969.

Walker, David B. *Toward a Functioning Federalism.* Cambridge, Mass.: Winthrop, 1981.

Wallace, Robert Ash. *Congressional Control of Federal Spending.* Detroit: Wayne State University, 1960.

Wasby, Stephen L. *The Impact of the United States Supreme Court.* Homewood, Ill.: Dorsey Press, 1970.

Welch, Susan, and Peters, John G., eds. *Legislative Reform and Public Policy.* New York: Praeger, 1977.

Wolanin, Thomas R. *Presidential Advisory Commissions.* Madison, Wis.: University of Wisconsin Press, 1975.

Wolfinger, Raymond E., and Rosenstone, Steven J. *Who Votes?* New Haven, Conn.: Yale University Press, 1980.

Wright, Deil S. *Understanding Intergovernmental Relations.* Monterey, Calif.: Brooks/Cole, 1982.

Yates, Douglas. *Bureaucratic Democracy.* Cambridge, Mass.: Harvard University Press, 1982.

Zeigler, Harmon. *Interest Groups in American Society.* Englewood Cliffs, N. J.: Prentice-Hall, 1964.

Selected Analyses of Domestic Issue Areas

Abrams, Charles. *The Future of Housing.* New York: Harper & Row, 1946.

Ackerman, Bruce A., and Hassler, William T. *Clean Coal, Dirty Air.* New Haven, Conn.: Yale University Press, 1981.

Amsden, Alice H., ed. *The Economics of Women and Work.* New York: St. Martin's Press, 1980.

Anderson, Bernard E., and Sawhill, Isabel V., eds. *Youth Employment and Public Policy.* Englewood Cliffs, N. J.: Prentice-Hall, 1980.

Anderson, Martin. *Welfare.* Palo Alto, Calif.: Hoover Press, 1978.

Axelrod, Regina S., ed. *Environment, Energy, Public Policy: Toward a Rational Future.* Lexington, Mass.: Lexington Books, 1981.

Banfield, Edward C. *The Unheavenly City Revisited.* Boston: Little, Brown, 1974.

Barker, Lucius J., and McCorry, Jesse J., Jr. *Black Americans and the Political System.* Cambridge, Mass.: Winthrop, 1976.

Battan, Louis J. *The Unclean Sky.* Garden City, N. Y.: Doubleday, 1966.

Bendick, Marc, Jr., and Struyk, Raymond J., eds. *Housing Vouchers for the Poor: Lessons from a National Experiment.* Washington, D. C.: Urban Institute, 1981.

Blechman, Barry M., Gramlich, Edward M., and Hartman, Robert W. *Setting National Priorities: The 1975 Budget.* Washington, D. C.: Brookings Institution, 1974.

————. *Setting National Priorities: The 1976 Budget.* Washington, D. C.: Brookings Institution, 1975.

Bradbury, Katharine L., and Downs, Anthony, eds. *Do Housing Allowances Work?* Washington, D. C.: Brookings Institution, 1981.

Breyer, Stephen. *Regulation and Its Reform.* Cambridge, Mass.: Harvard University Press, 1982.

Brown, Harrison. *The Challenge of Man's Future.* New York: Viking Press, 1954.

Browne, William P., and Hadwiger, Don F. *Rural Policy Problems: Changing Dimensions.* Lexington, Mass.: Lexington Books, 1982.

Bullock, Charles S., III, Anderson, James E., and Brady, David W. *Public Policy in the Eighties.* Monterey, Calif.: Brooks/Cole, 1983.

Carmichael, Stokeley, and Hamilton, Charles V. *Black Power.* New York: Random House, 1967.

Carson, Rachel. *The Silent Spring.* Boston: Houghton Mifflin, 1962.

Christianson, Jon B., and Marmor, Theodore R. *Health Care Policy: A Political Economy Approach.* Beverly Hills, Calif.: Sage Publications, 1982.

Chu, Franklin D., and Trotter, Sharland. *The Madness Establishment.* New York: Grossman, 1974.

Crandall, Robert W. *The U.S. Steel Industry in Recurrent Crisis: Policy Options in a Competitive World.* Washington, D. C.: Brookings Institution, 1981.

————, and Lave, Lester B., eds. *The Scientific Basis of Health and Safety Regulation.* Washington, D. C.: Brookings Institution, 1981.

Cronin, Thomas E., Cronin, Tania Z., and Milakovich, Michael. *U. S. v. Crime in the Streets.* Bloomington, Ind.: Indiana University Press, 1981.

Culhane, Paul J. *Public Lands Politics.* Baltimore: Johns Hopkins University Press, 1981.

Dales, J. H. *Pollution, Property, and Prices.* Toronto: University of Toronto Press, 1968.

Davis, David. *Energy Politics.* New York: St. Martin's Press, 1982.

Dillman, Don A., and Hobbs, Daryl J. *Rural Society in the United States: Issues for the 1980's.* Boulder, Colo.: Westview Press, 1981.

Downs, Anthony. *Who Are the Urban Poor?* New York: Committee for Economic Development, 1968.

Dupre, Stefan, and Lakoff, Sanford. *Science and the Nation.* Englewood Cliffs, N. J.: Prentice-Hall, 1962.

Elshtain, Jean Bethke. *Public Man, Private Woman.* Princeton, N. J.: Princeton University Press, 1981.

Esposito, John. *Vanishing Air.* New York: Grossman, 1970.

Feder, Judith, Holahan, John, and Marmor, Theodore. *National Health Insurance: Conflicting Goals and Policy Choices.* Washington, D. C.: Urban Institute, 1980.

Fitch, Lyle C., and associates. *Urban Transportation and Public Policy.* San Francisco: Chandler, 1964.

Freeman, Myrick A., III. *The Benefits of Environmental Improvement: Theory and Practice.* Baltimore: Johns Hopkins University Press, 1979.

Freeman, S. David. *Energy: The New Era.* New York: Vintage Books, 1974.

Fried, Edward R., Rivlin, Alice M., Schultze, Charles L., and Teeters, Nancy H. *Setting National Priorities: The 1974 Budget.* Washington, D. C.: Brookings Institution, 1973.

Garvey, Gerald. *Energy, Ecology, Economy.* New York: Norton, 1972.

Gelb, Joyce, and Palley, Marian L. *Women and Public Policies.* Princeton, N. J.: Princeton University Press, 1982.

Gilford, Dorothy M., Nelson, Glenn L., and Ingram, Linda, eds. *Rural America in Passage: Statistics for Policy.* Washington, D. C.: National Academy Press, 1981.

Gimlin, Hoyt, ed. *America in the 1980s.* Washington, D. C.: Congressional Quarterly, Inc., 1980.

Giraldo, Z. I. *Public Policy and the Family.* Lexington, Mass.: Lexington Books, 1980.

Glazer, Nathan. *Affirmative Discrimination.* New York: Basic Books, 1975.

Goodwin, Craufurd D., ed. *Energy Policy in Perspective.* Washington, D. C.: Brookings Institution, 1981.

Gordon, Kermit, ed. *Agenda for the Nation.* Washington, D. C.: Brookings Institution, 1968.

Guthrie, James W., ed. *School Finance Policies and Practices/The 1980's: A Decade of Conflict.* Cambridge, Mass.: Ballinger, 1980.

Hadwiger, Don F. *The Politics of Agricultural Research.* Lincoln, Neb.: University of Nebraska Press, 1982.

Hale, George E., and Palley, Marian L. *The Politics of Federal Grants.* Washington, D. C.: Congressional Quarterly, Inc., 1981.

Halperin, Morton H. *Bureaucratic Politics and Foreign Policy.* Washington, D. C.: Brookings Institution, 1974.

Harrington, Michael. *The Other America.* New York: Macmillan, 1963.

Haskell, Elizabeth H. *The Politics of Clean Air: EPA Standards for Coal-Burning Power Plants.* New York: Praeger, 1982.

Herber, Lewis. *Crises in Our Cities.* Englewood Cliffs, N. J.: Prentice-Hall, 1965.

Herfindahl, Orris C., and Kneese, Allen V. *Quality of the Environment.* Baltimore: Johns Hopkins University Press, 1965.

Higbee, Edward. *Farms and Farmers in an Urban Age.* New York: Twentieth Century Fund, 1963.

Holloman, J. Herbert, and Grenon, Michel. *Energy Research and Development.* Cambridge, Mass.: Ballinger, 1975.

Jacobs, Jane. *The Death and Life of Great American Cities.* New York: Random House, 1961.

Jencks, Christopher. *Inequality.* New York: Basic Books, 1972.

Krasnow, Erwin G., and Longley, Lawrence D. *The Politics of Broadcast Regulation.* New York: St. Martin's Press, 1973.

Krier, James E., and Ursin, Edmund. *Pollution and Policy.* Berkeley: University of California Press, 1977.

Lave, Lester B. *The Strategy of Social Regulation.* Washington, D. C.: Brookings Institution, 1981.

Lawrence, Robert, ed. *New Dimensions to Energy Policy.* Lexington, Mass.: Lexington Books, 1979.

Leichter, Howard M. *A Comparative Approach to Policy Analysis: Health Care Policy in Four Nations.* Cambridge, England: Cambridge University Press, 1979.

Levy, Lillian, ed. *Space: Its Impact on Man and Society.* New York: Norton, 1965.

Manvel, Allen D. *Housing Conditions in Urban Poverty Areas.* Washington, D. C.: Government Printing Office, 1968.

Mechanic, David. *Mental Health and Social Policy.* Englewood Cliffs, N. J.: Prentice-Hall, 1969.

————. *Politics, Medicine, and Social Science.* New York: Wiley, 1974.

————. *Public Expectations and Health Care.* New York: Wiley, 1972.

Morris, Robert, ed. *Allocating Health Resources for the Aged and Disabled: Technology versus Politics.* Lexington, Mass.: Lexington Books, 1981.

Murphy, Earl F. *Governing Nature.* Chicago: Quadrangle Books, 1967.

Nadel, Mark V. *The Politics of Consumer Protection.* Indianapolis: Bobbs-Merrill, 1971.

Nader, Ralph. *Unsafe at Any Speed.* New York: Grossman, 1965.

Nathan, Richard P. *Monitoring Revenue Sharing.* Washington, D. C.: Brookings Institution, 1975.

National Academy of Sciences. *Science and Technology: A Five-Year Outlook.* San Francisco: W. H. Freeman, 1979.

Ng, Larry K. Y., ed. *The Population Crisis.* Bloomington, Ind.: Indiana University Press, 1975.

Noll, Roger. *Reforming Regulation.* Washington, D. C.: Brookings Institution, 1971.

Owen, Henry, and Schultze, Charles L., eds. *Setting National Priorities: The Next Ten Years.* Washington, D. C.: Brookings Institution, 1976.

Owen, Wilfred. *Transportation for Cities.* Washington, D. C.: Brookings Institution, 1976.

Paarlberg, Don. *Farm and Food Policy.* Lincoln, Neb.: University of Nebraska Press, 1980.

Patterson, James T. *America's Struggle Against Poverty, 1900–1980.* Cambridge, Mass.: Harvard University Press, 1981.

Pechman, Joseph A. *Federal Tax Policy.* New York: Norton, 1971.

————, ed. *Setting National Priorities: The 1978 Budget.* Washington, D. C.: Brookings Institution, 1977.

————. *Setting National Priorities: The 1979 Budget.* Washington, D. C.: Brookings Institution, 1978.

————. *Setting National Priorities: The 1980 Budget.* Washington, D. C.: Brookings Institution, 1979.

————. *Setting National Priorities: Agenda for the 1980's.* Washington, D. C.: Brookings Institution, 1980.

————. *Setting National Priorities: The 1982 Budget.* Washington, D. C.: Brookings Institution, 1981.

————. *Setting National Priorities: The 1983 Budget.* Washington, D. C.: Brookings Institution, 1982.

Poole, Robert W., Jr., ed. *Instead of Regulation: Alternatives to Federal Regulatory Agencies.* Lexington, Mass.: Lexington Books, 1982.

Reagan, Michael. *Science and the Federal Patron.* New York: Oxford University Press, 1969.

Redford, Emmette S. *The Regulatory Process.* Austin, Tex.: University of Texas Press, 1969.

Rhoads, Steven E., ed. *Valuing Life: Public Policy Dilemmas.* Boulder, Colo.: Westview Press, 1980.

Ripley, Randall B. *The Politics of Economic and Human Resource Development.* Indianapolis: Bobbs-Merrill, 1972.

Roberts, Leigh M., Greenfield, Norman S., and Miller, Milton H., eds. *Comprehensive Mental Health.* Madison, Wis.: University of Wisconsin Press, 1968.

Rosenbaum, Walter A. *Energy, Politics and Public Policy.* Washington, D. C.: Congressional Quarterly, Inc., 1981.

————. *The Politics of Environmental Concern*. New York: Praeger, 1973.

Rubin, Eva R. *Abortion, Politics, and the Courts: Roe v. Wade and Its Aftermath*. Westport, Conn.: Greenwood Press, 1982.

Schultze, Charles L. *The Politics and Economics of Public Spending*. Washington, D. C.: Brookings Institution, 1968.

————, Fried, Edward R., Rivlin, Alice M., and Teeters, Nancy H. *Setting National Priorities: The 1971 Budget*. Washington, D. C.: Brookings Institution, 1970.

————. *Setting National Priorities: The 1972 Budget*. Washington, D. C.: Brookings Institution, 1971.

————. *Setting National Priorities: The 1973 Budget*. Washington, D. C.: Brookings Institution, 1972.

Seligman, Ben B. *Permanent Poverty: An American Syndrome*. Chicago: Quadrangle Books, 1968.

Silberman, Charles. *Crisis in Black and White*. New York: Random House: 1964.

————. *Crisis in the Classroom*. New York: Random House, 1970.

Steiner, Gilbert Y. *The State of Welfare*. Washington, D. C.: Brookings Institution, 1971.

————. *The Futility of Family Policy*. Washington, D. C.: Brookings Institution, 1981.

Stevens, Robert, and Stevens, Rosemary. *Welfare Medicine in America*. New York: Free Press, 1974.

Stockwell, Edward G. *Population and People*. Chicago: Quadrangle Books, 1968.

Straetz, Ralph A., Lieberman, Marvin, and Sardell, Alice, eds. *Critical Issues in Health Policy*. Lexington, Mass.: Lexington Books, 1981.

Taggart, Robert, III. *Low-Income Housing: A Critique of Federal Aid*. Baltimore: Johns Hopkins University Press, 1970.

Tatalovich, Raymond, and Daynes, Byron W. *The Politics of Abortion: A Study of Community Conflict in Public Policymaking*. New York: Praeger, 1981.

Thomas, Norman C. *Education in National Politics*. New York: David McKay, 1975.

Thompson, Frank J. *Health Policy and the Bureaucracy: Politics and Implementation*. Cambridge, Mass.: MIT Press, 1981.

Thurow, Lester C. *The Zero-Sum Society*. New York: Penguin, 1980.

Watts, William, and Free, Lloyd A. *State of the Nation, 1974*. Washington, D. C.: Potomac Associates, 1974.

Wholey, Joseph S., et al. *Federal Evaluation Policy*. Washington, D. C.: Urban Institute, 1970.

Wildavsky, Aaron. *How to Limit Government Spending*. Berkeley: University of California Press, 1980.

————, and Tenenbaum, Ellen. *The Politics of Mistrust*. Beverly Hills, Calif.: Sage Publications, 1981.

Wise, Arthur E. *Rich Schools, Poor Schools*. Chicago: University of Chicago Press, 1968.

Young, Oran R. *Natural Resources and the State*. Berkeley, Calif.: University of California Press, 1981.

Selected Studies of the Policy Process

Alford, Robert R. *Health Care Politics*. Chicago: University of Chicago Press, 1975.

Allison, Graham T. *Essence of Decision: Explaining the Cuban Missile Crisis*. Boston: Little, Brown, 1971.

Amrine, Michael. *The Great Decision: The Secret History of the Atomic Bomb*. New York: Putnam, 1959.

Anderson, Martin. *The Federal Bulldozer*. Cambridge, Mass.: MIT Press, 1964.

Art, Richard. *The TFX Decision*. Boston: Little, Brown, 1968.

Ashford, Douglas E., ed. *Comparing Public Policies*. Beverly Hills, Calif.: Sage Publications, 1978.

Bachrach, Peter, and Baratz, Morton S. *Power and Poverty: Theory and Practice.* New York: Oxford University Press, 1970.

Bailey, Stephen K. *Congress Makes a Law.* New York: Columbia University Press, 1950.

————, and Mosher, Edith K. *ESEA: The Office of Education Administers a Law.* Syracuse, N. Y.: Syracuse University Press, 1969.

Baldwin, Sidney. *Poverty and Politics: The Rise and Decline of the Farm Security Administration.* Chapel Hill, N. C.: University of North Carolina Press, 1968.

Ball, Howard, Krane, Dale, and Lauth, Thomas P. *Compromised Compliance: Implementation of the 1965 Voting Rights Act.* Westport, Conn.: Greenwood Press, 1982.

Bardach, Eugene. *The Implementation Game.* Cambridge, Mass.: MIT Press, 1977.

————. *The Skill Factor in Politics.* Berkeley: University of California Press, 1972.

————, and Kagan, Robert A. *Going by the Book.* Philadelphia: Temple University Press, 1982.

Bauer, Raymond, de Sola Pool, Ithiel, and Dexter, Lewis A. *American Business and Public Policy.* New York: Atherton, 1963.

Bellush, Jewell, and David, Stephen M., eds. *Race and Politics in New York City.* New York: Praeger, 1971.

Bendiner, Robert. *Obstacle Course on Capitol Hill.* New York: McGraw-Hill, 1965.

Benveniste, Guy. *Regulation and Planning.* San Francisco: Boyd and Fraser, 1981.

Berman, Larry. *Planning a Tragedy.* New York: Norton, 1982.

Bibby, John, and Davidson, Roger. *On Capitol Hill.* New York: Holt, Rinehart & Winston, 1967.

Caputo, David A., and Cole, Richard L. *Urban Politics and Decentralization: The Case of General Revenue Sharing.* Lexington, Mass.: Lexington Books, D. C. Heath, 1974.

Carroll, Holbert N. *The House of Representatives and Foreign Affairs.* Pittsburgh: University of Pittsburgh Press, 1958.

Chamberlain, Lawrence H. *The President, Congress, and Legislation.* New York: Columbia University Press, 1946.

Clark, Terry Nichols, ed. *Urban Policy Analysis: Directions for Future Research.* Beverly Hills, Calif.: Sage Publications, 1981.

Cleaveland, Frederick, ed. *Congress and Urban Problems.* Washington, D. C.: Brookings Institution, 1969.

Crecine, John P. *Governmental Problem Solving.* Chicago: Rand McNally, 1969.

Crenson, Matthew A. *The Un-Politics of Air Pollution.* Baltimore: Johns Hopkins University Press, 1971.

Dahl, Robert A. *Congress and Foreign Policy.* New York: Norton, 1950.

Daneke, Gregory A., and Lagassa, George K., eds. *Energy Policy and Public Administration.* Lexington, Mass.: Lexington Books, 1980.

Danhof, Clarence H. *Government Contracting and Technological Change.* Washington, D. C.: Brookings Institution, 1968.

Danielson, Michael. *Federal-Metropolitan Politics and the Commuter Crisis.* New York: Columbia University Press, 1965.

Davidson, Roger H. *Coalition-Building for Depressed Areas Bills: 1955–1965.* Indianapolis: Bobbs-Merrill, 1966.

————. *The Politics of Comprehensive Manpower Legislation.* Baltimore: Johns Hopkins University Press, 1972.

Davies, J. Clarence, III, and Davies, Barbara S. *The Politics of Pollution.* Indianapolis: Bobbs-Merrill, 1975.

Davis, James W., Jr., and Dolbeare, Kenneth M. *Little Groups of Neighbors: The Selective Service System.* Chicago: Markham, 1968.

Derthick, Martha. *Policymaking for Social Security.* Washington, D. C.: Brookings Institution, 1979.

Dommel, Paul R. *The Politics of Revenue Sharing.* Bloomington, Ind.: Indiana University Press, 1974.

Donovan, John D. *The Politics of Poverty.* New York: Pegasus, 1967.

Dye, Thomas R. *Politics, Economics, and the Public.* Chicago: Rand McNally, 1966.

Ehrlich, Everett M., and Scheppach, Raymond C. *Energy Policy Analysis and Congressional Action.* Lexington, Mass.: Lexington Books, 1982.

Eidenberg, Eugene, and Morey, Roy D. *An Act of Congress.* New York: Norton, 1969.

Etzioni, Amitai. *Demonstration Democracy.* New York: Gordon and Breach, 1970.

Fenno, Richard F., Jr. *The Power of the Purse.* Boston: Little, Brown, 1966.

Freedman, Leonard. *Public Housing: The Politics of Poverty.* New York: Holt, Rinehart & Winston, 1969.

Frieden, Bernard J. *The Environmental Protection Hustle.* Cambridge, Mass.: MIT Press, 1979.

Friedman, Lawrence M. *Government and Slum Housing.* Chicago: Rand McNally, 1968.

Fritschler, A. Lee. *Smoking and Politics.* New York: Appleton-Century-Crofts, 1969.

Gans, Herbert J. *The Urban Villagers.* New York: Free Press, 1962.

Gray, Virginia and Williams, Bruce. *The Organizational Politics of Criminal Justice: Policy in Context.* Lexington, Mass.: Lexington Books, 1980.

Green, Harold P., and Rosenthal, Alan. *Government of the Atom.* New York: Atherton, 1963.

Greenberg, Stanley. *Politics and Poverty.* New York: Wiley, 1974.

Greenstone, J. David, and Peterson, Paul E. *Race and Authority in Urban Politics.* New York: Russell Sage Foundation, 1973.

Greer, Scott. *Urban Renewal and American Cities.* Indianapolis: Bobbs-Merrill, 1965.

Gryski, Gerald S. *Bureaucratic Policy Making in a Technological Society.* Cambridge, Mass.: Schenkman, 1981.

Hadwiger, Don, and Talbot, Ross B. *Pressures and Protests.* San Francisco: Chandler, 1965.

Hardin, Charles. *The Politics of Agriculture.* New York: Free Press, 1952.

Horwitch, Mel. *Clipped Wings: The American SST Conflict.* Cambridge, Mass.: MIT Press, 1982.

Hunter, Floyd. *Community Power Succession: Atlanta's Policymakers Revisited.* Chapel Hill, N. C.: University of North Carolina Press, 1980.

Huntington, Samuel. *The Common Defense.* New York: Columbia University Press, 1961.

Ingram, Helen M., Laney, Nancy K., and McCain, John R. *A Policy Approach to Political Representation.* Baltimore: Johns Hopkins University Press, 1980.

Ingram, Helen M., and Mann, Dean E., eds. *Why Policies Succeed or Fail.* Beverly Hills, Calif.: Sage Publications, 1980.

James, Dorothy B. *Poverty, Politics, and Change.* Englewood Cliffs, N. J.: Prentice-Hall, 1972.

Johnston, Michael. *Political Corruption and Public Policy in America.* Monterey, Calif.: Brooks/Cole, 1982.

Jones, Charles O. *Clean Air: The Policies and Politics of Pollution Control.* Pittsburgh: University of Pittsburgh Press, 1975.

Karnig, Albert K., and Welch, Susan. *Black Representation and Urban Policy.* Chicago: University of Chicago Press, 1981.

Kash, Don E., and White, Irwin L. *Energy Under the Oceans.* Norman, Okla.: University of Oklahoma Press, 1973.

Kettl, Donald F. *Managing Community Development in the New Federalism.* New York: Praeger, 1980.

Kweit, Mary Grisez and Robert W. *Implementing Citizen Participation in a Bureaucratic Society: A Contingency Approach.* New York: Praeger, 1981.

Labunski, Richard. *The First Amendment Under Seige: The Politics of Broadcast Regulation.* Westport, Conn.: Greenwood Press, 1981.

Langbein, Laura I. *Discovering Whether Programs Work.* Santa Monica, Calif.: Goodyear, 1980.

Latham, Earl. *The Group Basis of Politics.* Ithaca, N. Y.: Cornell University Press, 1952.

Lee, Robert D., Jr., and Johnson, Ronald W. *Public Budgeting Systems.* Baltimore: University Park Press, 1977.

LeLoup, Lance. *The Fiscal Congress: Legislative Control of the Budget.* Westport, Conn.: Greenwood Press, 1980.

Levine, Adeline Gordon. *Love Canal.* Lexington, Mass.: Lexington Books, 1982.

Levine, Charles H., and Rubin, Irene, eds. *Fiscal Stress and Public Policy.* Beverly Hills, Calif.: Sage Publications, 1980.

Lipsky, Michael. *Street-Level Bureaucracy: Dilemmas of the Individual in Public Services.* New York: Russell Sage Foundation, 1980.

Logsdon, John M. *The Decision to Go to the Moon.* Cambridge, Mass.: MIT Press, 1970.

Lundqvist, Lennart J. *The Hare and the Tortoise: Clean Air Policies in the United States and Sweden.* Ann Arbor, Mich.: University of Michigan Press, 1980.

Maass, Arthur. *Muddy Waters.* Cambridge, Mass.: Harvard University Press, 1951.

Mann, Dean E., ed. *Environmental Policy Formation.* Lexington, Mass.: Lexington Books, 1981.

————. *Environmental Policy Implementation.* Lexington, Mass.: Lexington Books, 1982.

Marcus, Alfred A. *Promise and Performance: Choosing and Implementing an Environmental Policy.* Westport, Conn.: Greenwood Press, 1980.

Marmor, Theodore R. *The Politics of Medicare.* Chicago: Aldine, 1973.

Mazmanian, Daniel A., and Nienaber, Jeanne. *Can Organizations Change?* Washington, D. C.: Brookings Institution, 1979.

Meehan, Eugene J. *The Quality of Federal Policymaking: Programmed Failure in Public Housing.* Columbia, Mo.: University of Missouri Press, 1979.

Meranto, Philip. *The Politics of Federal Aid to Education in 1965: A Study in Political Innovation.* Syracuse, N. Y.: Syracuse University Press, 1967.

Meyerson, Martin, and Banfield, Edward C. *Politics, Planning, and the Public Interest.* New York: Free Press, 1955.

Mitnick, Barry M. *The Political Economy of Regulation: Creating, Designing and Removing Regulatory Forms.* New York: Columbia University Press, 1980.

Mitroff, Ian L. *The Subjective Side of Science.* New York: Elsevier, 1974.

Moynihan, Daniel P. *Maximum Feasible Misunderstanding.* New York: Free Press, 1969.

————. *The Politics of a Guaranteed Income.* New York: Random House, 1973.

Munger, Frank J., and Fenno, Richard F., Jr. *National Politics and Federal Aid to Education.* Syracuse, N. Y.: Syracuse University Press, 1962.

Nakamura, Robert T., and Smallwood, Frank. *The Politics of Policy Implementation.* New York: St. Martin's Press, 1980.

Nelson, Barbara J. *Making an Issue of Child Abuse: Political Agenda Setting for Social Problems.* Chicago: University of Chicago Press, forthcoming.

O'Brien, David M., and Marchand, Donald A., eds. *The Politics of Technology Assessment.* Lexington, Mass.: Lexington Books, 1982.

Oppenheimer, Bruce I. *Oil and the Congressional Process.* Lexington, Mass.: Lexington Books, 1974.

Palumbo, Dennis J., and Harder, Marvin A. *Implementing Public Policy.* Lexington, Mass.: Lexington Books, 1981.

Peterson, Paul E. *City Limits.* Chicago: University of Chicago Press, 1981.

Pierce, Lawrence C. *The Politics of Fiscal Policy Formation.* Pacific Palisades, Calif.: Goodyear, 1971.

Piven, Frances Fox, and Cloward, Richard A. *Regulating the Poor.* New York: Pantheon, 1971.

Polsby, Nelson W. *Political Innovation in America: The Politics of Policy Initiation.* New Haven, Conn.: Yale University Press, forthcoming.

————. *Community Power and Political Theory: A Further Look at Problems of Evidence and Inference.* New Haven, Conn.: Yale University Press, 1980.

Pressman, Jeffrey L., and Wildavsky, Aaron B. *Implementation,* 2nd ed. Berkeley, Calif.: University of California Press, 1979.

Preston, Michael B., Henderson, Lenneal J., Jr., and Puryear, Paul L., eds. *The New Black Politics: The Search for Political Power.* New York: Longman, 1982.

Price, David. *Who Makes the Laws?* Cambridge, Mass.: Schenckman, 1972.

Rainwater, Lee, and Yancey, William. *The Moynihan Report and the Politics of Controversy.* Cambridge, Mass.: MIT Press, 1967.

Redman, Eric. *The Dance of Legislation.* New York: Simon and Schuster, 1973.

Reid, T. R. *Congressional Odyssey: The Saga of a Senate Bill.* San Francisco: W. H. Freeman, 1980.

Rossi, Peter, and Dentler, Robert. *The Politics of Urban Renewal.* New York: Free Press, 1961.

Rossi, Peter H., and Lyall, Katharine C. *Reforming Public Welfare: A Critique of the Negative Income Tax Experiment.* New York: Russell Sage Foundation, 1976.

Sanders, M. Elizabeth. *The Regulation of Natural Gas.* Philadelphia: Temple University Press, 1981.

Schattschneider, E. E. *Politics, Pressures, and the Tariff.* Englewood Cliffs, N. J.: Prentice-Hall, 1935.

Schick, Allen. *Congress and Money: Budgeting, Spending, and Taxing.* Washington, D. C.: Urban Institute, 1980.

———. *Reconciliation and the Congressional Budget Process.* Washington, D. C.: American Enterprise Institute, 1981.

Selznick, Philip M. *T.V.A. and the Grass Roots.* Berkeley: University of California Press, 1949.

Sharkansky, Ira. *The Politics of Taxing and Spending.* Indianapolis: Bobbs-Merrill, 1969.

Silverstein, Arthur M. *Pure Politics and Impure Science.* Baltimore: Johns Hopkins University Press, 1981.

Spanier, John, and Uslaner, Eric M. *How American Foreign Policy Is Made.* New York: Praeger, 1974.

Sproull, Lee, Weiner, Stephen, and Wolf, David. *Organizing an Anarchy.* Chicago: University of Chicago Press, 1978.

Steiner, Gilbert Y., ed. *The Abortion Dispute and the American System.* Washington, D. C.: Brookings Institution, 1983.

———. *Social Insecurity.* Chicago: Rand McNally, 1966.

Sundquist, James L. *Politics and Policy.* Washington, D. C.: Brookings Institution, 1968.

Tobin, Richard J. *The Social Gamble.* Lexington, Mass.: Lexington Books, 1979.

Van Horn, Carl. *Policy Implementation in the Federal System.* Lexington, Mass.: Lexington Books, 1979.

Vladeck, Bruce C. *Unloving Care.* New York: Basic Books, 1980.

Wenner, Lettie M. *The Environmental Decade in Court.* Bloomington, Ind.: Indiana University Press, 1982.

Westin, Alan F., ed. *The Uses of Power.* New York: Harcourt Brace & World, 1962.

Wildavsky, Aaron. *Dixon-Yates: A Study in Power Politics.* New Haven, Conn.: Yale University Press, 1962.

———. *The Politics of the Budgetary Process.* 3d ed. Boston: Little, Brown, 1979.

Williams, Walter. *Government by Agency.* New York: Academic, 1980.

———. *The Implementation Perspective: A Guide for Managing Social Service Delivery Programs.* Berkeley: University of California Press, 1980.

Wilson, Graham K. *Special Interests and Policymaking.* London: Wiley, 1977.

Wilson, James Q., ed. *The Politics of Regulation.* New York: Basic Books, 1980.

———, ed. *Urban Renewal.* Cambridge, Mass.: MIT Press, 1967.

Wirt, Frederick. *The Politics of Southern Equality.* New York: Aldine, 1970.

———, and Kirst, Michael W. *The Political Web of American Schools.* Boston: Little, Brown, 1972.

Wolman, Harold, *Politics of Federal Housing.* New York: Dodd, Mead, 1971.

Index